SOJOURNS IN IREL.

First published by this author:

The Life and Times of Francie Nichol of South Shields
George Allen and Unwin, 1975
Futura 1977
TUPS BOOKS, 1997

Claret and Crossbuttock
George Allen and Unwin, 1976

Tommy Turnbull – A Miner's Life
TUPS BOOKS, 1996
The History Press, 2012

The Making of a Microbe Hunter
Smithwhite Books 2007

Poms and Pakehas
Smithwhite Books, 2008

A Difficult Man to Work with
Smithwhite Books, 2009

Sojourns in Ireland and Spain

A Memoir

JOSEPH ROBINSON

This book is published by Joseph Robinson.

All rights reserved. Copyright © Joseph Robinson 2020

A catalogue record of this book is available from the British Library

ISBN 9798635342589
Printed by Amazon

*

Disclaimer

To avoid the risk of anyone featured in this book feeling they have been in any way unfairly treated, and to preserve everybody's privacy, all names have been changed, including the author's. I, for reasons of consistency appear as 'Jack Smithwhyte', a fairly common name within my family, and I trust this minor artistic licence will cause no confusion for the reader.

*To Hannah,
conscientious proof-reader who hounded me to get
this book done*

PREFACE

Fifty years ago, enchanted by Henry Morton's travelogue, *In Search of Ireland*, monologues by Irish writers like Millington Synge and tales by various acquaintances who had visited the country and spoken so favourably of its easy ways and friendly people, I brought my family to live in a land that on a five-day recce appeared to be much as depicted by its apologists and just the sort of place we were seeking to begin a new life. Some things would take a bit of getting used to: not least the relevance of the Catholic Church, seemingly the ultimate authority in every domain from education to health, and politics to sex; its officials not as conspicuously venerated as in former times, though their pious uniforms still commanded more respect than any other authorities'.

Whether from town or country, every Irish man and woman manifested an affinity with the earth, and a glance would be enough to inform them as to the best use any acre could be put – particularly somebody else's. 'Good land,' they would aver, 'is the greatest of gifts', though many also had considerable affection for ice-cold cash. When we arrived, the country had only recently joined the 'Common Market', as it was then known, and was still only sparsely populated, so land and property was cheap and available compared with England; but because her entrepreneurs had not yet discovered how to exploit the situation sufficiently enough to become the nonpareil of beneficiaries, she was part of the Common Market's 'third world'. However, with a government night and day pleading need that left others high and dry when it came to beseeching, and the emergence of fly-by-night financiers who set up offices guaranteeing to obtain a grant of one kind or another for anybody who could do with a bit of a fill-up, it would soon achieve enviable success. When it rained, farmers would obtain a grant for land drainage; when it didn't, they would obtain one for irrigation – that sort of thing. Everything qualified, it was just a matter of devising the right spiel and forever broadcasting it.

Although rather narrow-minded, thanks to the Church, the average Irish were friendly and hospitable and it seemed that every other man or woman could play the fiddle, sing, or talk the hind leg off a donkey; so where one would provide company, two and you were in the midst of a party; sociable and obliging to neighbour and stranger alike, they were as ready to amuse, inform or lend a hand, and getting dirty or shedding a little blood was of little consequence.

Long before any personal acquaintance with the Emerald Isle, my indirect introduction had been via teachers at the Catholic school I once attended where the strict masters and buxom soft-hearted mistresses were invariably Irish; but my wife Helen, a 'hard-faced Prod', as some old Taig biddy would one day refer to her, would have to wait until we got there. Weird though it might seem, the physiognomy is a give-away when distinguishing the two, the latter's underlying bone being arguably that much closer to the surface.

Helen and I had grown up in an England that after the War had becoming increasingly and stiflingly English, and emigration to the dominions concomitantly attractive, so after qualifying as a microbiologist, incidentally not my first choice of career, we spent several years in New Zealand, Australia and Canada, eventually returning for family reasons. After a spell in Scotland I obtained a position at a teaching hospital on Tyneside, but during the course of research into a group of virulent and highly infectious bacteria, contracted *Brucellosis melitensis*, a tropical disease which, after two years of various but ineffective treatment, was classified by the DHSS as chronic, probably incurable and I as 'fifty-percent disabled for life'. At the time we had three small children, had invested everything in a reasonable house and settling down, in addition to financially supplementing research that was entirely voluntary and done in my own time. So apart from my suddenly being plunged into poor health with no prospects of ever again obtaining the kind of employment I was qualified for, we were left with very limited financial resources. My main concern was of course for the welfare of my family, and after much futile medical treatment and medical and industrial tribunals primarily designed to dispose of me, I realised we were going to have to make a different life and somewhere else.

Helen and I had always liked the country and reasoned that if we could buy a smallholding perhaps we could eke things out by producing as much of our own food as possible and selling the surplus, and the fresh fare and open air would be good for all of us. Once we had established a garden with a few fruit trees and bushes, installed a poultry house and a couple of beehives, plus whatever else seemed promising, I should be able to attend to more cerebral matters. Previous to becoming ill I had written a couple of biographies, one of my grandmother who had married into a boxing family, run lodging houses and had a hard but interesting life, and one of an uncle who had been a Durham coal-miner whose life was no less hard or interesting. I had also had a number of sculpture exhibitions. Neither venture had created much of a flutter, but given the change in my situation maybe I would do better now.

However, a search throughout Northumberland and Durham soon revealed that commuter investors had gobbled up almost everything we could have afforded and were frantically converting houses, villages and surrounding areas into a kind of 'Sussex of the North', a holiday-home habitat where glasses of wine replaced mugs of tea, genteel vocal sounds supplanted guttural Northumbrian vowels, and politically correct sniffs usurped phlegmatic howks.

Reckoning that if we could not find somewhere in the county we already lived in, the most sparsely populated in England, we were unlikely to find anything anywhere else, and given we were becoming increasingly disenchanted with England anyway, we began looking in Irish newspapers and learned of a place in County Wexford, in the south east corner of the island. It sounded idyllic, though Helen had misgivings about such adjectives, and we jumped in, all hands to the fore.

Life in the country, working for ourselves, doing so many things we had never done before, from husbanding a range of domestic animals that included milking goats, bees, sheep and poultry, building and making all kinds of utilitarian things, was so different from being confined to a hospital laboratory and living in a city, that it wrought the manifestation of previously never realised but very welcome abilities.

After more than twenty years, during which we survived on a typically minute English invalidity pension supplemented by what we could earn from our smallholding and my art, Helen and I had managed to rear four healthy children, two boys and two girls, have them university educated and, hopefully, by virtue of their upbringing in the country by urban parents, ready for the world at large. In no time they then all seemed to disappear and without their invaluable input the farming work quickly got beyond their mother and me. The Irish weather, particularly the enervating humidity, would at times wreak havoc with me, and leaping ditches after screeching geese, wrestling goats among briar and gorse and manhandling donkeys – often in wind and rain – was a lot less fun, and what was once healthy exercise became more of an ordeal.

We reduced the most physically demanding livestock and sought to supplement our livelihood via more sedentary endeavours, like the art, with me doing the fashioning and Helen the selling to hotels, art shops and 'big houses'. I had neither the neck nor knack to knock on doors myself, whereas she could happily turn her hand to arranging exhibitions of oil paintings and ink drawings, obtaining commissions for sculpture, and cold selling items like stone sundials and brass weather vanes. But there was a limit to how many weather vanes a district could support, one highly erected vane more or less serving the whole community, and the 'art trade' was too seasonal. We then tried forestry, but trees took a lot longer to grow than lettuce and rhubarb, and required much more energy and know-how.

At this stage we considered it expedient to make one last move before becoming totally defunct, and Spain was the choice, a sunny, warm and salubrious place, a wildlife paradise and interesting culture we had visited long ago during the era of General Franco who, as champion of the garrotte and practitioner of longevity, had almost strangled the country he stole by coup. But at last, having had the benefit of practically every medical and Frankenstein Ian procedure known to medicine, plus the orchestrated appeals of regiments of praying intercedes, even God wearied of him and the country was now apparently as safe as Scotland.

Despite inevitable drawbacks, Spain was wonderful, and when we eventually returned to Ireland, it was for the same reason we had come back to England from abroad – family.

People who had not lived in both countries, perhaps not even visited, claimed the Irish and Spanish were very similar; but we thought them quite different. The Irish tended to be soft-spoken whereas the Spanish were frequently loud, almost bellicose, in conversation, especially when eating. The Spanish were also alleged to be big drinkers, but this was not the case either. Gourmets, yes, but because they hated to make fools of themselves, they were very aware of the downside of drinking. Their counterparts, on the other hand were quite content to be drunk and seen to be, and would readily boast of their loss of *compos mentis*.

Spanish public servants relished saying 'No', while their Irish counterparts, at least in the lower ranks, went out of their way to make a 'no' into a 'yes'. The Hispanic language was beautiful, dress sense immaculate and manners often exquisite, but their total conviction that their academic or technical qualifications in any field were superior to the rest of the world's, ipso facto their IQ, was less appealing and not entirely convincing. Whatever, they were the exotic country of Europe and their culture mesmerising if at times rather brutal.

Not many man-made things the world over can truly be classed as perfect, but coffee anywhere in Spain is surely as close as anything gets, and it is cheap; and the men who serve it, like the men who, for some reason usually serve comestibles, are quite as magnificent as any in flying machines. It might seem like a small thing but in fact says a lot.

This book is a memoir of the generation I lived in Ireland with my wife and family, and then for more than a decade in Spain with only my wife. It is by no means a family saga and has been written from a personal point of view, recounting experiences that illustrate the existence Helen and I suffered and enjoyed as English expatriates in Hibernia then Iberia. At this point I should confess that although we never considered ourselves to be hammy 'expats', no doubt that was how we came across to more than a few of our various hosts.

Our children especially did not want me to speak for them because they felt their individual experiences, feelings and opinions, were private matters, and I have respected this by committing the writer's sin of treating them as cyphers, although I think they are perfectly rounded human beings, decent, loyal and, despite having a martinet for a father, more than merely affectionate.

When we first arrived in Ireland we were more or less halfway through our lives. It was a wonderful year for weather and an auspicious one for a move that would lead to our longest sojourn abroad, plus a spell in another country where circumstances were very different and perhaps show distinct sides to a human being. There again, perhaps not so, and the reader, with his more objective judgement, can perhaps infer similarities that have simply eluded the writer.

PART ONE

A GOOD LIFE

ONE

On the 2nd July 1976, a glorious summer morning, my thirty-seventh birthday and Helen's and my sixteenth wedding anniversary – we sailed into the Port of Dublin on the overnight ferry from Liverpool. The previous day, in the wake of a removals van carrying half our chattels, driven by its fastidious owner, Arnold Fenwick, and accompanied by my youngest brother, George, riding shotgun, we had travelled from Newcastle-on-Tyne, our home town, in a previously oft-owned Morris Mini that had been acquired in rather too much haste the week before. I say 'in the wake' because Mr Fenwick had been so scared that his precious new Mercedes Benz van, the spoils of an inheritance, might have been severely traumatised were the weight of its contents to have exceeded the manufacturer's recommended limit, or been other than perfectly evenly distributed, that he insisted I follow closely behind him to make sure the level of the top of his van was continually in line with the horizon. I say 'half our chattels' because when he had come to the house to estimate their weight and volume, he had arrived without a tape measure or scales of any kind, and had calculated everything at a glance, a talent normal customers were usually impressed by.

As a consequence, after a dramatic five hours trying to get the furniture into a space painfully too small, and my reluctantly disposing of the excess to neighbours lending a hand, Mr Fenwick had finally conceded he would need to make two trips and I was thus obliged to retrieve what I could of the more lavish bestowals I had been making, without too headlong a fall from grace, though the brown ale that our next-door neighbour had provided was by then well beyond recovery. Had my father, who was one of the volunteers, been in charge of the operation, he would not have allowed any partaking until after the job was done, but as it was somebody else who had supplied the wherewithal, I had not felt I had any authority regarding its disposal.

By eight next morning we were crossing the old Tyne Bridge among convoys of huge lorries heading north and south, the bridge being the ancient gateway into Newcastle and on to Scotland, and for Novocastrians like us presented a very sentimental view of the quayside and southern part of the city. Many was the time I had crossed the bridge by train, or on my 197cc Ambassador motorbike when I was scarcely more than a lad doing National Service in the Royal Army Medical Corps. I would be returning to camp after a weekend pass, and a few years later when I had completed my military obligations and was working in London, I would be back to see the family whenever possible, now on a 500cc AJS.

This time I was probably leaving the North for good, though I did not dwell on the thought as I looked down on the river with its considerably fewer ships than yesteryear, and the far less busy banks of Gateshead, a mere precinct of the once great city and long before the imposition of a crass eyesore on a hill overlooking the highway that had no relevance to either side of the Tyne, past or present, though it had ludicrously replaced the Old Tyne Bridge as the icon of the North. The artist responsible had moved on to planting naked, mainly middle-aged and old females – real ones – on beaches, along promenades, up and down stairways and in various other places with a view. Sculpture had always been a hobby with me but most people were hesitant about expressing an opinion on anything with a third dimension, considering it too demanding to judge.

We had spent our last night at my parents' house but it had been too much of a scramble getting the children ready and last minute things packed, to spend much time lamenting our approaching departure. Besides, Helen and I had left too many places too many times to grieve too much about leaving anywhere; our new destination was not that far and parents and friends could come over to see us when we were settled. Mind, the natural selfishness of youth and preoccupation with the minutiae associated with departing always made these occasions easier for the leaving than the left.

My illness, a chronic and incurable tropical infection, had many symptoms: some distressing, such as incessant pain; some embarrassing, like the oft-times gross flatulence; others just plain disagreeable, like the drenching nocturnal sweats; though none so perverse as the drastic loss of stamina which affected everything from shovelling the snow away from the front door, to writing a letter in pursuit of getting something back from the life insurance policy I had been paying into for years. The latter was something that at one time everybody felt obliged to subscribe to, even though insuring against one's demise is probably one of the most unrewarding investments known to man.

British governments had never been sympathetic to victims of industrial disease or accidents, no more than they were to casualties who had volunteered or been conscripted to fight their abominable wars for them. Consequently I had received no more than the equivalent of four months salary in compensation, so at thirty-six years of age the prospects for the second half of my life, with a wife and three small children, were pretty bleak. On top of that, more than a few relatives, friends and neighbours were becoming more than just a little peeved at having to stomach incomprehensible and indefinite illness in someone so fit and full of life that he was still able to walk and talk and move his arms up and down.

Both our parents had tried to dissuade us; not only because they felt we would be plunging ourselves into a situation so unfamiliar, as well as physically demanding, that we might be making things harder than ever, but because they were concerned about 'The Troubles', which they, like most people in England, thought engulfed the whole of Ireland. After all, we would be urban English entering a very rural region deep in the south at a time when relations between North and South were very strained because of Thatcher's policy of internment in Ulster. However, my determination to create a new and utopian life over-rode all opposition. I expected problems, I knew we would be doing all kinds of work we had never done before, and because of financial constraints, doing it ourselves, but I was dead keen; I had spent nearly two years on my behind getting stale and going nowhere while waiting for the medical and industrial tribunals I had attended to be decided, and at last we were moving on.

An onerous journey by day led to a pleasant summer night passed at sea, something we had grown to appreciate the time we sailed to New Zealand and spent more than six weeks of nights lulled by deep and blue oceans. Some years later we had taken a rather less exciting ten days crossing the Atlantic on our way home from Canada. This voyage had been shorter, colder and bleaker, with cobalt grey skies, herring gulls instead of albatrosses, and fish that behaved like fish rather than miniature dolphins. We could have stood on deck, closed our eyes and never for a moment imagined we were on the Indian Ocean.

Next morning the sun was rendering the coast of Ireland wild and wonderful, the sky a lovely pale blue and the sea a dark grey green flecked with white horses, most of them stallions.

'Land ahoy!' some fool shouted.

George had spent a rather uneasy night in the same cabin as Arnold and could not wait for him to disappear to take his nostra so he could acquaint us with details, Arnold having established himself as worthy of the brunt of most of the humour. Apparently his case with the red cross emblazoned on the front was full of bottles of vitamins and over-the-counter medications, some of them ancient and including semi-precious baubles and figurines. He had obviously decided George should be under his wing because he constantly preached to him in maxims about all manner of things, but George was a tolerant chap and only responded with a smile.

'Can you give me a hand with this, lad?' Arnold had said before clambering early into his bunk. He was heaving at the bottom of one of the posts on which the bunks were mounted, his one long eyebrow beetled into a frown, his thick heavily oiled hair dangling in front of him, and beads of sweat dropping on to the floor. He was short and stocky, hands huge and hairy, fingers tattooed with 'LOVE' and 'MOVE', and each thumb with 'I'.

'What's up?' George asked. 'Are the bunks wobbling?'

'Na, it's so we can put wor shoes underneath, so if anybody comes in during the night to pinch them, they'll wake us up. And these boots are ex-Northumberland officer's, so I certainly don't want to lose them.'

'Aren't the posts fastened to the floor?'

'Ahht! Looks like it... Stupid nowts!'

Wasting minimal time on breakfast, the Smithwhyte party excepting George, were soon crammed into the Mini, trying to contain our excitement: Helen silent and calm, maybe a trifle grim, and the kids trembling in anticipation of their wonderful new life; even Harry was aware that something big was imminent and had lost the power of speech, though that would not be long gone. Helen was accusing me of 'nudging' other vehicles when I was merely giving nobody an excuse for alleging I might be creating a gridlock.

Suddenly there was a swell of people at the point of disembarkation and a general hush as they waited for the boat to shudder to a halt. Young foreign couples laden with rucksacks bulky enough and secure enough to ensure that in the event of a calamity they would drag their wearers straight to the bottom of the sea, middle-aged Irish couples whose overheard snippets of conversation indicated they were parents returning after a trying fortnight as grandchildren minders, a motley of elderly Americans and Australians, a range of squabbling children having a last go on fruit machines, and last of all, the peripatetic alcoholics who had slept on the floor until the very last moment and did not seem to care whether or not they got off at this end.

Smoothly I eased the Mini down the ramp, staring straight ahead and keeping at dead on 5 mph. Although Helen and I had passed through plenty of Customs before, usually on a motorbike, I had never been seriously stopped and it would be a couple of years of Irish conditioning before I had grown a dark beard, taken to wearing rural Irish clothes and had evolved an 'Irish face on me' that would never allow me to escape being taken aside and interviewed by Irish guards at one end, and Special Branch at the other.

On this occasion the smug smile which I always strove mightily to deter must hardly have faded from my face when the blast of a whistle and several shouts from the Customs booth called me back. Arnold, honest Arnold, no smuggler he, had seen fit to blab to Customs that our car, the pathetic previously multi-owned little Mini which had a petrol leak and several other quite serious impediments, was short of an import licence, something I would have thought its current value would not have merited.

Without any semblance of negotiation, the guardians of Irish Revenue peremptorily slapped IR£400 duty on us, and because I was unable to pay, ownership of everything we possessed immediately passed to the Irish state. What a start! The car had only cost the equivalent of IR£325, the petrol tank patently leaking and the chassis clogged with rust, which made me wonder if they had not simply drawn a number with a pound sign in front of it, out of one of their large, upturned peaked hats from under the counter. Huge vans and lorries were rumbling past with God knows who or what on board, and no more than a wave and cheery exchange between their drivers and the same Customs officers who were giving us the big stick. Meanwhile my pale-faced little crew was staring out of the steamed-up windows of our little heap of corroding contraband, mortified in case we were going to be sent back on the next ferry; or perhaps scuttled with all aboard.

It took two and a half hours to persuade our tormentors, a tiny junta of semi-militarised civil servants, for whom arbitrariness, like in no other profession, forms the basis of judgement, to let us borrow our car, and Arnold's van, for a week, to allow us to complete our journey to our new home, and it was the arrival of their lunchtime that clinched it. Everything we possessed now belonged to the Irish Inland Revenue and somehow or other, after a week we would have to return the car and van to them back here in Dublin. The only satisfaction the trauma provided was that Arnold's fuckin' van, even though licensed, was also impounded and he would be shitting himself with a capital 'S' for a week.

At last out of the shadow of the shed which looked like something out of a cold-war movie, and a mile into the sunshine, we were thoroughly traducing the only category of Irish who, at no matter which border, would never treat us with less than surliness because we were English and, as far as they were concerned, the everlasting enemy.

Right behind us crawled the bright Ulster-orange removals van with its two pale grey faces behind the windscreen, George's skinny arm half raised in triumph and wan smile indicating that he and Arnold and the van would be following us.

'Three cheers for Dad!' Walt yelled, as we headed for the city.

'Hush, Walter! Do you want them coming after us!' Helen chided.

Driving through Dublin was like driving through a town in the midlands of 1950s England, grimy and subdued but respectable with a decent upper-working-class air about it. Buildings were very conservative and obviously owed more to conscientious English architects and painstaking artisans of another century, than to egocentric councillors and their building cowboys of this. Surprisingly, many of the cars were quite big, perhaps because of the large families we had heard about, or maybe so occupants could give the impression of being well-to-do, cars being more attainable indicators than houses. Many of the shops, especially the specialised ones, had clearly been in the hands of families for generations and were a reassuring presence. Buses were of an older vintage than in England and all traffic moved that much slower, but pleasantly so. People were generally dressed more conservatively than what we were used to, and nobody seemed in a rush, frequently walking across the road without bothering with pedestrian crossings or looking first left, then right, then left again, and nobody was honking horns at them. Most noticeable and so nice was how everybody we spoke to was so friendly; if there really was a grudge against the English, these Dubliners did not seem aware of it. Whenever we asked for directions, they would supply far more information than requested, and stretch their reply to a commentary on the weather, forecast included, and an enquiry into our roots and the purpose of our visit.

With little traffic and few traffic lights on the N11 (the main trunk road to the south) in no time we were in County Wicklow and it was a joy to drive in. The countryside, with its many old and frequently decrepit farms, dense-foliaged and sweet-smelling hawthorns, huge and powerful beeches thrusting over the road from unkempt hedges, asymmetric fields with little square hay bales scattered willy-nilly as if dropped from the sky, and paddocks with one or two horses and often a foal, were so very different from the prairified tracts in England that were once wonderfully bucolic stretches between towns and cities. Every so often the traipsing traffic was punctuated by tractors and other agricultural vehicles, trails of straw and hay, dung and mud, indicating who was doing what this week and nary a horn was sounded. It made me think of Australia and the fights we had so often seen in the middle of roads because somebody had impeded the traffic, and how these days lorry drivers no longer gave a damn for their sentimental old eponyms as 'knights of the road'. And every few miles, even on a highway such as this, a lone elderly woman would be seen plodding along with neither stick nor dog, head down, basket on her arm, along the scarcely twelve inches of gravel between concrete road and weedy undergrowth. Driving overall was erratic but unaggressive.

A month prior to coming to Ireland I had read about an Anglo-Irish landowner, Charles Carleton-Borris Esq., who was letting cottages on his estate to artists in an effort to beget a 'community of creativity'. It hadn't sounded like the kind of situation that would ordinarily have had my tongue hanging out, but it might have provided somewhere for us to live while we looked around for something more permanent. I had studied sculpture at Maidstone and Melbourne so had written to this Irish de Medici, care of the newspaper, and two days later received a telephone reply in Oxbridge English. Although my dialect was as thick as any of Breughel the Elder's peasants with a Geordie inflexion, it did not seem to bother him. He said he was delighted to hear from me not only because I was the only non-Irish 'candidate' and he was in favour of 'cross-fertilization', but because he regarded a sculptor to be a real find. As a consequence he was prepared to offer us the best accommodation on his estate, 'with perks'.

'You're not a monumental mason?' he had tentatively enquired after we had made arrangements to come over for a viewing. I almost quipped: 'Why, do you want a headstone made?' but stopped myself in time; not everyone appreciates a smart-arse.

In less than a week my family and I were walking around the 'abode' our prospective patron had described so captivatingly, and Helen was quite taken with him, finding him 'quite handsome and charming'.

Comprising the remnants of a small and derelict farm was a house made of marl (clay) and stone, a number of ancient outbuildings of richly-coloured river stone and near petrified timber arranged in the shape of a quadrangle enclosing a south-facing yard. Beyond, two south-facing meadows sloped gently down to a small meandering stream with the remains of a corn mill straddling part of it.

From the outset, where I saw charm and promise, Helen saw mess and expense and cautioned me about showing so much joy at the sight of so much ruin: overgrown relics of agricultural machinery alone, apart from the rotten floorboards in the loft, apparently making a number of 'near death-traps for the children'. But, like some manic 'developer' before the word was poached and became opprobrious, I could visualise animal pens arising from scrap timber, sculpture from rusting ploughshares, and classically interlocking dry stone walls from heaps of rubble. In the palm of one hand I could imagine a fat edible carp scooped from a wet and reedy area that had been deepened into a pond, and in the other, an exquisite egg from a rare breed of game fowl that was nesting in the renovated stable. And as I listened, I could imagine the contented ruminating murmur of an affable herbivore that would, at the end of a productive life, be humanely rendered into steaks and school satchels. I could hear our own *agua* potable cascading from the ancient but currently non-functioning pump, Italian bees buzzing around hives oozing honey, and catch the whiff of freshly plucked garden produce. In a stone house converted into a dairy I could picture Helen squatting on a little wooden stool rhythmically drawing down the teats of a large pink udder, its contents noisily splashing against the insides of a shining enamel bucket, while, after their chores, the kids teased each other with gorgeously fragrant strands of golden hay just in from the meadow.

Consequently, despite one of the children rather too easily putting their hand through a bedroom wall and waving to us outside as though this were yet another bonus, and then shortly after, the announcement that a laurel was growing in through the kitchen wall, I said we would take the place, but only if we could buy it. We would be leaving a fine terraced house in Newcastle, and although I was prepared to work day and night to make the dwelling into an attractive and comfortable home, restore and modify the outbuildings and repair anything else that needed it – and that meant virtually everything – I was not prepared for us to be evicted on some whim should landlordism ever come back into favour. Thus it was agreed and the papers signed before we returned to England a few days later.

I knew little about horticulture but had worked for years in the Veterinary Division of the English Ministry of Agriculture and Fisheries, and had always kept pet animals as a hobby. I knew little about construction but was familiar with steel, cement, plaster, fibreglass, resin and other building materials, through my sculpture, and had bought John and Sally Seymour's beautifully illustrated book on self-sufficiency, for Helen for her next birthday. She had barely glanced at it so far, with its back-breaking images of a dungareed-and-wellied middle-aged, middle-class woman picking swedes, plucking geese and weaving wicker baskets from reeds; the kind of reeds which I first, and then the children, would be cutting while waist-deep in the river which was less than half a mile away.

I had read the book from cover to cover and absolutely wallowed in it. Every aspect of husbandry to do with common and not so common farmyard animals, plus the cultivation of all kinds of small crops, including tree and bush fruit, was covered by this highly industrious, country-loving couple whose intention was to create a temperate Garden of Eden long before EEC grants would lure more than a few other couples disillusioned with the 'rat-race', into attempting something similar, though so far more than a few had already come to grief for one reason or another. In return, as a kind of tit for tat, Helen got me the Reader's Digest DIY manual, and I had also been through that, even though it was directed more at the kind of prissy householder I had never really been, rather than the provident, small-time, self-sufficient, farmer-builder I was intending to become.

Everyone over two years old, including George who had just finished art school and had come to help us get started before returning to England to do teacher training, had his or her work schedule for the rest of the day typed out in my back pocket. As soon as we arrived, Helen would be bringing down cobwebs and sweeping floors ahead of George who would be painting ceilings while Arnold and Walter were unloading the van and I establishing a garden and planting it with seeds of every kind of edible plant, including ones I had never heard of that could be sown this late in the season. Reliable little Alice would be carrying messages to and fro and keeping Harry out of mischief.

John McCormack had always been a favourite of my father's family, so as we drove down in the glorious sunshine, and the strains of his beautiful voice came over the Mini's radio singing The Old House, we all joined in. I cannot say what was going on inside the removals van, or even if it had a radio, but I doubt if there was quite as much merriment, Arnold being somewhat of a depressive as well as a 'worrit'.

But was it the Count? There was something ever so slightly different – not inferior, just different – about the voice, and Helen and I disagreed about it until the singer's name was announced to be Frank Patterson, someone we had never heard of but would not easily forget, his notes just the tiniest bit sweeter than his long dead peer. It was perfect and we regarded it as a good omen, and by the time we entered the county that would soon be ours, we had gone through our full Irish repertoire and were well into the old Tyneside ballads. When we had lived abroad and done a lot of travelling even by Triumph T110, Helen and I had always sung, sometimes for hours on end, when conversation for that length of time would invariably have turned rather sour.

We arrived at our new home shortly after three in the afternoon to find everything pretty much as we had left it, except that the charmingly shaped crab-apple tree at the side of the house had been uprooted and removed, along with a patch of comfrey I had noticed when we first came, plus a small woodpile of well seasoned ash. I trusted the thefts had been by somebody other than our host.

No sooner had we refreshed ourselves, than we set about our tasks, Helen creating clouds of allergenic dust mixed with thousands of fossils of long-dead spiders, daddy-long-legs and flies, George's ceilings soaking up emulsion like gigantic wads of blotting paper and his brush bringing down huge flakes of stratified generations of whitewash that exposed intimidatingly wide cracks running in all directions. As for my garden, it more resembled a patch of no-man's land than the neat workman-like allotment I had envisioned. The place I had chosen turned out to be more clay than soil, and with the sunny weather had become like one very big brick that could have done with a kilogram of TNT before yielding to hoe or rake. 'God help the seeds trying to make inroads into this,' I muttered. 'Maybe I'll have to get at it with a pneumatic drill and sledge hammer.'

It was not until we sat down for our first meal that I truly became aware of the flip-side of 'quaint', this being the only laudatory term I could conjure to describe a combination bathroom and toilet that abutted a kitchen-cum-living-and-dining room, and we had just started eating when through the particularly ill-fitting door, which had a one-and-a-half-inch gap at the bottom, came the sound of adult bowels being violently moved, even though Arnold had said he was only going in to wash his hands. Putting finger to lips, I quickly motioned to Walter to fetch the Bush transistor radio and stand it on the chair beside the bathroom door from whence it would prove to be a scrambler thus initiating a long and well respected tradition, many a radio programme on both sides of the Irish Sea seeming perfectly devised for the purpose.

By the time we went to bed that night, the van had been emptied, major electrical items wired up and large furniture found a halting place. The six-foot aquarium I had made for my jack pike was still in the middle of the yard waiting for Helen to relent and have it indoors, something she had never done and never would. The life-sized concrete Christ on the Cross was relaxing against the outside wall of the bathroom with similarly little chance of being admitted, and John the Baptist was in the field facing the road, letting the locals know that the English missionary sculptor and his family had arrived.

In minutes Helen was asleep. For her, lying in a comfortable bed at the end of a busy day, with the cover of a crisp cotton sheet drawn up to hide her from any prowler with murder or worse on his mind, was as effective at producing sleep as a general anaesthetic. She would soon be back in her childhood, half a mile from the Tyne, reliving the memories that always restored her and prepared her for what the next day would bring. I, on the other hand, would be reviewing the day's proceedings and planning tomorrow's before letting go, and this night was certainly no exception.

As I lay, utterly content with the way the day had gone, I was suddenly aware of an overwhelming silence coming from outside. There were no domestic noises, nothing to indicate there were others in the house or anything outside: no owls or other nocturnal creatures such as I had anticipated; just the silence, as though everything was waiting to see who or what would make the first move. It was perfect.

TWO

AFTER BREAKFAST, WITH INVOCATIONS for a safe journey home and back again, we saw Arnold on his way, and everybody returned to their tasks. The children were still just kids so I might have let them play a while to find their bearings and get used to their new home and the very different scenes and sounds, but I felt they should practice the principle of work before play, right from the start. I had abruptly cut us adrift from our previous life, and if we were to survive we would have to fully apply ourselves, learn quickly and adapt where necessary. I would be referring to my hagiographies of the great self-sufficers, Bakunin, Thoreau and Seymour, the public library, and whatever useful leaflets we could pick up from the Department of Agriculture. Every little thing would be planned in advance to save wasting valuable labour and resources, both of which were of course in very short supply.

I was confident that if whatever we did always advanced the restoration of the house or promoted the creation of our little enterprise, even to just a small extent, it would not only further the development of our skills, but would save money. It would all go towards the forging of character, but I would have to be careful I did not become a martinet. Helen would mock my Dickensian rules and I would cackle to imply good humour, but I would soon discover that at times she shed bitter tears at the way our life had changed so drastically, and wonder if we might lose more than we had gained. Certainly I was aware of being necessarily much more involved in the running of the household and bringing up the children than ever before, but that was the way I felt it had to be. For all Helen's virtues, which included acknowledgement of the need for pretty strict discipline, she was not a strong disciplinarian herself and always tended to give way rather than risk a row. That was the way she had been brought up by both her parents, whereas mine, particularly my father was different. He came from a boxing family, had a loving but tough mother and had been a soldier during the last War. Being the eldest of five lads, and having also experienced the discipline of army life, I felt the brunt of his principles where order and obedience was concerned, and by the time I left home appreciated what I often had not liked.

I began my chores on our first full day as Irish peasants by tackling the petrol tank. 'Peasants' was of course an assumed designation which won me no simpatico from anybody except Walter who was still young enough to regard me as an omniscient hero. My father had discovered the leak on his path just before we left, but because we had not had time to take the car to a garage, I had patched it up with chewing gum and a mixture of ancient glues from his shed and it had held for most of the journey. Now that I could get a good look at it, I could see the whole tank was so badly rusted it was on the brink of disintegration. We were only a mile from the village shop but it only carried basic items like bread, milk and safety matches, not petrol tanks for a 1968 Morris Mini. The town was five miles away and there was no public transport that might have got us there. It would not be long before we would discover that had we stood outside the front gate and waved an arm, the majority of motorists would have stopped. But that was in the future and we needed food and all sorts of supplies immediately.

Digging up a five-gallon drum I had noticed three-quarters buried at the back of the house, an item surpassingly difficult to get pristine clean on the inside, I fastened it standing up in the back of the car with elastic spiders, inserted one end of a length of silicone tubing, bypassed the tank and connected the other to the carburettor. I doubt it would have passed an MOT, but it would have to do until I could get another tank, and it would help me stop smoking. I had given up drink and cigarettes the previous night because I could no longer justify either on grounds of health or thrift, and 'cold turkey' was the method I chose for addictions after seeing Frank Sinatra in The Man with the Golden Arm years previously. The drum would give sterling service for years, that being how long it would take to locate a second-hand tank. Filling up at petrol stations was something we would always do ourselves, so eyebrows were rarely raised; in any case, this was not England, here one could do things like that and get away with it.

Anyway, as soon as I had installed the new fuel injection system – cleaning the drum took all morning – we all headed into town for household provisions and a variety of bits and pieces that would allow us to get on with the more urgent tasks in and around the house, and there were certainly plenty of those.

'Look at this, Dad!'

'There's something wrong here, Jack!'

'Have you seen this, Daddy?'

'Is this any good?'

For every exclamation that made the heart leap – such as the sighting of a bullfinch, something I had never seen in the wild – there would be three or four that caused it to stop; but there were only so many things one could concern oneself about at any one time and the list of priorities continually changed as features of rural life were experienced for the first time, more holes emerged, inaccessible corrosion was detected, areas with rotten wood exposed, and ever more bolts and fastenings found in need of unjamming, straightening and de-rusting. But it was going to take more than a few trips into town and rather more material in our sparse bank account, before we could make serious inroads into tackling these.

Wexford was a little market town at the mouth of the River Slaney, whose most prominent buildings were two Catholic churches, and most memorable oversight the absence of traffic lights. Our patron had said there was a strong Viking influence in the town, but apart from young bucks' hairstyles and boorish manner towards girls, it would have taken keener senses than mine to discern it. In years to come, when EU heritage grants would pay school-leavers on FAS (government trade school) courses to build fake archaeological sites, plant evidence of primitive habitation and bury homemade armour and items from pre-history, for the benefit of tourists, it would be different, but at the time of our arrival, although execrable language could be heard everywhere, crass-helmeted Norsemen could hardly have been credited with its introduction; that was more likely due to the influence of the Catholic Church in whose culture bad language, particularly of a profane variety, always seems to thrive. For instance there would come a time when while watching a primary school hurley match Walter was playing in, where the language of players and family spectators was so atrocious I would ask a priest standing by, why it was allowed, and he, smiling patronisingly, would tell me that words like 'fuck' and 'shag' were mere olde English 'obscenities', as opposed to 'blasphemies', and therefore quite acceptable to God. Several adults were close enough to hear everything we said, but nobody said a word; like him, they had the same supercilious smiles on their faces and minutes later one of them would be cursing his head off at the referee while smiling ever so graciously at me.

The main street of the town, which ran from east to west, was fairly narrow and had even narrower side streets leading up to residential areas; from the other side they descended to the quay from where a railway ran down to the ferry port of Rosslare. All along, from the threshold of nearly every pub, unkempt conversationalists tottered, sometimes spending as long as ten minutes taking their leave and orientating themselves before blending with the throng meandering along the street. Everywhere there were small shops with Celtic names captivatingly inscribed, friendly staff and customers, and at no time anywhere did we hear a disparaging word.

For some reason there was a disproportionate number of pharmacies and hardware stores as well as pubs, yet all were busy and Colman Doyle's hardware shop allowed us to bring away several sizes or types of various items on the understanding that we would return any that proved unsuitable, and only then would any money change hands. We were quite dismayed however to notice, more so than on our previous fleeting visit, that everything was more expensive than in England, and fruit and vegetables, particularly potatoes, which were considerably outnumbered by the clods of earth and stones in their sacks, were of exceptionally poor quality, though Helen considered the mutton looked good.

Creatures of the cloth were everywhere: whispering pairs of nuns covertly carrying out consumer surveys presumably for the convent, solitary monks who, as is so often the case, appeared down on their luck, rummaging through tack, and better-off priests oozing pious geniality in exchange for discounts on digital and other high quality trifles, the kind of stuff they presumably usually purchased duty-free when in civvies on an overseas duty-free holiday.

Vociferous Anglo-Irish ladies, bearing themselves as though they had once served as officers in the Women's Royal Cavalry, patronised the classier shops where the staff were extraordinarily biddable and remained largely mute whilst their goods and service were being unfavourably compared with their equivalent across the water. Young Scandinavian couples with hitch-hikers' tastes and various currencies in very secure leather purses, were peering through windows of places that catered for customers seeking bargain antiquities, but if they had heard Ireland was a paradise for the poor tourist, they would be getting quite a shock. Elsewhere, jovial groups of expensively tackled coarse-fishermen from Bradford and Cardiff were coming out of an old cycle shop that sold cheap bait, kidding each other about prowess as opposed to luck, as they shoved cartons of maggots between cans of beer in backpacks especially tailored for the purpose.

The town was certainly busy but there was no noise or bustle, and the few visible boy and girl police appeared to be functioning as guides rather than law-enforcers. Slim and effete with overgrown black hair, they were a far cry from the big, tough ginger coppers we had expected, and seemed totally incapable of dealing with any real baddies.

All in all the town left a pleasing impression, as did the wonderful drive back home, past the estuary and along the river with its luxuriant stands of thatching reeds. Off the bridge near the road that led to our house, fathers and sons were catching bass, while crabs, eels and other rejects were flinching and gasping on the bridge's narrow path. Everybody seemed to be catching something.

We were back home having lunch when Mr Carleton-Borris called to see how I was progressing with my first piece of Irish art, that, after all, being the reason for our being here, and he pointedly lead off with a complaint about the 'skinny little potter' in the lodge near his mansion, a frail nursing mother whom we had met on our previous visit.

'I must say I'm a wee bit disappointed. She hasn't turned out a single pot in over three weeks.'

'It'll take her a while to get set up though, won't it?'

'He's supposed to be a handyman and building a new kind of kiln, but he's gone off somewhere. Whenever I go round she's messing about with the babby. No doubt I'll be looking for a substitute potter before long… Ah, well, must be off. I've a meeting with the Town Clerk in twenty minutes and I'm sure you'll be anxious to get on with your sculpture.'

He was civil, though I could never see us becoming bosom pals.

'Some intriguing characters out here, I see,' he remarked as he stepped into the yard and nodded towards the Baptist. Then, chuckling: 'You do do secular stuff as well, I presume..? Ha, ha. Well, don't let me hold you up. Toodle-pip.'

And off he went with 'his man', a slovenly dressed, badly bucktoothed jack-of-all-trades who trailed behind him at a respectable distance as he sauntered up the path in his food-stained pale blue suit with tightly knotted varsity tie, cherubic face beaming and raft of lank aluminium hair flapping. I had not made up my mind about him yet. Although he was more than likely half Church of England, half nothing at all, I could well imagine him playing local dignitary from his 50-punt pew at the back of his church, no doubt guaranteeing he would be given the village equivalent of a state funeral when his time came. Before we arrived, I with my concrete saints, he might have presumed from my English background in science that my broadest stripes were similar to his own. Taigs (Irish Catholics), like tinkers, were something he would always have had to live with, just as we English Catholics – hardly a designation in England – always had to live alongside Protestants. Religious differences, however, did not matter to us; it was the reckoned differences in class that bothered us, and Carleton-Borris's was certainly different to ours. He had men working for him whom he and his wife treated like servants, the way big landowners in England treated their employees. When I first started work, which was for the Veterinary Department of the Ministry of Agriculture and Fisheries, I often had to visit large farms to take samples of blood, faeces and other bits and pieces from the animals, and the owners, frequently ex-senior officers in the Armed Forces, treated our vets as though they were 'lads just out of college', and referred to all of us as 'Ministry wallahs'. Their own people they regarded as stock. The odd one would invite us to 'sup' from a mug of tea after we had spent hours in the snow, wind or drizzle working in his fields while he remained indoors, but the invitation was never extended to his shepherd without whom we would never have been able to manage his hundreds of sheep or scores of cows. This poor chap was never even given a glass of warm water while he waited in the yard for us to come back out, and we, standing in a nondescript little room that looked as though it had been designed specially for petty commerce with nobodies, would be taking our beverage in mugs decorated with Disney caricatures while the master drank whatever he was drinking from a vessel embellished by George Stubbs' horses. 'And who's the lad's favourite: Mickey Mouse or Donald Duck..?'

Carleton-Borris had very early on told us he had been to Cambridge where he had read classics rather than agriculture; maybe he thought what Homer and Plato did not know about artificial insemination and copper deficiency in Swaledale x Blackfaces, was not worth knowing. But he seemed genuinely interested in art and always strove to manifest an urbane manner which he managed to bring off at least to Helen's satisfaction and I had to admit he could twinkle his eyes in an attractive way.

On our previous visit we had briefly visited the local school and met its headmaster, a hearty fellow from Galway called Phelim O'Hanlon who had been delighted when we knocked on his door to tell him we were hoping that two of our children might soon be joining his little constellation.

Mr O'Hanlon's father had served in the RAF during the Second World War and had passed on to his family a qualified respect for the British; as a consequence Phelim seemed to consider the prospect of a duo of Allied pupils joining his school, to be a real bonus. He had called his wife from her class and the two of them had hardly been able to contain their excitement: he, a burly, good-natured fellow, and she, Marie, a tall, nervous but attractive woman smiled at virtually everything we said.

Alice, our least enthusiastic pioneer and previously very content with her school in England, would be in Mrs O'Hanlon's class and as such was whisked away to be paraded in front of it, accompanied by proclamations of virtues calculated on the basis of such evidence as the colour and style of her hair and ability to answer simple questions in a confident clear voice 'devoid of the slightest trace of deceit'. As far as Walter was concerned, maybe I had laid on the potential for adventure a shade too thickly before we came, because he was convinced he would be living the life of an Irish Huckleberry Finn where school would prove an infinitesimally small part of life – a misapprehension that would need to be corrected pretty soon.

While we had been discussing our intentions concerning our new life, the classes had become a trifle restless and the 'ash plant' in Mr O'Hanlon's hand was beginning to oscillate as if divining the need for castigatory service, and he suggested it would be apt for us to now call on Fr Cathal Foyle, parish priest and manager of the school. Seemingly all state schools had to have an ordained priest as principal if they were boys' schools, and mother superiors if they were girls'. As commonly, the local church was only a few yards away from the school, so Fr Foyle would have been well aware of us by now, and right enough, the local spiritual shepherd had come out to greet us before we reached his presbytery door. White-haired and rubicund he came straight off a postcard depicting a nineteenth-century Irish country cleric.

Scarcely had we introduced ourselves before he asked if we played whist, but because we considered card games, along with scrabble, solitaire, golf and other ways of wasting one's valuable time on earth to be a waste of valuable time, I shook my head; I had enjoyed the odd hand of poker when I was a soldier but could not afford to be cavalier with resources nowadays.

'You'll have to come by on a Wednesday night and we'll learn you,' he persisted when I apologised. 'Our parish is famous and challengers come from far and wide. Not least for the delicious supper prepared by our ladies of the parish.'

He then asked a few convoluted questions patently geared to determine whether, given my scientific background and nationality, I and my little family relied more on logic than blind faith to make our way through life, and when I assured him we were pretty much 'kosher Catholic', he beamed a truly beatific smile. He seemed an affable chap, totally different to the callow, tough, ex-hurley playing missionaries they used to send over to Tyneside to strike fear into the hearts of young Catholic parents when they were encouraging them to expand the Catholic population. He revealed a sense of humour and, judging by the many and various musical references in his reception room, would almost certainly have been able to turn a tune on something. However, I could not imagine him at an old folks' Christmas party on Tyneside rendering the kind of pseudo-bawdy ballad his peers – though rather more worldly missionaries – used to win hearts at the Young Catholic Men's Club in Newcastle.

When after a pleasant exchange we took our leave of him, it was to find the beaming Mr and Mrs O'Hanlon waiting for us, morning lessons now over, keen to continue their polite but comprehensive interrogation. Although I suspect half the things we were asked or told were to test our naivety or demonstrate Phelim's, he was manifestly devoutly religious, his curiosity unlimited, and his regard for the English reassuring.

When I was attempting to circumspectly explain, in answer to his question about 'what I did', that my activities were modified by a chronic malady, he asked if I had ever been to Lourdes.

'Yes', I said. 'Helen and I visited it years ago during a tour of France.'

'Ah, but was that before your er, er… A miracle would have been surplus to your needs then, I suppose? Lourdes doesn't function as a 'prophylactic', as you medical people might put it. You should give it a visit now. I guarantee you'd find it worth your while.'

He then recommended a number of Irish shrines where various wonders were currently being worked, though probably without sufficient clout for anything terminal. Nonetheless, they might be able to yield palliative support to tide me over until I could arrange a pilgrimage to headquarters. Thus we amicably parted.

The local village was nothing like the ancient, thriving, picturesque community we associated with the English definition, being no more than what looked like a temporary post-office and couple of tawdry closing down shops with countless cobwebs and piles of dead flies and wasps, old notices, remnants of Christmas decorations and other bits of refuse, as well as the little church and school, but it had seemingly produced a corps of great men, both living and dead, though unfortunately no females worth a light. 'Pickerel', it was called, though how much this had to do with that species of fish, and how much to pure whim, probably only God would know. Whatever the derivation of 'Bastardstown', a small village not far enough from where we lived, little imagination seemed to have been spent on place names in the past and if their selection had referred to the nature or business of the town, in some cases it hardly spoke too highly of the citizenry.

The kitchen of our low-ceilinged house was beamed with second-hand oak heavily tarred in patches to inhibit parasites, the floor of uneven stone flags patched here and there with concrete, and the open fireplace with its huge chimney, totally lacking any comforting aggrandisements that could often otherwise provide heart-warming features. Without a grate or any kind of containing structure, a fire might have been set in any of several places that could not have long been left unattended, although the odd smouldering faggot tumbling onto a stone flag was not likely to have caused much consternation when there was only an old woman sitting by who had spent large tracts of her life praying to be taken.

According to the O'Hanlons she had been a servant to the family who owned the house and farm and they had left everything to her in their will. By then she was quite infirm and able for little other than to manage the place from her chair with the sporadic assistance of a couple of local lads to mind the livestock and tend the modest crops. Meanwhile she had sat cooking in the fireplace, gradually assuming the jaundiced pallor brought about by the smoke of the coarse turf she used to keep the fire constantly alight.

With three small children unused to fireplaces of this sort, a nearby river and the collapsing ruins of an ancient mill, a haggard which was a graveyard of metallic remnants that could so easily cause tetanus and gangrene infections, plus the kind of dangerous tools we would inevitably need, I was going to have to establish safety rules without delay.

Notwithstanding its superficially aesthetic appeal, the house had been put together without much regard for architectural constraints, crude building techniques being adequate for a few simple humans and beasts; in any case, it was highly unlikely the owner-builder possessed either the skill or resources for anything more lavish. To avoid paying housing tax, the abode would originally have been erected and thatched as a single storey building in the course of a single day. Subsequently a tiny room would have been added at each end, and, much later, an upper floor. Ultimately the roof would have been slated when alternative accommodation for the animals had been provided outside and more humans took up dwelling inside, and the slates made from slices of wonderful Bangor stone. At that time, the main coachway to town passed by the front door and a limited amount of refreshment trade carried on before a road of sorts was made. The habitation itself was never more than a dwelling for a small family and a few edible scavengers, such as a fattening pig, a few poultry, and the occasional small milking cow.

The real charm of the place lay in the outbuildings, all of which had plenty vestiges of ancient furniture and trappings: leather belts, iron chains, hooks, bars, agricultural implements and remains of very worn tools whose identity and use would tax the most knowledgeable of agricultural museum curators today. From the one and only door, the quadrangular yard sloped southwards towards town, surrounded by the house and various small animal houses and stone buildings, which were quite sound except for the slated roofs all of which needed attention, and the internal trappings.

Most agreeable to me was the evidence of honest wear in everything, whether it be of iron, timber or stone, and it was in the outbuildings where past inhabitants had left their most enduring marks which included carved initials done perhaps during a shower of rain by work lads in ill-fitting, several times handed-down homespun suits, or whilst in a huff and hiding from the mistress back in her more mobile days. It was very likely she who had pinned up the St Bridget Crosses in the dairy and poultry house to keep the 'Divil' out of the milk and eggs, though plainly they had had little deterrent effect on his legions of rodent, insect and mould, and it was possible to scoop handfuls of the loathsome powder – mainly faecal and cadaver remains from countless generations – out of the woodwork. No reeds cut from the nearby river and sanctified in the church, had prevented inanimate agents like corrosion from attacking the metal and mortar in vital structural parts; nor had the paint or creosote which of necessity had been used so sparingly, because there was not a single hinge or door fastening that did not need repair or replacement because of it. It was going to take time and ingenuity, as well as muscle and money, to attend to it all. Even thinking about it would cost us peace of mind.

THREE

After a week that seemed like a lifetime, to our great relief Arnold returned. Someone had told him there was no Customs on the Stranraer-Larne route – meaning there was none in Larne, not that there would be none when he crossed the border into the Republic – and his luridly orange van might be a sight for sore eyes in the north, but not in the south. Thus he had been driving in lovely country for miles without a care in the world, when he had suddenly come upon a little Customs shack where the occupants were Southern Irish – Republican Irish – and would not let him in. This time it was because of a metal trunk whose lid was jammed, causing the Customs officers and Arnold to think it was locked, but for which Arnold had no key. The trunk, for which there never had been a key, contained underwear according to the bill-of-lading, but because the lid would not open, they deduced the contents to be some kind of contraband. From his previous experience Arnold had gleaned that saying too much could prove worse than saying too little, and we had primed him before leaving the previous week to keep his mouth shut and let the bill-of-lading do the talking. Nothing could go wrong we had assured him, because the issue of the Mini was being dealt with by us. But his introducing that matter by way of explanation only confused the Ulster men who had not the faintest idea what he was 'gabbling on' about.

After an hour and a half parked in front of the Dundalk Customs where the colour of his van must have got up the noses of every bounty-hunting one of them, the ever-redeeming Customs' lunch break arrived, and as they were getting ready to go off, one 'with a really nasty face who spat when he spoke', told Arnold they were going for lunch and absolutely wanted no problems waiting for them when they came back. Sound counsel is rarely any use unless implemented, and instead of making himself scarce as soon as they went, Arnold got out his packed lunch, bottle of Newcastle-on-Tyne tap water and Newcastle Journal, settled down to his own repast, and waited for his tormentors to return.

When they did, 'without a friendly "Hello" or anything', Arnold apprised them of an excellent idea he had conjured to solve the problem of the locked trunk: he would get Alice's 'foldy-up' bike from the back of the van, ride down to Wexford on it, get the key from us and ride back with it. The Customs could then open the trunk, see everything was in order, and he could continue on his way. How old was the girl, they wanted to know.

'About nine or ten, but big for her age.'

'And you mean to tell us that a six-foot feckin' eejit is going to ride all that way on it..? How far do you think Pickerel is from here?'

They then went off without waiting for an answer and a couple of minutes later Arnold could hear them laughing.

'On your way, pal, before we lock you up,' one shouted.

Suspecting a trap, Arnold cautiously engaged first gear and crawled away at no more than three or four miles an hour until his inquisitors and their shed were completely out of sight. Changing gear, he then put his foot down. From then on he did not have a speck of bother until, instead of taking the route down to us that we had marked out for him, he took what he reckoned would be a shortcut, and got lost. After going round and around a couple of roundabouts because signposts were often in a 'foreign language', he managed to find a road going south.

'And here I am!' he declared with a grimace. 'And everything better be in there 'cos I can tell you I'm not coming back to this place again. At first I thought I might make this a regular run… But not now, brother. Not after what I've had to put up with.'

For a moment I thought he was going to cry, but he was just wiping away some engine oil that had managed to get in his ear.

The following morning, as soon as he left, I levered open the lid of the trunk. While he had been telling the tale I had felt an icy hand gripping my heart. On top of a pile of unmentionables was my old New Zealand .22 rifle, one of the last things to be shoved in after days of stewing over the best place to hide it.

'He isn't as unlucky as he thinks,' I muttered to George.

'Genie, neither am I, I suppose,' replied George, whistling through his teeth.

The very next week we received a letter from the Inland Revenue Commissioners demanding the levy on the car be paid immediately or the car delivered to Dublin Castle as forfeit.

Embarrassing though it was, we decided there was nothing for it but to seek Carleton-Borris's advice, not least because part of the letter was in Irish, something we would come to realise was a common ploy with the Irish Civil Service when they wished to intimidate their correspondent. Our patron was surprisingly helpful and suggested we go to see one of the local TDs (members of the Irish Parliament), on Saturday night at the Labour Hall in town. Apparently not only was this person a TD, he was also *Tanaiste* (deputy Prime Minister) and leader of the Labour Party. We thought it incredible that such a personage would involve himself in something as flimsy as this. Imagine a constituent of Winston Churchill's having plied him with such a request? He would more than likely have turned a machine-gun battery on them.

'You mean the deputy Prime Minister of the country..? For an old Mini..?'

'That's him, and that's what he's there for. You're a constituent of his now and there's no depth to which he won't stoop if he thinks there might be a vote in it.'

So on the Saturday evening, with no small misgivings, Helen and I went to see the second-highest person in the land about our second or maybe half-dozenth-hand little car – an apparently small step for an Irish politician, though a giant leap for us – and after waiting no more than ten minutes, a big handsome man in his fifties, with thick combed-back grey hair, who looked as though he had done a bit of boxing in his time, came to the door and invited us in, name Brendan Corish. It was a very Spartan place with no secretary or anything, just a small table, a couple of wooden chairs and a telephone.

No sooner had we got started, than the telephone started ringing and it rang incessantly throughout the time we were with him. The way he dealt with the various callers, plainly according to their station and situation, was straight off the stage: with some he was genial and reassuring, with others as solemn as a hanging judge, and throughout he winked, pulled faces and made daft gestures for our benefit.

'Calm down, Miley! You know what an eejit he is… Give me a bell tomorrow morning if you're still in. There's nothing I can do at this time of a Sarriday night.'

He put the phone down and turned to us with a snort. 'God knows how many times that feller's been locked up for knocking in shop windows. And who does he contact when he's allowed a call..? Not his solicitor, I can tell ye!'

Helen and I looked at each other, wondering what kind of 'eejits' he would decide we were when he had heard our tale.

But we would soon learn that Irish TDs were not only accessible but accountable and never forgot where they came from; most certainly their constituents would not allow any such lapses, just as they would never overlook a failure to attend the funeral of anyone in the constituency who was not a total nobody. A wise man with a digger would submit a tender for a job with the Department of Forestry and then tell his TD he had better see to it that he got it, while rivals might have placed more store by the rosary, and missed out.

We kept the Mini, the registration plate and the oil drum, and never paid anybody a penny. Whenever anybody in uniform asked – and they did, often enough – we just told them the Deputy Prime Minister was dealing with it and they either grinned or leered, depending, we supposed, on what political party they supported.

Before we came to Ireland I had told my brother Michael that virtually every window frame in the house was rotten and he said he would come over and give us a hand to replace them, meaning he would do it all himself. He was a civil servant but carpentry was his hobby and he had a few days left out of his annual leave, so on the Monday of our third week, within three-quarters of an hour of arriving on his Norton 500cc, with his box of pristinely-maintained tools in his pannier, Michael was in his overalls, complete with Stanley knife-blade creases, and on the job; and every day he was here, he was first up and at it, continuing until only dusk threatened to slight his wonderful workmanship. He had come to work, he said, but the surroundings made it a perfect holiday and he was thoroughly enjoying himself, so I just left him to it. Where I was satisfied with doing things so that they functioned and would endure indefinitely,

Michael insisted on doing everything perfectly, meaning using teak rather than pine, and mortise-and tenor joints instead of nails; and if he had to use a metal fastening, it would have to be a brand new pure brass screw with all its threading intact, and most definitely not one of my reconditioned iron nails.

Because the Age of Disposal was descending on Ireland the way it had descended everywhere else inside the 'developed world', one could get virtually nothing that matched anything over six months old, so much had to be replaced in pairs or sets, which added considerably to the expense. Nevertheless, by the end of Mike's week we had beautiful handmade teak windows, mahogany shelves and cupboards, albeit on lumpy walls that were unworthy of them, and he was looking around for anything else to fill in his time right up until the moment of departure. Everybody enjoyed his presence, not least the children who found him a good-humoured uncle who always had something interesting to say to every one of them. He gave Walter a flying apprenticeship in carpentry, and when we saw him off on the Friday, there were many more tears than carpenters usually get when they finish a job. It had been a wonderful opportunity for the children to get to know their uncle and establish memories they would never forget, and his high standards would haunt me long after he left. Regularly I would be reproved with things like, 'Uncle Mike said you should always dovetail something like that,' as I whacked a hundred-year-old nail with its original tip rusted off and a new one roughed on with a file. 'I know, son,' I would explain, 'but it doesn't matter for this...as long as it works. What your Uncle Michael was doing was pure carpentry. This is joinery, a different skill altogether. But still valuable.'

We would have George for two months yet, and the children until they started school; after that, the children only for an hour or two in the evening and at weekends. So much of the work would soon be up to only Helen and me. My minute invalidity pension would not stretch to hiring skilled tradesmen or unskilled labour, and we would only buy what we could not make – when we could afford it – supplemented by beachcombing in scrapyards and dumps. Fortunately it was an age when councils still appreciated people taking away and using stuff that had been dumped, and every time we went we would come away with something useful, or potentially so. It never ceased to surprise me how people regarded so many utile oddments as rubbish, and we would always find enough for a rabbit hutch, a poultry feeder, or little wrought iron gate that I could repair with the DIY welder I used for sculpture.

Walter and George, one of whom would always come with me, would shout from the other side of a pile of newly dumped junk as it gushed out in a smelly torrent, from the back of a scrap lorry.

'What about this, Dad?'

'Is this what you were looking for, Jack?'

'Hey, man, look at this!'

As a sculptor I had visited dumps for years in search of scrap metal. I had always regarded it as honest and valuable recycling, now regarded it as providence and had no qualms about bringing it home, though Helen never felt the same when she saw me coming down the drive with all kinds of junk tied with ropes and spiders and hanging out of the back of the Mini.

Creosote was expensive, but paint dregs, of which there were always masses, could be pooled into a thick grey sludge and used to protect timber in rough outside jobs. Huge rectangular-headed nails, no longer manufactured but ideal for some things, could be drawn from old wood, straightened and de-rusted, and screws that had lost their thread become nails or tacks. Old hinges, fittings and tools that could not be obtained any more, would be renovated in jars of phosphoric acid and made ready for brazing. Some stuff had never been used and plenty only wanted a simple repair. For us, Council dumps were Aladdin's caves, and it seemed silly to close them down, or put a fence around them and charge a ridiculous amount for depositing stuff in them, or for taking stuff away to make use of it.

Vanity had been one of the first casualties when my career went, so handing down clothes from one member of the family to another was never an issue, no more than it had been when, in a four-lad family during the Second World War, footwear in particular might begin with the youngest lad's discards from the family next door, and go down the line in our house until sheer hard wear had taken them well beyond the initial 'bit of scuffing'. Such things were a vital part of household economy, just like our mother's knitting and darning, until only clippy mats, dusters and floor cloths remained. At the end of its intended life, almost everything can be used for something else.

Things had changed greatly after the War when my father returned to continue his career and my brothers and I had grown up and begun our own. Now, after all the years, Helen and I often found ourselves referring to the old times of scarcity, rationing and sacrifice, but without moaning about 'hardship' – a word like 'stress' which, because of abuse and overuse, I could not abide. Anyway, luxuries like a decent car, television, telephone and other things which we had enjoyed before coming to Ireland, were not being dispensed with forever, only suspended for a few years until our ship came back in.

Repairing whatever we could, inside and out, buying only what was absolutely needed, and regularly scavenging, was always satisfying, though some of the stuff Helen saw us unloading in the yard would fill her with dismay.

'What's the point of tidying the place up one day, if you are going to turn it into a dump the next!'

'It's improvising, man.'

'Improvising? You never know who's been using it, and for what!'

In any one week we might clear a length of ditches, cement a floor, weld a gate and join a series of gutters; or creosote the timber in an outbuilding, hang a door, paint several windows and plaster a wall. We would do one job until we got blisters, ran out of materials or needed a change, and then turn to another, and I considered we were very lucky in this. Some days one felt more like working inside rather than outside, especially if the weather had changed, or doing one kind of job rather than another, perhaps a nimble-fingered task rather than a heavy one. During a tedious one, and there were plenty of those, we would chat to each other, listen to music, Irish news or magazine programmes, on the scrambler, and learn about the land we were now living in. As interesting or important items came over the air, we would be calling across the yard or through an open window to keep each other informed or entertained, and in this way felt we were integrating with Irish life. In a short time we realised, in a way we had never had occasion to realise before, how incomparably useful was the old Bush transistor, a technological marvel in its day and the first item Helen and I ever bought for each other. It had been around the world with us, got badly bashed out of shape after tumbling down a long and steep staircase during a slight domestic altercation, caught fire when having its battery livened up in situ on the hearth in New Zealand and had to be tossed in the sink to prevent it melting into a complete blob, but it was still doing its job.

When broaching a new task I always gave thought as to how best deploy our energy and other resources, and priorities constantly changed as we learned what was the best way to get the most out of what we had, given each other's ability. There was one principle to which we would always adhere, and that was never to make or repair anything as a temporary measure but always to fix or fabricate with a view to whatever it was lasting forever. Every farm we ever visited displayed examples of 'temporary measures' that were, in fact, permanent; by that I mean, tolerated until they fell to pieces and their atoms dispersed. Things in such a state of disrepair would look unsightly, fail to do whatever they were supposed to do adequately, and require more effort to continually repair than would have been the case had they been scrapped and the job done properly from scratch. The most common example would be the ubiquitous, flimsy bit of frayed and knotted blue baler twine being used to tie things together: things like a fence or gate used to contain seventy head of cattle desperate to be milked or fed. It will be a sad day when the depressed young men who are increasingly hanging themselves, begin using the stuff.

We would puzzle ingenious constructions that failed to perform until we understood how they were meant to operate, and would be delighted when we managed to restore them to full function. Sometimes, because of the availability of better materials or wider requirements, I would devise improvements on ancient designs only to find they had been made the way they were for a reason, and I would then have to undo what I had done and redo it the way it had been done in the first place. Probably the best example would be the hanging of a gate over uneven ground where the gate was rhomboid rather than rectangular. I would dismantle the old gate, which maybe really only needed a few new reinforcing spars, get out my T-square and tape measure and reshape it to make it perfectly symmetrical, hang it on carefully squared-up posts and creosote or paint it, as I did to every stick of wood around the place except what went into the stove, only to find it would now neither open nor close. It was obvious that far more initiative and care went into the making of so many utilitarian items manufactured fifty years ago than into the manufacture of the same item today. Even complex electronic devices which had required so much skill in their invention, often fell short when it came to assembling them, and poor design, clumsy fabrication and flimsiness would be revealed at every turn. Only packaging had improved, and that at considerable cost to the environment.

All the time we worked it was in fresh air, with the sun shining, birds singing and the calming drone of a tractor toiling in the distance. We could not know it then but that first year would turn out to be the warmest since records began and the sunniest we would ever spend in Ireland. It was the perfect way to begin a life in the country.

Every day would turn up something interesting: in the outbuildings or haggard, hedge, field or stream. On rafters and walls we would find copperplate handwritten accounts detailing payments for materials, records of artisans' services rendered in another century, caches of documents in pigeon holes left so long to the vagaries of time and exposed to whatever cellulose-addicts the building had harboured, and climatic forces that had intruded, that they would sometimes sadly atomise into puffs of dust before our eyes.

Occasionally we would come across names and dates scratched into a wall or on a cross-spar during the Civil War or Famine, and this would make us wistful for hours afterwards, for it was impossible not to imagine how things might have been for the autobiographical scribes then and for the rest of their lives. How many of them had emigrated to England, Australia or America to work on roads, railways or down mines; gone to Canada, New Zealand or South Africa and made fortunes, become brigands, hoboes or mere deserters from the ever-burgeoning families their lust and chivvying parish priest had helped create. Had they perhaps lost their way, or been born lost, and subsequently transported free of charge to work in the colonies of Van Diemen, or hanged by the roadside just a mile or two away. More than likely, how many had just laboured here until they were too infirm and had ended their days in the workhouse before sharing a grave with other unknown paupers. So many things were evocative of experiences only ever ideated in dreams or fiction, that it would have been only too easy to have unwittingly constructed an alternative history for oneself. Maybe my ancestors had something to do with it.

On our first Sunday in Ireland we had gone to Mass at the local church. Not only did it seem right, it might have been an opportunity to test the waters of neighbourliness and make ourselves known to the local community. We had hardly sat down before we realised the male congregation was sitting on one side of the aisle and the female on the other, and everyone was staring at our 'mixed' party boldly sitting in the middle of the male enclave where no female worshippers had ever dare sit before. The Mass had more or less ground to a halt and all was dead quiet while the celebrant and congregation waited for us to sort ourselves out. Never having experienced segregation in a church before, we did not care to be separated, so stuck it out, staring towards the front when standing, and at our feet when kneeling or sitting, pretending we were unaware we were defiling anybody's temple. But eventually the service picked up where it had left off and we only had the wide eyes of children plus a few sneaking glances from the more devout adults to contend with.

The church was quite unprepossessing and lacking in hallow, but when we came out it was to find our humble Mini, with its tartan rug still covering the oil drum, hemmed in by a surprising number of big and expensive cars, what, I understand, the police nowadays call 'kettling'.

Women in sombre floral dresses were already deep in gossiping groups, and men in ill-fitting suits with over-long flared trousers that swept the ground whenever they moved their feet, were lighting cigarettes before they were entirely out of the door. Country children in summer wear advertising either American universities or police departments, were clamouring to buy lurid edibles that posited disaster to both skin and teeth, from a little shop across the road. Nobody seemed to be without a 'redtop' (Sunday paper with centre-page photographs of girls with huge bare breasts) tucked inside a more conservative publication such as the Sunday Times, and the womenfolk clutching plastic bags containing cigarettes, bacon rashers, white pan and milk – breakfast for the communicants.

Meanwhile we sat trapped in the Mini, where, judging by the many glances in our direction, we were the topic of many a lively conversation.

A dozen young 'bucks' had remained standing in the doorway throughout Mass, cracking jokes, eyeing up the girls and sniggering at items in the 'redtop' that one of them had had the foresight to buy before the service started. When some months later I got to ask one of them why they bothered to go to Mass, he answered quite ingenuously that it was to be 'on the safe side, just in case', and nodded skywards.

By the time we had been a month in our new home, it was beginning to take on the appearance of a homestead and everyone apart from the mistress was itching to see some livestock running around, at least a dog and a few hens. As long as the place remained devoid of dependants, Helen felt we could just withdraw if necessary, and this was the reason more than a few items still remained unpacked. She did not realise I knew, but I knew. Counter to this, I felt that with even just a few animals housed and seeds planted, we were morally obliged to see them fulfilled, though I had insisted there would be no animals until we had made comfortable and secure abodes for whatever the beast; that included everything down to bedding, food and drink receptacles that would not easily get fouled or spilled, plus a means of tethering when the subject was out of its quarters. Consequently I had been working overtime – I always worked overtime – to convert the old WC at the bottom of the yard (the 'khazi') into a substantial, timber and cement kennel, and every week had been scouring the local paper and looking through adverts in shop windows for a good pup, such a creature being a lot harder to locate and detect than one might expect. Virtually all pups, like most young creatures, were irresistible, but assessing, their most important feature, their character, was difficult at this stage, and whereas a good dog is a treasure, a poor one is a nuisance as well as useless, especially around other livestock.

At the same time as I was making the kennel, we had been restoring the poultry house, and one day, Tod Doyle, who lived with his wife Sarah in Carleton-Borris's lodge, came to navigate us to a farm over-run by all sorts of poultry: these included the usual farmyard mix of crossbreeds, in-breds, casualties of farm accidents, and the odd outstanding specimen.

As on all farms, every man, woman and child who lived there, could identify every creature they had, but nobody had bothered to cull the runts or deformed specimens. Maureen, the 'boss-woman' Tod called her, a huge woman with massive varicose-veined legs ending in 'crankles' (ankles so thick they spilled over the back and sides of shoes) claimed that every last specimen had received all of its injections, and she was probably pretty much speaking the truth, otherwise, given their number and overcrowding, they would surely have wiped themselves out.

After we told her what we wanted, she steered us into a shed with a few hundred hybrid Rhode Island Red growers (young pullets) milling around an infra-red heater and huge grain feeder, and invited us to pick out a dozen. Then, in pinny and slippers I presumed were left on the doorstep when she entered the house, so thick were the soles which looked as though they had been hewn from petrified chicken-shit, she stepped into the huge pen, grabbed six, steaming hot, bald and scrawny birds in each hand, and rammed them into a woven plastic sack, followed by a thirteenth, making it a 'baker's dozen'. 'For luck, sonny,' she grinned at Walter and revealed a crooked yellow tooth in a sticky black maw.

Alice had remained at the door of the shed, too concerned about being drawn into the nine or ten inches of claggy ammoniacal litter, but Walter's feet were completely buried in it and his fully-dentate grin said it all as he took the bag from Maureen Bosswoman and proudly marched out with it over his shoulder, soft wet chicken crap dribbling down his back.

'He's not coming in the car with us, is he, Dad?' squealed Alice.

'How do you think I'm going to get back?' retorted Walter. 'Trot behind while even the chooks get a ride..? Anyway, you should be carrying half!'

Not that he would have allowed anybody to carry any of our precious primordial stock. But it shut her up.

After we had dropped Tod off at his cottage and returned home, we locked the birds in the henhouse for a few days so they would remember where they were well off when eventually we let them out. They would then be 'free-rangers' when real 'free-ranging' for poultry meant freedom to roam anywhere on God's good earth to consume healthy plants, insects, worms, fruit, seeds, seedlings and fresh water – as well as good grain. It certainly did not mean confinement in a rickety, rusty barbed wire pen where the water soon became fouled, nothing grew and rotten vegetables rapidly got mixed with mouldy grain and fellow captives' droppings.

'We're a farm now, aren't we, Dad?' Walter avowed as we all crammed together to look through the henhouse window to see what the new occupants were doing.

'No, we're not! Aren't we not, Mam? A few chickens doesn't make us farmers!'

Alice would no more admit to having a father and mother who were farmers, meaning a pair of old yokels who had relinquished all interest in life as we all once knew it, than after fifty years would she confess to being a countrywoman herself, or the tiniest bit Irish. Born in Newcastle of Northumbrian parents meant she was English, never wanted to be anything but English, Northumbrian and a Novocastrian, and no-one had better try to change her.

It was astonishing how much life passed by when, solely as a spectator, one remained on the same spot on a street or by a roadside; it was simply a matter of noticing. Now, after living for so long in a busy residential part of a city and working in the epicentre of a town, I had suddenly come to think of ourselves as remote country folk with the gate at the top of our drive, as our spot.

In the course of a single day, tractors laden with hay, lorries with building materials or squealing pigs, small furtive vans and tinkers' caravans – none with legible registration and some straight out of a fairy tale – post-adolescent girls with plump bottoms bouncing on horseback, helmeted middle-aged women on mopeds, teenage boys on racing cycles, old men on heavy, black, upright First World War machines, occasionally still the rural transport of choice of old guards and postmen who could have done with the new vans; pedestrians of both sexes and all ages, a dopey lad waving a stick behind a flock of sheep; a rogue bullock on the run, a prissily trotting truant donkey, and a troupe of furiously pecking hens removing all traces of a trail of spilt corn, all came by at some stage. One fragment of life would appear, make its way past and then disappear, and for a few minutes all would be still as the dust settled and everything became quiet until the next actor trotted across the stage. The inquisitive humans among them must have acquired cricks in their necks from so often straining to discern the nature of the hectic activity suddenly going on in a farmyard that had been so long in repose; and pedestrians and cyclists, old and young, male and female, rarely failed to greet whichever of us could be hailed from the road. Slow-movers would be only too ready to stop for a chat and find out as much as they could about us blow-ins, so they could enlighten familiars awaiting news at home or work.

'Fine bit of land there, sir. I suppose it's a few fattenin' cattle ye'll be puttin' in..? Mind, facin' south, wouldn't it be grand for a crop of onions or strawberries..? Did himself let ye have the whole field..? I was interested in acquiring the house meself at one time. He must have come down a good bit I expect?'

No matter who they were, they all asked the same questions and gave the same advice, even though the latter would mostly be admonitory, such as the need to dispose of the poultry before the fox did, or pull up the rhubarb we had just planted because the fairies would never tolerate the evil plant in this parish. And there were occasional areas, a few feet in diameter, where the grass grew poorly indicating an underground spring or patch of nutritional deficiency, but nothing convincing regarding the subterranean presence of a malevolent form of life given what the overworld already had to contend with.

To all of these, unaware of peers in front or behind, we would almost certainly have been the show, the travelling circus, and they merely the spectators. It all depended on one's position, vis a vis the gate.

Living in the country created the opportunity, and engendered the facility, to develop superstitions, and I can think of no better example to substantiate this than the local motor mechanic who told me that should I ever see a rat leading another one by drawing on the proximal end of a piece of straw, whilst its follower held on to the distal end, it would be because the second was almost certainly blind and responding to the 'humanity' of the first. When I asked him how then could he account for one or more of the same species ravenously devouring a still living but atrociously mauled *compañero* (companion) probably one of its own kin, caught in a gin trap, he thought for a moment and then replied that such an unlikely event could well be the equivalent of physician-assisted euthanasia, but he was smiling and I was not certain that he was not just pulling an Englishman's leg so he could entertain his own *compañeros* in the The Rook's Beak that night. What better for a party of Irishman to contemplate – better still, witness – an Englishman making a fool of himself.

FOUR

One day in September, a few days after George had left and the children started school, it began to rain, and it rained and rained as though it were never going to stop. Water swept down the yard in sheets, carrying away earth, leaving the cobbles bare, and flooding the outbuildings. For a week, fields at the bottom of the valley were turned into lakes and mud was constantly traipsed into the house and car. Thus it was that, like well brought-up Japanese, we began the worthy habit of leaving outdoor footwear in neat rows in the porch, and another very practical tradition was established that would last for long after our Irish days were merely a memory.

Despite having their own warm dry house, the pullets would come into ours whenever they glimpsed the opportunity, jumping up the steep step and depositing little piles of messy excrement on the doormat: not, like a dog, in order to mark its territory, but as a simple gut reaction to having to stretch their legs so far apart. On days when it rained forever and poor Helen had heaps more muddied clothes to wash, there would be nowhere to dry them except in the kitchen, the room where all of us congregated, and even with the Rayburn solid fuel cooker, that wonderful heart of Irish homes since the 1920s, the atmosphere throughout the house was like a 'soft day' (fine misty atmosphere).

Rainwater found spaces between tiles on the roof and the wall above the front and only door, and Helen and I spent a whole day burying a piece of iron railway track I had rescued from the dump, into a mass of diminishingly freshly-mixed cement we repeatedly clagged above the walls of the porch to bolster the plaster and chipboard ceiling which was collapsing under a major leak. Not five minutes after we got it up, down it would come, again and again, with the two of us standing below, splattered with cement clarts. With hands cupped to catch as much as possible of the continuously stiffening mess which slithered up inside our sleeves, we tried to clash it back before the next lot came down. Helen held up the broom whose bristled end was wrapped in a plastic bag for as long as she could – ideally until the cement had set in place upside down – while I strove to apply a plasterer's finish with a bent spade, cursing Isaac Newton and his infuriating law of gravity. Sporadically it held for about twenty minutes before a dull thud would announce another bucketful of sog had hit the floor, and for the rest of the day, despite my cursing, we had to endure the exasperating sound of plops and remember to lock the door every time anybody came in or went out in case they acquired a hairdo that would take a week to undo. Eventually, the last of the cracks settled into fissures, threatening but remaining, and we withdrew to a distance out of earshot to do something else. We had learned something about upside-down cementing, not least that 'chipboard does not a good ceiling make'.

That first wonderful summer lasted from May until September, and from then until spring, as rain took over from the sun and dictated how life had to be lived underwater. A feature of daily rain was that at about a quarter of an hour before dusk it would finally dribble to a stop, like a prostatic old man emptying his bladder, and the sky would temporarily lighten as though a very weak and transient sun were struggling to emerge but would fail. A lone cock blackbird would then hastily deliver a full verse of his scolding song, loudly but without much melody, signalling that for all intents and purposes the day was over. By the time the last notes had died, which they did as suddenly as they had begun, dusk had fallen perfectly seamlessly, and he was already heading to his roost.

One day there was no rain but the humidity was very high and a wonderfully delicate mist pervaded the whole valley. Matthew Sinnott, an old man who could have stepped out of any number of illustrated fairy tales, but owned the tiny village shop which stocked no more than one or two of every basic commodity, and nothing had a 'sell-by' date, had called with a few groceries and observed that it was a 'soft day'. It was the first time we had heard the epithet spoken, as opposed to written by someone like Patrick Kavanagh, and no translation could have been more apt than his observation under the circumstances. No matter how lyrical the metaphor, I could not dismiss from my mind the image of swathes of green fungi propagating in the timbers and even the mortar of the buildings, and the powdery black stuff consisting of millions of spores that produced indelible stains on any first-edition books, wedding photographs, decent clothes and articles of leather, in the corners of wardrobes and drawers. Oh, Ireland and its H_2O… I am a biologist yet confess to preferring aridity to humidity any day.

Matthew had been trained for the priesthood but was remarkably humble for such a profession. He had taken a shine to us, as we had to him, and would sometimes stand in the yard, looking towards the hills, a small, bald-headed figure in late middle age, murmuring a few tantalising verses of Irish poetry before turning around to face us with a smile, confident his gentle soliloquy had been appreciated. Locals said he had only had two loves in his life, and when a superior at the seminary had found letters from the secular one, it had cost him both. He was a sad figure, with his anciently tawdry little shop and few scraggy cows, living in a cottage with as badly a disintegrating thatch as his own, but was wise and gentle and a shade less modest, I think, than he tended to convey. Helen heard he had dozens of little red 'tick' books under the counter, recording debts that were rarely if ever cleared; it seems he was so clement that customers felt obliged to take advantage of him, with the result that instead of being credited with uncommon generosity, he was more often taken for a chump.

Like anybody who came to our door, he never stated outright the purpose of his visit and never directly asked a question or answered one. At times he would call with an item he did not stock in his shop but had picked up in Dublin on one of his weekly trips for supplies, because he thought we might like it. A total stranger would stand farther down the yard than someone like Matthew, and begin with something like, 'Grand day, sir. That's a fine-looking yoke' – meaning St John – and it would take at least ten excruciating minutes to get out of him or her what he or she wanted.

Harry was always there when anybody came and must have eased our passage through many an awkward situation by virtue of his age, smile and patter; most Irish men and women seemed to like children. To hear them, one would think he was an angel and a little genius, but I suspect that even he knew that when it came to complimenting, the Irish did not mean everything they said, and listeners could pretty quickly go through a sack of salt.

The Irish are hardy people and of all the white-skinned wretches unfortunate enough to be transported to slave in the colonies during the heyday of the British Empire, they best survived the privations of the journey. Even today, whether from town or country, many are capable of withstanding physical adversity and will go bare-headed, sleeveless and bare-legged on days when the wind would cut through most urban English flesh as through a frayed lace curtain. So when they came to the door, often enough in the rain and soaked because lousy weather will not deter them, it is never with an umbrella, and rarely with a hat or coat, man or woman, and the word 'stoicism' would never enter their head.

We must have given our postman more business than anybody on his route, because prior to the age of flyers and brochures from local supermarkets, mail for most people outside Advent was Government stuff, whereas we, habitually regular correspondents and now without a telephone, received letters most days of the week. Whether our man saw that as a good thing or bad thing, we never knew because he never spoke. From the day we came until the day he retired, this tall, flint-faced old man with his warhorse of a bike, never uttered a word except twice: once by accident when he grunted: 'Christ!' the time he slipped off his saddle and the hard steel pipe of his crossbar must have almost bifurcated his scrotum.

Had we not already surmised it, we were soon apprised by neighbours that for Old Pat, Satan was an Englishman: immigrant, tourist, or soldier. He would trundle his vehicle down the yard, clash it so hard against the side of the house that lumps of precious rendering would be knocked off, rive open the door without knocking, stride over to the table without a glance at any of us, and plonk whatever he had on the table. Once I placed a bowl of porridge and a plate of jam and bread on the edge of the table nearest the door, but he merely swept it aside with his long, trowel-like hand and clashed down what he had brought in its stead, streaking it with gobs of porridge, raspberry jam and the type of old man's snot that cascades in a torrent whenever they get excited.

'Let's hope that's not another invitation to a garden party at the Palace,' I might comment. But he took humour worse than anything.

'Good morning, Mr Byrne,' we would steadfastly chorus when he first started calling, but salutations always fell on deaf ears.

For all that, we knew there was nothing he liked better than a bit of gossip, because as we became friends with our neighbours they would tell us how from the first day he had been reporting our every move to all his customers en route: 'Wait till ye see the cock they've got. A divil that'll bring them no luck at all... And what d'ye think they've gone and done to the labourer's loft..? Stuck a feckin' bolt on the door..!'

He would be referring to the tiny room under the roof in one of the outbuildings where the casual labourers used to sleep in the last century, and where I was now storing tools. Perhaps he had spent many a night there himself in the past and resented the possibility that he might once again be sleeping there if he ever lost his job with An Post, perhaps through intimidating English correspondents on his route. Ten minutes before he was due to pass their house, fellow countrymen, who rarely if ever received any post, would nevertheless put an extra bit of turf on their stoves to bring the kettle to the boil for his cup of tea which he would quaff as he brought them up to date with the news he had gleaned on his round.

The one time he actually ventured a sentence in my hearing – not to me personally but to the atmosphere as he was swinging his long leg over the saddle – it was couched in a retort: 'That swarm in the sceach (pronounced "skyok" and meaning hawthorn) should be got down in a hive.'

'You can have it, if you want it,' I replied, smiling as graciously as I could.

The thought of him completing his round with a swarm of bees, the size of a large pumpkin, hanging from his crossbar, amused me no end. His reply was to mutter something suitably incomprehensible and ride off. I say 'ride', though I never saw him do anything other than walk by the side of the bike and push it.

He was very likely an old Shinner (Sein Finner) who had been tortured by the English at one time, and the mere sight of one of us now probably caused his vocal cords to seize up. Sometimes we would be walking or driving along the road and pass him on the way to the house. We would offer to take whatever he might have, but he would never part with anything, merely narrowing his eyes and gritting his teeth. Whatever he had belonged to him until he reached its destination, and I am sure he would rather have died than surrender it before he got there. Imagine him sacrificing his life to make sure we received a birthday card or promotional offer from Dunnes Stores. Apart from Mr Byrne, the only reluctant conversationalists we ever encountered were tinkers, but even they would only open their mouths to ask if we wanted to buy something they had or could get.

'A fine carpet..? And ye could do with a field gate. What about a pair of brass bedsteads, then..? No..? Well do ye have any brass bedsteads for sale? Or anything made of brass...? What about iron bedsteads? Or that yoke over there? (John the Baptist). How much would ye be wantin' for him..?'

They could tarmacadam the drive and make a wonderful job, no estimates. They would do it and then we would come to some arrangement regarding payment, like true gentlemen. As they talked, their progeny would be wandering around the yard, in and out of the buildings. They were tough and they were rough and the women could change their facial expressions from comic apathy to defensive ferocity in an instant. None of the local farmers liked them and we were always being given unsolicited advice about not encouraging them, though they did not seem bad, merely different from the rest of the population. Before setting foot in Ireland I had read everything I could get hold of by Millington-Synge, and as a consequence in our house we had a rather romantic concept of the people Synge referred to as 'tinkers', even though some people saw the term as pejorative. Apparently the tinkers themselves preferred 'traveller', as though such an individual were more respectable than a repairer of kettles and pans, and the Government used 'itinerant', though that seemed awful to us. In England they were invariably called 'gypsies' and that seemed the best term of all; but it was only a word and hardly an insult.

One day I was welding in the yard when one who often called, came hobbling down the drive with a companion behind urging him to approach me. The principal was short and thin, as though sorely undernourished in infancy, and I guessed his age would be about thirty-eight, near enough to my own, though he surely looked a good deal older. When out of their teens the race tended to look twenty years older than they actually were, especially the girls. This fellow was darker than most, with claggy black hair, beautiful brown eyes almost buried in a face fissured with strife, and a lopsided body that made his limbs appear of unequal length.

He was wearing the same filthy brown suit he always wore, the same patched white rag of a shirt with odd-sized buttons and no collar, and odd boots that had lost most of the thread that held them together and in any case were far too big. His huge, badly-stained, rotten and incredibly crooked teeth seriously impeded his speech, causing him to dribble saliva and thoroughly spatter any face within a yard. His left trouser leg was torn and soaked with sticky black stuff, and he kept putting his hand down slowly as though to draw my attention to it without having to explain too much.

'What's the matter?' I asked.

Without saying anything, he slowly drew up his trouser to reveal a large gash with a splinter of bone thrusting through the skin like a stick of young celery, and a stockingless boot glued to his leg with pus and dried blood. All he wanted was some ointment to make it better. A jackass had been trying to mount a mare in foal inside the horsebox he also had been travelling in, and it had gone mad, kicking and biting the mare half to death, and he had got in the way.

He urgently needed an analgesic, an antibiotic and an anti-tetanus injection, but would not let me take him to the hospital or do anything other than provide him with the magic ointment, and when I failed to provide it, his face crumpled even more in a mixture of agony and despair. I pleaded with him and threatened him with the consequences of not submitting to proper treatment, but he was adamant. Eventually and very gradually he withdrew, utterly disillusioned, and as he grotesquely limped back up the drive to his friend, with me following, I felt sick and embarrassed by my own futility. They got into a battered little van and drove off and I never saw either of them again.

Notwithstanding their fear of hospitals, whenever a tinker was admitted, a whole party came to visit every day and spread around his or her bed in defiance of hospital regulations and the complaints of other patients and their visitors, but they would soon get bored and wander through the other wards to see if there was anyone else they knew.

I always insisted our family be friendly to tinkers, and we never had anything stolen by them or bother of any kind. George became particularly friendly with them because they made ideal subjects for drawing and painting and loved to hang his portraits on the walls of their caravans. Walter made a friend of one of their lads and the two of them would be pals for many a year until a series of wild experiences followed by retribution loosened the knot; the lad was then swallowed up by a religious cult, disappeared in England, and died before he reached middle age. The tales we heard from Walt as he grew older and closer to his friend were invariably sad, though some tragically funny, and he told of many who died early, often from horrendous accidents.

It was nigh on impossible to draw a tinker into conversation and if you tried to raise a topic other than what they had come about, they would ignore you completely.

Farmers resented them letting a few horses into one of their fields at night, even though they only ate the long tough stuff, like couch grass that neither their cattle or sheep would touch, and even though the same farmers would look away when fifty of their cows broke into a forestry plantation or a neighbour's meadow – including ours – a happenstance they called 'grazing the long acre'.

A small gang, with a middle-aged woman as spokesperson, was the way they dealt with authority, and few young doctors were able to cope with them. Our first GP, very much an 'old hand', would have had little trouble. Most of the locals thought him a tyrant but he always treated us with respect and I could not imagine him treating tinkers that differently from anyone else. His heavy sagging face, with its deep purples and reds, was like an expressionist portrait in the days when syphilis was rife, and his burly build and gruff demeanour was probably just right for a medical man in his neck of the woods. Bombastic and brooking no demur, especially in his surgery where, with the door always ajar, occupants of the waiting room could not fail to acquire details of their predecessor's ailments and transgressions, medication and punishment, and reputedly that was why some in need of medical attention would rather have died than call for him. His skills, like his patience, were limited, but many considered such deficiencies to be amply compensated for by his readiness to leave a warm bed and haul his arthritic old joints into the cold, wet, and wind in the middle of a wild night whenever warranted.

One of the village's many Marys, and Helen's first friend, told us of a woman with a large family who had been very weak after a confinement, and because they had no money coming in, Dr McDonagh paid her husband's wages for a week so he could stay at home to look after her. On another occasion he had been short with a 'demanding old bugger' with a multiplicity of geriatric ailments, and although at the time he had been very busy, he had come back the following day to apologise. Contrition has no more of a place on the syllabus in medical schools than it does in seminaries, and according to Mary, apologising was very hard for an Irishman, especially to a woman.

Imagine a doctor in his late seventies suffering a heart attack while climbing the steep stairs of a tenement on his way up to a bed-ridden patient, and expiring halfway. A half-century ago our family doctor in Newcastle did just that and I suspect Ronan McDonagh would have done the same had his number been called in such a situation.

Mind, ordinary Irish people, and that certainly includes strangers as well as Samaritan familiars, could be extraordinarily friendly and helpful.

One Sunday our car conked out on the way back from an expedition up country to suss out a gander allegedly 'as big as a horse' which turned out to be no bigger than a duck, and I was kicking a tyre in exasperation when a car pulled up and a skinny fellow in his thirties, wearing best bib and tucker, got out and came over.

'Grand day, sir,' he said. 'Are ye right?'

Without waiting for an answer, he stuck his head under the propped-up bonnet and began tapping and riving at this and that until the long strands of his sparse hair were trailing across the sticky black parts of the engine, swiping up little clots of gunk and depositing them on his collar and neck.

In response to my repeated enquiries as to his opinion, he confessed to knowing very little about 'these kind' of cars, so all I could do was nevertheless thank him for his help and apologise for not having a rag to clean himself up with. 'No worries,' he said, pulling a pristine ironed handkerchief out of his pocket with a greasy black hand. But somebody else had stopped now, somebody who could and did fix the problem, and the first chap, smiling graciously with a face smeared in gunk, wished us luck and departed, probably for tea at his girlfriend's where one could only hope he was not on his way to ask some cantankerous old sod for his daughter's hand – if they still did such things in Ireland. At one time in England one's vehicle could hardly come to a rest anywhere by the side of a road before a saluting, impeccably uniformed AA or RAC patrolman would have been standing by one's vehicle with his box of tools. My Singer Coupé, acquired when I came out of the Army and started courting girls of a haughtier type than those always ready to throw their leg over a motorcycle pillion, only cost £27 but its brake fluid always leaked out after a few miles, meaning the cost of the car should have been reckoned in terms of litres of brake fluid. In such situations both the AA and RAC angels of mercy could be an excruciating embarrassment when you did not have sufficient money to pay them and had to commit to joining their association for a whole year or, at the very least, a three-months' trial.

It was not necessary to know an Irish person to strike up a conversation, because the majority walked along the street with their mouths already open ready to greet somebody – anybody – and it only required the slightest acknowledgement to get them going. If you were next to one in a bus or train, a waiting room or queue, they were always ready to opine on almost any topic. Years later on a visit to Spain, a Catalan would complain that the Irish greeted everybody they met, including strangers, in an unforgivably genial manner. Such a liberty, he declared, was nothing short of an invasion of privacy; anybody should have the right to pass anybody else anywhere on earth without having to acknowledge their existence. Mind, the Spaniard – both Catalan and Castilian – a race that specialises in contrariness, can be very affectionate to people they hardly know, reaching out to pat one's shoulder, grasp one's forearm, or rub the back of one's shoulder as though trying to revive the part. There may be hesitation initially, but once the threshold has been crossed, the Spaniard quickly warms to whomsoever he considers has become, or will become, a new friend. The Irishman, on the other hand, though superficially very friendly, can very easily withdraw from the encounter and think no more of it. More than almost any nationality, the Irishman will dole out invitations to visit his home without the slightest intention or expectation of the offer being taken up; it is merely a way of their taking their leave.

FIVE

By now Walter and Alice had settled into school and were having to deal with Gaeilge, (the Irish language) as an academic subject. Considering English was clearly and legally the working language of the country, the prominence given to Gaeilge in all official documents seemed irrational, and, apart from anything else, the sheer cost of duplicating every communication, unreasonable. That bonus points could be earned in school and state examinations by answering questions in any paper, no matter the subject, in Irish, seemed academically crass and grossly unfair. We were in favour of Gaeilge being taught as a European language of choice, as was, for instance, Welsh in Wales, but not when it meant that someone born in the Gaeltacht (an Irish speaking area) or with a talent for Irish, could score higher in geography, history or anything else, than someone with a greater aptitude in that subject than the candidate with a superior aptitude in Irish.

While Alice devoted herself to being a good scholar, with or without Irish, Walter sought to establish himself among the scamps, and the O'Hanlons were kind and helpful to both of them, as indeed they were to Helen and me. Because they passed our house on the way from theirs to the school, they frequently gave them lifts to and fro, a favour unimaginable from a school teacher, let alone a headmaster, in England or anywhere else we knew of. Meanwhile, Harry's nursery school was the yard and field, and his peers the pullets.

By the time we had been in Ireland a couple of months, nearly everybody in the parish and somewhat beyond had found an excuse to come to the door, introduce themselves, and offer their help should we ever need it. A woman and her mother from Yorkshire, with no connections to the area, had come to live in the village but the mother had passed away within a couple of weeks. The daughter was beside herself, not knowing anybody or what to do, but the locals had got together and done everything for them, from arranging the funeral, readying the house, getting the flowers, baking and preparing the refreshments, all in such a homely manner, never leaving the bereft young woman alone until all was well over. Some time after, she told Helen she had never known such kindness, not least from people who until then were complete strangers. No doubt there are people all over the world given to such acts, albeit they are more likely to be from among the primitive or poor, and the Irish would surely be among the best of examples.

Ever since we landed, Marie O'Hanlon had been trying to persuade Helen to join the ICA, the Irish Countrywoman's Association, a rustic ultra-conservative sort of sisterhood, but Helen feared it would turn her into a kind of 'Stepford Wife'. Yet in spite of what she maintained and probably believed, none of us had adapted to the new life better than she had. According to her, even the washing smelt better after drying on the line I had strung across the yard, than it had ever done in Newcastle. But even though she was very sociable by nature, the ICA seemed too great a leap as yet and she would hold off a little longer until she had more confidence. Marie excused herself for not being a member herself, saying Helen would understand, though she never did.

In the meantime, George, who had returned after his last course of study in England, had become pally with a chap who bred Staffordshire bull terriers and on learning we were looking for a dog, gave us the choice of a male pup out of a litter he was weaning. We picked out a brindle with a great head and called it 'Sullivan', after John L., the famous Irish pugilist, though he eventually proved unequal to the tribute. He was a magnificent looking little beast with an enormous vulgar appetite, the only dog I ever knew to eat cat, but he never bothered with rats, the quarry his breed was once famous for.

To deal with what I considered to be far and away the vilest animal on earth, we advertised in shop noticeboards for 'good ratting cats', and ended up with sacks and boxes of moggies fit only for mauling the sweetest of songbirds, and Sullivan put paid to most of them. Over a period of months the only feline out of at least fifty that was any good, was a huge tom that, like many a cat in the country, got run over when crossing the road.

Before long, Sullivan was emitting the classic Staffordshire bull-terrier howl at night. Greed, plus want of spirit and intellect, were the main vices of the modern breed, but the howl, which sounded as though the beast was being throttled, took some beating. When one recalled that a hundred years previous this animal was the quintessential ratter that provided so much brutal entertainment for the 'sporting man', it went to show how the selective breeding of dogs, in particular, by so-called 'fanciers', had resulted in the loss of so much character. If the dog had any value as a guard, it was due to its deterrent appearance. That said, when Declan Lorcan, the replacement Anglo-friendly, banjo-playing, bee-keeping postman asked if – after Sullivan tried to bite him – we would mind if he whacked him with the hurley he carried for carnivores, I said no, as long as he appreciated the dog's motives were also primarily defensive. I thought it might be good training for him:

defence against the armed intruder. However, notwithstanding Declan's accusation, and Sullivan's well proven tilt to cat, I never for a moment thought he had it in him to take a wedge out of a human.

Our first Irish Christmas was as traditional as we could contrive, and indigence undoubtedly contributed to the primitiveness; certainly it made us more creative than we had been for a very long time. Helen and I resorted to the kind of ploys perpetrated on us by our respective parents during the Second World War, such as the stuffing of narrow stockings with bulky exotic items such as a couple of Jaffas (the oranges with skin as thick as a doormat) or a packet of non-luxury (tank grey or khaki) plastacine. Helen tried her hand at oragami animals but parcelling them up meant the recipient had to remake them from scratch. I had a go at what should have been absurdly easy – the wonderful trapezist who traditionally did his stuff by squeezing his wires – but the wire obviously was not the right grade and merely bent to leave the figure dangling as though his neck and all his limbs were broken. The one unalloyed success was the fabrication of paper-chain decorations made from several weeks' Wexford Echo.

We had no television, but the 'scrambler' still served us well, both entertaining us and instructing us about the Irish way of dealing with Christmas, such as the 'wran boys' who used to catch wrens and impale them on hawthorn hedges – and apparently still did in places like Cork and Kerry, but I never caught any. It was our first introduction to the *seanachai* (storyteller) in the person of Eamon Kelly, a Kerryman favourite with RTE, the Irish radio station, and although his dialogue was strictly stage Irish, it was hilarious to us. His talent resided in his ability to create an atmosphere by describing ordinary things in marvellous detail with only a tad of cynicism, and peppering his tales with Irish maxims. Resorting to very little sexual, political or religious innuendo – anything vulgar or contentious – he invariably ended his tales with a denouement that was acceptable to all tastes and ideologies, and even the kids liked him.

Leading up to Christmas, we had scoured the countryside around for holly and mistletoe and ended up with enough to have started a small business. The tiny, expensive sprigs we used to buy from greengrocers in Newcastle rarely had more than one or two bruised and battered berries, and even their tough leaves showed the rough handling they must have had from being daily humped in and out of the shop, suffering maximums and minimums of temperature and humidity every day for a month, constantly having bits nipped off by enterprising kids, and being discoloured and tainted by mongrels peeing on them.

It was my first Christmas without alcohol or tobacco since I was an eighteen-year-old soldier, and although I have to say I particularly missed a drink at this time, we must all have benefitted, for it had become somewhat of a problem since I contracted my illness. But we had a little spruce, enough to eat, ginger wine to drink, sing-songs, and the mah-jong set I had bought in Hong Kong many years ago, the playing of which had become a Boxing Day tradition. Boxing Day in Ireland was called 'St Stephen's Day' but none of us from England would call it that. Had we remained in England, perhaps the old traditions of singing and making our own entertainment would have gradually died out, television having eliminated many home-brewed initiatives. That said, now that we had no television, I convinced myself we did not miss it, though I was almost certainly the only one. It would be a year before we felt justified in buying a set, and then it would be a tiny second-hand, black-and-white version.

Tod and Sarah Doyle, whose main reason for living seemed to be so they could open and close the gate for any car coming in or out of the driveway to Carleton-Borris's estate, lived in his lodge just inside the gate, that consisted of two rooms, a little stove, no running water and an outside toilet. Every day Sarah walked to the village to attend Mass and thank God for his munificence, and both of them agreed with everything any higher-ranking passerby – i.e. just about anybody – said, which we presumed was also one of their duties. We invited them for tea on Christmas day, but either they had no clock or were simply desperate for company, because they arrived about three hours early, just as we were finishing dinner which was about two in the afternoon. We had been told they knew the life histories of everybody who had ever lived in these parts so reckoned they would be a fount of bucolic tales, but because of their dread of indiscretion, they were like fossilised clams when it came to leaking the kind of information that could have had us gasping in wonderment or chuckling with glee. Instead of spending the one day of the year playing games with our offspring, we exhausted ourselves in a three-hour interview of two old people who might as well have come from another planet, and even when they had had tea and been taken home, for the rest of the night we could not dispel the awkwardness. It must have felt like half a day in the Star Chamber for them, all for the sake of a few tinned salmon sandwiches, a piece of icing cake and a glass of wine with nary a drop of alcoholic cheer in it; even the crackers, none of which detonated, had all been pulled and ripped to shreds by the time they came. If only we had had them for dinner instead, at least when they went home they could have spent the remainder of the day digesting the contents of full bellies while Tod wallowed in the sports page of the local newspaper and Sarah savoured the anniversaries and obituaries.

In continuance of our own traditional Christmastide, at ten minutes to midnight on New Year's Eve, I went out into the cold pitch-black night in overcoat and trilby, clutching a small brown paper bag containing the first egg laid by one of our hens – which from now on and forever would be preserved as a fossil – a lump of peat, a crust of soda bread, and a punt (Irish pound note). These represented tokens of sustenance for the coming year. Inside, eagerly awaiting midnight and Helen's ringing our old school bell whose peals would call me back in and allow the festivities to begin, was my excited little family. First-footing was a North of England and Scottish tradition which Helen and I had always observed, no matter where we were, and had a tall, dark and handsome stranger, instead of an infinitely less attractive figure, been first to cross the threshold, it might well have brought good luck. Nowadays, the phenotype seemed few and far between, and even on Tyneside requirements had been revised in favour of short baldies with wiry grey hair tufting out of their nostrils and ears. Nobody remotely resembling Gregory Peck or Lawrence Olivier had ever chanced across our doorstep.

The contents of the paper bag were meant to signify a hoped-for abundance of comfort, security and wealth. My father used to take out a slice of fruitcake, a lump of coal and a pinch of salt, and even though the seven of us could never have survived long into the new year on such limited provender, the gesture was considered to be at least as vital as a Mass to celebrate docking a foreskin, however divine.

There was a slight drizzle so I could not see any stars, and as I felt my way into the woodshed to wait, I mused on how long the tradition was likely to endure on our limb of the Smithwhyte family.

After an age, the bell rang and I stepped out of the five-feet high shed and into a mound of Sullivan's excrement, a pipistrelle flew out and, legendary radar notwithstanding, brushed my face with its creepily greasy little furry body. Having been searching for mammals of a much viler order, I stumbled backwards into something else and made haste indoors, casting shoes and socks as I went, and doing the kissing, speeches and auld-lang-syning in bare feet. So much for pagan traditions; the St Bridget's crosses were probably vibrating with fury.

Snow was scarce enough to be a treat, unlike Northumberland where it snowed most years, and by the time I had knocked up a couple of sledges – a man-sizer's and a toddler's – the snow had nearly all gone. But at least we were ready for it next time, and when it returned, which it did a couple of days later, I had them down from where they were hanging in the garage, before the ground was covered. It came in blizzards, the heaviest since 1947, and a neighbour with a tractor came without being asked, and hauled the Mini up the drive.

Helen and I had had plenty experience of snow throughout our lives, including five solid months of it in Ontario, but I could never recall it creating more wonderful scenes than it did with the farm buildings, gates, railings and trees, the way it did here. It really was good fun, snowballing and sledging with the kids and then having it disappear before it became a nuisance. The Canadian experience, which was far more exacting than anything in the north of England, had made us well and truly aware of the disadvantages of the stuff and nowadays I could certainly do without it, but must confess to finding the profound cold and stilly silence that came at the end of the day when dusk had fallen but no more snow, and the scene matured, absolutely mesmerising.

The Rayburn cooker, the solid fuel stove in the kitchen where we ate and largely lived when indoors, was not only central to our comfort but critical on the too frequent days when we had no electricity to cook with because of strikes by constantly whingeing ESB employees who clearly, but without justification, considered themselves the kings of the working class. 'Whingeing Poms' was what the Australians used to call us English, so God knows how those masters of withering slang would have designated the stalwarts of the Irish ESB.

The Rayburn had been our first and most important capital purchase. With an oven as well as a large hotplate, it easily managed our meals while drying the clothes hanging above and thoroughly warmed the kitchen. It was the only heating we had, so in winter all windows upstairs and in every other room downstairs had ice on the inside. Sitting by the side, where I had an old armchair wedged between it and the wall, I could lean over and turn the draught-wheel that acted as bellows to ramp up the degrees. The trouble with this was the hole that led down into the earth beneath served as a centrally heated highway for mice until I had rammed sufficient wire-netting into it. Everybody loved the Rayburn as it radiated power and exuded personality from where it stood in the centre of a huge open fireplace that led to what locals said was the widest chimney in Wexford, as though that were easy to establish and of some significance.

Peat was the commonest and cheapest fuel, and considered, along with bread and milk, to be vital to life. But it was a hell of a pollutant and everybody warned us that our predecessor, Bridie, the woman who had lived in the house for years prior to our arrival, and spent most of her last years sitting in the fireplace next to an open fire – a kind of campfire that smoked as though fed on tractor tyres – apparently had skin the colour and texture of a dirty walnut. Now, however, when we came in after the last of the chores had been completed on a cold, wet and thoroughly vile evening, to lean back while standing, hands grasping the long smooth, shiny bar in front – teeth of the dragon – which would be warming one's pyjamas while a hole would be threatening to burn in the seat of the trousers one was wearing, was sheer bliss.

On the way home from school one afternoon in February, Walter and Alice saw a goat hopelessly tangled up in a barbed-wire fence by the road, and ran all the way home so they could tell me. I immediately covered the oil-drum petrol tank, grabbed a length of rope, and with Walter and Alice all the while urging me to make haste in case the goat somehow disappeared, off we went.

The poor creature was still there at a bend in the road, entrapped and badly ripped but neither struggling nor making a sound, and although various vehicles were slowly passing, none were stopping or any their occupants saying or doing anything beyond staring. It would probably have been different had the unfortunate creature been a calf or a lamb. It was a female with a large distended udder that was badly lacerated and bleeding profusely, and quite a task getting her off the wire. But she did nothing to hinder us. Instead, she just lay there, waiting, breathless and totally exhausted, her intelligent eyes seeming to understand what we were doing. It was a 'scrub', or semi-wild type, and heavily pregnant, so we heaved her up into the back of the Mini as carefully as we could.

When we got home I stitched her up and dressed her many wounds, during which she never flinched. Then we put her in a clean dry shed with a few armfuls of beautiful dry, sweet-smelling hay in a rack on the wall, and a few sprigs of fresh glossy green ivy, into which she tucked immediately though gracefully while standing on very wobbly legs. She was so fastidious that unless the food was up in the rack, she would not touch it, and even though the ground was clean and covered with fresh straw, she was able to determine if anything had touched it, simply by sniffing.

Two nights later she produced a billy and a nanny kid, and by the following morning when we went to see how they were getting on, they were already suckling and hobbling about. 'Gertie', as we called her, was endearing herself to us as much as any of the many animals that would eventually come into our lives over the following decades.

Within a few days the kids were astonishingly active, running around the yard and climbing up steps and walls for the sheer delight of jumping off while kicking their legs in the air. I found it hard to credit they were so closely related to sheep, animals I had so often worked with in my veterinary days and long since concluded had IQs on a par with woodlice, though most certainly not ants or bees.

Through time, after we had been introduced to many others of her species, along with the magpie among birds and border collie among dogs, the goat would prove its intelligence and its stoicism, especially if it was a scrub; and if it bleated, you could be sure there would be something wrong. Both the buck and the doe were extremely stubborn and even though one could drag them or they could do the dragging, one could never haul them the way one might a ewe or heifer; they had to be allowed to lead and at their own pace. Some of the goats we subsequently acquired would be infuriatingly slow and pretend they were on their last legs until they saw the rose bush outside the dairy, when they would race ahead to nip off a bud or flower before we could get them in the door; the sharper the thorns, the more enticing the plant, seemed a truism. Some would stand and ruminate like statues concreted to the ground, and we would have to implore them to take a step; swearing got one nowhere and I certainly tried it, although, of course, none of our own kids (the children) were allowed.

By now Helen was coming to regard our Irish domicile as home, and it had not taken very long. The ICA, which she had tentatively joined, had introduced her to most of the local women, and although some of its traditions would always remain beyond her, she was learning various skills and rustic lore, like who in the parish possessed the largest button, who was related to whom – the answer to the latter being almost everybody to everybody else – and how various ones voted. It seemed to me to be a kind of rural multi-denominational women's guild and a limited 'useful' leisure activity for those who rarely got off their farms or met anybody new, this being, for many, their only outing and opportunity to talk about something other than lambing, vermin, milk quotas and blight. Helen had expected they would be competent darners, knitters and bakers of good bread and scones, and was delighted to learn that despite their circumscribed contact with the rest of the world, some of the women were not only remarkable embroiders and crocheters, but lovely bakers capable of making delicious decorated cakes that would have held their own in the best of English teashops. The local ICA branch, of which there were branches throughout the whole country, was often called upon to make suppers for whist drives and other celebrations in the village, and proud so to be, giving of their own time and providing ingredients, flowers and decorations, all for nothing.

Because we had a young family and there were no shops near where we lived, it was often necessary to make trips into town for the kind of domestic necessities that frequently ran out, and without ever complaining, every time she went, Helen would call at the greengroceries for leaves and left-over fruit and vegetables for the goats, to the fish market for the plentiful scraps the hens relished, the bakeries and confectioners for the stale bread and pastries that every creature on the farm would eat, and finally to the timber merchants for the sawdust we would fling down as litter for the hens and goats, a task even Alice relished.

It cannot have been a joy for Helen, but it was an excellent way of using good food that had often been discarded not because it was bad, but because it did not conform exactly with the diameter or colour of an EC model carrot; or some other stipulation made by a Brussels civil servant that had nothing to do with quality and everything to do with appearance.

All livestock food needed some supplementing, no matter how good the pasture. Goats, for instance, needed salt mineral licks, and poultry good grain, and there were always veterinary requirements, all of it expensive. So by doing what she was doing, Helen was not only saving us money, she was preventing unnecessary waste and the shopkeepers seemed to appreciate it. Not many countrywomen did what she did, no matter what their background, and she did it with grace. I supposed she was respected for it, but did not care if she was not; I certainly admired her for it and always encouraged her not to pay much attention to the deprecations of others, friend or foe.

Although I often referred to the Seymours, and Helen had at last read their book, without exactly 'devouring' it, we did not do everything they did. Apart from differences in taste, whereas we started with nothing, I suspect the Seymours started fairly flush. John Seymour, a proficient though rather vainglorious narrator, irritated me with his assumption that at the end of the day every agrarian male worth his salt would need to quaff a redoubtable quantity of home-brewed liquor – or proprietary stuff if he had over-quaffed his own. He seemed blithely unaware of how much harm alcohol could do, whether brewed in a country kitchen or bought in a bar, and I suspect his continual endorsement was due, as much as anything, to a pretty hefty macho element in his nature.

Helen kept reminding me that she had heard the Seymours had split up, implying it was likely the upshot of too much self-sufficiency, in his case the outcome of doing everything according to the tenets of his own book. But maybe Mr S had modified some of his ideas since publication, because we had also heard that he had moved to Ireland with a pretty girl a fraction his age. I suggested his current rants might be dealing more with raddling and tupping than previously, but Helen did not think that at all funny, not least because there might be a shred of truth in it. Nevertheless, the fact that he had moved to Ireland was heartening, indicating we were in the right place to live the self-sufficient life. In any case, having used his unquestionably valuable book to get started, we were now learning from our own experience and changing whatever we felt was warranted. Many important things about animals and plants could be learnt not from books, but by observation, noting what they needed and liked, and what bothered them.

Walt was now going to a secondary school in town. It was also a seminary, one at which the present cardinal of the country had attended, so although its academic record was one of the highest in the country, and its sporting achievements renowned, religion was still the most influential. The main problem for us was that, unlike in England, even school education was costly. There, everything was paid for by the state; here, everything except the tuition had to be paid for by parents: textbooks, notebooks and instruments, right down to the last pencil. In addition, there were fees for internal examinations, including 'mocks', which were examination rehearsals, expensive uniforms out of which pupils of course grew long before they were worn out, and very pricey sporting gear. On top of this were the 'contributions': variable amounts paid every year towards the running of the school. Poor kids had to seek help from charities like St Vincent de Paul, and settle for the 'Tech', the school that cost the least, so again unlike in Britain and including Northern Island, no matter how clever the child, if he or she were poor, apart from the occasional miracle, he or she would never be well educated. On top of this, inflation was nearly twenty percent and subsidies being phased out on many basic items.

Whatever Alice thought of Ireland and the Irish, she never confided it to me; some things she liked and some she did not, and no one could coerce her one way or the other. Knowing how much it meant to me for us to succeed, she tried desperately not to disappoint, but there were certain things, particularly the leaving of her grandparents to whom she was very attached, that were very hard. It was therefore a pleasure and relief to Helen and I to see the way, so very young, modern and English, she adapted to Irish ways in spite of herself. She could turn the local accent on and off like a tap, depending on who she was with, and when we eventually got the telephone, we could tell who she was talking to by the way she talked and the accent she used, even by the supporting gestures she made. It was as though she were auditioning for roles on the stage; though afterwards when we kidded her on about it, she would get really vexed, especially when Walt would imitate her and grossly exaggerate.

Large families were always encouraged by the Catholic Church, yet when their children started school, even the catechism had to be paid for by the parents. I was well acquainted with this awful little rule book from my own days as a Catholic schoolboy and, like most pupils, had hated and feared it. At least my parents never had to pay for it because, like all other books used at school, it was lent by the school, had been used by many before me, and by many a one after.

Because in Ireland pupils had to buy the books they studied from, we sought to obtain second-hand copies of textbooks, but there were problems with this. The main one being that because syllabuses and books were invariably written by Irish schoolteachers and therefore constantly 'revised' – reprinted – they soon became obsolete. Another was that because most teachers encouraged pupils to scribble notes in them, by the time the term was over they had become most unattractive items and Helen would have to spend hours erasing pencil marks and Tippexing silly ink doodles, ironing badly creased pages and cellotaping torn pages and covers. When she and I had been school-children, defacement of a textbook was a serious offence, practically on a par with debasement of the coinage, and any pupil who marked or damaged one was severely punished. Years after, when Walter and Alice had started school, educational materials were still supplied by the school, belonged to the state and, like the teachers themselves, treated with considerable respect – if not quite as much as in Helen's and my time. Parents were generally content with the way corporal punishment was meted out, and it certainly helped keep school text books in near mint condition.

Most of the pupils in our area were children of farmers who, despite platitudes attesting to penury, were every month becoming wealthier as their shrill representatives pleaded special considerations. Whatever their lot in the Nineteenth Century, poor pupils were usually from the town nowadays and often enough with unemployed parents.

'Saving' was a verb farmers reserved for getting in the hay; care of material things, including money, was an idiosyncrasy. Extraordinarily long summer school holidays, initially conceived to allow children to assist fathers bring in the harvest in the days before automation, were long appreciated by pupils and teachers with much higher salaries than their English peers, and spending holidays in Australasia and South America. As a consequence, more than a few pupils found it difficult to get through the syllabus without resorting to 'grinds' – an unfortunate term for private tuition in their own homes – and extramural courses for weeks at a time in special schools in Dublin, necessitating the additional expense of accommodation, transport and subsistence for those who lived outside the capital. We certainly could not afford extra tuition, and were against it in principle, so our kids studied at home during their holidays.

I felt that any money we had spare should be invested in more plants and livestock, though Helen did not always agree. Accordingly, whenever we could afford it, we would buy a better strain of milking goat, a new gander or superior tup, always improving stock the cheapest way, by replacing the studs. Likewise, if ever an odd half acre of adjoining land came on offer, we would take it if we could, and find some use for it.

We all drank goatsmilk now, and as the total produce increased and became surplus to our own needs, we not only used it to help nourish the other animals, but sold it from the door, then from shops, and people bought it for all sorts of reasons: children for whom the mother could not produce human milk, the surprising number of children who could not digest cow's milk, ones with allergies and skin complaints, amateur body-builders, and greyhound owners who fed their pets better than they fed themselves.

Eventually we had tried all the common varieties of goat and found the Saanen to be the best milk producer in terms of quality and quantity. Some goats were nice-tempered but poor yielders, others lovely to look at but stubborn as mules; every one had its own personality. Unlike with human beings, most creatures tend to have a personality typical of the breed, which means that with the likes of a 'pure-breed' pup, as opposed to a mongrel, one would have a pretty good idea of what its nature would be, long before it matured.

With only a few animals of each kind, we got to know individuals well and I insisted they have a contributory role to play, rather than merely to exist as like pets in a menagerie.

Although being part scrub, Gertie's yield was never high, we never had a goat of any breed that was anywhere near as good a mother, that produced milk anywhere near as nutritious, or was as tough or lived as long. Each of us had our favourite animals to which we became especially attached, but Gertie was more human and probably more lovable than any bar Jake, the border collie which would replace Sullivan. Both creatures were intelligent, though in different ways, and the 'understanding' that existed between animal and human being was almost superhuman. My maternal grandmother was a tall and dignified Victorian woman with lovely bones and long silver hair, and Gertie always reminded me of her.

Although we did not have much in the way of resources, I had decided right from the start to try as many different animals and plants as possible to find out what and which best suited our needs. After reading up about a newcomer, fauna or flora, so we could have the right place ready for it, we would seek a specimen or two – preferably a male and female – and carefully observe them for a season. Whatever it was, we knew it would be necessary to keep it throughout a year to discover its strengths and weaknesses, how much care it might need under untoward conditions, and how difficult it would be to propagate. We would then decide whether to persevere with it or try something else.

All animals were easier to look after in the summer when food was abundant and the weather better, but at particular times, such as in winter when weather conditions could sometimes be quite harsh, and then in spring during the breeding season, they would require special care, and sometimes a lot of it. And all animals and plants required constant attention. Grass was never enough for a grazer, nor foliage for a browser, and because the earth would have been stressed and messed around with over a long period and thus be really deficient in some respects, supplements would be needed.

New geese would fly several fields away, for the sheer hell of it, and have to be herded back by tortuous routes, and it was impossible to convince sheep that the grass over the fence was unlikely to be any more succulent than what they were standing on. As a result they would regularly and persistently break through hedges and fences that would then require laborious reparation. They would desert the sweetest pasture to leap onto a piece of wasteland or stony path thirty feet below, and break their legs or back; others, perhaps the lot of them, would then hurtle straight after them.. A bleat might be an ovine cry for help but it would invariably be ignored by anything except a predator. By any measure, the sheep, closely related to, but very different from, the goat, could not be compared with any other life form when it came to intellect, and this 'feature', coupled with apathy, was one of the reasons why every one of us, with the exception of our eventual youngest. Medbh, who loved every animal and plant God ever devised – even those that had been extinct for millions of years – considered them the most exasperating forms of life. However, easy-going Harry disliked them the least, and when he turned eleven became our shepherd.

Sheep were the animals I had worked with most when I began my working life in the British Veterinary Investigation Service, but it was not until now, when we owned vast numbers – fourteen to be exact – and had to deal with one ovine problem or another every day that we fully realised what they were: obstinate, greedy, ill-mannered, messy, pathetic, vulnerable, criminally neglectful parents with shitty behinds. And most of all, profoundly stupid. It explained the perverse nature of the shepherds we had to deal with when a team of us from the veterinary centre were sent up into the Cheviots in a January blizzard, to take blood and faeces samples from hundreds of them. Manically depressed, man and beast, with diarrhoea streaming out of the latter due to the nematode worms with which they were heavily infested, they could not have been less cooperative.

Notwithstanding all of this, when the 'miracle of birth' produced the annual torrent of lambs, everybody was delighted, and each night we would tot them up and talk the big talk of the American herbivore barons back in the days of the Wild West when fourteen ewes would have produced at least twenty-eight lambs on the basis of two apiece, balanced out with the odd singleton and set of triplets. That particular biological rule never applied where we were, not like the one that dictated that were a ewe to seek out the tiny stream that ran along the bottom of the meadow, wedge itself in and contract pneumonia or drown, it would always be the best one and leave behind three orphans. When it fell, it would not make the slightest effort to help itself, but would simply lie there until death came to relieve it.

I could not shear sheep as I had done once upon a time, Walt did not have the patience, and Harry was not big enough, so in the early days we had Danny Molloy, a local shearer, come and do the job in the yard, followed by their dipping in a fly-dip Walt welded up from an old oil tank. Harry thought the world of him. He was rough but friendly and although he was so shy none but Harry could get a word out of him, he talked to Harry as though he were a man, and Harry loved it. Harry and Jake would drive the sheep into the yard and into a corner, the way that suited the man himself, and would not have anybody interfering; nobody was even allowed in the yard when he was 'busy with Mr Molloy and the 'yeo's', as he and Mr Molloy called them. Even the commands of his mother, female equivalent of the 'bossman', standing in the doorway, fell on totally deaf ears.

When the shearing was over and the fleeces rolled up and tied in the proper manner, Helen would take them to the Farmer's Co-op where they would be weighed and she would be paid. This was something she liked, for she had none of the dirty work to do. She would take in the fourteen fleeces on the back seat of our little Mini, have a bit of a chat with the farmers' wives coming in with their hundreds, in their big jeeps and trailers, and feel quite the part.

When we decided to keep an old sheep for ourselves, we would truss it up, tying its legs crosswise, put it in the back of the car with Harry in his old clothes and wellies sitting on it, Helen in the front with his school uniform and shoes on the passenger seat, and they would take it to Keanes, the butcher's. They would then go to Harry's school and drop him off at the back where he would slip into the ablutions to get washed and changed and join his class.

Whenever we needed to replace any sheep, we would buy them from an old sheepman from a nearby village who would bring them one by one in his daughter's car on a Sunday evening. Why it happened this way, I do not know, he was a funny old blighter and nothing he did was ever determined by me. He would be about eighty, six feet tall if he straightened up, and had a long face under one of those caps that eventually become part of a man's head, the kind you could not have pulled off without yanking off tufts of hair and lumps of scalp.

He never smiled and was totally devoid of any graces, yet he was courteous in an old fashioned way. He would arrive, arguing with his daughter and her husband as they came down the path, and then open his conversation with me by criticising how too long or too short I had allowed the grass to get on the meadow 'his' sheep were on. But he was a perfect gentleman with Helen and she responded to it like a little girl. I warned her he was a waffler and had probably been a notorious philanderer in his day, but she would have none of it. He was amazingly fit and I had to rely on Harry to keep up with him as he strode through the yard and out into the field as though he owned the place. Although his daughter would be nagging on to him to come away so they could get back and she could get on with their tea, he refused to leave until he had inspected every last sheep and blade of grass and commented on their well being. It was obvious he knew what he was talking about, so I would not argue with him. The time for that was when he came back into the yard and we had to 'do the business'; that is, we had to decide how much we owed him for the sheep he had brought, and how much he owed us for those he had previously taken to market and sold for us.

We then had to go through his trading ritual, even though it drove me mad. First he would ask me how much I wanted and I would ask him what he thought was a fair price. This always put him in a quandary. His son-in-law would then come up and remind me 'the old bugger' was mentally incapable of being honest and fair, for that was not the way one did the business with sheep. Apparently with sheep, the idea was to buy them for less than they were worth, and sell them for more than they were worth. It was a very simple formula and I would have to learn it if I were to succeed in this business.

'For God's sake, man! Just give me a figure…any figure you like… And we'll be satisfied with that!' I would nearly shout at him. 'We trust you!'

'That's the problem,' the son-in-law would intervene. 'He cannot do that or he'd be cheating himself.'

'You see to him, will you, Helen?' I would moan. 'I've had it.'

Helen would then turn to Old John and they would settle the matter without any further fuss.

'See, he's just an old man,' she would say as she waved him off. 'He's a canny fellow if you treat him right. You just need to show him a little patience… And deference.'

'Aye, right. Patience..! Hmmph.'

Next time, same thing. He never learned and neither did I. He had his principles and I had mine. But he was becoming an extinct breed and I shall always remember him with affection.

If the term 'peregrine' had not been secured for the greatest of all falcons, it would surely have been commandeered by the duck, for the latter were forever taking off and waddling in the direction of foxes that, for the sake of consuming one or two, would slaughter the whole flock. If the ducks were feeling more adventurous, they would scramble under the hedge, out onto the road, and straight under the double-wheels of an articulated lorry.

Apart from being comically attractive, the youngsters were delightful the way, within no time of hatching, their young would plop into the old horse trough in the yard that I had made into a micro pond for sticklebacks and tiny lilies, and take off into the middle like toy boats. As adults they were of course delicious on a dinner plate with a few fresh vegetables. But time and again, after we had spent months raising, feeding, guarding, and herding them back up the road after some passerby had called to warn they were emigrating, we would lose the lot without a quack; whatever the species, they were all doomed. If the magpies had not ripped them to pieces while they were ducklings – ducks were very poor parents and their chicks far better fostered by an old broody hen – the foxes, which killed and maimed for the sheer brutal pleasure in it, had been kept away by Jake, and the flattening pig lorry had missed them, one day I would have to play butcher and did not care for it. Ducks belong on a lake, not in a farmyard; they do not thrive without constant access to a large body of water.

Animals with hooves have to have them cut regularly, and although we just shoved goats and sheep on to their sides to do them, the only way to do a donkey was to take its hooves, one by one, between one's legs, and trust it not to do anything so ungallant as to suddenly withdraw its huge hard foot, or kick one in the back of the head, while one laboriously cut hooves that were like lumps of granite. While struggling with such a powerful animal, surely the parent that bestowed the gene responsible for incredible stubbornness, on mule offspring, I would try to think good thoughts and remind myself that this same animal had the most beautiful breath of any creature in the world, and that included Helen. The first donkey we ever got was won by Helen at a local fair. Everybody liked it and when it foaled we were done for, donkey farmers – breeders of big stubborn beasts that stripped the bark off the trees until we could not bear it any more.

When animals escaped during the day, Walter and Alice would be at school, so Helen and I would have to find them and herd them back ourselves. But there were limits as to how fast and far we could run, and chasing goats which would keep separating and doubling back to lead us some very merry dances, would frequently end in my collapsing in a heap, and their continued freedom. Some days we would have to keep going out with the binoculars every hour to see if they had moved into view, so we could tell Walter when he came home, and he and his dog would inevitably retrieve every one. For us it was a bane; for him, a caper. Jake was of course the perfect dog, Sullivan having proved himself entirely unsuited to the agricultural life and gone to the tinkers for a more adventurous life chasing vermin.

Owners who treat dogs as pets or toys, and not as working animals, have fanciful ideas about how they should look, and continually breed out naturally evolved virtues, along with their most serviceable physical endowments, and produce instead, grotesque creatures utterly devoid of character. When one day I saw Sullivan, an English, Nineteenth-Century, pure-bred Staffordshire bull terrier and fighting dog, dozing in the yard, instead of tackling – with one paw tied behind his back – three mongrels who were savaging our hens, he had to go. All of the family were upset but I could not abide such a creature for maybe twelve or thirteen years.

I knew the Border Collie, a Scottish and Northern English sheepdog, was a highly intelligent breed that could run, jump, scramble, swim, dig, fight, catch foxes and rabbits, and make an excellent guard dog, so decided to do what I should have done in the first place, which was to resist all pressure and wait until we had come upon a litter of 'real farm dogs', instead of going for the Staffordshire Bull Terrier which was a soft-hearted, fine looking animal, but that was all. Jack Russells were good for rats but given to worrying anything that moved, including human ankles, and the risk of their infecting someone with the vile Weil's Disease, commonly called 'Ratcatchers' Fever, plus the destructiveness they never grew weary of, was something to be seriously borne in mind.

Acquiring the Border Collie was achieved in a perfectly Irish manner. We had seen an advert in the local newspaper before

Sullivan had demonstrated his breed's tolerance of looters, but had not taken notice of the seller or his address, only the district. Instinct told us that the way to find that out would be to phone the newspaper, but experience should have taught us they would have lost the address, and we ended up phoning the local post office to see if they could guess the address from the scant data we were able to supply. An hour later, they telephoned back to say they had contacted the local police who had come up with three addresses they were prepared to contact on our behalf. We were only too glad to have their help because finding our way via Irish signposts and local yokel's directions, was something we had not yet mastered, and a few hours later, Walt and I were conducting that most difficult but enjoyable of tasks, selecting the best of eight pups, six of them males, at a farm in Wicklow.

Five punts the 'little feller' cost us and the farmer gave Walt a shilling for luck. I found this to be a common practice with country people, and always therefore worth having Walt with me. Sometimes we also had Alice, depending on what she might be having on her lap or crawling all over her, but Walt who loved anything to do with animals and never missed a chance to go out in the car was always with me. For him, the rarer and more fierce the newcomer, the better.

The pup was quite randomly given the name 'Jake' on the way back, a good name for a dog, but I would henceforth devise a more democratic method for deciding the name of an animal, one which would exclude the names of all relatives and friends, living or deceased, and all silly names; I believe animals are susceptible to insults and humiliation and respond accordingly.

I trained Jake, as I did all the animals, Walt exercised him, everybody loved him, and it only took us a few months to realise that whatever a Border Collie is or is not, apart from a brother his own age, it must be the greatest of companions for a country lad, and a lad probably the best companion for the dog.

A dog was always entertaining, as were the kid goats until they stopped being kids, but there was no animal more fascinating than the common 'hen' or 'chicken' – 'chooks' we called them, the way they had in New Zealand; 'hens' was already used for all female birds. These half-running, half-flying, tough, cheap, gregarious, greedy, individualistic and sometimes gorgeous multifarious creatures, forever squawking with triumph or outrage, made a farmyard the way nothing else did. Just half a dozen, especially if one were a broody with chicks, would fill it, because they would go everywhere and were curious about everything.

Every minute of its life, the hen – the female chook – was under the supervision of an observer who strutted about with his chest thrust out, head thrust up with wattles engorged with the blood of lust, having his way with any of his kind whom he always regarded as family whenever he fancied the exercise. A first rate opportunist, he would race to their aid after any mishap they had suffered, and promptly violate them.

Fowl, and certainly geese, were among the toughest of farm animals, yet their young, especially goslings, were probably the most delicate. In an environment where so much was going on contrary to the welfare of living creatures, from maiming and killing machines, careless and clumsy humans, and hostile other animals, it was so gratifying to have those which overlooked minor assaults and get on with life. Reasoning as an amateur but committed naturalist, as well as an erstwhile professional biologist who endeavoured to regard animals and plants from various perspectives but always pragmatically, I found myself increasingly inclined to the view that 'nature' was as 'bad' as it was 'good'. Nature contained as many predators as prey, as many poisonous weeds as food or medicinal plants, extremes of geography and climate, and every possible variation of homo sapiens. Indescribable beauty and grotesque horror existed side by side, like death with birth, yet so often did one hear reassurances that spoke of the ineffable 'goodness' of Nature or of God.

It would take a more comprehensive explanation than 'It's just their nature' to satisfy me as to why a sheep that stumbled would fall and stay put, whilst an insect would struggle unto death to right itself; or a bird, particularly poultry or a corvid like the magpie, would endure the most appalling injuries without a squeak and require the minimum of assistance to recover. And after the assault, only the chook would be prepared to immediately tolerate a dose of carnal knowledge from its guardian, old 'Cock-a-Doodle-Do'.

One Christmas Day our gander, Deacon, had gone to the aid of his harem – a typical avian trait – after five of his subjects had been badly mauled by a Jack Russell we had borrowed to 'teach' a terrier we had recently acquired, how to catch rats. 'Deacon' had also been attacked but kept battling the dogs until we arrived. The wings of several of his charges were broken, viscera exposed and entrails trailing on the ground, and I spent all afternoon stitching them up assisted by Walter and a friend from England who had come to spend Christmas with us.

Some of the work we did outside but when it began to rain we had to shift the theatre indoors. The table had been beautifully set for dinner, with a new tablecloth, all the best cutlery and crockery, candles, crackers and other memorabilia, and Harry and Medbh already seated with a cracker in each hand and tongues hanging out. Everything had to be quickly removed to a safe place elsewhere, and an oilcloth covered with newspapers put on in their place. Meanwhile, our friend, Chris, Walt and I stood by, hanging on to rain-soaked, tied and taped geese, while I gave instructions to the indoor staff – Helen and Alice.

It took two and a half hours to apply tourniquets, staunch wounds with charcoal powder, stitch and apply antiseptic – mainly tincture of iodine – splints and sticking plasters, and by the time we were finished the poor creatures were quite subdued. And when we had settled them on hay in wooden crates in their shed to immobilise them, we were likewise. But all ended well. Not only did none of the patients expire, but in less than two months every female laid a clutch of perfect fertile eggs, and apart from a bit of time juggling, the table was restored, the fare preserved, and the meal thoroughly enjoyed.

Like goats, geese have very different personalities, one from the other, and one good or bad one can change the way one feels about the whole species. Once, but only once, we bought livestock unseen when we arranged to have twenty-two geese sent by rail from the far end of the country, Donegal. It was too far for us to have gone for them ourselves and the Mini was by no means roomy enough to have transported them, so we had decided to take a chance, even though from the time, as lads, my brother and I several times learned the bitter lesson that there was hardly a more crooked creature roaming the earth, than the livestock dealer. It was late at night when the geese arrived, and the station master, who had had to stay behind long after the last train had gone, was not a happy man. But at least he waited and did not just let them all out and go home.

Next morning, when I got a good look at them, they were in an awful state: every one of them an emaciated little runt with broken flight feathers, covered in blood and shite, hungry, thirsty and honking like mad. As soon as we let them out, they took off, half flying, half running, and had to be hunted down and herded back. And every day the same routine. After trying unsuccessfully to fatten them up for several months, we sold them, sight unseen, to a restaurant in town where they never appeared on the menu and the chef resigned shortly after. At least Helen and Alice scavenged enough feather and down to make a small duvet.

Early on in our life with farm animals, we discovered the value of 'mooring' a new animal to a remote area with food, drink and shelter, on the understanding it would return to it when released. It almost always worked and was particularly effective with geese. The exception was with Deacon, the gigantic 17-year-old Embden who should have spent his life in a travelling freak show. He had got off to a bad start, undignifiedly arriving in great anger and humiliation in a sack in the back of a pick-up with scores of squealing piglets.

He had a massive head and beak, huge horny legs and feet that could have served as models for those of fossilised pterodactyls, and when resting on his honkers looked like an airship that had been shot down. In the middle of his first afternoon, after only a few hours in his new abode, he was disturbed by half a dozen rogue cattle that had come stampeding along the road and down into our drive, and we were just in time to see him take to the air with twenty feet of cord and an iron picket dangling from his leg. How he managed to yank out the picket and get up was testament to his strength, and how he managed to stay up, fetters and all, was little short of a miracle, but eventually, as though cantilevered into the clouds, he disappeared. About seven o'clock that evening, Alice, our 'goose girl', a title that brought her not one whit of pride, came running in to say Walter had espied Deacon high in the sky, heading towards our field, and Jake was keeping an eye on him. All of us rushed out, I telling everybody to turn their heads away because I was certain that when he landed – which should have been on deep water – he was going to plough a furrow that would resemble the entrance to a drift mine, and we were going to be digging up splinters of his bones for years. But not a bit of it. He landed as though on skis, without breaking a feather, the rope and steel picket trailing from his ankle like a hauled-in anchor. Phillip, his son and the first gander we bred, never at any time left the ground but he once chased four-year-old Harry up the field, through the gate and up the yard which had quite a slope on it.

'Don't run, Harry!' everybody shouted. But Harry was every inch as stubborn as a donkey, goose or goat, and when he saw Phillip lurching behind him in great strides, neck outstretched and parallel with the ground, bright orange beak snapping and making a sound like two African wooden bowls with concavities facing, being clashed together, he did a rapid toddle towards the house, as fast as his bandy little legs would carry him. But Phillip nailed him before he had got halfway and grabbed the flab of his chubby little behind. Speechless with paediatric rage, Harry dragged him all the way into the kitchen. It was hardly a capital offence and nobody paid any attention to Alice's demands for a trial, especially considering hot-tempered Phillip had previously had to suffer some kid tossing stones at him from the road.

SIX

Eventually I gave in to Helen and the kids and agreed to get a second-hand black-and-white television if the shop could fit an aerial and obtain a satisfactory reception.

'Who's the bossman round here?' a short stocky man with a mass of ginger hair called out from the window of his van.

I nodded.

'Here we are then, Johnny. One television in near perfect condition. A bargain at fifteen pound.'

His attitude immediately irked me.

'We were told we paid when you got it working.'

'It'll work, Johnny. My word on it.'

'And why are you calling me by my first name?'

'Oh. Sorry, John.'

I did not like people I did not know calling me by my Christian name, yet everybody did it in Ireland: insurance agents, the plumber, electrician… I had been brought up to address strangers by their title and surname, and expected the same back.

After he had been on the roof for about twenty minutes, singing and yelling to his mate, he shouted 'Right, then, John! That picture suit ye?'

There was something but it was not good enough, so he came down the ladder and into the kitchen where he fiddled in the back of the set until he was satisfied.

'That's a lot better,' he announced.

'Better than nothing, you mean?'

'We're gettin' there, we're gettin' there. In this country we have somethin' called "patience". Isn't that right, Brendan?' he called to his mate. 'It's invaluable in this line of work.'

I left him to it, returning after a while when he called. He was putting his tools in his box and nodding towards the picture on the set, which was now much improved.

'There y'are, now. Ye won't get better than that.'

I paid him and it was not until he was going out the door that I noticed the heavily laden flypaper had detached from the ceiling and was now coiled around the back of his head surrounded by masses of sticky flies. Trying not to laugh, I thought it civil to at least mention it, but he merely brushed the back of his head with his hand, leaving the flypaper hanging like a ponytail from the back of his neck.

'Aaaht!' he grunted, indicating 'So what?' and off he went.

By the time we had been six years in Ireland, we were not just surviving: we had completed all of the major repairs except for the outer rendering of the house walls which had proved physically beyond me. We owned a variety of livestock, small in number but thriving, and a garden and orchard highly fertile due to the land having previously been used only for pasture. And we were producing so much more than enough for our own needs that we were able to sell the surplus, be they sheep, honey, rabbits, goats' milk and kids, poultry, eggs, rhubarb and berried fruit; and all but the sheep, from the house. There was insufficient land or stock to make a living out of it, but what with the modest takings, my small disability pension, and the little I made from my art and writing, we managed to eke out. The pension by no means reflected the deficit caused by the loss of a salary, because although compensation for industrial injuries suffered in Ireland was extremely generous with its jury-determined awards, especially in a medical case like mine, industrial injury compensation in England had never been more than a pittance, this for everything from war wounds to pit accidents. It changed, but not by much and not until long after I was able to benefit.

We survived by living frugally, never taking any holidays, never going out for a meal or to a show of any kind, making everything last by judicious use and repair, and limiting gifts to ourselves. Thus we had enough for our needs but nothing more, and we never borrowed a penny.

Fr Foyle had several times commented on my sculpture in the yard, so I thought I might try to do something to adorn his austere little church and see if I could cheer it up a bit. Certainly no future Cromwellian marauders would find my concrete saints as easy to demolish as the ones his Roundheads destroyed when visiting the area in days of yore. Fr Foyle seemed keen on the idea, so I suggested doing a penitent kneeling before God on Judgement Day, and although he nodded his head up and down, it was very slowly. Within a few days I had made a maquette in clay, set it up on a makeshift plinth on the table in the parlour, and invited him to come and have a look. He came but took a long time to say anything, and I thought he must be intending to go away and meditate on it, maybe ask God's opinion. Finally he said, 'And where had you in mind for it?'

'Above the altar would be fine.'

'The altar..? Oh..! Inside the church?' he stammered. 'I thought you meant for the car park.'

'The car park.?!'

I was not happy about doing anything for a car park and realised that perhaps we should have discussed the site first. That way I could have quickly knocked up some grotesquerie that he would have had to reject, and that would have been the end of the matter: gesture made, gesture appreciated though declined; matter briefly entered in parish records. End of story.

'Don't you like it?' I almost snapped.

'It isn't a question of "liking",' he sniffed. 'It's just that while the penitent figure is suitably enough er, er… the God figure is just a bit too er, er…'

It wasn't until he was up the path, safely and comfortably back in his car and electrically lowering the window, that he managed to finish what he was saying: 'Menacing… A shade too menacing, don't you think?'

He was turning on the ignition but I was buggered if I would let it go at that. I would not have minded so much had he said he thought it was tripe, I could have put that down to a warped sense of humour or sheer lack of taste.

'You're right of course. But that's the point.'

'But God isn't like that,' he said with such a disarming smile, as he continued to fire up his super-duper charger. 'He is just and kind and welcomes all sinners. Things have changed,' he beamed as his leg went down and the engine roared. 'There isn't a Hell or Purgatory any more.'

'You must be joking..!' I found myself almost jeering. 'Who said that..? If that were the case, there'd be no point in anything any more.' I was cantering alongside the vehicle with my hand holding the window down. 'Purgatory was always problematical… Like Limbo. But there would be no repentance at all without Hell. One cannot have a Heaven without a Hell,' I almost shouted as I stood in the road and let the car go.

'I can see we'll have to have a chat sometime,' he called back. 'Such matters cannot be debated in the middle of the road.'

'Certainly not when one party is already driving away,' I muttered as he drove off in a car I thought altogether too well upholstered for a priest, and wondered what channel his

German cassette radio was set at. It seemed to me that if these chaps were not actually thinking about what they were going to say when they got to where they were going, they should at least have been praying or meditating, and not listening to pop music or supercilious chat, during working hours, which for them should be right around the clock.

At least I could not imagine him scolding an eight-year-old girl at the altar and refusing to call her by her given name just because she had been born illegitimate, the way some of his colleagues in rural parishes did. Nor at Sunday mass reading out the names and amounts of parishioner donations for this or that, including the ones who gave nought. No priest in England would ever have come out with anything like that. Nor, 'How's wee Alice getting on,' to Helen at Confession immediately before granting absolution for her sins.

The maquette was put in a plastic bag in a corner of the workshop where in time the bag would come apart at the seams, the clay would dry and crack, gradually breaking into small chunks which would eventually crumble into powder that would ultimately merge with the dust. Ashes to ashes and dust to dust, and all that.

Ever since we arrived, chunks of ancient lime rendering had been falling from the outer walls of the house. Parts that I had been able to reach from the ground or with a ladder, I had patched with mortar, but the patches were becoming dislodged by the surrounding disintegrating lime. Wind got under the loose flaps, shaking them like wet sheets, and rain washed them away. As a consequence, what with broken straws and horse hair poking from its bell-shaped walls, a clay and muck base where countless beetles lived and the chooks scratched and pecked, our home was increasingly coming to resemble a Three Little Piggies' abode. The pity of the property was that because the house had been the first structure built, and in the most frangible material, whereas the beautiful outbuildings, like the upper storey and extension on the end of the house, had been constructed at a later period and entirely of river stone, the outbuildings were more formidable and considerably more attractive than the house.

My father and mother were concerned about us living in what they referred to as an 'old shanty' which they were convinced would collapse one night during a storm and bury the lot of us, and had repeatedly tried to get us to accept their offer of help towards the cost of having a 'proper builder come and do it up'. My father had died not long after we came to live in Ireland and now that my mother was coming to live with us, she tried to persuade us to do what he had urged, but we still declined. However, we realised it certainly needed doing up, and decided to see if we could find someone to do it. Few were enthusiastically recommended, so we settled for one who praised himself up to the skies.

Helen had become so exasperated by my rejecting one candidate after another that she was sure we were never going to get the job done, so when this one came down the path looking around as though to make sure the place was worthy of his trowel, she started nudging me to prevent me asking questions she knew, like with the others, he would never be able to answer. She was quite ready to overlook quirks of personality if he were able to do the job; in any case, would he not be outside, up a ladder and out of sight for much of the time. The thing was, I wanted a good personality as well as the skill.

'Ye'd be just as well pullin' it down and buildin' a bungalow,' were his first words. 'I could have it down and back up in a couple of months. As it is, it's scarcely more than a pile of horse's hair, soil and clay. And old stones.'

He sauntered towards a wall, obviously to give it a kick, but I held him back.

'If you can't do it, forget it,' I said. 'There's plenty good plasterers around.'

'Huh! Not like me, there's not. It's cowboys, you're talkin' about, mate. Ones waitin' for suckers with more money than sense...'

'English, you mean?'

He sniggered. 'You said it.'

I looked at Helen to make sure she could see why I was considering telling the blighter to beat it before I set the dog, the Rhode Island Red cock, billy goat and half a dozen more ill-tempered beasts on him.

'Ye'll need a bent plumb-line for this.'

'A bent plumb-line?'

'Hah! I can see ye've never even heard of one... But that's what it needs, and I'm one of the few around here knows how to hang one.'

And so we were already in the throes of the first of many excruciating disputes with a tall, gangling man in his early forties, with a tuft of hair that arose from his scalp like an upturned industrial grade sink brush, huge flapping ears, obscenely hairy nostrils, and ill-fitting lips that prevented his mouth from ever shutting properly. And we had not even started him.

'Being "bent" would defeat the object of using a weight. A "plumb-line" depends on gravity and is a metaphor for a vertical line,' I stated calmly.

'That's what you think because ya're an Englishman and don't know the first thing about building. All the fine houses where you come from were built by Irishmen.'

'Roads, wasn't it?'

'Roads, canals, railways. You name it.'

I should have called it quits at this point and prepared myself for a spat with Helen once he was off the premises, but who was to say the next candidate – if we had not already exhausted the list – would be any better. I desperately wanted to get it over and done with, so tried him with the crucial question. Pointing to one of my cement patches on a bad part at the base of a wall, I said, 'Could you do as well as that?'

He glanced at the wall and then looked at me witheringly.

'If I couldn't do better than that, I'd take a rope and hang meself.'

It was pure impudence of course, and not a bad idea, but I had to admit he was a bit of a clown, and a fortnight later, in the absence of any other contenders, we hired him and thence began months of unadulterated torment. Ken Scully was his name, and the following Monday, armed with a quantity of very well kept tools and accompanied by a mate, a smaller, older man with a ferocious face, called 'Tiggy', dead on time he came strolling down the path. He did not announce himself, discuss his schedule or even call to say 'Coeee, sir! I'm here, reporting for duty'. He merely got started and the ghosts in the walls must have rubbed their hands.

Tiggy's job, apart from making tea, mixing cement, shifting ladders, erecting the scaffolding entirely by himself, and roughly 'cleaning up' while Ken smoked a cigarette and watched, was the audience for Ken's loudly expressed opinions on the meaning of life, the mistakes of history, the devastating future for mankind and, most importantly, the problems created the world over by Englishmen. When he was not expressing opinions, which was rarely, he was bitterly complaining about the job and me, me whom within days he was referring to as a slave-driver.

One of his major foibles, an odd one given the nature of his work, was that he could not abide anybody watching him out of a window, or coming out to inspect his work under the guise of seeing how he was 'getting on'. And he absolutely hated anybody interfering by coming out during the frequent rain showers to cover up a bag of cement with a sheet of plastic, just because the bag was still almost full – a chore beneath even Tiggy. Such thrift showed 'the mean streak you always get with the English'. Better to let the stuff metamorphose into a heavy, shapeless, almost immovable rock to be disposed of each day after he had gone.

He insisted on knocking off at exactly 1 p.m. and 5 p.m., whether there was a load of mixed and wetted cement waiting to be slapped on, or only a little bit that would have completed an area. And always, in the steps of his master, when he had knocked off for lunch, or at the end of the day, Tiggy would leave the water hose running, rather than go into the field to turn off the tap he had turned on and left on since first thing that morning.

Scully could not bear not to hear his own voice, so as he trowelled, he blathered non-stop. Most of the time only Tiggy would be within earshot but I doubt if he paid any attention to the philosophy and views on everything in the news that continually came his way, and shudder to think what might have occupied his mind during the brief periods it was left to its own devices. Whenever I was in the yard and Scully was carrying out the critical procedure of 'laying on', with about as much panache as MichelAngelo preparing to execute an upside down mural in the Vatican, he would be prattling to the log of wood below which went by the name of 'Tiggy' and Tiggy would be nodding grimly.

'You have to stand up to these English,' Tiggy would be repeatedly advised. 'Or they'll have you working like a bloody slave.' Thankful for small mercies, I was relieved he confined himself to the lower register of swear words. If it had been a matter of 'Fuck this, fuck that, fuck him and fuck you!' I could not have tolerated it. But, as he frequently assured us, he had his principles. If only they had been as striking as his faults.

Helen still believed he was only a harmless fool whom we should not let bother us because it might be impossible to get somebody else to finish what he had started, and she might have been right. I tried to bear it in mind when he came down the ladder and called to his sidekick, 'Could himself do better then, d'ye think? Hee, hee, hee.'

It would have been so easy to give the ladder a kick, and heart-warming to see him hurtling through the air on his way to dashing his brains on the concrete yard and the ravenous chooks rushing up to see if there was anything worth pecking at. The thing is, Helen had very little to do with the blighter, and when she did, he would perform more like one of King Arthur's knights – albeit an Englishman – than an Irish plasterer with Kleneze-brush hair and ears like Dumbo the elephant.

When I offered them any produce, be it eggs, vegetables or whatever, Scully would unfailingly spurn it with a wave of the hand, leaving Tiggy to hastily stuff both shares into his grotty little haversack. Scully obviously hated the English with commendable sincerity, although he accepted work and money from us, so I suppose he thought of himself as employed during a kind of Occupation where subversive little gestures could contribute to the Resistance.

By the time autumn came and it was colder and damper but still good enough to work in, the two of them had become really cocky and developed a ploy where they would meet at the top of the drive, have a cigarette and chat for about ten minutes, then disappear for several days. Soon they were doing it several times a week. Glad though we were of the relief, we simply could not afford to let the house remain in the state it was in throughout the winter, with large areas of wall exposed and winter fast approaching.

From the moment the two of them had come into our lives, everything had changed. The scaffolding detracted from the house, most members of the household, as well as certain animals, had had accidents with the ladders and cement-covered planks, and we could no longer have a conversation in the vicinity, this being the only time Scully kept his own mouth shut and both lugs orientating like hydrophones on a submarine to pick up the signals.

One day, after the two of them had been AWOL for ten days and come swaggering down the path 'without a word of apology or explanation', I just 'let them go' – as the Irish have it – and Scully almost burst into tears. Tiggy just shrugged, he could have survived on rabbits and berries if he had to, though with the generous allowance Irish Social Security doled out, it would hardly have come to that.

Shortly after, we got somebody else to finish off. He was no master craftsman but was much easier to get on with, and got the job done with a minimum of pain. What a difference it made, getting our house, farmyard, and peace and privacy back.

People had seen how we appreciated our smallholding, that we were trying to restore it without altering anything fundamental, that we had reintroduced animals and poultry to make the farmyard live again, and they seemed to respect us for it. To remember the yard the way they all were once upon a time, when nowadays there were very few like it anywhere, clearly pleased them and won over those who had initially been suspicious, if not hostile, on our arrival.

Many a time when working in the yard we would glance up to see passersby, often tourists, looking over the front gate, watching the antics of somersaulting acrobatic goat kids, a broody hen chivvying her chicks while chasing a murderous magpie; or chuckling at the sight of Deacon, old but not yet impotent, leading his geese away while 'honking' at the intruders. The same ones would remark admiringly when they witnessed the all too rare sight of a whole family working together, such as when we were out on the road, cutting and laying the hedges. Although methods had changed over time, especially with so many multipurpose tractors that could power all kinds of devices to greater or less effect, there were plenty retired farmhands who would be able to recall the old days with fondness and might well have lain odds that we would have come to grief long before now. Locals would have seen us tackling one thing after another, sometimes the 'wrong' way, seen our young children whom they would have recognised as city children, engaged in tasks totally foreign to them, seen us in mortal combat with animals they knew to be 'difficult' to manage, and in addition, species of fruit and vegetable they had never seen before and therefore declared guarantors of bellyache.

To top it all, there were these strange scarecrows, heroic (life-sized and larger) yokes made of steel pipes and concrete, sitting meditating, or standing playing musical instruments, on good pasture, the likes of which would never before have been abided in God's fields or farmyards. Mind, it would not have taken an old-timer to concede that the hacking of trees and hedges by casual labourers riding machines, was shockingly bad, not only aesthetically, but as far as the health of the bush was concerned. From the very beginning, when first we started laying saw to branch by hand, our hedges were superior and people would ask if we had had it done professionally. Skill had a lot to do with pruning, as with building dry stone walls, but much was down to certain basic principles being applied with care and common sense, and while there was little instruction via the boxing of ears and cuffs about the head, there were wonderfully illustrated old books without puerile scribbles or teacher's chidings in the archives of libraries, and I would not consider it a boast to admit to being a compulsive reader.

Most Europeans, and particularly the English with their reputed eccentricity, involved themselves in many things that were only remotely associated with their occupation or environment, so it was a disappointing surprise to find the Irish – like, subsequently, the Spanish – to be much narrower in terms of leisure interests and hobbies, and the opportunity to indulge them, their spectator love of sport drawing by far the most, if not the only, interest. The Irish were good at rugby and English football (soccer), probably due to their popular gaelic football game, one similar to the Australian. Cricket they seemed to be useless at, but there was one ball game they played magnificently, and that was hurling, a game played with a kind of hockey stick made of ash – hence the 'clash of the ash'. Boxing and judo were sports I came to Ireland already liking, and boxing, which my forbears were famous for, Walter would one day become passionate about, was something for which the Irish had a natural talent for. But hurling, as a spectator sport, captivated me as soon as I had seen a few games. It was hard, fast, skilled and some of its moves truly spectacular.

Neither of our lads took up hurling at school, but I think it was because it had to be in the blood. The cracking – and almost splintering – sound as ash struck bone was at least as martial as ash on ash, so God knows what rearranging it did inside the ears. Like fighting, it was a sport for the tough – but with a weapon – and I considered it more dangerous than boxing, so did not encourage it.

We had all been sitting in the kitchen about ten o'clock one night relaxing before going to bed, when there was a knock at the door and there was Phelim, headmaster O'Hanlon, beaming with a cardboard box under one arm and a battered wooden box under the other. When he told us what he had brought, we were all as excited as we had ever been about any living thing introduced during our incumbency. It was a swarm of bees and an old hive empty save for a few moulded wax combs hanging inside, and he had commandeered the former after being notified of its having alighted in a neighbour's barn. He had shaken it into a cardboard box at dusk and brought it to the house in his car.

Under his direction, with the aid of a torch we sited the hive in a quiet spot near a hedge in the field, opened its doorway, propped up a white sheet pinned to a sloping board leading to it from the ground, gently poured the clump of bees on to it, and then quietly and carefully came away so as not to cause any further upset. The idea was to let the bees enter the hive in their own time and settle in to create a working colony.

In just two days the hive was a factory vibrating with life. The new, recently mated queen that had prompted the swarm to leave its old nest, whether from a hive or a hole in a tree, had marched up the white slope amidst her subjects, like invaders up a drawbridge into a vacant castle, and was already laying hundreds of eggs while her workers were bringing in nectar and pollen. It was wonderful to see the hundreds of airborne bees coming in, landing on the ledge in front of the entrance, pollen baskets on their legs packed with subtly different, pale-coloured powder, depending on where they had been foraging: mainly yellows, pinks and oranges, but greens, violets and blues as well. At the same time, other bees, relieved of their burdens by workers inside the hive, were departing to seek more supplies. It was perfect harmony, perfect discipline and perfect horticulture.

Phelim told us we would need several hives to create an effective apiary, so when, a couple of weeks later, we heard of a 93-year-old bee-keeper who had a spare hive and colony, we arranged to go to his house at twilight to get it. We had seen him during the day when his spectacles were so smeared with honey, wax and a variety of non-apian debris, that his vision could not have been much worse then than it had been during the day, but he moved so slowly and carefully, without appearing to disturb so much as a blade of grass, that he seemed to be navigating by some instinct he had perforce absorbed from his personnel. As we made our way through an overgrown patch of wasteland he called his garden, we did so very slowly, and the anticipated knocking upside down of one or two hives and the releasing of legions of furious armed-to-the-hilt defenders, never happened.

He was such a nice fellow and would not accept a penny because he said he was only too pleased that a new home had been found for his excess employees. Indeed, so grateful was he that he had his daughter make us a gift of their home-made blackberry jam. There was nothing more we could do, since he would accept nothing other than our thanks and well wishes for his good health and continuing long life, and when we finally took leave of him and his daughter at their front door, after much feeble grasping of my elbow to hold me back while he imparted yet another morsel of advice gleaned from a lifetime of medieval beekeeping, he was waving in the opposite direction to where we were supposed to be going. How he managed to manipulate his hives, I could only guess, but he was another blow for my anti-anthropomorphic rationalism. He had worn no beekeeping garments, no chainmail or blacksmith's leather, nothing inimical between him and the hundreds of thousands, among whose forebears were surely some who might have stung some of his own into total submission, if not death.

Easy and amusing to visualise, was his skeleton stretched out in his garden, wax combs packed with raw honey and pollen and gorgeous healthy brood dangling from bleached frail bones that had once constituted his skull, ribcage and spine. He was absolutely fearless, and that, combined with his gentle touch, must have had a salutary effect on his dear friends.

George, who had completed his teaching diploma and was back in Ireland as resident artist at the town's art centre, had come to help and was sitting next to me in the Mini with the hive on his knees. I had given him instructions as to what to do and more importantly what not to do, although I must confess this was the first time I had ever transported bees. As always, George was obliging and game, though understandably not just a tad apprehensive, especially as all the way there I had been entertaining him with Edgar-Allen-Poesque tales of apian horror.

On the way home, before we had gone a mile, bees were flying around in the car and we were both getting stung, particularly poor George. He wanted to open the window and let a few out but I would not let him in case we lost the queen, upon which the colony would have behaved like a flying, blundering, headless porcupine whose spines had been dipped in vitriol, and we would have lost the lot.

I warned him not to sweat either, for that would rile them even more.

'You're kidding though? You never told me that!'

'Don't make a fuss, man! We've got to stay cool and dry. That's the way to transport these blighters. Even if they're inside your pants.'

By now, the ridiculously over-armed little monsters were flying in my face and I was having to try to detect the queen, in the dark, while driving, but we eventually made it back intact, set the hive near the other one, and left the car doors open so any stragglers would be able to join their brethren at dawn. We would then know if the queen was still with us: if she was, the hive would be humming and the occupants buzz-whistling the 'Off to Work' song that the seven dwarves serenaded Snow-white with. If not, all that remained would be an empty box with the odd, bad-tempered old bee, flitting around searching for something or someone to stick its sting into.

Of all the livestock we ever kept, the bees were probably the most fascinating and exasperating. We could spend every other Sunday afternoon throughout the summer looking for queen cells, catching, marking and clipping them as soon as they hatched and had been mated, and becoming tremendously excited when the colonies built up to numbers so large that the hives were practically boiling over like pans of treacle toffee. But more often than was just, when the 'nectar flow' should have been in flood because the forage plants – mainly hawthorn and clover in our area – were at their peak, rain would descend in torrents and the bees become deranged because they could not go out. The biology would continue unabated inside but we would be unable to open the hives to destroy surplus queen cells and prevent swarming because the hives would have been drenched and cooled, and comb and brood destroyed. Then the wayward sun would come out for maybe fifteen minutes between showers and the desperately waiting emigrants would instantly swarm.

Occasionally we would get a swarm back, but that depended on the weather and where they landed. When bees could not get out to forage, thousands would consume the honey stores, and if untoward conditions continued, in a few days there would be nothing left. So 'wintering' had to begin with the teeming in of proprietarily denatured sugar to keep the colony alive until spring. Yet we could feed them hundredweights of sugar over the winter, only to find in spring that half had died of hunger and the rest were in such a debilitated state they were ready to succumb to infection by bacteria, viruses or fungi, infestation by mites, or predation by wasps and mice. Sugar was not as vital as honey, and the bees' metabolism could no easier be fooled than we could.

Although Ireland was anything but good bee country, occasional years were magnificent and we would bring in hundredweights of liquid gold, stripping frames and scooping the glorious stuff into buckets while a few hundred aggrieved minders hung around outside the back door waiting for one of us to come out and be punished for theft, rather like St Sebastien on the doorstep. Even when we bought expensive mated and clipped queens from reputedly superior stocks abroad, like Italy, France or England, the temperament of the colonies changed entirely after a daughter queen had mated with the wild drones of an unknown genetic nature waiting high in the sky.

Sometimes the new community would be predominantly excellent workers but vengeful psychopaths; others might be sweet-natured but feckless. It was 'lucky dip' methodology and all depended on the anonymous fathers.

Every so called 'worker' bee was capable of behaving like a kamikaze pilot and this was the impetus most often manifested after we had been manipulating their hives. They would fly back and forth over the yard for hours, waiting to sacrifice their lives for the sake of hurting somebody – anybody, preferably in the neck, nose or lips, and then depart to the happy hunting grounds where their stings would remain forever sheathed. Not a very worthwhile exchange, but Nature never had much time for fair play.

When manipulating particularly vicious colonies we had to make sure the dog was not tied up or they might have stung him to death. If he were free, and as intelligent as Jake, he would tear down to the river and lose them by diving straight in.

One year we had an exceptionally bad-tempered colony that one afternoon got into Alice's long thick hair when she was bringing in the goats, and stung her so badly we had to take her to hospital for anti-histamine injections, and while we were away, they stung two new-born goat kids and a dozen goslings to death. A colony like that could take over the whole place for half a day.

For every year that we had a good crop of honey, there were at least three disastrous ones but, like most disenchanted beekeepers, I was loath to give them up; not only because of their honey, but because whatever the weather, they were still valuable pollinators, manufactured gorgeous brood combs in various stages of maturation accompanied by perfectly symmetrical cells packed with subtly different coloured pollen, and performed wonderful antics as they toiled, danced, groomed and defended their home unto death. On a sunny afternoon, if I had allowed myself the time I could have watched them for hours.

We had not been in Ireland long before we were aware of the significance of funerals, and there never seemed a time when somebody was not being sent off to the place where even green cards were redundant. In most countries we had lived in, funerals were something to be got over and done with as soon as possible. They were distressing, embarrassing and inconvenient; by no means were all mourners strictly grievers, and there was always some longstanding dissent. No doubt there were elements that soured commemorations in Ireland, but there was also more, a lot more.

If someone's life had been worth anything, surely something more than a bit of ritual was justified, and in the European sphere nothing surpassed the Irish. Respect and attention was not only paid to the deceased, but to the mourners as well, and no matter who they were, the latter were treated with hospitality and kindness. A restrained party atmosphere, with recitation, singing and interesting conversation, would take over towards the end, so mourners would depart the host's premises more like well treated guests than distraught relatives and friends. Most of all, the deceased would have been 'waked', and until their physical remains had been properly disposed of, there would always have been a family VIP guarding them day and night. Nobody who came to pay their respects would be turned away, and that included politicians and representatives of various organisations with whom or with which the deceased or his intimate had been associated. Although this meant that the average citizen was a potential mourner many times over, we never ever heard anybody moan about having to go to two funerals in a week. It happened, and at funerals outside Ireland, but not so often as to generate chapbooks of platitudes. Travellers, itinerants, gypsies or 'tinkers' – the term I preferred – were champions when it came to funerals, and would go to great lengths and expense to celebrate the death of one of their number.

I was once at a funeral in County Wexford where the deceased had been the mother of a player on the County hurling team, and after the interment, her nephew, a lad with a ukulele and a voice that had not yet broken, started singing their anthem, the 'Purple and Gold'. All around was deathly silent apart from the faltering tones of the nervous performer, until one of the grave-diggers standing by suddenly joined in in a pitch like a Volga veteran's and was gradually followed by various bystanders in little more than a murmur.

When my father died, my mother came to live with us. Canada, where one of my brothers lived, was too cold and far, and Australia, where another lived, was too hot and far, and George had not decided where he was going to settle. Michael still lived in Newcastle but appreciated that because of Mother's love of nature, Ireland would probably suit her best, particularly with my being at home all day. However, before making her mind up, she decided to come over and have another look. Instead of telling us in advance, so we could have met her at the airport or from the train, she just materialised at the door in a taxi at about 9.30 p.m. when we heard her gentle knock on the door. Her first words were to ask if we had change for the 'taxi-man' who we assumed was intending to rob her blind. The two of them had come all the way from Dublin, but she was such a gentle soul she must have won him over during the long journey and stifled whatever designs he might have had on her purse, because his fare was surprisingly reasonable.

On her return to England after a fortnight, she and George, who had taken her to the airport, had been chatting, forgot the time and missed the boarding call, and the pilot had already started his checks when one of the airport staff telephoned to tell him the missing passenger had turned up. Mother, who had always been shy, was greatly embarrassed and could not apologise enough. However, the airline she was booked on was Aer Lingus, the Irish airline, and they decided to take care of her. The pilot held back the take-off – I think 'abort' is too strong a word here – and an official drove her out to the plane in his own car. The plane door was opened, the gangway lowered and my mother admitted and helped to her seat before being given a cup of tea by a steward. We would never forget Aer Lingus for it and whenever any of our family were in a discussion about airlines, we would always regale them with the tale, so remarkable we thought it.

Shortly after my mother came to live with us, our second daughter and last child, Medbh (Maeve) was born and a wonderful but all too short relationship began between them, both grandmother and granddaughter loving life in our Irish home.

SEVEN

By the time we had been a decade in Ireland, we had had many kinds of domestic animal and bred from all of them. Getting creatures to reproduce was for me the crux of success in husbandry, and I never saw anything hatching from an egg, or being born with a placenta, that did not delight me; nor fledgling take flight or mammal take its first steps. Our children witnessed all of the livestock through their whole life cycle and helped raise their orphans when necessary – invariably the case with at least one species. They not only learned the natural food of every animal, but also what constituted a treat, the best persuader. They learned the right conditions for comfort and security and the best method of restraint, how to deal with common injuries and illnesses, how to encourage breeding, how to train them, and how to humanely and swiftly bring their lives to an end – although I invariably performed this unpleasant chore.

Each of them in turn, depending on their age, milked the goats and put them out to graze before going to school in the morning, and then brought them in for the night and milked them again, when they came home. They had other chores as well, preferably ones which suited their natural ability, but they were all taught to do everything so they could stand in for each other, or help one another when necessary. Heavy dangerous work, such as with cutting machines, was always done by me or the boys, though the girls took their turns with dirty jobs, such as mucking out the animal houses, and nobody ever complained about their assignment. Everything was done as fairly as possible, nobody doing more or less than anybody else, and they all understood the principles behind everything, even though they might have thought I was rather hard at times. They all worked hard at their farm duties and on their school work, but they always had some leisure when all the work was finished, though it often did not amount to very much. The place was not run like a factory, it was a home, and they realised they were working for themselves and their family. They learned about the wonderful wildness of the countryside, which, even on a modified scale, was always present. Many things they learned by unconscious absorption, and even though they sometimes pulled a face when some task meant they could not go off with friends, they acquired a love for the animals and a respect for the tasks of the country that they would never disown, and as they got older and became physically farther away, so did their loyalty, pride and affection grow for all these things.

One day, so I hoped, they would look back and be proud of how hard they had worked, value the knowledge they had learnt, appreciate the discipline they had acquired, and be grateful for the loyalty and love of a mother and father and brothers and sisters who had shared it all with them. This is what I told myself and Helen when we had had an upset, and we did have them. Nothing was easy, and the handicaps we had brought with us, to do with the loss of my career, health, financial resources, and isolation from our culture and other family and friends, were always in the background.

In the beginning, when we were seeking to buy stock, if we could not obtain it locally we would have to resort to the newspaper, and because we had no telephone, would have to go through the shenanigans of 'horse-dealing' via the public telephone in the village, counting ourselves lucky that, unlike in England, country telephones were usually not vandalised. Mind, telephoning was not the ideal method of doing business in Ireland, because the prospective seller would always insist on being told what the prospective buyer expected to pay, rather than confide the minimum they were prepared accept.

Dealing in animals was always a rather unholy affair, and although it was something I deplored because I so often found myself disliking the people I had to deal with, plus it was risky buying animals with no provenance, we had no other choice. Bringing animals in from Britain was problematic because although they were invariably better specimens and the choice much greater, the vendor was not necessarily any more reputable, and bringing them over was a right palaver, what with the transportation, Customs, and pedantic Department of Agriculture.

One night when the rain was teeming down, a drenched scraggy little fellow with a plastic sack under his arm, came to the door to say he wanted to see the Rhode Island Red cockerels we had for sale. We did not have any at the time because we did not keep cockerels once they had matured sufficient to indicate the kind of specimens they were going to turn into, and it was two years since we last had any for sale. When I told him, he said 'Well, this is the place. I remember that yoke' – John the Baptist –standing there. It was dark and scared the daylights out of the wife when she saw him sneering over the fence.'

I said I was sorry but we had none.

'Me mother used to keep them when I was a little feller.'

'Did she..? That's interesting, but…'

'I only want a couple. One for me and one for me neighbour, Pat O'Connor. He used to play for Adamstown Terriers. I promised him I'd fetch him one back. He was one of the best hurlers Waterford ever had… How much were ye askin'? They wouldn't cost an arm and a leg, would they?'

'Not if we had any.'

'There's one!' he shouted excitedly, pointing at a hen sheltering in a doorway.

'It's a hen.'

'And there's another!'

'That's a hen as well, and they're not for sale.'

'I don't want a hen, I want a cock. Two.'

'I'm sorry but we don't have any cocks for sale. You can't keep more than one cock at a time.'

'Then why did you put them in the paper?'

'They're not in the paper!'

'I saw them.'

He reached into his pocket and started fumbling with some crumpled newspaper cuttings.

'When did you see them?'

'Not that long ago.'

'How long?'

By the time I had proved my case he was absolutely saturated, but there really was no point in inviting him in or I would never have got rid of him. Besides, I had been listening to a traditional music programme on the radio that I listened to every week and wanted to get back in. But here he was, standing with his bag and no doubt a knotted mass of baler twine inside. Actually, it was a wonder he had brought anything to carry them back in, most people brought nothing but the boot of their car full of all kinds of farmyard rubbish and kids' stuff. I could have wept at the sight of him standing with the rain dripping off his eyelashes and the end of his nose and such a look on his face. But, 'Get a broody and I'll let you have a clutch of fertile eggs,' was the best I could come up with.

'There goes somebody convinced I'm a typical Englishman,' I thought as he trudged back up the drive.

Carleton-Borris had sold his mansion and we had not heard anything from him for a long time, so had no idea whether or not he was still involved with art and the nurture of artists, but one night at about ten o'clock when it was quite dark, a couple of weeks before the annual Opera Festival, a hoity-toity Anglo-Irish woman with close-cropped hair and large uneven teeth came to the door. She was clad in a thick woolly jumper tangled with bits of hay and straw and flecks of dried dung, tight-fitting jodhpurs enclosing a big flabby arse, and filthy wellingtons, and introduced herself as an associate of Carlton-Borris and a breeder of Jacob's sheep. Apparently we should have been keeping them instead of wasting time on scrub goats and lowly breeds of sheep. No doubt this meant she was fed up with her Jacobs and saw us as potential dupes prepared to relieve her of her own.

I was not very enamoured of sheep of any description and certainly did not like Jacobs. I thought them ugly with their piebald colouring, troublesome because of their multiple horns, and because they were so rare, probably hopelessly inbred and suffering some genetic neurological diseases common to the species. She had a lot off about their 'wonderful characteristics', the way female breeders of bizarre canine species often do, but after half an hour of trying to find a topic of mutual interest, I felt our hospitality had been stretched to the limits and began to wind things up as courteously as I could.

At this point she started on what I suspected was the real purpose of her visit. Having heard that George and I were artists, she asked if we would like some free promotion for our work, namely the opportunity to submit paintings on boards with large frames that could be used to display oysters and other marine shellfish.

'I beg your pardon?'

Then she explained the real reason for her visit. She had a load of oysters and other shellfish from Connemara, which she wanted to sell during the festival from a temporary oyster bar she was rigging up in the old gas show-rooms, a place much better suited to the hire or sale of dicey plumbing accessories. If we wished, we could put up some of our paintings – provided they were framed – on the walls, 'little bits of sculpture here and there, as long as wouldn't impede customers from moving freely'.

The paintings would have to be well varnished, 'of course', so none of the paint would come off onto the oysters. Afterwards they could be cleaned and would be as good as new; we would only need to make sure the cleaner we used for the shellfish grease would not dissolve the paint. It was, of course, up to us to see to that.

George stood there with his mouth open, not knowing what to say, and I laughed, but she did not seem to realise why.

'I'd need to see the standard of your work first, of course. Do you have anything you could show me. Art school diploma stuff even, just so's I could…'

'George has quite a bit of stuff stored in the rubbish bin,' I teased, 'but mine generally goes for litter in the poultry house.'

Her expression had changed from 'Hooray Henry' to 'bloody irritated' and she turned her attention to George, probably hoping he might have a more serious business head on him. However, I could not tolerate her in the house any longer, what with her composty smell, her hairy warts and spluttering teeth, filthy fingernails constantly digging into the biscuits, and most of all – despite her airs – her bad manners. After assuring her we were interested in neither her sheep nor her oyster-driven art sales, I showed her to the door. There she stood snorting in front of the yard gate that we always kept closed to keep the animals from straying up the drive, her fat freckled arms folded and fresh hospitality food droppings sticking to her jumper.

'Aren't you going to open it for me then?'

'How did you get through when you came in?'

'I had to damn-well climb over!'

'Then why not damn-well climb back over,' I said, although I was sorry almost as soon as I had said it; she was a woman and I had been brought up to treat women like ladies. But how could God create women like this and expect ordinary men to lay down their cloaks for them.

Although I like most birds, there is one that really thrills me, and that is the Spar (female sparrowhawk). This lightweight little bird with its grey-brown back feathers and striated underparts, its long yellow matchstick legs, needle sharp talons and hooked beak, hard frowning eyebrow and ferocious yellow eye, is magnificent. The term, 'wild as a hawk', is meaningful, for there are few creatures more wary of man than the hawk, and this one was no exception. The female, larger but lighter than a pigeon, would take prey as tough as a crow, as well as a pigeon, but the diminutive Musket (male), so delicate it was considered by the austringer (hawker equivalent to the 'falconer') to be unsuitable for hawking, was something else. Equally proficient at hunting, though its prey was much smaller, it was a superb flier. Both Spar and Musket were abundant and easy to trap in the area where we lived, and I would catch one, train and fly it for a few weeks and then let it go before replacing it with another; thus I learnt things about the sparrowhawk I could never have learnt from books.

Hawking and falconry were rare sports in Ireland at the time I caught my first bird, because of the predatory policy of the British RSPB (Royal Society for Protection of Birds) which almost maniacally outlawed birdkeepers throughout the British

Isles, putting out propaganda and tales for the media to take up without question or demur, to the effect that raptor eggs were worth thousands of pounds, and that raptors were being ill-treated and trafficked throughout the world. Conniving with the police, they raided the homes of suspected austringers and falconers, turning their beds upside down in the middle of the night and treating them like terrorists instead of what they were – working-class fellows with a love of a certain genus of bird in a country that allowed its wealthier citizens to hunt foxes and other animals – both quarry and predator – in the cruellest and most unsporting fashion.

Eventually I was raided. Early one Monday morning a gang of high ranking officials from the Departments of Agriculture, Veterinary Science, Wildlife, RSPB, Customs, and Office of Public Works descended. After several hours of a surprisingly civilised discussion-cum-investigation, with all of them sitting in our front room asking all manner of questions and my being threatened with imprisonment if I did not give them the answers they wanted to hear, they 'confiscated' my stock. This meant I was expected to feed all of my raptors and look after them until my tormentors had made arrangements to remove all eight of them, all of one of which were nesting in aviaries, and return them to England, when 'return them to England' meant they would be transported at my expense to England where they would be given away to various English raptor-keeping friends or associates of my persecutors.

Instead of losing my temper and expressing outrage that they should expect me to 'turn my wife in' – an offer they had the neck to offer me – to spare myself by stating she was an accomplice involved in the transport to Ireland of a legally purchased, captive-bred South American desert bird – a 'Harris', which is not native to Britain, though commonly bred in properly licensed falconry centres. I decided to make it obvious how ridiculous the whole thing was – the horrendous waste of money in expenses by all these Dublin people, mostly travelling in chauffered cars and claiming first-class subsistence for several days 'feckin' round after a couple of old crows', to quote the two very senior Customs officials.

Because of their high individual rank, all but the representatives of the Office of Public Works – who alone came across as most unreasonable and vindictive – were amenable to rational explanations, and after a good deal of talk, things were pretty much sorted out.

Apart from anything else, most of the birds were in the middle of breeding and any fuss would almost certainly have disrupted them. Also, I was by now well known in the south, including by the local wildlife warden, as somebody to whom sick and injured birds of all kinds could be brought. I would treat them, feed and look after them and then return them to their owners, without charge. When I worked for the English Veterinary Division of the Ministry of Agriculture, twenty-five years previously, I had gained plenty of veterinary experience.

Nobody in Ireland provided such a service, and private veterinary fees were far too much for the average raptor fancier who tended to be of very modest means. If they had taken their bird to a vet, not only would they almost certainly have been putting it in the hands of an incompetent, but more often than not they would have been reported to the authorities.

It was clearly an embarrassment to the raiding party who had come expecting to find a completely different situation, and they were obviously niggled at having to get involved in what they considered to be such a trifling matter. I became friendly with several of them, especially when I discovered two of them had a hawk or falcon themselves.

Both of my lads inherited my interest in animals and were valuable assistants when it came to holding the birds so I could carry out tricky procedures such as surgery for bumblefoot, a common disease of peregrines' feet that doomed them if untreated, or fitting broken legs or wings with splints or plaster casts. When we wished to test a healed wing we would sometimes arrange the many garden tools and heaps of scrap we stored in the old stable, so that the area between roof and floor was a morass of obstacles with scarcely a few inches between them, and either Walt or Harry, standing at one end of the stable, would cast a musket or whatever from the wrist of his leather glove. At the other end I would stretch out my arm and whistle, and in a second the bird would be standing perfectly perpendicularly on my wrist, its two skinny legs perfectly parallel, its fierce yellow eyes flashing and challenging after a flight of sheer dazzlement.

How I was able to catch a sparrowhawk, train it, hunt with it and then let it go, all within the space of a fortnight, which was usually the case with a musket, and three weeks with the Spar except for stubborn individuals, was because of the wonderful bond that developed between us, a totally different bond to that between a shepherd and his dog, but a bond nevertheless that served the nature of both parties. It was a bond of dependency, not love, and the relationship one of colleagues, never master and slave; and the bond, as with any animal, was via the belly or the gizzard. Almost any creature when hungry can be persuaded, even to interception of loyalty.

Many a nine o'clock at night I would be sitting in my slippers in the armchair beside the cooker, book in hand, mammalian orphan in a cardboard box by my feet, while Helen darned or knitted and the children did their homework at the table. Heat would be coming up in visible waves, rendering the whole room a haven. Stealthily I would rise, sneak across the room, and prompt the musket to leave my fist and flit onto the bannister at the bottom of the staircase, or onto the top of the bathroom door. I would then slink back to my seat and tap my wrist with my forefinger. Instantly the bird would swoop down over the heads at the table and back upon my fist. Nobody moved or said a word, the blink of an eye or flicker of a smile the only acknowledgement.

Nobody could be seriously involved with raptors in Ireland without being acquainted with Darragh Doyle who knew more about trapping birds of prey than anybody I ever knew or heard about. You might not know him personally because he was anything but a public figure; but if you had raptors, he would be aware of you, and if you had anything he wanted, sooner or later he would be in your yard. He would be smiling and scruffy, appear when you least expected it, and in no time found out everything he needed to know about you and your stock. When he had gone, you would not know his real name, where he lived, what he did, how old he was, or anything worth knowing, except that without a doubt he knew more about birds of prey than you would ever know.

He might not have been the most profound, but was certainly the most consistent, liar I ever met, and like most people who bought and sold animals, particularly of the rarer kind, he was incredibly cute in his wheeling and dealing. Only fools tell everybody what they want to know, was his justification for prevarication; but there was rather more to it than that. For instance, were you to ask him the time, he would pause to consider whether it might be more advantageous to him to give the impression it was earlier or later than it in fact was, and only then would he tell you he was not wearing a watch.

Like a species of feral man, he was always in the same shabby leather jacket, scruffy trousers and well-worn boots, his greasy hair lank and uncombed, fingernails long and shiny black, razor-sharp bones poking out of his cuffs, dried and discoloured bechin (tiny piece of meat to tempt a raptor) between his fingers. Yet his large, long-lashed eyes moistened and shone when he smiled his frequently winsome smile and his ears waggled. His moustache drooped over the corners of his mouth and hair covered the tops of his dirty ears. I never saw him eat anything, never saw him go to the toilet, and believed him when he said he had never taken any medication in his life.

He was infinitely knowledgeable about all Irish raptors and their quarry, especially the peregrine, though the knowledge was anti-academic, based on his own experience, and so jealously guarded that he would have had to have been tortured before he would have yielded a whit of it. He was pathologically secretive and lacked the ability to reason, making it impossible to trust him or have anything approaching a friendship with him, yet he was highly intelligent in a creepy way and it behove you to get to know him if you wanted to know about getting around the law regarding raptors.

He told me he had dreams of being a female gyr, though why not a male or a peregrine he could not say; he was certainly a near genius at catching them and trading them and spent most of his sleeping hours doing so. As soon as he was old enough he had taken a mountaineering course so he could dangle over cliffs to manipulate eyries, removing young wild birds and replacing them with ones he had bred himself in order to overcome the problem of imprinting which can be a curse with birds raised in captivity.

The principle of imprinting was first described by Konrad Lorenz, the great German biologist, who, through the behaviour of his Greylag geese, noted that young animals, particularly birds, transferred feelings normally reserved for their natural parents, to human beings, and sometimes other creatures or inanimate objects, which the youngsters regarded as parents. Such 'imprints', because they are not afraid of humans, can often be very aggressive towards them, and because imprinting is a sexual thing, they will try to 'mate' with humans rather than with their own kind, females crouching and submitting as in the wild, and males by ejaculating on the head of the substitute.

Leaving aside strictly imprinting, when my young brother and I were nine and ten years old and kept canaries and other aviary birds, we wrote to the old Duke of Bedford who was a famous aviculturist and columnist for the aviculture magazine, Cage Birds. His special interest was in developing the homing instinct in all birds, and the sight of flocks of exotic foreign birds he had bred, flying free over Woburn Abbey where he lived, made him renowned world-wide, though I suppose his title contributed to it..

He had written an article on the homing instincts of jackdaws, and because my brother and I were fascinated by these wonderful intelligent and easily tamed crows, we had written to him to ask if he could help us get one. Very courteously and elegantly, but sensibly, he wrote back saying that when we were old enough and experienced enough to catch a young jackdaw ourselves, we would then and only then be entitled to keep one. However, because he realised how disappointed we would be, and wished to dull the blow, he sent us a wonderful brand new book about birds and animals entitled, King Solomon's Ring by Konrad Lorenz, which, in addition to a chapter on the jackdaw, contained information about Lorenz's theory on imprinting which we probably learned at an earlier age than all the scientists who ever worked in the field.

My brother and I were overjoyed and so proud to be the recipients of such a gift, though our father, who had been a soldier in the British Army during the War, was not too happy because the duke had strong German family connections and had been a Hitler sympathiser which the papers said was the reason he went out on his huge estate one day with his double-barrelled shotgun, and shot himself.

To return to Darragh, who, like the Duke of Bedford, was a strict loner, but unlike the duke, a non-socialiser with very little money in his pocket, he was in pretty thick with a band of German falconers who lusted after the Irish haggard peregrine falcon (wild-caught adult) and did not give a fig for Darragh's risky physical and illegal undertakings on their behalf. They could be pretty generous with someone who was not only able to provide the perfect bird, but prepared to take every risk transporting several to their hunting lodges in the Black Forest, from Darragh's own bunker in Kerry. He provided them with first-class peregrines and they him with second-class goshawks.

Darragh went over so many times with some of the best hunting falcons in Europe and returned with some of its best hawks, which he would bring back in sacks in the boot of his car, that had the RSPB ever laid hands on him, they would have strung him up.

Meat was the expensive food on which raptors were fed, but Darragh would have arrangements with Irish butchers, 'manufacturers' of dead day-old chicks – companies who bred day-old chicks but only kept the pullets (females), so sold the males to all kinds of carnivore keepers – and the many farmers who let his squads of crack-shots shoot over their land to reduce the crows, pigeons and rabbits. The birds among them were rated 'vermin' when it suited the hypocritical bird protection societies, who likewise turned a very blind eye to the massacre of hundreds of thousands of so-called 'game' birds by landowners who bred pheasant, grouse, quail, partridge and other 'table' birds for the sole purpose of producing live targets, many of which survived, maimed by lead shot, when they could easily have been killed humanely were there any justification for raising them as livestock targets; as were raptors punished, often cruelly, for taking the relatively few 'game' birds among their much commoner quarry, the many pigeons and crows.

Because peregrines, and to a much lesser extent, female sparrowhawks, occasionally took homing pigeons, pigeon fanciers would shoot both, even in their nests with their young.

Falcons, like the peregrine, are long-winged birds that hunt from on high by stooping and striking; short-winged hawks, such as the sparrowhawk and goshawk, hunt by short rapid pursuits close to the ground. Both are spectacular in appearance and action.

Although he dealt with wealthy people, especially Germans and Italians, I never saw Darragh with money in his hand and doubt if he ever carried more than enough for a telephone call. He would boast that he had never spent a penny on his mania for falcons and hawks, acquiring everything he had by barter and guile. People who had done business with him said that every other word he spoke was a lie, which, I suppose, was something of an achievement, but I am sure he was speaking the truth when he said being 'caged' – a situation he must often have had occasion to contemplate – would have killed him. I could imagine him visibly wasting away day by day among ruffians who would treat him with neither respect nor affection; unable to wander freely in all weathers, leaping ditches and wading streams, surveying the horizon while dangling over cliffs from the pendulating bosun's chair he had rigged to allow him to access eyries; and the abrupt cessation of daily communion with the wildest of birds, birds which soared and stooped from high in the sky and tore into a cloud of crows. It would have been unendurable, for such was his oxygen, his reason for living; he wasn't just a hobbyist or fancier, nor a mere zealot; he was a fanatic, mad and a fiend where birds of prey were concerned.

Unappetising though he was when ensconced on one's sofa in a tidy, well-appointed sitting room, he was a delight to watch out in the wilds spotting predator and quarry, pointing at targets the shooters had missed, and moving like an animal himself, stealthily loping along with a stride just short of a canter, head lowered and forward, keen eyes squinting, body crouched and arms hanging loosely by his sides. Many was the time I tried to imitate such a gait and found it quite impossible, so exquisite the beautiful coordination required. For all his social gaucheness under domestic conditions, once over a fence and into a field, or up a mountain, he made you feel like an oaf as you traipsed far behind, skinning your shins and spraining your ankles. Birds have marvellous eyesight, and none better than the falcons, but Darragh was a species unto himself, *Hominis darraghus* could have fittingly been the binomial for the only mammal to match his wonderfully sighted avian cousins.

As well as the day-old chicks he obtained by special arrangement with the foreman at the day-old chicks' abattoir – and goodness only knows what kind of deal he had to strike to guarantee him first preference with those hundreds of thousands – Darragh's gangs of shooters would fetch him deer, goat, rabbit, pigeon, magpie, jay and crow. These were mainly members of local gun clubs, plus some less respectable outsiders, and when their periodic 'vermin shoots' took place, they were something to behold, especially when their cargo was dumped in the kitchen of a little house on a claustrophobic council estate.

At the end of a shoot, thousands of shattered feathered and furred bloody carcases would arrive in Darragh's backyard in bin liners, and be dragged one by one into the kitchen where his wife was cooking and the kids playing. In no time, the carpet, furniture, walls and ceiling would be covered with feather and fur, beaks and bones, tissue and blood, as Darragh and his kids plucked and eviscerated the vitals with their bare hands, and flung the best of it into bags that were crammed into huge deep-freezes in his backyard. Hour after hour, without a single break for a snack or mug of tea, the legs and lower parts of the squatting pluckers would be enveloped in a moving sea of bloody fluff, with bits of bone and tissue in their hair and stuck to their faces. Nobody interrupted the operation even to relieve themselves, and nobody talked because they could not afford to let the stuff get into their lungs. If I were there to collect what I had paid for, I always helped. One could not just sit and watch them, and Darragh would not dispense any shares until his own massive portion was processed; then you could hop it and do your own stuff at your own place.

I would do ours in the field when I got home. I let the wind blow away the fluff, and the hens and crows dispose of the bits and pieces, though remnants of Darragh's quota would still be upholstering his sofa when the next season's bounty arrived. He could skin a donkey by himself in little more than half an hour and there would hardly be a drop of blood left when he had finished, certainly not enough to be incriminating, and the end product would all be packed in plastic boxes in storage. If a whole fleet of his ships had come in at the same time, he always had somebody who would store stuff until his freezers had room, and they would be paid in venison or other prize game, no questions asked.

Through time I dealt with quite a few falconers and austringers – English, Scottish and Welsh – some of whom considered themselves celebrities and dressed like Robin Hood; they would hire themselves and their birds out to historical film makers, documentarians, fairs and festivals, and loved to talk the talk. But never a one who could hold a candle to Darragh Doyle whose only costume was the greasy, filthy and tattered leather jacket he had once swapped for a one-legged goshawk. The Germans and Italians came over every year to snaffle Irish game and expected our raptor men to act as beaters and general dogsbodies. Except Darragh. Darragh beat for nobody and nobody beat for him. I would not have been surprised if Darragh had evolved directly from the bird of prey and skipped the ape and the others altogether.

EIGHT

DURING THE PERIOD WHEN pesticides were used with abandon in Ireland as elsewhere, the exquisite Peacock butterfly was virtually wiped out, and when we came I never saw a single one. Tortoiseshells, yes, but no Peacocks. We had many patches of lush nettles, the natural foodplant of the Peacock as well as the Tortoiseshell, which I extended with nitrogen fertiliser. I then bought several score of Peacock eggs from a lepidoptera farm in England, made a dozen large square butterfly cages from fine black netting, which I suspended from the ceiling in a well ventilated greenhouse I had made from scrap glass, and bred Peacocks first by the hundred, and then by the thousand. Saving only enough of the best specimens to produce the next generation, I would release them on a sunny morning with the family in attendance, and it was a stupendous sight to watch them fluttering off in little clouds; then a few weeks later to see them breeding in colonies on our own patches of nettle and wild nettle in surrounding fields. We did this again and again, and it was so gratifying.

However, as nature has it, every living thing is prone to predator and parasite – many predators and many parasites – particularly ones in captivity and in large communities, and the degree of infestation and predation is directly proportional to the size and density of the community.

In the case of the Peacock butterfly, the nonpareil parasite was – and I cannot help slipping into anthropomorphic mode – the evil Ichneumon wasp, an insect which inserted its long ovipositor through the spaces in the netting of the cages and into the bodies of the sedentary hibernating chrysalids, a single Ichneumon egg for every Peacock chrysalis. The egg hatched and the larva developed inside the chrysalids over the winter. While the larva was developing, the Ichneumon larva was also developing – but with a superior mechanism – as it grew and metamorphosed inside in tandem. Eventually the Ichneumon wasp developed into its imago, an adult wasp that emerged leaving a mere transparent Peacock chrysalid shell. The only felicitous feature about the creature was that it was in turn parasitised by the Ichneumon ichneumon wasp which destroys its quarry, the Peacock Butterfly's natural parasite, in the same way its host destroys the butterfly. People who know little about biology will marvel at the perfection and 'goodness' of nature, rave about its beauty and recommend leaving it to cure all ills, when the truth is that so many of its natural processes are absolutely barbaric. Perhaps the only rational way to regard nature is to do so entirely without sentiment.

Father Foyle had never again mentioned the sculpture for his church – or rather, his car park – and neither had I. Meanwhile I had done various modest commissions around the town and county: heroic freestanding sculptures for the fronts of hotels, bronze reliefs for restaurants, keystones for private houses, and memorial statues and reliefs for various other patrons. Items like sundials and weathervanes, I sold through exhibitions. My painting themes were usually working-class scenes done with what I hoped would pass for good humour rather than inferior technique, though the sculpture was rather more serious, tackling different issues. The latter was my first choice, preferably of heroic dimension – 'heroic' in the sculptural sense of size – but its sheer weight and bulk required a maker of more heroic dimensions than mine, and my physical strength was not increasing. As a consequence I was now doing more painting and drawing and had several exhibitions abroad, including one in America in Washington DC.

During the latter Helen and I stayed with an Irish American lady with 'connections' who owned a couple of my paintings, was very hospitable and had arranged for the Irish Embassy to supply a crate of whiskey. Incidentally, when during the opening speech he realised I was English, and my wife too, he looked as though he were gearing up for a stroke, and I heard he had made enquiries to see if some of the whiskey could be withdrawn and replaced with something fizzier. Whatever, he soon disappeared. There were more important things in the world than oil paintings.

Helen got on so well with Frances Howard, the sister of the late Hubert Humphrey and friend of Mary Lynn, our very hospitable host, that Mrs Howard, seemingly a powerful woman in Washington political circles, arranged a further exhibition for me at the National Institute of Health. It turned out that Mrs Howard had considerable sympathy for coalminers, having accompanied Eleanor Roosevelt when she took up their cause in Virginia in the 1940s, so I thought I would push my luck somewhat further and ask if she would write an introduction to a book I was writing about coalminers in County Durham, a body of men for whom I had the greatest admiration. She said she would be only too delighted, but when we returned to Ireland and I sent her a copy and she saw I intended to have Arthur Scargill write an introduction also, she hastily replied saying she was sorry but for some reason could no longer oblige, and the romance ended abruptly. When, for some reason, Arthur Scargill then declined, I asked Tony Benn, and he agreed and wrote a very fine piece without any fuss or conditions. So it worked out well in the end and I could not have asked for better. Nobody among my readership would be likely to have heard of Frances Howard, nee Humphrey, but everybody would have heard of Tony Benn, nee Anthony Wedgwood Benn, Viscount of Stansgate.

Because I was doing more oil painting, I decided to have a couple of skylights put in the roof of the barn, a good place to work I thought. As a consequence, in response to an advert I put in the local paper inviting quotations from roofers, two young brothers came to the door, and I soon realised that the eldest and more intelligent was the one I was going to have to deal with.

One might expect a small stature not to be a disadvantage in anyone working on high, though a less than basic IQ would hardly be an asset, and the younger brother quickly revealed his by his contrariness. No sooner was he up, than he was sending the large irreplaceable Bangor slates his brother had taken off and stacked in neat piles, into my rubber-sheeting-lined koi carp pond. These days, because proper slates were very hard to come by, broken originals had to be replaced by rubbishy asbestos substitutes, flexible pond-liner was extremely difficult to repair perfectly, and huge, multi-coloured but guillotined, koi impossible to suture.

When I saw what was happening, I rushed out and told the little guy to lower the slates gently so they could go back where they came from, but for some reason he did not like doing this, and the next time I told him I could tell he was sizing me up, slate in hand, contemplating the feasibility of an accident wherein a wonderful Bangor slate might separate an overweening Englishman's head from his body. Then I caught the two of them putting in the deal skylights without first creosoting them with the stuff I had supplied, on the grounds that they could not creosote them upside down without the creosote splashing on their faces. And this was the way things went. While they were up, all sorts of debris came down into the yard on one side, and into the pond on the other, and the whole vicinity was constantly flooded with non-stop inanities.

On the third day there was suddenly a lot of shouting and yelling and when Helen looked out of the window, it was to see the younger brother hanging from the guttering, legs kicking the air, head lurching from side to side as though in a fit. The unholy rumpus he was making had attracted a swarm of bees which were buzzing around his head and bare chest, shirt open to display a gold medallion and a couple of ginger hairs, but he was frightened to come down because the dog was waiting for him at the bottom of the ladder, growling and baring its teeth. Meanwhile from above, the elder brother was shouting at me to do something.

'Tell him to let go and drop down!' I called out of the window.

'The feckin' dog'll get me!' yelled the one who had filled my lovely koi and lily pond with rubbish, smashed innumerable irreplaceable slates, and never stopped making cracks about St John and his retinue of concrete saints.

'Quick, for God's sake! Get the feckin' wasps' – which he pronounced as 'waasps' – 'away! They're bitin' me all over!'

'They're not "waasps"!' I corrected him. 'They're bees!' – as though it made the slightest difference – 'And they don't bite! They just sting!'

'He's allergic to stings!' shouted the eldest brother.

'Everybody is!' I called back. 'It's just a matter of degree!'

It was hard to be overly sympathetic when writing, especially with the young one howling as though he were being stung to death, so I went out and chained the dog up.

I do not know how many rungs he engaged coming down, but it could not have been many, and when he hit the ground, he leapt straight into their van and slammed the door. Half an hour passed before he could be persuaded to come out and make a run for the house so that I could treat his stings, and after I had finished, the two of them raced off for the rest of the day. When two days and half a dozen phone calls later, they returned, and the one with no brains was getting out of their van, a bluebottle buzzed by and sent him yelling up to the house and straight in the door. Twenty minutes later, after some serious talking, they returned to the roof and from then on worked in relative silence. I had warned them that a lot of clashing and gabbling at roof level was sure to annoy any passing wasps, as well as bees, and the dog was so intolerant of people fussing about that he was likely to snap his chain, and they seemed to accept it. To tell the truth, I was surprised they had come to finish the job, although I felt I had made it clear that I would not be paying them a penny unless they did, and from then on there was no more noise other than the tapping, clicking and clacking of a couple of elves. In a week the roof was finished and we never saw them again.

NINE

Because the land at the bottom of the two fields we owned flooded several times every winter and hardly ever dried out, we decided to plant it with water-tolerant trees like willow, hazel, spruce and alder, and where it was higher and drier, with as many species of native deciduous tree as feasible. But a few weeks into the back-breaking work proved too much for Helen and Medbh, the only one of our children still at home, and myself, and we had not yet started on the real labour. Fortunately we learned that the EU was giving grants for afforestation so that farmers with land unsuitable for crops or pasture could put it to use by growing trees they could sell in a matter of thirty years. As a consequence, private forestry companies were opening up all over the place and advertising their services in the Farmer's Journal and local newspapers. It was apparent it might be a pretty dicey business, so we interviewed those that seemed to know what they were talking about and settled for Coillte, a state forestry company. Not only did we favour state ownership as a principle, but felt they would be more reliable than the private firms, most of whom seemed like chancers from their patter. Coillte would bring in diggers to cut herring-bone drains, spray the weeds, fence around the borders, supply and plant the trees, and we would be responsible for the aftercare which consisted of maintaining the fences, pruning and replacing duds, control of pests and weeds, and anything else that threatened the welfare of the crop. It seemed like a generous offer, and like all generous offers from the Government, was largely financed by what was now being called the EU.

Coillte kept telling us that not only were they the experts, and everybody else the 'cowboys', but that they would provide muscle as well as 'know-how'. Perhaps, but I loved trees, had learned everything I could from good books on silviculture, and had no intention of sitting back and handing everything over to somebody else, especially when I discovered their way of working was to be given carte blanche to plant whatever they wanted, however they wanted and whenever it suited them, as though the whole thing were a personal favour we were being done. Also I soon found that for every 'expert' – a staff member who had been to college or had worked his way up through the ranks – there were probably a dozen unskilled labourers from the local employment centre who knew absolutely nothing about trees, and cared even less. The expert would tell them what to do on a Monday, leaving them to get on with it until the following Monday when he called to set them on with the next part of the job. It was a perfect way to create disaster, given that in a week half a dozen men can plant an awful lot of the wrong trees too deeply or too shallowly, the wrong distance apart – and upside down.

The main problem was that even Coillte were new to afforestation on this scale, and knew nothing about dealing with private investors. Previously, when they worked for the state, they had had nobody to chivvy them, and the technical quality of their work, along with the economics of planting trees for profit, was left to their own initiative. Worse still, the majority of their customers were farmers who knew nothing about trees and were not interested in knowing anything. They were content to leave everything to the forestry outfit, and glad to get paid something for land they had always considered wasteland, useless for anything except shooting over.

When Coillte came to do our land, they got a hell of a shock to find that not only could we tell the difference between an oak and an apple, we would be taking an interest in every stage of the work and insisting on joining every discussion regarding it. From the very start, we would be out every day to see what was being done and if we approved of it. As a result they would soon realise that as far as we were concerned, we were their employers, not some paymaster in Brussels who would never see a single tree they planted, and not give a damn whether it was the right way up or not.

Draining the wetland by cutting trenches with a digging machine caused the first of many headaches, not least because although the driver had no experience of this kind of work, he had plenty of big bad ideas. Having cut his way in, but forgotten to leave access to and from the road in order to get out and back in again, he attempted to rectify it by abruptly changing the directions of trenches when so many were already dug, and this proved catastrophic. I suppose we should have been grateful the casual unskilled labourers were not issued with JCBs as well as spades, because the planters not only got species mixed up because labels were scribbled in ink that quickly washed off in the rain, but because many of them were illiterate – certainly as far as Latin binomials were concerned – and because it was winter, few, if any, leaves remained to help even the 'experts' identify the saplings. As a consequence, a good many went in with their roots in the air and crowns in the earth.

The plants arrived when it suited the supplier, not when the planters were ready, so they were sometimes left in bundles above ground with, at best, a shovelful of earth tossed over them. Rain and wind soon washed that off and Jack Frost then took over. Because the saplings were merely little sticks without leaves and only a whisker of a root, not only were they beyond identification, it was impossible to tell if they were dead or alive, and stiff stems of weeds, such as docken and gorse, were not infrequently planted.

When the 'slaves' – as unskilled Irish workmen are wont to refer to themselves when working for a foreigner – had gone, and spring arrived, we could at last see which saplings were alive, plus which species were what, and what which, thus providing evidence of error by long-gone planters who were now cowboy plasterers on building sites, cowboy plumbers or landscape gardeners.

Now we were confronted by other agents of exasperation, ones we had scarcely reckoned on, certainly not in astronomical numbers. Sticky slugs might only have had a slimy layer of mucous to protect them, but they had rasping jaws sharp enough and tough enough to gouge canoe-shaped wounds in incipient wood. The forestry advisers had overlooked mentioning something they would have been well aware of, which was that because of the permanently damp climate, an immature tree plantation in Ireland was paradise for a slug, whereas for the human owner to go out with a powerful torch and survey the same scene on a misty night, was the equivalent of *Walpurgisnacht*, and if he stood stock still and did not make a sound, he would be able to hear their nano sloppy munching, belching, puking and farting. The expensive anti-slug pellets with which each sapling's base had to be encircled, were not only poisonous to birds, dogs and other animals, but quickly dissolved in rain, so to be effective the circle had to remain unbroken until the sapling's stem had become a trunk.

After the marauding slimy blobs came the rabbits and hares, and, like all predators, instead of eating their fill by consuming the whole plant so that it would have to be replaced, like a rat in a clamp of potatoes, a goat in a vegetable garden, or a wasp among apples, slugs just browse, moving from one food source to the next, nipping off the succulent leader, thus guaranteeing the sapling's turning into an ugly bush, rather than an elegant tree.

After trying dozens of remedies, orthodox and alternative, sophisticated and ludicrous, we started collecting plastic bottles from the council dump and using them as sleeves. Although this was extremely tedious and looked ridiculous, it protected the sapling against slug and rabbit, though not, of course, from the many species of fungi which adored the high humidity provided, or a herd of cattle. It was, however, a partial solution because fungi were by no means as bad as slugs, and the wind which often shook the bottles like the percussion section of the Berlin Philharmonic, aerated the insides, thus subduing most of them.

It took a year of such travails, by which time most of the failures had been rectified by a process called 'brashing', which I think is a rather unpleasant word for a pleasing and worthwhile task where bad specimens are removed and replaced by healthy new ones, something we mostly did ourselves, before the situation improved and by the summer of the second year we had row upon row of saplings that would one day transform the landscape.

Now we had the farmers to deal with. We had established a little plantation of lovely native trees that already enriched the area we lived in, but irritated our neighbours. Trees turned out to be a red bull to our 'pcers' who thought they were a ridiculous waste of land, albeit our land and even waste land. When EU subsidies favoured cattle, cattle, or grain for cattle, was what land should be used for; and if they favoured emus, emus and emu fodder were all land should be used for. Unfortunately trees by virtue of their immobility were highly vulnerable. Plant lusciously delicate Ash saplings in a field separated by a rickety baler-twine fence from a pasture overstocked with Friesian cattle, and see who wins. You won't have long to wait.

Notwithstanding the preference of our neighbours however, by the time we had been planting trees for a few years, excessive food production in the EU with its policy of dumping mountains of it to feed the vermin rather than selling it cheaply, or better still, donating it to countries with starving populations of human beings, generously grant-aided tree plantations were becoming a popular way of utilising patches of spare land, and the *Farmer's Journal* asked me to write a series comprising four articles recounting our experiences. After just two, they withdrew their request because of pressure from the Department of Forestry and other parties with an interest in afforestation, because potential planters were being deterred by the 'hardship' I detailed. Had the editors been more stoic and waited until the last article, they would have learnt the answer to depredation of trees by rabbit and slug – and other problems – all of which I dealt with in a helpful and cheerful manner. But they only read as far as the bad news, and panicked. They were too dyed in the wool, too used to cultivating creatures that crapped in kilos and peed by the gallon, that transmitted diseases that killed humans as well as their own kind, and produced comestibles that were increasingly becoming disavowed on grounds of costs and health.

After all the hassles with experts and incompetents, parasites and perversity, and long months of waiting to see what had survived, to stand in the midst of our nursery of native trees, and think of how before long their prunings would be giving warmth and comfort to the house, birds would be sheltering from the rain and roosting and nesting in them, was a wonderful thing to go to sleep with. Imagine how in later years their mature timber would be felled, mostly to construct and heat homes, some, later still as hardwoods, to create lovely furniture and perhaps carved sculpture, gave me a powerful Johnny Appleseed feeling. And then how some would eventually sink down into the earth and turn into peat that would provide fuel a million years from now for descendants who will regard us as neo-Neanderthals...and, who knows, perhaps preserve one or two members of the family as bog bodies, though hopefully without the braided cord around their necks that have in the past so often ritualised ancestors' decease.

I truly believed we had done good, returning the land to what it had once been, perhaps even better.

PART TWO

COSTA PENSIONISTA

TEN

By 1996 Helen and I were going on sixty, and the depletion in her stamina, as well as mine, could no longer be ignored in a life which made so many physical demands. Things I had relied on her to do, she could no longer do, or not do as well, and the 'easy' ways of doing things that I had long since developed for myself were increasingly becoming inadequate. The deterioration in my spine meant I could no longer turn my head sufficiently to reverse the car, lift anything heavy, or wrestle a female goat to the ground without ending up with its udder, or worse, in my face.

But it wasn't only we who had changed. Changes in society that had been gradual, were after twenty years becoming overwhelming, and as the end of the century approached Ireland was an altogether different place to what it had been when we arrived. A metamorphosis every bit as striking as the caterpillar into the Peacock butterfly – or rather, the Death's Head moth – had occurred outside our front gate and I, more than anybody else in the family, seemed to have been unaware of it. While I had been striving for the past, towards an archaic idyll, everyone and everything else had been galloping in the opposite direction, and the place we had come to with God, we were now contemplating leaving without, largely because He seemed to have disappeared from so much of it. But also because my life tended to be much more solitary and stationary than anyone else's.

We had created a poor man's garden of Eden, a place that functioned as a livelihood and source of pleasure, and had reached the point of having done as much as possible in terms of our capabilities, but had not left ourselves sufficient time or energy for dalliance, for the opportunity to saunter beneath the trees, trail our fishing nets in the ponds, or explore with binoculars and microscope the fascinating periphery that, left to itself, would have yielded more. And now that the weather seemed colder, wetter and windier, and life rather more hostile, I realised it was due as much to my own shortcomings as to climatic, biological and societal changes.

After contracting my illness, and particularly since becoming older, I had become very sensitive to changes in temperature, especially to cold; and night and day I was continually having to change my garments because I was too hot and drenched with sweat, or too cold and clammy. It was a nuisance but apart from superficial adjustments, there was little I could do. The weather was the key arbiter, especially the dinning humidity and its habit of changing so frequently and abruptly.

Neither Helen nor I had ever got over the salubrious years in New Zealand and Australia: the huge green vegetables of the former, and gorgeously ripe fruit of the latter; life outdoors, swimming in oceans and steeping in thermal springs, camping in the fresh air of mountains and tramping in bush.

The more we thought about moving to a country with such a climate, the more it appealed. I liked Australia and had a brother there but Helen thought it too macho and far away, especially with the children now making lives of their own in Ireland. But Spain was a possibility. It was relatively close now there were so many reasonably priced flights, we liked the culture and the food, and whereas the pernicious humidity of Ireland was a killer, the sun and aridity of Spain would be good for us. Until recently, the dictator Franco had still been bloodying his hands with the kind of people we would have been had we been Spanish, but by 1998 had thankfully disappeared into the long dark night himself, though not gently. The country had then been leavened by a Socialist government, become a member of the European Community, and was the most popular place under the sun for retired English couples.

The relief from physical labour would be a boon, and the opportunity, within limits, to travel, something we had once so enjoyed, was most welcome after so many relatively sedentary years. So after discussing it with the children and getting their approval, we decided to investigate the prospects.

Leaving Helen to look after the farm, I went on a month's recce to the Costa Blanca and came back having put a deposit on a villa in an *urbanización* (housing estate) in Las Pajaras Rojas (Red Songbirds) a few miles inland from El Jemina, a seaside town in the province of Alicante. The Romans, who left behind many instances of their occupation, though not as many as the subsequent Moors, called Alicante 'Lucentum – 'City of Light' – because of the wonderful natural light. It was the capital of the province and its airport only a few miles from El Jemina. It would surely be a good place to pick up art again, though I had no illusions about my stuff selling like hot cakes. I had a primitive style which some people called 'childish', rather than 'naïve' – and I portrayed subjects in situations of mild confrontation, such as the quarrelling that goes on between husband and wife, two sisters, or employer and employee. It was intended to convey humour, something many viewers consider to be cartooning, therefore not real art. Furthermore, female models should be much easier to obtain; they were certainly very difficult to procure in Ireland, especially without a full length skirt, woolly cardigan and a blouse buttoned up to the neck.

The villa I had so hastily put a deposit on, as though it were the last chance saloon, an inexpensive three-bedroom bungalow built by an English couple who were now raising a bigger house on a plot next door. The *urbanización* was quite modern and situated in what was described as a 'rural' environment, which meant a treeless and barren area, apart from a few patches of cactus and scrub. The only shop in the area was a bar, a desperate lean-to that sold a few brands of bottled beer, bottled gas, stale bread, 'foreign' cigarettes, blow-up pool toys and sanitary towels, and it was always open. A couple of miles away was the ancient pueblo of Los Pajaros Rojos which had a town hall, police station, hole-in-the-wall post-office, bank, down-at-heel family doctor practice, small restaurant, pharmacy, hardware store, pet shop, ice-cream parlour, butcher's, all of them tiny. The houses, like so many in Spain, were of a mixed variety owned by people of various nationalities which, by virtue of their style and the state of their little gardens, tended to indicate the provenance and nature of their owners. The icon of the area was a large golf complex with all the trappings of the nouveau riche, and during our first few days in Spain, our host, a dignitary of the local freemasonry and vice-captain of the golf club, insisted on showing us everything the club had to offer, a remarkably unseductive tour.

'Thanks, but no thanks,' I said at the end. 'As I said, I'm not really a golfing man.'

'Just you wait,' he gleefully assured me. 'You'll see.!'

I supposed he was referring to the utter euphoria I would be wallowing in after wasting half a day in his and his sporting oppos' company playing a silly game with a little white ball covered in indentations.

Moving from a four-bedroomed house with many outbuildings into a tiny house without a garage or shed meant most of our possessions would have to be disposed of, and over the next few months, everything – from all our animals, including the dog, the furniture and most of my collection of books, records and art – had been either sold for next to nothing, or given away. Finally, the old house in which we had reared our two sons and daughters, plus all the many animals, birds and plants, went along with the outbuildings, fifteen-acre forestry, koi ponds, hawk aviaries, mews, hives and many other outdoor things we had made or acquired. It was like having shreds of ourselves ripped off with pincers, and we had to continually remind each other why we were doing it.

'You're doing the right thing,' the children would say. 'If it helps Dad's health, it'll be worth it.' It became a mantra and, like all mantras, began to wear thin after a while. For my part, I went at it like Henry VIII's minions dissolving monasteries without considering the emotional or financial cost and not wanting to think about anything other than getting the job over and done with as soon as possible.

It is surprising how many people like looking inside other people's houses, and we had plenty of them treading in and out of ours every day with no intention other than to see how we had been living. It is painful having total strangers push past you into one room after another, looking into private places as though rummaging through the dregs of a closing-down sale in an old bookshop, some with their noses up, murmuring among themselves, others nodding towards us as though we were rival viewers sharing disapproval of something. At times I had to fight back the urge to announce the show was over, that we had decided to stay and wanted everybody out immediately.

Sometimes a nice quiet family with well behaved children would enter after tentatively tapping on the open door, or a respectable couple who clearly appreciated country life and expressed wonder at seeing what we had done, would wave as they passed by the window, and we would not be able to help smarting at the thought of giving it all up and allowing somebody else, maybe someone we did not like, to take over everything. It was not always easy to distinguish the genuinely interested prospective buyer from the nosey blighter sussing the place out.

Two months of this and nothing happened; nothing, that is, apart from a large, very fashionably dressed lady who had for some reason been poking around the septic tank in the yard, lifted the lid, and fallen in up to her fleshy thighs. The first we knew was when she came up to the house in an awful state – garments, handbag and person dripping and stinking – to apologise and very politely explain what had happened. Naturally we were beside ourselves and could not express enough regret, but she just kept smiling. What does one say when an exceptionally well-dressed lady falls into your septic tank? What words, what inanities are available to soothe the troubled breast of a middle-aged dowager standing in front of you with the lower part of her person filthy and stinking due to her being drenched in the excrement of your household? Would the sale of the house and land realise enough to cover the fine and court costs?

As I was filling the bath and trying to keep everybody outside and occupied, Helen was looking for a decent set of clothes from the time before she lost weight, clothes not too expensive but good enough to make the poor woman look nice. Astonishingly she seemed content with the bath and the clothes which she assured Helen she would have laundered and returned, but that just made us even more embarrassed.

'Oh, no! Just burn them!' I told her while Helen almost choked.

Because the bathroom lock, which was always iffy, decided to play up, the poor woman, who, amazingly was still not distraught, could not open the door from the inside and Helen had to whisper instructions from the outside while I was hosing down her boots and clothes at the back of the house. Even though I had given up on God several years past, as on several previous dire occasions, I welched, and sincerely and wholeheartedly prayed that He would not allow anybody else to come, and make those hanging about hurry up and get off the property.

All the same, we were still on tenterhooks until eventually we were thirty thousand feet above the Pyrenees and all our belongings either in the cabin luggage compartments above us, or in a lorry aboard a ferry proceeding in the same direction.

Long before this, however, as the weeks went by and nothing positive happened bar a number of tentative phone calls – always at night – from viewers who were proposing we ditch the estate agent and deal directly with themselves, thus saving us a good bit of money, so we were assured.

Gradually it became clear that the state agent's enthusiasm was waning, so because we needed to sell soon or would lose the deposit and the villa, we agreed to his suggestion to go for auction. There were no signs of the incredible boom in property prices that would soon shake the whole country from top to bottom, and he could only muster half a dozen bidders, but at least it was sold, albeit for a quarter of what it would eventually fetch.

Onc cannot insist that something he or she is selling be subsequently treated in a certain way, despite the most impassioned of pleas and assurances. Yet it seems wrong that somebody should be able to substantially alter something just because they have paid money to own it; it is like buying a Renaissance masterpiece and pouring creosote over it just because one likes the smell of creosote. Some things have a right to exist pristine forever, no matter who the custodian. For someone to change physically and spiritually something which has taken years to create, and been sanctified by the love and care of decent custodians could be totally changed physically and spiritually by strangers, seems a mortal sin.

ELEVEN

On the 2 July 1998, twenty-two years to the day we came to Ireland, again and equally insignificantly, my birthday, and Helen's and my wedding anniversary, we arrived at Alicante airport to be met by Lew Spiers, an Englishman with a sloppily large nose, ears and mouth, who was selling us the villa, and embraced us as though we were relatives he had not seen for many years. Standing beside him was his 'oppo', Colin, another Home Counties man, who was to be our chauffeur. Colin looked as though he had been knocked about somewhat, perhaps done a bit of time and not fared too well.

Lew's conversation was directed entirely at me, plainly he had no use for women, and he gabbled nonstop about how 'chuffed' I was going to be when I 'clapped eyes' on the area's newly refurbished golf course, membership of which he had arranged to begin for me the following week. He bustled us into a battered old car and we headed straight into wasteland. On my previous visit I had assured him that golf was 'not my thing' – my polite way of conveying I hated the silly game – but he obviously considered that was impossible because anybody who did not think the way he did, was a fool.

When we stopped at a petrol filling station so Colin could get himself some cigarettes, Lew utilised the opportunity to apologise for Colin's being rather tipsy as well as not very smartly dressed, and explained that he had only hired him because his own car was off the road. When Colin came back, Lew decided he wanted to go for something, thus giving Colin the opportunity to point out that Lew was not really a 'friend', he was just doing him a favour because that was 'the sort of thing expats did for each other'.

In minutes we were in hot, deserted scrubland, with the airport and all other signs of civilisation gone, and as we drove further inland into the mountainous area we were to live in, with our heads filled with Lew's inane cockney bragging, and our lungs with Colin's breath mingling with the sickly car deoderiser, I was imagining life in close association with people like these.

Helen, who sat in the back and never said a word, told me later that with every kilometre we were being hauled farther away from Ireland, her heart had felt closer to rupturing. I saw her sneaking glances at Lew's face with its large bony nose sprouting hair matted with dried snot, and thick dribbling lips barely able to contain his Labrador-like tongue. The hair on his head was long and greasy and stank of what I assumed was golfing gel, his huge hands spread out over the back of Colin's seat, black-nailed fingers impatiently roving. Everyone and everything we passed, he leered at, occasionally nodding or waving a finger at an attractive woman, as though we were passing through his domain and we should know this one and that one were his, or destined to be.

When we arrived at the villa we were to live in for the next six months while ours was being built – a 'misunderstanding' had caused a change in arrangements – we were met by Mrs Spiers, a hard-faced, sturdy little blonde of about forty, with eyes like arctic marbles and hands like a bricklayer's: all fingers the same length and squared off as though cropped with a trowel, fingernails like small uneven tiles.

Over a cup of tea, while sitting on boxes of chattels we had sent on ahead, she told us we would have to pay extra charges for electricity because of another 'misunderstanding', and Lew followed up with a warning that we should be on the lookout for, though not worry about, an Englishman who was currently going around with an axe with which he had recently put his wife in hospital. Seemingly the chap bore the Spiers a grudge for some reason they could not divine, or rather, would not divulge. It was late and we were tired but before we retired I had to insist on learning the axeman's name, and being given some idea what he looked like, in case he happened through the bedroom window during the night. But Lew was 'reluctant to say too much because of the law of slander'.

'So, we keep an eye open for a dingbat with a chopper..? Otherwise everything's hunky dory.' I really did not know whether I should be chuckling or manifesting genuine anxiety. 'Are there many wife-cullers around these parts? And are they all expats?'

Lew guffawed and slapped his massive thighs.

'"Wife-cullers"..? That's a laugh, eh, Val..? That imbecile!'

So we had to go to bed guessing. However, I assured Helen there was probably nothing more to it than a bit of aggro between Lew and a neighbour, and he was trying to enlist our support before the other fellow got his neb in.

But by the time the two of them had left to go into the caravan they were living in, which was beyond a massive pile of builders' rubble a couple of yards from the villa we were in, where I was merely disconcerted by everything so far, Helen was practically in a state of shock. We were lying on a bed surrounded by plastic bags of clothing and a whole lot of beach paraphernalia, and unable to sleep because of the heat and the racket caused by hundreds – or was it thousands – of cicadas sizzling like sausages in the trees outside. I recalled the night exactly twenty-two years previously, when Helen and I had lain in our bed on our first night in Ireland, after travelling from Tyneside: I had been listening to the sounds from a bog in the distance and relishing the wonderful summer night, and she had instantly fallen into what she described next morning as 'the most wonderfully peaceful sleep I've ever had'.

Before coming to Spain for the recce, I had written to the local English-speaking newspaper, asking readers for their views on life on the Costa Blanca, and among the glowing replies were a number of invitations to come for tea and a chat, including one from a Scotsman offering to rent me a flat for the month I intended to spend in El Jemina. I had taken him up on his offer and was met ten days later at Alicante airport, by a skinny but very fit-looking fellow in his seventies, T-shirt and shorts, who clearly delighted in informing me he was 'always in shorts in November'.

His bank manager had assured him that because his flat was on the fifth floor, none of his tenants would ever have anything to fear from malaria, yellow fever or any other of the mosquito-borne diseases, 'because the little buggers can't fly any higher than the fourth floor'. I presumed his flat had previously been repossessed by the same bank.

He then told me he was a Glasgow Rangers supporter, presumably to deter me from asking the times of Sunday morning Masses in case I were a papist.

Finally he introduced his charlady wife, a sad, skinny worn-out looking soul standing a couple of paces away. She would be cleaning the flat; that had always been her occupation back in Scotland, so she was well used to it. People mistook her for his mother, he joked. He might be in shorts but she was no bikini bimbo and it was a wonder he did not have her in clogs and a pinny.

On the way to his flat, in a car that was way too big for him, he had filled me in on his attributes, tastes and achievements, the latter consisting mainly of how he made money from expatriate car repairs, expatriate property extensions, and a bit of other expatriate this and that. 'She makes a few pennies an' all, but I wouldna' hae her cleanin' up slops after any diego, I can tell ye that. Would I, pet..? We hae wor pride.'

After a bit of tourist guiding, he suddenly blurted out with: 'I bet ye've brought nae food wi' ye..?' 'And ye dinnae knae Monday's a bank holiday, di' ye?'

'Food..? Er, no. I don't usually bring food when I go on holiday,' I said, thinking he was joking. 'Most countries I go to tend to have food.'

He looked at me with something approaching a sneer.

'Well, if ye de'int think ye can last till Tuesday, we'll see if we cannae find ye a wee supermarket open,' he chuckled, nudging his wife with his bony elbow as we drove up to a scruffy little supermarket where I was able to get enough 'expired' provisions to make a cup of tea and a sandwich for my supper.

'You'll be pretty fluent in Spanish after seven years?' I suggested, in an attempt to break the awful silence with a sentence or two of acceptable small talk.

'The only lingo I know, is "*cerveza*", which means "beer". My motto is, "If they want my loot, they can bloody-well speak my language".'

The following morning he arrived, uninvited at 8.30 a.m., to show me around town; this consisted of a tour of bars and cafes owned by various of his mates.

'They mightn't be the poshest, but ye won't find anywhere cheaper,' he vouched. 'An' that's all that matters te me.'

I found myself nodding at his various homespun adages, then wishing I had grimaced instead.

He must have thought I could be trusted with a tad more personal information, because he confided that although he did not expect 'wee wifey' to manage it, he expected to survive at least another ten years himself, what with the weather, food and easy life.

'She's hardly what ye'd call in tip-top shape, poor lass. Always worked her fingers to the bone, and still does. We both have. But I'm takin' it easy now. She disnae knae hoo.'

The following day I came back from my first foray on my own, to find him sitting in an armchair reading my paper, while wee wifey was doing something in the kitchen. I was rather taken aback and told him. 'I told ye he wouldna' like it,' came a tired voice from next door.

He, however was really narked and maintained that since it was his property he could enter it whenever he wanted. I tried to get him to appreciate that I had a right to regard the place private for as long as I was paying rent, but as the first tenant in his new career as landlord, it was an uphill battle and I never saw them again until the day I left when he suddenly arrived to make sure I was not stealing his chipboard furniture or nylon sheets. There was evidence enough that they were making inspections when I was out, so I suppose he was watching my movements from a parked car somewhere; but I did not think he was dishonest, merely mean and distrusting.

After we had parted, thankfully early on in our relationship, I had explored the town and environs and called on the better-looking estate agents, though it was quite impossible to carry out a meaningful survey through their double windows, of the masses of villas, apartments and *fincas* (farmhouses) displayed. I then decided to follow up on some of the invitations I had received following my letter in the paper, and sample some of the expatriate culture, travelling by the excellent cheap and frequent little '*Tramvia*' train, but when I began telephoning to confirm, more than a few seemed to have forgotten their invitation, or changed their minds; perhaps my plebian Geordie accent was a deterrent. But this still left a few genuinely friendly respondents and a few more just wanting to show off.

Interestingly, but not surprisingly, most turned out to be middle-class or fake middle-class, certainly no palpably working-class, at pains to acquaint me with the local customs they had adopted, the foremost of which – and I never thereafter encountered an *extranjera* (female foreigner) who had not adopted it – was the double kiss seemingly imposed by Spanish women on all men.

Being English and therefore reserved, I was not accustomed to grappling with bossy women with lurid plumb-purple lipstick trowelled on to cheeks devoid of lips and frequently overhung by a nose with hairs impaling drops of mucus, who thrust themselves at me so that I could plant a big wet *beso* (kiss) on each of their sagging, pink-powdered cheeks while notifying me that 'This is the way we do it in Spain.' There were lots of things Spanish ladies did that English ladies did not, so why pick on this one? For instance, if you begin to sit down beside a Spanish person on a seat in a park or at a concert, they will invariably greet you, man or woman. So why not just do that..? And if one addresses a Spaniard in the street, say, to ask directions, they will always react with a greeting appropriate to the time of day; it is done a tad reprovingly but not rudely.

English people never do that, although they might open with 'Excuse me.' That said, most people, certainly including the Spanish, think the English are the most polite of Europeans, even though the era of the Lager Lout and Sangria Slapper were, at this time, still far from over.

A couple I visited on the Altea Hills had a house that jutted out from the side of a cliff in a sort of reservation surrounded by a high wire fence that was probably electrified. All four of their en-suite bedrooms had gold-plated plumbing which I suppose was better than gilt-edged bonds in that they got to feel the stuff; but for somebody who grew up in a council estate, in a world of lead and copper with only an occasional glimmer of brass, and winced every time he heard the phrase 'en-suite' pronounced in English, it was quease-making. Added to that, three separate little Alhambras just to eliminate in, which must surely more eloquently distinguish ape from human than any superficialities like the want of a tail, or a tad too much hair on the back. Yet, so typical of their class, when I let out that I had once worked for the Veterinary Department of the Ministry of Agriculture and Fisheries, without inquiring to make sure it was not in Administration, the matriarchal expatriate immediately declared that I could cut her Chihuahua's claws to save their having to pay the vet to do it; the thing's claws certainly needed doing, it ran up my inside leg like a squirrel and twice during the meal I had to stand up to shake it off.

Middle-class English are never satisfied with their neighbours. If they are worse off than they are themselves, they disapprove of them; if they are better off, they despise them. So to live beneath a German old enough and wealthy enough to have been an officer in the SS, whose hacienda protruded from the top of an overhanging cliff like the main turret in 'The Guns of Navarone' to cast a permanent shadow over one's banyan tree, must have been 'hard chancre', in military parlance, even though he was seemingly in a coma and had been left by his wife years ago.

'Because of his evil shadow, I can't get the hibiscus to flower,' my hostess bleated. 'When we came, we were assured that for purely geological reasons it would be impossible to build any higher than us. Then Herr Bigshot comes along with his ill-gotten gains and monstrous digging machines…no doubt made by Krupps…and "Shazam!" anything is possible.'

Some of her odium must surely have floated up to the old boy's south-facing intensive-care room and poisoned the air he breathed, notwithstanding his battery of de-ionisers, but, try as I might, I was unable to muster much sympathy for either of them.

The day I was invited to a 'tavern' in Calpe, the woman showed me how well she and her husband had integrated by going for a siesta five minutes after I arrived. She was only in the next room and must have spent the whole time listening to what he and I were talking about, because when she eventually came out, dressed as though for a royal garden party, she constantly alluded, with no small amount of scorn, to various things we had said, though repeatedly confusing *Feng Shui* with yoga, and Dublin with Belfast. She was a cat person and I, who had kept canaries in an outside aviary as a boy, was not. Three of a hirsute breed capable of harbouring many zoonotic parasites, kept raising their tails and rubbing themselves past my face in some kind of hideous foreplay. They were very clever at reading people, according to 'Mummy', yet failed utterly to detect the urge I had to swipe them straight through the window, because they repeatedly came inches away from having it demonstrated. Both host and hostess affected to deplore the English, though very English themselves, a common enough contradiction, but she was also a misanthrope, something I found unbecoming in a woman. The two of them boasted of shunning all English shops and any Spanish that had a section devoted to English goods and, however crass their facility with the Spanish language, whenever they were addressed in English by an English person, they would always reply in Spanglish, object being to stymie any attempt by a fellow countryman or woman to strike up a conversation. They were ex-restaurateurs intending to establish a bed-and-breakfast business, but had not got very far with it yet; and no wonder, given the short shrift any prospective English customers would have got, plus the unappealing nature of the fare to any Spanish.

In over three hours they only managed to whip up one stale bread roll soaked in rancid olive oil, and a badly smeared glass of peach-and-melon juice, the cheapest of all *zumos* (fruit juices), with a specific gravity similar to lava: it was warm, so had probably been kept at room temperature and fermented because by the time I got back to Jemina after a fifty-minute train journey, my entrails were heaving. My only thought had been how to get back to Jock's flat with my intestinal contents still in my intestines, and throughout the mile trek from the station, which included some very uneven waste ground, a leap across a wide drain, and finally dragging myself up four flights of stairs because the lift was out of action, I went through minor agonies.

Every day from then on I called into every promising-looking estate agent's, until eventually I was attracted by a photograph of a 'chalet' owned by Lew and Val Spiers, a Cockney couple who had built it themselves. According to the spiel it took very little looking after, the proximity of the sea and mountain air made it like living in a health resort, it was close to the town of Jemina, the city of Alicante and the airport, and the price was very reasonable.

There were many such properties, I had already seen a number of them and was only supposed to be gathering information. But deep inside my ear a demon was taunting me with 'If you don't buy now, you'll never again find anything as wonderful as this'. So I telephoned Helen and told her I thought I had found the ideal place. From the start, she had not been that enamoured of moving to Spain and had been hoping that a year or two of global warming might step up Ireland's climate, but I had kept reminding her that she had not liked the idea of moving to Ireland either until we got there, but had soon fallen in love with it. We talked several times over the next twenty-four hours but I was too enthusiastic to be as objective as she needed me to be. I could hear the anxiety in her voice, but anxiety is no match for fervour and she knew I was getting impatient with her stalling, and eventually gave in.

Lew Spiers, a backslapping fellow with a goofy grin, was delighted. Even Val, with her Barbie hair and ice-cold eyes, had been pleased, though for some reason had tried hard not to show it. He said he was going to build a bigger house for themselves and that when we came to live, they would move to Benidorm until it was finished, which he expected would be in June of the following year.

Considering we were to be next-door neighbours at least for a while, I thought it would show good faith to offer to defer coming until July so they could build their house with minimum domestic upheaval. It would also allow us more time to do the many things we would need to do to wind up things in Ireland. So I 'very generously and unusually', according to Roberto, the estate agent, offered to pay the deposit and let them stay where they were until the following July. 'Oh, that would be so, so kind!' Lew Spiers had yelped with comic gentility. 'I can tell we are going to be great friends. You and your lady-wife are just the kind of people this place needs… educated, no dogs or kids, and nature-loving with a medical background. Couldn't be better.' When he clapped his hands I should have heard alarm bells ringing, but I did not know then what I would learn soon after and never forget, which was that the Spanish sun, language and culture all conspired to concoct quick and foolish decisions in ancient Western European skulls.

During the recce I had become very friendly with Roberto Hernandez, the son of the owner of the *inmobiliaria* (estate agency), who had been brought up in England and worked in Ireland, and he drew up the contract, arranging it so that Helen could immediately send a bank draft for the deposit, which in Spain is always paid to the owners, not the estate agents, balance to be paid when we took up occupancy. I then returned to Ireland to work on enthusing Helen and reassuring the family, and begin the painful process of selling up, which is quite contorted when a farm with outbuildings, land and livestock is involved.

During the long months we were dismantling our home and gradually disposing of various items, the Spanish villa being much smaller than our Irish house, we kept in touch with the Spiers by letter, and in one of theirs, which were always written by Val Spiers, a solicitor's daughter, it came out in a very abstruse way that the house they were building for themselves, which was on the plot next to our, was going to exclude the view of the Mediterranean, one of the main positive features of the villa.

'Exclude' in this instance did not mean 'interfere with' or 'partially hide', it meant 'completely blot out'. So I immediately telephoned to protest and at the same time sent a fax to Roberto Hernandez. It was obvious the Spiers knew all along this would happen, and even admitted it was 'a bit of a dirty trick', but begged us to 'forgive' them and allow them to make amends by building us an identical villa on another site they owned in the same street, one with an even better view than the one on which we had put the deposit. It would have the same extras, we could choose the décor, and we could stay in the original villa rent-free until the new one was ready to move into. It was an opportunity to withdraw if we wanted to, but by this time we felt we had gone too far, so when Roberto telephoned the following day to say he and his father had inspected the new site and it seemed a good alternative, we accepted. Roberto had then sent an amended contract in Spanish and English, saying the Spiers had agreed to build us a chalet that would be of *mismo diseño* (same design) and *exactemente iguale* (exactly equal) in every other way to the one we were originally going to buy, and the deposit and all conditions in the initial contract would transfer.

So we carried on with our arrangements, sold up and left, pretty much exhausted by the time we were done. We had lived in Ireland for almost a quarter of a century and were leaving behind many things we could not dispose of. Most of all, the children. But it was only an hour and a half to the airport, two hours and fifty minutes by plane, and then half an hour's drive to the villa. Five hours total from closing one door and opening the next.

TWELVE

'ARE WE REALLY HERE?' Helen asked despairingly. The blinding sun was streaming in the windows and the white walls and wardrobes made it feel like the annex to a tropical hospital.

'Remember the last time we woke up like this?' I said cheerfully.

'I hope you're not talking about New Zealand..?' Helen replied. 'That was civilised! The chalet was lovely… The fridge full of food… Birds singing… Here the fridge doesn't even work!'

'Give it a chance, dear. It's probably not switched on. And you can't expect the birds to be singing with all that banging and clashing going on. When they've finished building, which can't be that long, it'll be like paradise. Remember, I've seen it the way it can be.'

There was a knock on the bedroom door. It was Val wanting to know if we were ready to go to the *Ayuntamiento* (Town Hall) to register ourselves. It was ten past eight.

We knew living in Spain was going to be very different from holidaying in it, but were totally unprepared for just how different. It was so hot from noon until five, for instance, that most people took a siesta, and all the shops and offices, apart from the large supermarkets, closed from 1 p.m. until 5 p.m. when they opened again until 8 or 9 p.m., though government departments, banks and post offices shut at 1 p.m. and stayed shut until 8 a.m. next day.

Other countries in the EU were doing all kinds of things to smooth out difficulties arising from cultural differences between neighbours, but Spain was stubbornly insisting on preserving them. Instead of the polite and affable hotel receptionists, waiters and travel agents, the kind of Spaniard one deals with as a holidaymaker, we were now going to be dealing with *funcionarios* – civil servants and officials from the nether world of the *Ayuntamiento* and (Oficina de Extranjeros) (Immigrants Office) who were anything but obligers. None of these Spaniards seemed to realise that we citizens of fellow EU countries coming to live, were not claiming refuge or political asylum, or social security benefits – which had to come from their own country – and it was their duty to facilitate us. Hardly any spoke a word of English, though all recognised the language, and when they heard it they often scowled as though the sound of it was the same as being stabbed in the groin.

While we were registering at the *Ayuntamiento*, and then again when we were opening our bank account, Val, who was nearly fluent in Spanish, and her ten-year-old daughter who was fluent, did not have the savvy to turn away from the various computer screens when financial and personal information about us was being screened, and one way or another were able to learn more about our financial and other private matters *vis-à-vis* Spain than we were. It would have been discomposing to suggest she move her chair away, because things were happening so quickly and we had no idea that Val had a stake in us because account-holders introducing prospective ones were entitled to discounts. But Val, the 'private school teacher' who was in fact no more than an assistant to a primary school secretary, was turning out to be quite wily, and we would soon find out that 'reinvention' was a common ploy with the many expats who claimed consequential pasts. Not only was it useful for gaining esteem in all kinds of situation, it could be very impressive when establishing relationships between sexes – and we would soon learn there was plenty of that.

    I was becoming increasingly vexed the way Val and her precocious little daughter had their heads thrust in front of ours and as close as possible to the computer, eyes wide as they uploaded all kinds of facts that had absolutely nothing to do with them. It was all I could do to refrain from dragging their chairs back, but apart from the fact that we were presently almost entirely dependant on them, and they seemed to be doing what they could to help us get started in our new life, it would have been impossible to do or say anything without creating a to-do right there in the bank. Had I created a fuss, Helen would have been put out and she was already in a highly friable state.

We had been told by the DHSS in Newcastle that as soon as possible we should register with their Spanish counterpart, which the Spiers said was in Xixona, about twenty miles further inland, so on our second day we drove there in a car we hired. The Spiers would have known that Calle Churucca in Alicante was the main INSS (Instituto de Seguridad Social) office where all the expats went, and much nearer, but for some reason misled us, something they would do repeatedly in the days and weeks to come. Why, we had no idea, unless it were with the intention of undermining our confidence and extending our dependence on them. Maybe I had been too friendly and accommodating from the start and they had leapt at the chance of taking advantage. It would not be long before we would learn from umpteen sources that because of his size, masonic connections, barrow-boy-wisdom picked up from his association with the underworld of London, and her superficial familiarity with the law and lawyers, and natural cunning, almost everybody was afraid of them. We would hear all kinds of tales, some seeming far-fetched, others quite credible, but all disquieting, and the characters who were always calling to their caravan, and sometimes by mistake to the villa we were in, were not the sort one would want knocking at one's door at yon time of night.

Xixona, with its downbeat local industries – government offices, *turron* (almond nougat) and disposable diaper factories – was hardly a tourist town. The atmosphere was gloomy and incestuous, in the way of small isolated towns that make one feel awkward and conspicuous simply by walking along the street or going into a shop.

Although we were the only customers, claimants, supplicants, *vagabondas* (down-and-outers) or whatever else the Spanish social security department perceived us to be, we had to wait unacknowledged for almost half an hour before finally taking the initiative and approaching a totally uninterested middle-aged woman at her desk, addressing her with an apology for my abysmal Spanish and attempting to explain our mission. Naturally I expected her to be gracious enough to greet us with something such as: 'Please don't worry, Senores. Your Spanish is grand. It's just silly old me. I'm always a scatterbrain before my first morning coffee break. Especially in the presence of VIPs.'

It would have put us at ease. But this was not Ireland, it was an EU office; so general information and questionnaires should have been printed in English as well as twenty-odd other languages. But everything here was only and entirely in Spanish. Without the slightest gesture towards attending to our enquiry, she waved us off in the direction of a colleague who was quite tall but by no means tall enough to justify so much difficulty getting me into focus that he had to screw up his eyes and pull a face. This was what had probably come of the universal belief that the under-nourished Spanish were the 'little people' of Europe. It was only now, after so many years privation, that they were starting to lay hands on some decent EU nutrition, as had the giant, Príncipe Felipe, plus, so the 'truth' magazines stated, his daily ration of growth-promoting complexes.

'No, no, no, no, no', he muttered, as soon as the documents were in his hand. ('No' is the Spaniard's favourite word, and he or she will repeat it four times, as through a Gatling gun; they do the same with 'Si' (Yes) but definitely prefer the 'No' word.

Suddenly the soaring, impeccably groomed fellow saw something he obviously recognised, possibly a symbol that reminded him that he, like us, was in the European Union now and our respective countries had obligations to each other, and he called to the woman who turned towards him with a face like a baby's recently smacked bottom, and summoned us with a flick of a many-bangled wrist. With questions curt and almost accusatorial, fingers drumming impatiently on the desk whenever we had to rummage through a bag or pocket for an item of information, she began a comprehensive questionnaire as to our circumstances and other, quite irrelevant matters. Suddenly and abruptly, after a quarter of an hour's tediously slow writing, she plonked down her pen, picked up the form and slowly tore it into confetti-sized pieces in front of our faces, before dropping them into a wastepaper basket at her feet. Because we did not have a *residencia* (permanent residence permit) we were ineligible for medical treatment, the main social security benefit we were seeking, and that was that. Out. She had already turned her back and was doing something else.

As we departed, I mused on the fact that there would almost certainly be no trace of our ever having passed this way, let alone having applied for anything. The filing cabinet was probably a refrigerator full of iced drinks and chilled vile gazpacho soup – something I would one day have to struggle to keep down when persuaded to 'be a bit more adventurous for a change and try it', as though it would give people to think I was a local.

Our visit to this huge office, empty save for two paltry human beings, confirmed an old adage which would be exquisitely illustrated on so many occasions during our life in Spain, and that was: 'Humiliation is a fine art whose nuances are never better appreciated than by the underling'. Within days we would discover that other than impoverished Spaniards usually pronounced *'funcionario'* – 'the tyrant on the bottom rung' – with a spitting sound.

When we returned to the villa, it was to find a Telefónica (semi-state telephone monopoly) van parked outside. The main telephone line to the house had been severed and was lying in the drive, and there was debris in the form of empty cartons, bits of wire and aluminium fittings, all over the place, as if the van had had its annual clean-out while its driver had been suffering a fit of rage.

The living room was full of cigarette smoke and there was fag-ash everywhere. The telephone was in pieces on the floor, along with the contents of a toolbox, and a sturdy fifty-odd-year-old man in shorts, with eyebrows like Mexican moustaches, was fiddling with the connection box. Three times I asked him what he was doing, before he turned around, and when he did, it was to demand a drink of water. At this stage we did not realise it was a crime to refuse anybody such a request, or an injured person on the highway a lift to the nearest hospital if you happened to be passing in a vehicle. Val had pointed this out while Helen was acceding to his request/demand; she spoke in English, so he did not understand. I must say I was touched by such a humane law, the only humane law I had ever heard of; we did not have such notices in England, only the likes of 'Keep off the grass', 'Trespassers will be prosecuted', etc.

When 'your man', as we say in Ireland, had drained the glass and thrust it at Helen, and I had repeated my question, he growled at Val: '*Oiga, Rubia! Digales!*' (Tell them, Blondie!). '*¡De todas formas, es demasiado caliente para que trabaje!* (Anyway, it's far too hot for me to be working!).

'What?' I said to Val. 'Is he saying it's too hot?'

'He is! And you'd better believe him!'

'But he's Spanish, isn't he? If he can't stand a bit sun, who can? Even I could fix a fuse in this weather.'

She shrugged. 'Tell him that and he'll be gone.'

While we had been putting our affairs in order, so that were we to experience a medical contingency we would be able to count on the Spanish authorities to look after us, he had been transferring the villa telephone to the Spiers' caravan, and Val now advised us that if we wanted another, we would have to apply to the telephone company to have a new one installed. This meant that in the meantime, contact with Ireland or anywhere else would have to be made via a public telephone, and the nearest was in town. And if we needed to make an international call, we would have to prevail upon the kindness of the Spiers, or do without. Fortunately, Helen was able to produce the inventory Roberto Hernandez had made out for us as part of the contract, and this clearly included a telephone, so after a week's argy-bargying, the Spiers were obliged to arrange for another to be installed.

The following morning we went to the Oficina de Extranjeros in Alicante to apply for *residencias*. It was a grotty place with a small, very old, heavily fortified door in a narrow street near the port, in an area where many of the walls were pock-marked with machine-gun holes. Close against the wall leading up to the door was a long queue of Moroccans, Algerians and South Americans in small groups, and a number of elderly white couples. Helen and I had not queued outside a building since the 1950s in England when we were courting and used to go to the posh cinema, and before that, as a kid I used to queue for my family's rations during the Second World War. There had been no embarrassment associated with it then because everybody did it and there was humour as well as community spirit.

We arrived at the *oficina* at 7 a.m. when the door was opened by a fat armed guard, a number of people counted in, and the door closed again. A group of Moroccans then got very agitated and raised such a clamour that the guard came out, and while he was dealing with them, we slipped in behind. A man with his feet up, reading a newspaper and eating a sandwich, was occupying a tiny kiosk just inside the door. He refused to look up when we called to him, and was turning the pages and shaking the paper so as to create as much noise as possible, so we knocked on the glass until he imperiously looked over spectacles which looked to be heavily flecked with fly dirt. Without moving or stopping eating, he called: '*Vuelvan mañana!*' (Come back tomorrow!) and splattered the glass with sticky, half-masticated morsels.

An American woman, halfway up the stairs, called out that they were only doing thirty today, and more than that were already in; any still queuing outside were wasting their time. 'You have to be here before seven o'clock to have a hope of getting in. I've been here three days in a row and this is the first time I've got past the door. These *schlemiels* like nothing better than giving you the run-around.' She waved her hand when she saw us glancing at the guard. 'Don't worry about him. None of them can speak any language but their own. If that.

It's a government department for foreigners and immigrants, so you won't find anybody in the building who speaks a word of anything except *castellano*. And they only work mornings. Come one o'clock and you've had it either way.'

The following day we were back at 6.30 a.m. This time I counted the number of people in front of us, almost all of whom were Arabs. There were eighteen. Half an hour later there were as many again as ones and twos casually sauntered up to talk to companions and then forgot to continue to the end of the queue.

'I see you not like us,' one of them said challengingly.

'What you see is that I don't like queue-jumpers,' I replied.

'What means this "q-jumpers?"'

I wasn't inclined to get into a ludicrous wrangle with anybody; it was too early in the day. I was tired and he had already made up his mind. I shrugged but he persisted.

'Those my friends. They go for coffee. Now they come back.'

From then until the time we got to the door, we had to stand and watch while he went up and down the queue apprising his comrades of the English redneck behind, and presumably canvassing for a vote, while their faces turned towards us with pained animosity, the equivalent of a psychological lynching.

We failed to get in that day, but did so by a hairsbreadth on the one after, after getting there at 6.00 a.m. After an hour and a half in a dingy room with hard wooden benches and a huge ventilating fan blasting like an Arctic wind, we spent an hour on the staircase waiting to get to the top where we were brusquely screened by a woman smoking a cheroot and flirting with a podgy guard a deal younger than herself. She gave us a number and showed us into a stuffy little room that was the antechamber to a place that reminded me of old photographs of Ellis Island's reception hall.

At 1.45 p.m., by which time we were sure the knell was about to toll and we were going to be told to clear off and try our luck another day and probably somewhere else, our number was called and we were beckoned to the desk of a crew-cutted burly man in a room with seven or eight other desks, each with an interrogator sitting opposite two or more thoroughly chastened human beings of various nationalities. He had hands like legendary Spanish *jamones* (hams) with thick black hairs growing out of them, a tank commander's neck, and an expression that could well have won awards for discouraging the most fugitives from wanting to settle here. Without inviting us to sit down, or so much as glancing at us, he put his hand out. I nearly made the mistake of shaking it but aborted just in time when I realised he was reaching for our papers. Throughout the interview he made telephone calls, growled, barked to colleagues across the room and frequently got up and went out in the midst of saying something to us, or our trying to say something to him. I use the word 'say', but in his case, communication took the form either of thick-finger pointing, or a vigorous shaking of the thick head. We were offering him one thing after another, as though trying to appease a savage chieftain: originals plus copies of identity photographs, birth and marriage certificates, passports, bank statements, pension payment cheques, and various other items. But anything presented out of the order that suited him was not merely set to one side until he was ready for it; it was waved away as though useless, and sometimes we would be left with our arm outstretched and hanging in the air, a vital survival document dangling from our fingers like a used bookie's slip.

When at last he seemed to be on the point of conceding we had a right to be in his country – or was merely teasing us – he sat with his finger to his lips and slowly went through everything one more time to make sure there was not the tiniest impediment – a comma perhaps that had not come through a hundred percent on the photocopy, or some other crucial reason for making us come back at dawn on another day and submitting all over again, by which time we might have had second thoughts about settling here and disappeared off the face of the earth instead.

While standing in the queue outside we had overheard that it was necessary to pay money into a particular bank nearby to cover the cost of the paper that the Oficina would be using to process us. Seemingly, if one did not also obtain a receipt to prove it, one would end up back in the street, on one's ear; it was the very last fence but one which frequently brought grief to otherwise well-prepared applicants. We were learning that one can never come out of a Spanish government office without paying for something, even if it was only a contribution towards wear and tear of door knobs or the floor.

One might have been forgiven for thinking that since we were retired we would not have been competing with him or any of his fellow-countrymen for work, and highly unlikely we would be attempting to dilute the bloodstock. Surely all we were seeking was the right to pay our pension and life savings into his country's coffers. Perhaps when he and his colleagues were chalking up scores over lunch, he might get a tad philosophical and posit that without the likes of us foreign riff-raff, he and his *compañeros* would be out of a job. Whatever, heaving himself to his feet to administer the final humiliation, he curled his finger at Helen, indicating she was to follow him to the desk with an inkpad the size of a small "WELCOME" doormat on it. This was what she had dreaded most of all. Fingerprinting has always been nothing less than a physical and mental violation as far as my wife is concerned, she hates it so much that her face was twisted in agony while it was happening, and when afterwards she stepped back to examine her fingers, apart from a trace of lipstick, it was deathly white.

'Tattooing is more civilised than that!' she muttered.

Then he did me, and I imagined he muttered '*Híbrido!*' (Bastard!) under his breath. I suppose there is only one way to fingerprint anybody, and that is to make sure they have enough ink on their skin before applying enough pressure on their finger to make an impression on the paper; but it never feels less than being criminalised. I had made the argument to Helen that it was a Hispanic convention of less significance than in England, and she would remember that very clearly a year later when Pinochet of Chile would be 'spared that indignity out of courtesy', in the words of Jack Straw, the British Labour government's Home Secretary, a courtesy he and the party we always voted for, withheld from millions of decent people.

To tell the truth, I was grateful to get away without having to produce a semen sample, a feat many males seem capable of obliging with at the drop of a hat, and under almost any conditions, but one I would have found absolutely impossible to accomplish anywhere inside the Oficina de Extranjeros.

At the end, there was not even a handshake, let alone a hearty embrace with a kiss on each cheek. Just a not-too-unfriendly snort. But we were not finished with yet, our application and documents now had to be subjected to the scrutiny of the backroom boys, a task that would take many months.

'At least we didn't have to salute the flag,' I blabbed with relief as we stepped into the street.

THIRTEEN

OF ALL THE THINGS we had to contend with, the most frustrating was our inability to communicate adequately. It had been our intention to learn sufficient Spanish not only to get by on, but to be able to make friends, read newspapers, go anywhere, and join art and cultural societies – though leisurely enough, say over a couple of years. The problem with learning the language of an adoptive country is that all the critical things to do with life and death and the giving and receiving of important information, have to be done immediately, before one possesses the means of adequate communication. They involve dealing with people who are always busy, often impatient, invariably officious and too often xenophobic; and if they have a smattering of a second language, likely as not it will not be yours. In Spain, even those one suspects of being able to speak one's language will save it for a more worthy occasion. No one in any police station, or the central railway station, central bus station, head post office, bank or government office – not even the huge, posh department store called 'El Corte Ingles' (the English way) – could or would speak a word of English. It was hard to credit that the Costa Blanca, an area that had for decades thrived on English-speaking tourists and residents, managed on such a sparse familiarity with its bread and butter.

The deficiency affected everything. It robbed us of the ability to make complicated requests, persuade, defend or justify ourselves, and it neutered both intelligence and self worth; it was like suffering a stroke without the physical symptoms. We felt helpless in a way we had never felt as tourists, misunderstandings then usually being occasions for humour or opportunities for empathy or sympathy. As it was, not infrequently the person we were talking to would get impatient and jump to the wrong conclusion, and our own exasperation would spill over as our vocabulary blacked out, which it did practically every time. An apology would then be required, hands waved to convey 'Don't mind us old fools. Just serve somebody else!' and we would come away feeling like banging our heads against a wall. My 'Teach Yourself Spanish' only taught how to talk like an automaton on holiday in the 1950s during the *Franquismo* (Franco dictatorship) when people addressed each other with far more respect than they do now.

Not only the language, but many other things were so different from how they were anywhere else we had ever lived, that we felt vulnerable and foolish for not knowing what everybody else seemed to know. We had no friends and no home and most of our worldly possessions were in cardboard boxes piled up outside the villa. Our connections to the kind of support we could have counted on, were all in Ireland, and although we had endeavoured not to burn any boats, we must have accidentally scuppered a couple of fleets and caused not a few others to become unseaworthy.

Languid though the pace of life often was, it was anything but on the road, with Spanish drivers treating the highway the way we used to treat other dodgems at the fairground in South Shields. Bumper-nudging, horn-blasting, thumping radios, arms swinging out of windows and giving all sorts of homemade signals, plus continuous lane-hopping, were all part of the game, with degrees of observance at traffic lights consonant with whatever Spanish drivers reckoned they could get away with. For a time we assumed motorcyclists must be exempt from traffic codes, for they not only drove through traffic lights, but on pavements and other pedestrian ways. Traffic roundabouts must have been a recent phenomenon because the Spanish had no idea how to conduct themselves when faced with one.

The number of times we pulled up at a set of traffic lights that had turned red, only to have the car immediately behind us, and often the one after that also, pull out in front of us and zoom over the crossing, was beyond belief. Many but by no means all of these anomalies, were gender-based. A male could not bear to look at the back of a white-haired head, especially if it were a woman's, because a white head meant an undyed old head; most often an ancient *extranjera's* head, something that had to be overtaken at all costs, even if it meant a diversion. Elderly drivers were sexed on a basis of hair colour, Spanish males using lampblack or leatherette brown, or wore a badly matching, ill-fitting wig which looked as if it were on back to front, or, even more horrifically, side to front. Spanish females styled theirs on burgundy-coloured candy floss. Grey was outside the spectrum because it smacked too much of the Grim Reaper. For a nation with outstanding dress sense, it was astonishing how few men knew how to cope with their scalps.

Pedestrians were always thoroughly disdained and motorists drove over zebra crossings in spite of the imprecations of the 'little coloured men'. Like everybody else, if we were on foot and wanted to cross, we had to grit our teeth, brace ourselves for a severe impact, and keep on walking, otherwise they would never stop. Even while one were crossing, they would race over the zebra stripes in front and behind – provided they missed.

Parking was worse: engines left running in vehicles left on corners, at traffic lights, half on pavements, and on zebra crossings; parked two and three abreast, frequently blocking in other vehicles, parked in the middle of the road with hazard lights on, doors wide open and often with the engine running. And there were always tales of people being knocked down and killed on zebra crossings without the driver stopping, and of drivers paying relatives or unemployed friends to take the blame and 'do their time' for a fee. The only time we ever knew a pedestrian to win was on an occasion we actually witnessed at a very busy crossing in the Port of Alicante.

It was the height of summer and there were masses of people waiting to cross both ways, but no vehicles were stopping because the traffic lights were out of order. After nearly ten minutes of moaning, swearing and much agitation by the two opposing throngs, a huge fellow with great muscular arms, a massive belly inside a perfectly ironed white shirt topped by a powerful head sporting a seal's moustache, suddenly stepped out into the road and onto the crossing, with his arm held up. Striding slowly and deliberately, without a word or a glance to left or right, he proceeded ahead, and every vehicle, be it bus, van, car, motorbike or bicycle, screeched to a halt as though up against the kind of barrier that once divided the Red Sea, or in more recent times had been encountered in episodes of Star Trek.

A moment later, both hordes followed suit, tentatively at first, some with their eyes tight shut, then proudly converging deadpan and without a flicker, as though such miracles happened to such brave souls every day at the same time.

But when our man reached the other side, everybody applauded and no vehicle moved until every last pedestrian was safely across to each side. Only an ex – or off-duty civil sergeant guard, or Jesus, could have done what he just did. Nonetheless, on or off the road, in vehicles or out of them, everybody is at the mercy of anybody behind a Spanish driving wheel, a place where egos inflate faster than airbags.

Public transport was excellent in that it was clean, efficient, punctual and cheap, but it did not serve estates out of town, and its buses never stopped when they scraped corners of narrow streets or the sides of parked cars. So for one reason or another we decided to get a car and surmised a Spanish model would show good faith.

All cars were cheap compared with Ireland's, and we had sufficient money from the sale of our two-year-old VW Polo before we left, to be able to buy a new Seat Ibiza with air-conditioning, and that included tax, insurance and other extras. But when we went to the main Seat dealer on the road to Alicante, it was 2.30 p.m., so they were shut and would remain so until 5 p.m. It was a mistake with business hours we would make on a number of occasions, each time swearing at their laziness, before coming to appreciate the advantages of evening shopping.

As it was, it left us with plenty of time to have a real humdinger of a row about the whole idea of coming to Spain, following which Helen decided to sulk on the grass verge outside the dealer's compound while I stomped off to see if I could walk to Alicante and back before five o'clock. Twenty minutes into my walk, I received my punishment – so Helen later rationalised – when a coach came rushing past and struck me the slightest but most shocking of glancing blows to the side of my head which, though thankfully miraculously superficial, knocked me into a ditch and made me as sick as a dog. When through time we came to know the kind of people who drove buses in Spain, we would realise the driver would most certainly have stopped and given help had he been aware of my plight, but in this case he must have been completely unaware of it. However I fortuitously filled in the time until five o'clock, convalescing in the ditch before heading back to the dealers to find my wife continuing with the sanction.

The right side of my shirt had a bloody patch and was covered with oily dirt, but because we approached the salesroom from different doors, Helen was unaware of it. Inside the palatial sales office, with its salubriously fragrant air, it was so deliciously cool that I immediately felt better and such pleasure at being treated so courteously by a grandee of the sales department, until I saw a reflection of myself in a wall-to-wall mirror, standing beside him in one of my most demeaning of postures.

Without so much as a glance in the direction of my debris dropping on to the papers on his desk, Sr. Grande de Huella-Marchin, spitting image of the handsome, thickly brilliantined English cricketer, Dennis Compton (when he was still alive) nudged a box of tissues towards me while ever so discreetly nodding towards the toilets, as though bleeding and bedraggled customers were an everyday fact of life. It was only then that Helen apprehended my injury, learned what had happened from brief whispers, and began to manifest a trifle of concern; but there was no way I could explain to the salesman, so I played out the role of injured party for the duration.

After I had cleaned up we looked at the cars and brochures and had a long chat with Sr. Salesman who demonstrated how one can make a foreign language easier to understand when the will exists. We had a couple of test drives for comparison and settled for the Ibiza, reckoning a VW engine always made sense, and with everything else Spanish it should have stood us in good stead with the *guardia civil* should we ever find ourselves over a barrel for some transgression. Funny how naïve one can be.

Our only quibble was that we were not allowed to buy it. Everything was hunky dory, with everyone smiling, we ready to pay and he ready to receive, when suddenly he asked for our NIE, and that was the end of the matter. We were allowed to buy a used car – even one costing twice the price of a new one – but not a new one at any price. Apparently the law did not allow a new car to be purchased unless the buyer had a NIE number, evidence of 'fiscal registration', whatever that meant.

When we got back to the villa and told the Spiers, Val said it would take months to get a NIE, but if we were to use her number and then exchange it when ours came through, 'Voila!… It seemed a reasonable and very friendly solution, so it still being during early days of the relationship and we continuing with all round naivety, we accepted Val's offer and acquired the car. However, when we returned our rental vehicle to 'Sunderland Edi', the proprietor, he embarrassed us by castigating Val in front of his staff and customers for doing what he alleged was a dirty trick that would cost us dearly one day. We believed she was only doing it as an act of kindness but Edi would say no more, other than that we had put ourselves in a very compromising position because Val Spiers was a well known 'so-and-so', which left us wondering if maybe Edi was the notorious 'axe-man'.

That night, feeling we could do with a treat, we went to an open-air guitar recital celebrating Federico Garcia Lorca that was being held in the port. Walking along the pavement towards the venue, by which time it was quite dark, the whole of my right sleeve was suddenly ripped out of my best shirt by a huge nail that was sticking nearly three inches out of a plane tree trunk, and before I could regain my balance, I stumbled into a hole surrounding the tree, and was flung headlong into the road. Fortunately the main injury was to my dignity, something that might have been considered 'near fatal' had it happened to a Spaniard, but for me was infinitely preferable to being almost trepanned by a rusty nail.

The streets were crowded with well-dressed promenaders and I was leading the way, weaving my way with my left sleeve rolled up to the shoulder and my right stuffed into my pocket, a large elastoplast from a *farmacia* on my forehead, which also covered the bus wound, and a limp. I had a monster of a headache but could not be persuaded to enter the Cruz Roja (Red Cross) booth with its attractive young volunteers looking like Born-Again Christians and charging nothing for their services.

'If only the Irish were here,' I observed to Helen. 'They would make a fortune out of that nail. A minute crack in the pavement and an Irishman would take a dive and then sue the County Council. They'd have been queuing up to impale themselves.'

The recital ended at 11.45 p.m., much too early to go home in Spain. The streets were full, people playing on the beach, strolling around the port and teeming in and out of restaurants and cafes that were fuller than at any time during the day; even little children were out, though all with their parents and better behaved than in the shops and supermarkets hours earlier. Yet it was not noisy. The sound was of talking, hundreds of human voices conversing in small groups, pleasantly and earnestly; no shouting or yelling, shrieking or guffawing. No pushing or shoving, kicking balls or riding bikes into elderly people, and absolutely no violence.

Normally I would never have a coffee at this time of night, nor at any time of day for that matter, but for some reason I really felt like one. Normally I do not like the smell of cooking, not outside anyway, but there were so many enticing smells of so many unobtrusive flavours, not least the coffee. So we found a little place on the promenade, one of many with spare seats, and ensconced ourselves, sensuously rubbing our toes with the dry sand inside our sandals.

An aged, ex-matinee idol of a waiter, who looked as though he had waited at some pretty big tables in his day, appeared with a freshly ironed teacloth over his arm. It was near midnight and only a tiny café, yet he was immaculate apart from the odd stray hair that made me wonder if he would be going straight home after he had finished. The main difference between him and a colleague a third his age, was that even at this time of night the younger man would have managed a pleasantry, whereas this fellow was just too old and tired. If they were going to tip, they would tip, and if they weren't, they wouldn't, and a platitude wouldn't make the slightest difference, not at this time of night.

I could never remember enjoying coffee, but would gladly have become addicted had it always tasted like this. Just the right temperature, the right amount of milk, coffee, brown sugar, and with a chocolate biscuit neatly wrapped in an origami flower – pointless but unquestionably elegant. And now he was bending over someone else, a shade more stiffly and his face a smidgen more weary.

We, however, felt like talking to somebody and trying a bit Spanish, so decided to have a go at the couple at the next table; I could reach them by simply leaning back and speaking half over my shoulder. They turned out to be English which perhaps was just as well.

When we had introduced ourselves and the man had managed to let slip his ex-Army officer rank – security guard in Marks and Sparks? – his good lady-wife took over.

'How big is your pool?' was question five of the standard profile questionnaire.

'I beg your pardon?'

They were both past the age when they should have been troubling themselves about how unattractive they looked, and should have been taking pride in other things, like souvenirs gleaned from cruises.

'Your pool..! How large is it..? You know…Length and breadth.'

'We don't have one.'

'You don't have a pool..?! Did the builder forget to put one in, ha-ha-ha?'

'We didn't want one.'

'You didn't want one..? Why? Is your plot not big enough?'

'Yes, but…'

'Where do you swim then, for God's sake? You can swim, can't you, the two of you?'

'In the sea.'

'In the sea! Whereabouts for heaven's sake?'

She was beginning to get under my skin.

'There.' I pointed to the Mediterranean.

'What about all the stingers and biters? And the poos and sheaths and disgusting body fluids..? Yaaaaaak..!'

Surely a bacteriologist could score something on this topic. Lend me a microscope and some basic microbiology apparatus, plus a single millilitre of their swimming pool water, and I would have had the two of them on the next plane back to England and the School of Tropical Medicine in London. But I didn't need to say any more, I had established our inferiority for their benefit, and that was all that mattered. It was time to get back to the villa.

The previous day we had come upon our first English *gestor*, a legal and financial advisor indispensable to English immigrants without Spanish. She had given us her business card, invited us to call her if we had any problems, and seemed as though she might be useful under some circumstances. We knew illiterate Spaniards had always used gestors to help them with documentation for all sorts of things, and now there were multilingual ones who served the whole expatriate community. She was blonde, the way Spanish men liked women to be – and would prove useful in negotiations – but no bimbo and no shrinking violet. She had strong opinions about the Spanish and other nationalities, particularly ours, and maintained the English were as dishonest as anybody in Spain and readily cheated their own kind, particularly recent immigrants because they were the easiest to take advantage of. Other nationalities did the same, she said, though not as much. She also said to beware of how expats described their pasts, as their memories were notoriously unreliable. Apparently she was happily married to a Spanish carpenter.

FOURTEEN

ONE MORNING WHILE HELEN was doing the food shopping, I was browsing the wonderful sandals in Pryca, the large, always crowded supermarket where every expat went at least twice a week, when I suddenly became aware of a most obnoxious smell. Looking around, I soon detected the source: in the middle of the floor near the fish counter, was a small pile of human excrement. Just then, a huge Scandinavian in shorts and jandals, who was expounding to a small group of kith or kin behind him, stepped into it, scooping garden-trowel-sized lumps between his toes and carrying them off while blathering, probably about the high standard of public health they had in Sweden.

Realising I had to do something public-spirited and quickly, I located a sales assistant stocking a shelf, and told her, but all she did was shrug her shoulders, pull a face and carry on with what she was doing. Maybe she thought I should mind my own business, and that given the quantity of the many canine brands in the streets, people should be inured to it. But because I might have mistakenly used the word *miedo* (fear) instead of *mierda* (faeces) – a common enough mistake with students of the language – and she had therefore misunderstood what I was trying to say, I took hold of her arm, which she most certainly did not like, drew her over to where she could see the remains, and pointed. Slowly she bent down, presumably to make sure it was what I claimed it to be, and not just a clump of half-chewed caramels or a bit of Mars Bar, stood up, looked at me with absolute disgust and pointed in the direction of the *aseos* (toilets) at the far end of the store.

'Si, si,' (Yes, yes,) I agreed, relieved she had confirmed my analysis. And then to let her know I had a sense of humour, continued, *'Pero es demasiado tarde,* ha-ha-ha' (But it's a bit late for that, ha-ha-ha).

She now took my arm firmly and led me to a spot where we could see the sign for 'Caballeros' (Gentlemen), pointing first at me and then to it.

'Wha..? *No moi..!'* I could not even think of the words in English, let alone Spanish. But she was already on her way, presumably to fetch somebody to sweep up, or maybe the security guard to escort me to the *aseos,* or even right out of the store, so I beat a retreat to find Helen; not just to tell her of the outrage, but so that if necessary she could bear witness to my character. I could imagine a blow from a lignum vitae truncheon on the back of my neck, the click of handcuffs as I slumped, being dragged half-conscious through the store into 'Caballeros' and flung onto the industrial-grade non-slip tiles, accompanied by the vituperative 'Feelthy old Gringo!' By now we knew that grey-haired foreigners were regarded by *funcionario* and citizen alike: senile.

The problems posed by retiring to a country with a language different to one's own were much harder to overcome than one with a different climate or superficially different culture. Climate could be partitioned into units and modified, and culture allowed for exceptions and could be enriched by them, but a foreign language is implacable and makes one feel as though one were hanging on to a disintegrating, unprovisioned raft, treading water in the middle of an ocean where everyone else is an acrobatic dolphin. The English and Spanish were probably the worst linguists in Europe, so communication between us probably worse than between any two nationalities.

I had plenty of books on Spanish grammar and a whole range of pocket Spanish-English dictionaries. Indeed, I could not resist buying one every time I came across a new one, under the illusion that the latest one would have an easier-to-remember vocabulary – maybe because the cover was a special tint of blue, or the main text was in an elaborately serifed font. We also had BBC cassette tapes, but they were really only of any use for helping with English pronunciation as it was before they replaced Trevor Howard's public-school English with Michael Caine's.

Helen thought personal tuition would be the best answer, so we tried various private people advertising in the local newspaper or on scrappy shop notice-boards. Most turned out to be coquettish Spanish wives of English plumbers who had not the faintest idea about grammar or teaching and could only speak 'builder's English', the variant they had picked up from their husbands; the rest were young Spanish graduates with secondary-school English, whose pronunciation was like a Hollywood Mexican bandit's, and whose rates were likewise.

The best we encountered was a highly cultured, rather racy Venezuelan ex-actress divorcée, but it was impossible to concentrate on the lesson with her Spam-tongued dogs licking our bare legs under the table, which we would afterwards find covered with a thin layer of a cellophane-like substance which had to be scrubbed off with Domestos, a powerful chlorine kitchen detergent. When we stopped going in shorts, they began nuzzling up my trouser legs and sticking their snouts under Helen's skirt, two at a time. And typical of female dog-lovers, just because we did not appreciate the mutts slavering all over us, our otherwise excellent teacher assumed we did not like animals, and there was no disabusing her of this.

One day in Quicksave, one of a chain of little shops that sold eccentrically English produce, such as Bisto gravy salt and Colman's mustard powder, preferably of Second World War vintage – supplements that preserved one's Englishness – and had a notice-board plastered with semi-literate spiels by English chancers and no-hopers, to some of whom one's heart nevertheless went out, there was one which read: 'Wanted: Elderly English Gentleman Who Would Like To Learn Spanish With An Elderly Spanish Gentleman Who Would Like To Learn English.'

I telephoned the number and the consequence was a visit the following Saturday from a jolly anglophile Spaniard – the first we had ever met – who turned out to be exactly a week younger than I was. As is the custom with Spanish guests, he brought a gift: a beautiful little cake. He did not seem to have expected that Helen would be taking an interest in our conversations, which were to be partly in Spanish and partly in English, but when she did, although rather awkward, he was extremely courteous. Many years previously he had attended a summer school in Hastings in Kent to learn the English language, an event which, though not a hundred-percent successful, was a major reference point in his life, and whenever we talked about England, he would invariably preface his comments with the words, 'When I was in Hastings…'

Seemingly I was the only person to respond to his advert which had been in the shop so long he had forgotten about it, and although Helen and I subsequently and independently made other Spanish friends, we never made one dearer. Although a few degrees short of a grandee, he was still a perfect gentleman, one of the gentlest human beings I had ever met in fact, and his name was Edmundo. He was short and fairly stout, with a balding sphere of a head covered at the sides and back with fine, well groomed hair, a constant appeasing smile with traces of food between teeth that revealed minimal professional maintenance, and everything about him, from the way he talked, moved and gestured, was redolent of a genial bishop who had abdicated some time ago and now reached stage 3 of re-entry into secular life. I am sure he would have been absolutely delighted to know here was a pukka Englishman who thought he would have made a perfect Dickensian Englishman. From that first Saturday on, he never missed our mutual lesson.

In many ways Edmundo and I were diametric opposites. He was very much the urban civil servant, armchair sport spectator, armchair adventurer, monarchist and Anglophile; in other important ways very similar: a humorist, agnostic, socialist; and in addition he was almost pathologically gentle and courteous. To his eternal embarrassment, his parents were *franquistas* although his many siblings were almost all socialists, and his wife was PP (Partido Popular) and successor to the Franquista Party) whereas his three children were all socialist. His wife was strong and strict, though generous and equally courteous. Generally Edmundo steered conversations away from his family, although he was very close to them, I think to avoid awkward topics. There was nothing I asked of him that he did not do immediately and it was only too easy to unwittingly take advantage of this.

By the middle of August the end-of-summer sales were on, so Val, who handled the Spiers' financial matters, insisted we choose the tiles for the '*vivienda*' – the term everybody used for the villa they were building for us.

Tiles were a major part of a house in Spain, being used in one form or another for roofs, paving surrounds outside the house, all floors inside, and the walls in kitchens, bathrooms and toilets. Unlike emulsion paint or wallpaper which can be changed every few years, they were more or less down for life and few markers more accurately dated a building. For anyone who has never had to choose anything other than a five-tile splash-back for a working-class Anglo-Saxon kitchen sink, it was an excruciating task. Some, such as those for the kitchen and bathroom floors, had to be highly slip-proof, and I imagined tiles anywhere would feature prominently in domestic accident insurance claims. There is a set for the lower part of a wall and another for the upper, divided by a border, with a 'wild card' every now and again to break the monotony. These had to match those on the floor, but different sets had a way of unexpectedly clashing. A bathroom design might have looked fine from inside the bathroom, but when one stepped into the passage, or into the bedroom, which looked all right before, it now had a way of looking hideous. It all depended on where one started: whether from the centre of the house outwards, or from the front door to the back door.

Without a computer to create a 'virtual tiled house', we designed ours at home with coloured pencils on paper, then in the store carried the proposed tiles from one end of the department to the other, or one floor to another, to balance them alongside others we had in mind, before rapidly closing and opening our eyes to allow our imaginations to conjointly fill in the details; but there must have been better ways.

One of the problems was that tile names were often long and ornate, like binomials in botany, written in chalk and invariably smudged, so we were continually having to have them deciphered, which sorely tried the salesgirl's far from infinite patience. And because the majority of Spanish people were on their annual holiday, tile shops were busy and it was difficult to capture the attention of sales staff. Given the option of dealing with a pair of loquacious Spanish yuppies and a couple of unintelligible foreign 'wrinklies' – the current media term for us – the Spanish yuppies were far easier and preferable to deal with.

Measuring up the *vivienda* in its primitive state, which we had to do ourselves because there were no plans, amidst open bags of cement and plaster, planks, ladders, tools, scaffolding and rubbish, after climbing into the house over a makeshift staircase we had to erect from broken concrete blocks, was an ankle-dislocating task. And because the Spiers had said they would not pay for any surplus tiles, we had to calculate in halves and other fractions. We would go into a tile centre early in the morning and spend until 1 p.m. planning a scheme for the whole house, only to find that when the sales assistant checked their supplies, one of the tiles we had chosen from the catalogue would be out of stock or in too short supply. This would throw everything out and we would have to spend the siesta redesigning before going back at half past four when they re-opened, and do the 'stock-taking' all over again. When we had designed the new scheme and been assured of the supply, then returned to tell Val, likely as not she would tell us they cost too much. There were many tile stores in Spain, she kept telling us, it was simply a matter of looking, and the exercise would be good for us. But as the days wore on, stocks of attractive tiles with an acceptable match were rapidly diminishing, so we said we would pay the extra if it would make the difference between getting something half-decent and something bloody awful.

Eventually we went to Porcelanosa, Spain's high-class tile store, and through the whole rigmarole again. The salesgirl checked the stocks, and we ordered. But because we had no NIE number, even though we were paying the extra, Val had to approve before the order could go through, and they told us they could not guarantee the supply for more than a day or two, so she would have to do it straightaway. The last thing we wanted was to have to go through the whole carry-on yet again, not with the choosing of electrical and plumbing accessories just over the horizon, so we endeavoured to impress upon her the need to telephone the store that night. Next morning when we went to confirm that she had done what we had asked, she would hoitily assure us that indeed she had. Later in the day when we called back to Porcelanosa to confirm the order, it would be to learn that indeed she had not, and we had lost the chance of those particular tiles. So we would have to do it all again, this time with just the dregs to choose from. 'Exasperating' was hardly the word for it. And why? Why was Val Spiers such a so-and-so? Lew kept right out of it. I sometimes wondered if right from the start she had been against his offering to build us another house and all the rest of it.

FIFTEEN

THE ONE SERVICE THAT met all expectations during the days that grew into weeks, whose *horario* (working hours) was totally customer friendly and never had to be paid a single *céntimo*, was the huge golden sphere in the sky from which every one of its millions of holiday-making prospectors on planet Earth got lucky. When we drove into Jemina in the mornings, the glistening turquoise sea provided a backcloth that would have glorified any scene, and on our return to Los Pajaros Rojos in the evening, it was the undulating velvet Carrasqueta mountains melting the horizon into heaps of constantly changing ochres and violets that brought such a wonderful end to almost any day, however long, trying or home-sickening.

Where in temperate zones it supported life, in others it dictated it and people had to live their lives in spite of it and yield the best part of the day to it. Mind, it was disconcerting to see how much Spanish skin was damaged by it, as though even after millennia of continuous evolution the human organism still had not come to terms with it. Yet judging from the way so many young and old exposed themselves to it, they obviously relished it the way Arabs and Africans, for instance, never seemed to do.

An incredible diversity of small creatures were sustained by it, particularly nocturnal insects. Yet the same sustainer and colouriser brought drought, pernicious creatures and cancer, bleached masterpieces, weakened cement in buildings and – I was convinced – weakened the character of its human subjects, just as I was convinced that snow and ice in other parts of the world fortified it. It annoyed people when I pointed to examples of different cultures to prove my point, but it seemed obvious to me, and I wondered in which ways Helen's and my life would change because of it. Would we become lazier and less adventurous in keeping with our decreasing faculties, perhaps tolerating things we once abhorred and eschewing things we once enjoyed. Would we become more selfish and less concerned about the rest of the world; might we recover our faith or become nonagenarian naturists? Or, no matter what we tried, would we merely pine for our family and Ireland until only senility dulled the pain while the health-giving sun extended its term.

So far there was not much to whet the mind apart from reading and listening to Radio Nacional d'Espana (Spanish Classical Radio) which was good for learning the language, for information on Spain, and especially for classical music. There was little for the non-Hispanic other than poorly transmitted expatriate stations whose ambition was hardly better than CB. English radio stations were very much English expatriate stations geared to suit this large but narrow-minded group, much like as though it were an underground pirate station on an island somewhere. The entertainment was about twenty-year vintage, the information Church of England in morality, and of local sports and indoor clubs in interest, plus obituaries of 'famous' locals and the C of E equivalent of beatification for charity work.

One afternoon we went to see the wonderful ruins of a sanatorium in Aigues de Los Pajaros Rojos, the next village to 'plain'

Los Pajaros Rojos in the mountains, and as we were walking by the railings that enclosed it, a very thin, unswarthy-looking man sitting writing at a table in the grounds, hailed us in English and invited us in. His name was Humberto Torres i Palau, and he was Catalan. (The Spanish have a charming way of composing their surname by giving first their father's surname and then their mother's). Humberto wrote books about his journeys in Catalonia and translated other authors into Catalán, and the peace and quiet of the precincts apparently suited him perfectly. He was acting as custodian until the premises were sold to a consortium of developers who wanted to convert the place into a hotel. It had a wonderful façade and it was a great shame the building was not being preserved as a hospital museum or something of the sort. The 'trouble' – if that is the right word – is that there were so many wonderful old buildings in fairly good condition throughout the land that Spanish people were rather cavalier about them and just left them to the sun to look after.

Humberto had a flat in 'Alacant', as he pronounced and wrote 'Alicante', but was originally from Barcelona, and in just a few minutes we learned we must not confuse Catalunya (Catalonia) with that voracious, egregious and untalented neighbouring country, Spain, because anything meritorious associated with Spain was due to the *catalánes*, and to an extent, the Basques.

Humberto's face, which was half boy, half man, tended to belie his middle-aged mannerisms, especially the numerous maxims, and though managing to be self-effacingly polite, he was quite brutally frank. He was also extraordinarily frugal, though not mean, and claimed to resort to a doctor or dentist only when, armed with a tin of bicarbonate of soda, a mirror, sharp instrument and pair of radio pliers, he could not sort the problem himself. His haircuts, for instance, were always better at the front and sides than at the back. So when he said thrift was one of his major principles, nobody took issue with it.

If he absolutely had to defer to a 'professional', the professional would be the very cheapest, such as an illegal immigrant who had obtained a certificate in, say, the Argentinian air force, but had no licence to practise in civvy street. He had studied at Toronto University, as well as in Madrid, and his English was equal to his wit as he revealed himself to be an astute observer of humanity, as well as of plant and animal life. He listened without interruption, spoke quietly and deferentially, though his humility was clearly a cover for some very strongly held views, especially about Catalan independence and global conservation.

He showed us around the sanatorium which had once been a TB hospital run by nuns for poor children, as well as a weekend spa for the local well-to-do. The remains of terraced gardens, groves, a little farm that had once produced food in excess of the sanatorium's needs, so earned an income, and a huge, deep, stone-built swimming pool on which the lady daughters of the patrons used to row little dinghies on their Sunday visits, had all endured due to the slow and gentle Spanish process of decay, and not with anything recognisable as conservation. Had it not been for the self-inflicted wounds of the relatively recent civil war, Spain's architecture would have been an even greater delight than it was, and that is really saying something. There is no place like it in Europe, possibly anywhere.

Jose Antonio Labordeta, poet, socialist politician and songwriter, introduced television viewers to places like the sanatorium in a wonderful series of videos of his walks through Spain – '*Un Pais en la Mochilla*' (A Country by Rucksack). Seeing him from an armchair, hiking and climbing and conversing with all kinds of interesting people, was a wonderful way of exploring Spain with arthritis or cardiovascular disease.

The whole area where the sanatorium was situated, high in the mountains, was quite spectacular, but although the air was reputedly fresh it did not, could not, have braced lungs the way spas in Switzerland or Austria did, because on any day we visited, it was always enervatingly hot.

The building itself, though in such a state of decay that it was in danger of collapse, was magnificent in its way. Many old hospitals I had visited in England had once been workhouses, and although there were nearly always parts of the buildings unable to shake off the austerity and gloom of their prime, there was always something reassuring about their not entirely obsolete discipline and moral fibre, as was often the case with old schoolrooms. I was aware that many people found these places oppressive but suspect much depends on the happiness or otherwise of their own childhood. Primitive iron beds, strong but simple wooden chairs and well-scrubbed tables, heavy doors, high ceilings, stone floors and cast iron fittings, created the vision of an age much harsher than today's, certainly in the way it was so uncomplicated and lacking in choices. Yet it was so easy to imagine the strict catholic nuns running the place efficiently and spotlessly, with the Lord present in every room from the gymnasium to the pharmacy.

As one who had once worked with tuberculosis, I was fascinated by the beautiful and scholarly kept records with details of treatments given, sometimes quite desperate and involving complicated concoctions, sometimes pathetically inadequate, but all requiring heavily augmenting doses of prayer, and I thought it such a pity that the prayers and hours given over to them had not been equally pedantically recorded. It was easy to allow that given the number of nuns needed to look after a place this size, with its considerable physical and emotional demands, there must surely have been at least one or two of truly saintly disposition, one or two capable of showing real love and kindness to the sick and mostly dying waifs who wandered around the wards, played in the yard, or lay on the grass under the trees, until their time came.

The records, written in wonderful cursive copperplate Spanish, in leather-bound books showing signs of age and marks of human contact, conveyed far more in terms of humanity than any non-serifed digital symbols on a computer screen, and I could not help perusing every one I could lay hands on. Other items – hopefully never including canes or other such instruments of instruction – were presumably long gone as souvenirs or eliminated as embarrassing evidence, so these wonderful literary artefacts were now the sole links connecting the building with its long-gone little inhabitants.

Come the advent of effective antibiotics like streptomycin, the tubercle bacilli would have retreated except from places like this, and in an age not noted for its altruism such places would gradually have fallen into disuse. The mineral waters whose conduits always needed regular skilled maintenance, remained still and crystal clear, closely filtered and purified into blandness by moss and aquatic plants. And now that the wonderful ruin had been taken over by a coterie of wealthy hoteliers, pests more pernicious than any bedbugs, cockroaches or rodents, its rather more comfortable cots would be supporting humans of a very different kind, its chefs producing paellas rather than broth, its roulette wheels and blackjack replacing tiddlywinks and snakes & ladders.

Although most of the wards and more robust places, like the dairy and stables, were not in too bad condition, special rooms, like the pharmacy and gymnasium, were in such a fragile state that they could never be restored; a strong blast of wind or torrent of rain would reduce them to rubble if the local vandals did not soon finish what they had already thoroughly begun.

Humberto was so full of irony that we were often unsure whether he was serious or not; he was fanatical about waste and pollution which he applied to everything including speech. Not only were there too many cars, planes, mobile phones, aerials, machines and dogs in the world, there were also too many words, and in excess, or where inappropriate, he considered them no better than toxins. His was the most excoriating denunciation of verbosity I had ever heard: nowhere near as neat as 'bullshit' but infinitely more memorable.

In keeping with his own canon, he spoke slowly and deliberately, clearly weighing everything before he said anything. This was fine and rare, except that he also listened intently to everything one said to him, and that was unnerving. Of course he was right, it was the civilised way to communicate. But to always listen like that, one would need some kind of robust filter for all the poppycock and twaddle that every day came one's way in any language. As well as being a conservationist, this particular Catalan was philosophical, ascetic and a loner, and it undoubtedly set him apart from the noisy, vain, frivolous, careless, gregarious and hedonist everyman rest of us. We had been telling him of a failed experiment we had conducted, which had consisted, for a whole week, of waving to everybody we met on our *urbanización* to see if we could encourage or oblige individuals to reciprocate. Nobody did, and he was neither surprised by the results, nor sympathetic. Why, in the street of a town in Spain or on a country road in Ireland, should people greet each other if they were strangers, he wanted to know; surely it constituted an invasion of privacy and was, at the very least, disingenuous. Whilst on the subject, the fulsome English expression of gratitude was another thing that irritated him highly.

"'Gracias" is never enough for you English. Not even "*muchas gracias*" (many thanks). It has to be "*muchisimas gracias*" (very many thanks). You even thank people who serve you in shops, and the clerk who sells you a ticket in a railway station. Why..? They aren't doing you any favours. They want your money and you have given it to them in exchange for an article or service. No party then owes the other anything at all. If you thank them, they'll think they've given you more than you deserve.'

'When do you thank anybody, then? And what's the point of having the word in Spanish?'

'The only time you thank anybody in Spain is if they have saved your life.'

'What about "Excuse me"..? The Spanish don't seem too keen on that either.'

'Just push, like everybody else.

'And "Sorry".'

He shook his head. 'Never. If you must, you confess to God when the time comes.'

But when I smiled, he smiled, so there was a bit of irony in there somewhere. Let me say he was a sincere skeptic, though not necessarily a cut-throat cynic. Sometime in the future I would tell him that instead of 'Many thanks', the Irish would usually say 'Thanks a mingying' (million). But he was not ready for that yet.

When he invited us to have lunch with him we should have guessed it would be different to what we were used to, though not necessarily inedible. Windfall, bruised and almost mummified fruit, stale bread moistened with a few drops of olive oil, and a few beans or nuts we had never seen before but looked as though they had come from a pet shop or under a tree, was the fare, and the whole thing turned out to be quite an ordeal, not least because before we started he announced he did not believe in talking during meals. We had nodded, said 'Fine' and then proceeded to talk as usual, only to be met with a wall of silence.

'Oh, we forgot. You don't speak when eating, do you?' I smirked.

He shook his head and carried on chewing, so much on the left and so much on the right: you could see it being moved over from one pouch-like cheek to the other, and I could imagine him fantasising about being a squirrel squatting in a tree. When we finished, he produced some raffia mat strips and suggested we have a siesta, but we could not relax with ants crawling all over us, so we retired to the car while he went into the derelict mortuary. There was no way we could nod off in an oven shaped like a car, but did manage to wile away some of the time reading his books and wondering whether we would want to be Catalan or Spanish should we ever be given the choice, especially given some of the differences between the two that our new friend had detailed for us.

When he awoke, refreshed, unlike ourselves who were now quite torpid, he showed us an old store containing hundreds of empty bottles labelled 'Marshall Plan', contraband from after the Second World War, relief that was never intended for Franco's Spain. He had guessed correctly that we would be astonished by the revelation. He talked of Barcelona's 'battles' with Madrid, and Catalunya's with Castile, of his own with institutions like the post office and corporate polluters, and of the ubiquitous *funcionario* whom he despised. Edmundo, our senior *funcionario* civil-servant friend never criticised Spain, although Humberto frequently waxed lyrical on the topic; I have no doubt he regarded strictures to be more genuine and effective than plaudits.

The morning after our very enjoyable trip to Aigues de Los Pajaros Rojos, we came clashing back to earth with a visit to the *vivienda*. In the few days since our last inspection, a grotesque roof had appeared on it. Instead of copying that on the villa we were occupying – the *modelo* (model) – it could hardly have been more dissimilar. When we complained, Lew said it had been too difficult for Miguel, the young Spanish fellow, hardly more than a lad, who had been contracted to do the building, and it would have cost too much. Because he had nothing in the way of plans for the construction of the villa model, or for the new one he was building, Miguel was having to keep coming across several times a day to measure a wall, a doorway or some other part of the villa we were in, and then using it as a specification for the one he was building. One fellow down below would be calling a detail to someone up aheight – over the noise of the radio, people shouting and things banging – and the one above would be asking him to repeat it, the two of them later disputing it. It was a method of construction fated for disaster.

'But it's nothing like the original!' I exclaimed when I saw the roof which did not require a tape measure to see it was completely different in both size and shape to the original. It's like a dog's kennel!'

'It's early days, old son. A lot can happen before it's finished. You have to allow for the Spanish way of doing things. Cross my heart, it'll be lovely when it's done. I can just see it nestling beside the bank, blue skies up above… You wouldn't want for more, I can tell you… Just be patient, mate.'

We came away, leaving him waving his arms about and bawling 'We all live in a yella submarine, yella submarine, yella submarine…' as though he had already forgotten what we were talking about and cared even less.

Two days later Helen and I went back with a tape-measure and notebook after the workmen had gone home, and checked everything. Apart from the very poor quality of block and cement work throughout, unaccountably there were two adjacent solid walls, twelve inches apart, in the main bedroom; the doorway into the kitchen had been put so far into the corner that it abutted the adjacent wall, leaving insufficient room for the door; the window in the lounge was far too small; the outer wall of the sun porch was so badly aligned that the floor was rhomboid, and the chimney was unbelievably crooked.

It was beyond belief that Spanish builders did everything so differently to every other builder in the world, and impossible to conceive how this mess could ever end up a 'lovely home by Christmas' or any other time. How on earth could it have been supervised by an architect and then passed by the Ayuntamiento's building inspector, also a qualified architect.

We told the Spiers we wanted to speak to the architect.

'He's Spanish, old son. Doesn't speak a word of our lingo.'

Nonetheless we wanted to see him. If Val did not want to translate, we were confident we could communicate our complaints to him ourselves. After a good deal of arguing, the two of them consented but said it would have to be at 7 a.m. because that was the time the architect came to the site. Right, we said, they could tell the architect we would meet him there the following day at 7 a.m.

The next day Helen and I were there at 6.30 a.m., and waited until 9.30 a.m., but there was no architect. We then waited in the villa for the rest of the day, positioning ourselves by the window so we could see anybody going to the *vivienda*. That night we went to see the Spiers again. They said we must have missed him because he was certainly there but was only a little chap and we could easily have missed him if we were not looking very hard. But he would not have stayed long because he had a meeting to attend in Valencia. The Spiers often said things that were hard to believe, but we had given them the benefit of the doubt because we wanted to believe them, but now realised we could trust them no longer. The walls would soon be coated with plaster on the inside, and cement rendering on the outside, and everything would be covered up; even a wafer thin layer would conceal the countless spaces between the blocks, as well as all the broken pieces that had been stuck in all over the place.

They said we would just have to wait until 31st December when the *vivienda* was due to be completed, before making any more criticisms. 'We could pull it down and completely rebuild it before then if we wanted to,' said Lew Spiers, 'and neither you nor anybody else could do a thing to stop us. You people don't even come into the picture until the completion date in the contract. You should read it, matey. You signed it.'

Every night in Alicante there were crowds of people in the streets, walking or eating and drinking at tables, yet never was there any drunkenness, never any voices raised in anger, no gangs of youths on the rampage or anyone intimidating anybody. People were noisy but it was only excited talk and there was never any aggression or any police presence.

It is hard for me to believe, though all the evidence seems to suggest it, that I am the only person in the world who does not like eating out, and by 'eating out' I mean anywhere outside my own home. In Spain, Helen informed me, every self-respecting expatriate ate out, and if I wanted Spanish friends I would most certainly have to overcome my aversion. But apart from anything else, hygiene had always been a priority with me. In domestic life, although most people appreciated the point of reducing germs, most would contentedly stroke a cat – which they invariably kept indoors – and then continue making the sandwiches with the same unwashed hands. If one had a depleted immune system, how could he explain that coming to tea might make the difference between you know what and you know what. In Spain, massive pans of fried yellow stuff are put on tables outdoors where the flies can get at it, and then everybody dives into it again and again, into their mouths and back into the pan, so that by the time the mush has disappeared, a massive exchange of bodily fluids, equal in microbiological measure to an orgy, will have taken place. Because food was cheap, waiter service excellent and restaurants plentiful, older English people who had rarely eaten out in their lives, apart from walking home with a bag of fish and chips, regularly ate out. Most of them consumed the same kind of stuff they ate back home, but cooked by somebody with a nom-de-chef like 'Viv from Penzance' or 'Babs from Hull'. Some, however, ate paella and then wrote home to tell everybody, the way they had done the first time they ventured to try tapas.

We never had cats at home, so hygiene was never a problem, but my mother's mother came from a family of bakers and confectioners and as a result my mother was a wonderful cook, putting all five of us sons beyond the pale when it came to eating anybody else's cooked meals. For all of us, school dinners, friends' birthday parties, the army, and girl friends' mothers' cooking, were ordeals. I had girlfriends whose mothers had various talents but never a one who could cook a decent meal, not compared to my dear mother who thankfully passed on many of her more modest culinary skills to her daughter-in-law.

After years of the good food we had produced on our Irish smallholding, we were now consuming the acclaimed WHO Mediterranean Diet. I very much liked fruit and could not ask for more than the all-year-round abundance and quality of what was obtainable here. Of course we scoured and peeled everything because we took it for granted that the Spanish would be heavy-handed with the agricultural sprays, and when they were in the fields and needed to 'go somewhere', they would go anywhere, and there would be no toilet rolls hanging from the trees, or taps with running hot and cold. I was also learning to take olive oil with salads and delighted to find it did not taste anything like the cod liver variety spooned down our throats every day when we were kids on the Second World War North Sea diet.

However, there was one thing I appreciated about eating out – by that I mean having a cup of coffee – and that was the *camarero*, surely the finest waiter in the world. Helen ate out with friends if she were going into Alicante to do some clothes shopping, and always praised the waiters. She usually went to the upstairs restaurant in El Cortes Ingles where there were small tables set along the side wall, perfect for people who ate alone, almost invariably women. I got so that I enjoyed having a Spanish coffee whenever we went out; not only because every cup tasted different from any coffee I had ever had anywhere before, but because of the way it was served. If ever we had had coffee in Ireland, not only would I rarely enjoy the stuff, or be impressed by the grooming of the waiter, though some were very pleasant, I objected to being moved on as soon as I looked as though I had drank most of it. In Spain proprietors are so reluctant to present a bill that one can go all night ordering refreshments and not pay a sosser until going out the door. Alternatively, one can sit talking for ages over an empty cup and nobody will keep asking if one wants anything else, or worse still, clear away one's cup. In new Ireland, the country of the so-called 'Celtic Tiger' – a less eponymous trope I cannot imagine – they would practically sweep you out the door, even if you and your party had just downed a three-course meal, to clear the decks for more customers with pockets full of capital. The days of the Irish grandee were not only long gone, they never arrived.

Generally, and especially in American movies, waiters and waitresses came from the lowest class, and even in high-class restaurants in Britain, Ireland and elsewhere they were not regarded as anything more than servants – 'fodder gofers' –

people to be bossed and messed about by anybody sitting at a table, be they a slavering demented old man or a spoiled brat.

In Spain the *camarero* is neither highly paid, nor particularly well treated by those he serves, but at least an appearance of pride endures and nobody treats him badly. Constantly on the move, full of gravitas but very little humour, the restaurant, bistro, café, airport and railway station bar are all his domain, and now and then, if it is very late or quiet, a few of the senior *camareros* will congregate almost out of sight, and steal a few puffs while exchanging a quick anecdote with their colleagues; always, however, one will be keeping toot to make sure no customer goes wanting. Yet although I would never fail to acknowledge his immaculate service, I once witnessed something that deserved the most scathing reproach, and I was unfortunate enough to be involved.

We were in Barcelona when we came upon a magnificent place that I hesitate calling a restaurant because through its huge ornate windows it looked just like what I imagined the dining room of a palace would look like. Although Helen's tongue was hanging out and she would have sacrificed a whole year of her life for one multi-course meal inside – or said she would, no power had ever exacted such a quittance from her that I was aware of – we simply did not have the money. But if they would let us in and allow us to sit at one of their beautiful tables with their gorgeously embroidered cloths, under those huge chandeliers – things I do not like but accept as proof of wealth – among such an ostentatious clientelle, while we took ages to drink a coffee which would probably cost as much as a full meal at an ordinary first-class establishment, then yes, I would certainly consider it. Perhaps they would take a framed photograph of us and we could write underneath: 'The conclusion of a deeply satisfying meal at Barcelona's most lavish restaurant'.

The thing was, how were we to find out if it were possible to have nothing but a coffee, there was nothing to indicate it on a menu posted outside because it was not the kind of place that resorted to such promenade-café promotion. In the finish Helen was so desperate to get in that she agreed to nip in, ask some waiter standing nearby and get a '*Por supuesto!*' (Of course!), I would join her with no further ado. Naturally I was a tad ashamed – I was one of those curs who sent their wives into Smiths bookstore to buy a copy of 'Lady Chatterly's Lover' when it came out – so I knew how it felt to be the architect of something so pusillanimous. But we found a nice table for two and I did something I very rarely do, which was to nip into the *aseos* first – maybe it was the excitement. The *aseos* were large and of course beautifully tiled and appointed, and as I looked into the mirror above the washbasin I was using, I saw behind me a particularly handsome waiter with slicked back hair, not unlike Federico Garcia Lorca, who darted out of a cubicle while the WC cistern was still flushing, and without washing his hands made straight for the exit. He glanced at me just before the door closed and I glimpsed what I took to be an expression of slight guilt as I followed him out and returned to our table. I could hardly wait to impart my experience to Helen and had no sooner sat down when, of all the aristocrats flitting about dressed as waiters with tantalising airs, who should come to take our order but Cackhands! I was shocked. Should we get up and leave? Should I reprimand him in bombastic English or halting Spanish? We certainly weren't going to drink from any cups he had handled.

Did he recognise me..? Yes, he recognised me all right
'Senor?' he murmured.

No matter how sumptuous the surrounds, I was a retired microbiologist and was not going to drink from his shitty cup, or have my wife do it,

He stood looking and becoming increasingly perturbed but I did not know what to say and of course neither did Helen because I had not had the chance to brief her yet.

'Hang on,' I said, and got up, leaving Federico leaning over the table, thoroughly discombobulated, and poor Helen, half sitting, half standing, and not knowing whether to follow me or sit down and wait to see what I was going to do next. Swiftly I strode over to the main desk and called for the manager. It took some time to get him, as I was offered various other subordinates first, the routine one invariably gets when one calls for a manager. I was already wishing I had chosen almost any other option, preferably one which involved leaving, rather than doing my public-spirited duty bit in a place like this, but there was already too much consternation and too many wannabe managers penetrating me with withering looks from the ring that had gathered around me. I was wondering whether to play the *'no comprendo'* card, signal to Helen to join me outside, and beat it, but the honcho himself arrived and seemed to regard my complaint with commendable concern.

Without argument or delay, he lined up every *camarero* in the place against the wall, and asked me to finger the one who had allegedly moved his bowels without washing his hands before serving us. Fortunately, or unfortunately, my man was not amongst them, although the bossman and his second-fiddles all insisted everybody was present. I just stood my ground, as much as anything because he was making a fool of me by keeping the non-bum-wiper out of sight, and after some excruciating disputation and a hunt that included a search of both *aseos*, two more heavenly waiters were produced and my man was one of them. He knew, and the rest of them knew as well. He denied what he had done, or rather, not done, and by now I was feeling sorry for him.

Mind, he was in his late thirties, old enough to know better and not to be showing the younger ones such a bad example. Perhaps it should have ended with him being given a stiff reprimand, even the sack. As it was, Helen and I left with the blade of an imaginary knife sticking between both our shoulder blades,

'God knows what he'll be slipping into the next ex-pat's coffee when he gets the chance,' I muttered.

'Well, if he does, it'll be your fault,' said my wife.

Any coffee, whether in a corner cafe or hotel bar, tasted excellent. As long as one did not think too much about E. coli, Enterococcus and other faecal contaminants. Humberto, our guru on Spanish mores, put it to us that since many of these waiters would come from poor homes not governed by hygiene, where toilets often meant holes in the earth without paper or running water, what could one expect.

I was well aware of the silly old adage about doing the same as the Romans were reputed to do if one were in Rome, but when it comes to dress, most Europeans could not hold a candle to the Italians. The thing with the Italians is that classy dressing is for the wealthy. Spaniards are different, every one of them can dress well, and *catalánes* best of all. Their sense of which pigments go together to produce a superbly subtle blend can only have evolved, because they all have it, rich and poor, old and young. The beautifully tailored suit is of the finest cloth, and suits are everywhere: the bank clerk wears one as he fills in one's details, the car salesman while he flicks through the brochures, and the plasterer at a wedding rehearsal. The shirt and tie could be as exquisite as the beholder could bear, the magnificently handmade shoes without saying, and who but the *catalán* knows that socks can be elegant. A Spaniard can, from any position, toss a raincoat over his shoulders and it will flutter down and alight like a cape, perfectly and without needing the slightest nudge.

I don't consider myself a prude but don't think old people should wear next to nothing in public places. If the purpose of 'under-dressing', i.e., exposing as much of the body as possible, is to titillate, then how can flesh that is withered, spotted, scarred, discoloured, malignant, or in some other way repugnant, be considered erotic.

To be in a bread shop, browsing the low racks where loaves are often displayed at a height where hairy little dogs can sniff or raise a skinny leg over, and find yourself staring down the tatty cleft of a seventy-seven-year-old Englishwoman's buttocks because she is wearing too loose-fitting a pair of shorts; or be sitting at a table having a drink when another bends over to pick up her bags and displays the other cleavage, the one that leads the eye down to a pair of flaccid flaps that look for all the world like expired dates, will surely make you wonder what is happening to the world. At their age both my grandmothers were wearing shawls and sitting in basket chairs indoors.

As for obese topless English men with well developed but utterly useless breasts that secrete only sweat, in top-class restaurants like El Cortes Ingles, standing at the bar in a pair of shorts and flip-flops amidst chicly dressed Spaniards who should make all other nationalities want to crawl under a table and disappear between the tiles, they should be arrested. If beautiful young women were until recently arrested for not wearing head-cover in church, or for wearing a bikini on the beach, why should grossers like these escape? Seriously though, in restaurants at least, security personnel should force them to cover up; and if this means being made to buy and immediately don a brassière from the ring of spares the guard has hanging from his belt, along with ties, so be it.

Helen loved going around the fruit and vegetable markets, and when Alice and Medbh were visiting, the three of them always went for a horchata, the reputedly nutritious drink made from tiger nuts and sold in what else but *horchaterias*. Obviously if a labourer in the tomato cloches is called a *'tomatero'*, what else should one call a place that sells horchatas. Every day of the week, some village held a market, and even though the food did not interest me much, I was very interested in the handmade hardware which included all kinds of ingeniously and deftly made cages and animal traps.

Because of pressure from the RSPB, that extremely powerful organization with well-known malicious elements which claimed to be making the world a safer place for birds, working-class men, such as the few coal-miners still labouring under dreadful conditions and kept a few singing native finches as a hobby, were hounded in Britain, fined large sums of money, and frequently jailed; this by magistrates who in the past were often coal-owners content to have the same little creatures die of gas poisoning down their vile pits. Coal-miners, who were among the very best the human race had ever produced, would come out of the pit to snatch an hour or two of fresh air and sunlight at the end of a long, dark and dangerous shift, stooping among the hedgerows for seeds of certain weeds for their pets, plants that would be favourites of breeding birds and medicine for those that were ailing. Whilst they stretched their legs through fields and tramped over wasteland, often in wind and rain, they would chat with their pals and enjoy a few lungfuls of air. These were the kind of human beings Margaret Thatcher and her gang insulted, abused and eventually destroyed. In Spain everybody loves singing birds, despite the harassment of the RSPB whose hooked beaks, long talons and vindictiveness nevertheless reached far beyond the borders of England, as indeed they had in Ireland.

On our previous visits to Spain, especially to Seville and Granada where birds of passage traversed during migration, street markets sold finches, traps, cages and ingenious appurtenances for aviculture; but all that was gone now. I had never taken pleasure in seeing the kinds of songbirds I would have given an arm and a leg to see when I was a boy, meticulously laid out on boards in a huge meat market as delicacies for the gourmet, but birds in cages for the simple finch fancier was a different matter altogether.

Whatever the Spaniards' love of songbirds, especially canaries and finches, their total mindlessness when it came to what most other nationalities regarded as blatant cruelty, was an incongruity impossible to explain, and it applied to birds, fish, reptiles and mammals. Witness their attitude to bulls where the scorn of other people infuriates them.

SIXTEEN

ONE NIGHT AFTER WE heard the Spiers go out, Miguel, boy builder of our *vivienda*, his wife, their few-weeks-old baby and an English interpreter friend, all of whom had been hiding around the back of the villa, came to the door. Miguel was in a pitiful state. After the normal Spanish pleasantries, much speeded up, he launched into a passionate diatribe against the Spiers, saying they had him under contract to build the villa for half what we were paying for it, including all materials, and they presently owed him more than a million pesetas. He could not even afford to feed his family, let alone build anybody a house. Prices were rising all the time, the only kind of *albañil* (building labourer) Miguel could afford was an *obrero*, the casual who had to be paid at the end of every day or would not come back, and he had no capital of his own. He was totally reliant on the Spiers to pay him regularly or he could not continue, and wanted us to persuade them to pay him. We were shocked to find how inexperienced Miguel was, that his work crew were just itinerant day labourers hired from nearby bars, and that he hadn't even enough to feed his family because he was always paid in arrears.

Standing there trembling and almost in tears, he could not have been more than twenty years old, though looked about eighteen with his slight figure, overgrown crewcut and pasty face. More appositely, he could not have built many, if any, houses before this, and could only have been hired because he was dead cheap. When we asked him about the ability of his workmen and the quality of the materials they were using, it was clear he wanted to say a lot more than he dared. Whether this was because it might reflect on his own capability and integrity, or because he was afraid of what the Spiers might do if he told us something that could get them into trouble, we could only conjecture, but reckoned it was probably a bit of both. He was defensive and critical at the same time and complained bitterly about the lack of any architectural plans.

'How can anybody build house with nothing but a child's drawing. I need proper architect's plans. For the money you are paying them, I could bring you a book of plans and you could choose a lovely chalet with balconies and terraces and nice tiles. That is what I wanted to build for you. Instead of that..!' He waved his hand contemptuously in the direction of the *vivienda*. We pressed him for details of the contract he had with the Spiers, but both his friend and his wife were continually giving him warning signals that stopped him saying more. Perhaps there never was a contract.

Next day I went to see the Spiers.

'Miguel said he'd accept half what you owe him, so things can get moving,' I announced.

'He can bloody-well go and jump!' Lew Spiers snorted. 'He's not getting another penny till it's finished!'

'But he'd nothing to live on!'

'What a load of bollocks! He's got all he needs to get on with it.'

'We aren't discussing that no-hoper with nobody. The arrangements we have with him have nothing to do with you and he has no business even talking to you.'

With that, he slammed the caravan door in my face.

The following day all work on the *vivienda* ceased, the workmen vanished and we were back to exasperation.

El Cortes Inglés was a superb department store and there was a branch in every city in Spain, sometimes several. It was big and imaginative and the only store we had ever been in that was arty and entertaining the way big stores in Tokyo were – well, not quite perhaps – and one could spend half a day wandering around and not get bored. One of those places where they claimed to sell anything if you gave them three business days – or something like that. I do not like big stores but I loved this place, and it cost nothing to get in.

Sales staff were of the same breed as *camareros* but more arrogant and regarded themselves – and were regarded by customers – as true professionals who perfectly acted and talked the part. The precept was for the customer to feel overwhelmed, intimidated and beholden; not the sales person. Saleswomen, such as those dealing in women's clothes and paraphernalia, carried their limited rank well but were excluded from masculine areas, such as IT where intelligence was required, and if a saleswoman were to be discovered there, or in another part of the man's jungle, she would very soon be ejected when spotted by a male. There was never anything as vulgar as '*Salga, bebé*.' (Butt out, babe!) or anything like that; not even an acknowledgement of their existence. She would simply be psychologically shouldered out of the way by a male already talking about the product before he reached the spot where the business was being conducted, and she, meekly and without demur, would simply evaporate.

Even male staff who were not dead ringers for Valentino or Tyrone Power, the latter being the epoch I came from, still looked like matinée idols because of their magnificent grooming. Spanish men – silk and leather aside – could be mistaken for Hollywood stars simply because of the way they combed their hair. Mature women, who would have been well on their way to biddydom in Ireland, were more chic than *chica* (girl). It was not that El Cortes staff were better informed than their counterparts in big stores in England, and far better than counterparts in Ireland – because they were not; it was because they looked and smelt a whole lot more attractive, and it definitely made a difference.

I have never liked using words that looked or sounded awful, even though they might be appropriate, and 'overweening' is one of them. This is because 'overweening' perfectly suits the disposition of male staff of El Cortes and I can imagine it being a quality high on the list of desired attributes among applicants for 'posts' in this great store, certainly higher than universities attended. So expensive, long and limited in choice, were university courses, that very few El Cortes staff would have been on one; but so what in a world where packaging was more important than education.

'The English way' in Spain was by no means a stuffy way, the way it tended to be elsewhere, for it catered for all sorts of people from those buying the cheapest and tackiest of items in the basement, to those where the sky was the limit, such as in the uppermost of heavenly floors. Even if not necessarily proudly, it dealt in the best and worst, and as one descended, so the décor became more supermarket and the goods more disposable, staff more market-stall, hair less immaculately dyed, teeth not so intensely bleached, and smiles friendlier.

I was once in the IT department looking for a dictaphone, which the male staff must have considered was a kind of toy and passed me on to a bimbo who did not even work in the department. I had some difficulty making myself understood, but she was very patient, certainly more than I was, and I eventually got what I wanted. But what did I want it for, she wanted to know. She was a pretty 'lass', if one can use that term for a Spanish girl with very un Spanish blonde hair, who was rather coquettish, though not in a way that should raise the pimples on a sixty-seven-year-old Englishman.

Had it been a male who had asked, I would have said something to the effect that I was writing a thesis on the plague of erectile dysfunction in Spain compared with the widespread priapism in England, something crass that would have jabbed his hubris. But she was nice and had been very helpful. When I told her I was writing a book about my experiences in Spain, including those in this very store, some of them worthy, some not so, she looked disconcerted. 'What about me?' she asked. 'Have I been of sufficient service?' Indeed she had, I said.

Without a moment's hesitation, she added 'Will you come back and take my picture and write a chapter about *las chicas amables del Corte Inglés*' (the nice girls of El Corte Inglés).

'Of course'.

The GP in Los Pajaros Rojos to whom we had been consigned by the Social Security Head Office in Alicante, was working under conditions no doctor from the last century would have done in England or Ireland. He had a tiny room, little more than a cubicle, with nothing in it except a rickety little table with a primitive computer that was out of order, and no other equipment except a hairy stethoscope, two chairs and a file bulging with papers. Outside was a small waiting room full of people sharing with a receptionist.

When shopping or waiting in a queue for a bus, usually the only time a Spanish woman respected the principle of first come, first served, was when she arrived first; but a mother whose precious little boy had scraped his knee and had a few specks of blood showing, would barge straight into a doctor's surgery, occupied or no, and if an old German happened to be in there with his pants down and the doctor's finger stuck between the haemorrhoids in his bottom, too bad.

Like a butcher and fishmonger, the doctor operated a ticket system which was only fully understood by locals who would employ every trick to get in front of an *extranjero* because they passionately believed *extranjeros* should not be allowed in at all, let alone in front of a Spaniard, especially a local.

One morning when an elderly Scotsman hobbled into the corridor to see the *practicante* – a male nurse in an even tinier room than the doctor's – a local with no teeth, thinking an *extranjero* was jumping his turn, pushed past and barred his way with his arm and a mouthful of *valenciano*, the local *catalán* dialect – which most Catalans insisted was a language distinct from *castlellano*. The Scotsman's wife then piled in with a dose of mercifully unintelligible Glaswegian, and the locals joined in to abuse the two of them – Spaniards will always enlist when a fellow countryman is having a spat with a foreigner, and it has absolutely nothing to do with right or wrong.

Suddenly the *practicante* came out and it was obvious the old Scotsman had only come for a dressing and not for anything as substantial as a consultation with el medico (the doctor). But no one apologised. The main difference between doctors' waiting rooms in England and Ireland, and in Spain, is noise, and it is a big difference. In England and Ireland, in deference to the doctor as well as out of consideration for fellow patients, silence prevails. In Ireland, waiting rooms were quiet not only because people were generally soft spoken, but because they regarded waiting rooms as ante-chambers to death, and only the doctor talked loudly. Here, however, it was like being in a bookie's shop, and every so often the doctor would come out, bang his fist on the door before waving it around threateningly, and then bawl '*Silencio!*' On one occasion, after Helen and I had been waiting over an hour and he had repeatedly come out and yelled in vain, he packed up and left. But just as he was going out of the door, he came back, histrionically threw up his hands and apologised to Helen and me. This gesture, something the locals had probably never witnessed before, transfixed them, and for a few moments, as Helen and I got up to go, they gawped at us walking out the door as though we were walking on water; not that it did us any good.

The first time we had called on this GP, it was with a letter from our GP in Ireland which I had translated into clumsy Spanish, giving a history of my illness. He had asked a few questions about how I had contracted the illness, commented '*Mal suerte*' (Bad luck) in a friendly manner – something no English or Irish doctor had ever done before – and then asked what medication I needed. I told him and he wrote out a prescription. He then stood up, shook hands and opened the door for us. Henceforth he was never other than similarly polite and friendly.

Eventually he had a nervous breakdown, partly related to his liberal socialist politics which were contrary to the young *alcalde's* (mayor's), people said, and he had to quit after a year. It was a pity because we never had another like him. Mayors are very autocratic personages in Spain, unlike in Ireland where they tend to be nobody special.

El medico had thrown his hat into the ring for the Left Party in an election where he hoped to get on the council, but his party was beaten by the PP (Partido Popular – successors to the *franquistas*) who, in that particular election, were bribing voters with condoms instead of, as previously, tokens for a free lunch; though whether that was only for male voters, I never managed to find out.

Our medical practice never seemed short of locums – mainly women probably serving some sort of penalty; it was space practices were invariably short of. Surprisingly for Spain, women doctors were renowned for their reluctance to carry out anal examinations on male patients and male Spanish patients were equally unwilling to submit, though for some reason Englishmen did not seem bothered.

One female locum was more or less forced out of the surgery by a *gitano* (gypsy) father who had stamped in and abused her because she had refused to continue signing his daughter's unending sick-notes, meaning the loss of livelihood for the whole family who, incidentally, lived on land they had illegally squatted and built a kind of animal shed-cum-dwelling on and avoided paying dues to the council by making threats against the staff. The female doctor had telephoned the police afterwards but was offered no protection so gave up and went somewhere else. It was surprising how much power gypsies had over the police, as indeed they had in Ireland. People said it was because the police were afraid of them, and this might well have been the case because Irish police were generally not as intimidating or tough as in other countries; some of the females, like the Spanish, were mere slips of girls, no more than 5 feet tall. Since the minimum height restriction had been withdrawn, at least in Ireland, there were lots of tiny female coppers and even average-sized males were scared of big bad guys, especially if they were tinkers, travellers, gypsies or whatever, notwithstanding police the world over seemed more brutal than they had ever been. Taser first, interrogate next, seemed to be the protocol.

The fact that Spain had twice as many doctors per capita than anywhere else in Europe probably accounted for the quality of its medical service; even the English expats, the greatest moaners in the world, praised it. As an example of Spanish care, from the outset we had been asked to sign a form agreeing to accept treatment at a private clinic should at any time public service treatment be unavailable within a certain period of time. If another were required, how about the Englishwoman who needed £400 worth of oxygen per week to be able to visit relatives in England, but could not afford it, and the English DHS would not even consider paying for it, so her local Spanish GP arranged for the Spanish Health Service to pay. Even under a Labour government, such a standard of medical service was only provided free in England for tyrants like Augusto Pinochet, by sycophants like Foreign Minister Jack Straw.

Unlike in Britain and Ireland, the excellent Spanish Accident and Emergency departments were never commandeered by drunks or thugs, and in all towns emergency health centres were always open. For good measure, Cruz Rojas (Red Cross Centres) were everywhere. After years of low expectation, the organization and efficiency of the medical service in Spain was astonishing. People said it was nothing compared to the French and German health services, but if this were so, all I can say is that the French and German services must have been of a very high standard indeed. Perhaps it had to do with the anarchic spirit, such as the wonderful right that anybody had to walk into any bar or restaurant, demand a drink of water and get it for nothing; or use their toilet; or flag down a motorist and demand to be immediately taken to a medical clinic in a case of emergency. Although Humberto warned that with the passing of the last whimper of anarchy, these little graces would pass into oblivion, Helen and I actually witnessed them within a short time of coming to live, and I have to say they were wonderful to behold.

SEVENTEEN

ONE MORNING IN OCTOBER Miguel telephoned to ask us to meet him at an office in Jemina where his English friend worked; he was afraid to come to the *vivienda* and sounded desperate. The Spiers still had not paid him any of the money they owed him but he was unwilling to say why; he just wanted us to arrange a meeting with them as soon as possible and for Helen and I to both be there. I rang Lew Spiers but it was only with the greatest difficulty that I could get him to agree. The arrangement was that we all meet at eight o'clock that night at our house.

The Spiers were first to arrive.

'Our contract with that little so-and-so is none of your business,' Val Spiers said nastily as soon as she sat down. I told her we only wanted to help sort things out and had no wish to pry into anybody's private affairs.

'Our business is our business,' Lew Spiers confirmed, glaring and making a big fist which he kept clenched on the table.

'We're involved whether we like it or not,' I replied. 'You're the ones who chose him to build the house that we are paying for.'

Just then Miguel arrived, more smartly dressed than we had ever seen him, and with so much lotion in his hair that it was running down his face, though some of it was probably perspiration. He was tightly grasping a briefcase, the sight of which very much bothered the Spiers. As soon as he sat down and began to open it, they got up from the table, plainly terrified in case we might see how little they were paying him, and how cheap were the materials he was having to use.

'That's it! Come on, darlin'!' Lew Spiers snapped. The only time we ever heard him use terms of endearment to Val was when he was annoyed with somebody and wanted her support. 'I love my wife!' he once embarrassingly informed us during an altercation. It was as though he could only argue for one or two rehearsed sentences before descending into a state of verbal destitution where all he could do was bleat about how besotted he was with his hard-faced *mujer* (woman, wife), as if that had anything to do with anything. Because of her refusal to ever yield on anything, she was little better, but at least she never stooped to the level of billing and cooing.

During the course of the next hour and a half we repeatedly had to appeal to the two of them to listen to what Miguel had to say, but they adamantly refused to let him get out more than a few words at a time. They would not address anything to him directly, everything intended for him being directed to us, as though he were not there.

'You know nothing about him!' Val sneered when I said he seemed a decent fellow.

'We know he has a wife and baby and that he's very unhappy about the *vivienda*.'

'Yeah..? Well, so are we, tell him. And he's the one building it!'

Eventually Miguel said he would resume work on the *vivienda* if they first paid him 500,000 pesetas, which was half of what he said they owed – a sum they had not denied even though he had quoted it several times.

Lew forced a guffaw and got up. 'Come on, my sweet. I don't know about you, but I've had enough of this.'

'What about our *vivienda*?' I retorted.

He shrugged his shoulders. 'If this "B" isn't here at eight o'clock tomorrow morning…without any payment…he can forget about ever coming back. Me and my mates'll finish it.'

We had shaken hands with them when they first came in and asked them to do the same with Miguel when he came, but they had refused, so when Lew now reached over towards Helen with his huge, shovel-like hand, she drew back, saying 'I don't want to shake hands with you. You are being unreasonable to this poor man and you have no right to finish the house yourself. You're not a proper builder and don't have a licence. If you have a contract with him, it's up to you to honour it.'

Lew Spiers was quite aghast. All along Helen had said little, leaving most of the complaints about the house to me. After they had gone, Miguel was near to tears.

'They very bad people. Tomorrow I bring *guardia civil*. My uncle a judge. They seal everything with yellow tape…*la vivienda, la parcela* (plot)…*todo* (everything).'

The following morning I went to see the Spiers. There was no tape, no sign of enforcers, nothing. The place was deserted.

'I'm not prepared to discuss it any more,' Lew Spiers snarled as he opened the caravan door.

'You've got no choice. It's our house and we're paying for it!'

He was already shutting the door in my face.

'We need to talk!' I called.

'Forget it!' he shouted from behind the door. 'Get lost!'

He had finally dropped the veneer of respectability and amiability now that he had lost faith in our gullibility. Right from the start, Val Spiers had resented any criticism of the *vivienda*. Even a query about something, the clarification or confirmation of some point, and her facial muscles would tighten, eyes narrow and lips withdraw inside her mouth. Although she was more intelligent and better educated than he was, where he had at first tried to come over as the friendly clown and ex-yeoman of England, she had never sought to make anyone like her. She was as stony-faced now, after our living next to them for months and seeing them every day, as on the day I first met her.

Everything about the construction of the *vivienda* was an eyesore, the overall impression being of a building coming down, rather than going up. The chimney, the steps, walls and floors were all cockeyed; the roof like a kennel's. One side of the house was crudely propped up with a few scaffolding poles because of a massive hole where a window had been crudely knocked out, and every few blocks there were gaps, many of which had fragments rammed in.

Convinced that no good could ever come out of anything to do with the Spiers, we decided to consult the English *gestor* we had met a few weeks previously, to find out where we stood legally. Janet, tall and slim with long fair hair, was married to a Spaniard to whom she seemed most ill-suited, he being a builder's labourer and not educated at all, and whereas she was always cheerful, he was invariably surly. He could not speak any English, so never said anything to us or to any English clients when we were there, yet he could be garrulous with a Spaniard. Nevertheless he gave the impression of being head honcho in what was Janet's office. Apart from being more good-humoured and likeable, Janet was like any professional Spanish woman in that she was elegant in dress and very self-assured, but different from other *gestors* we had met in that she appeared to be the genuine article.

Most of her work involved acting as an intermediary between *funcionarios* and English immigrants, other nationalities and any Spanish having *gestors* of their own. She told us there were hundreds of people throughout the Costa Blanca having to contend with problems associated with the purchase of property and vehicles, construction work and swimming-pool service, plus financial problems related to the payment of government dues – and there were umpteen of those. She said she knew of nobody who had been in Spain for more than two years without being swindled over something or other, mainly by their fellow countrymen – or at least people who spoke their language – because in a foreign country people readily trust people they would never have trusted back home. She also said she had heard plenty bad things about the Spiers, but because Lew was such a bully and Val so vindictive, nobody dare stand up to them.

'Most people, English or Spanish, are afraid of the Spanish system of justice because they are convinced they can never win. They accept their losses and forget about it. Quite a few go back. But I have a Spanish husband and two half-Spanish children, and I like Spain. I'm sorry to have to say it, but the English have the worst reputation of anybody. The Irish are much better liked.'

When we said we did not intend walking away and leaving our deposit behind, Janet warned that the legal system in Spain was horrendous even for a Spaniard, and the Spiers had the advantage of having lived here a long time. Val Spiers was not a teacher, as she claimed to be but she was employed at a private school, so would have contacts; and Lew was well up in the Freemasons. Another thing was that she was a solicitor's daughter. So nobody would know the score better than those two as far as the English in Spain were concerned. But if we wanted to have a go, she would arrange an appointment with an English-speaking *abogado* (lawyer).

The consequence was a consultation the following night with a lawyer in Alicante, a flashily dressed twerp who strode about his huge office as though delivering immortal lines from the stage; but we had been warned what to expect from no-win, no-fee, abogados. His advice was to look for another place to live as soon as possible and let the Spiers do whatever they liked with the *vivienda*, because there was nothing he or we could do until the day after the date of completion of contract, which was the 31 December, 1998. If the *vivienda* was not the way it should be in every respect according to the contract, then and only then would the Spiers have failed to comply with the terms of the contract and have to repay our deposit. We said we would think it over. Finding accommodation for an indefinite period, plus storage for all our furniture and effects, would be a heck of an upheaval and expense. But continuing to abide in the Spiers' house, given the expectations we now had about the *vivienda*, was untenable. Everybody was telling us how violent Lew Spiers was, even to his own wife, and advising us to leave. He knew I sometimes had to rest in bed during the day, and the bedroom window was facing where he was building his own house, which was right next to the plot where Miguel was supposed to be building the *vivienda*. Consequently he had stepped up the noise, banging and clashing things about, bawling out silly ditties all day, and frequently cutting off the water and electricity for hours at a time. At first we thought it must have been Iberdrola, the electricity company, because they rarely notified householders when they intended to cut off the power, but then we found that anybody can switch it off because the connection boxes are in the front street and anybody can get into them.

All the same, I did not like the idea of leaving the villa because I did not want the Spiers to think they could harry us into it. If they had until the 31st December to complete the *vivienda*, I reckoned we had the right to stay in their villa until then. But although Helen was not easily upset, things were now beginning to get her down, so we began looking for alternative accommodation and somewhere to store our effects.

One day we received notification by letter from the Spiers, via a *notario* (notary), informing us we would have to pay the balance on the *vivienda* and complete the contract on the 30th December, otherwise we would forfeit our deposit. We took it to Janet's lawyer.

'Throw it away,' he said, flicking his wrist and waggling his fingers.

'What if we get a note telling us to collect another one from the post office?'

'Don't go.'

'What if somebody comes to the door and insists we sign for it?'

'Tell them to go away. I told you last time: do nothing. Come and see me in January.' He was practically pushing us out of the door.

We decided to ring Roberto Hernandez, the estate agent, whom we had not seen since coming to Spain. He was very friendly and invited us to lunch with himself and his wife at an elegant Chinese Restaurant at the Port where we told him everything. He was sympathetic but said we should bear in mind that he was still the Spiers' agent, therefore could not say anything derogatory about them. However, he begged us for our own sakes not to even think about taking the matter to court. He was very handsome, testimony to what money can do to aggrandise what nature has already been more than generous with, and it was easy to imagine him getting his own way with people.

'You have no idea what you would be getting yourselves into. The waters of law run deep and murky in Spain, and are full of whirlpools and waterfalls. It could take years and cost you a great deal lot of money and trouble. You came here for your health, didn't you..? Well, the stress of something like this could make you both ill. I know, I've seen it happen many times. Please consider very carefully before you do anything. But there is one thing you must never do, and that is to ignore a *notario's* letter. A *notario* is a very important person in Spain and to treat one with disrespect is to ask for serious trouble. Why not just complete the contract in December, as though everything were all right, and then sell it?'

'Because it's full of faults and looks awful!'

'Spanish people don't care if the walls are straight or the roof is this shape or that. They buy a house because they enjoy being outside of it.'

'Maybe, but as far as we are concerned it wouldn't be fair, knowing what we know, whether they were Spanish, English or anything else.'

'Look, Jack, I don't want you to be unhappy in your new land. How about we sell it for you? We won't charge you anything. We'll sell it now for the amount you were going to pay, including the extras, and give you back your money, and the Spiers theirs.'

'It's not even finished.'

'That doesn't matter. People can see how it's going to be. We have many clients…foreigners and *madrileños* (citizens of Madrid)…wanting a little chalet like that to spend a few weeks' holiday in every year. They aren't fussy about how it looks. One of our salesmen is in the area with clients right now. If you like, I could give him a call and ask him to show it to them.'

We thanked him and said to go ahead, as long as he was sure nobody was going to be deceived in any way.

'No, no, no, no, no! Of course not! He'll show them everything.'

That night Roberto telephoned to say that although they had somebody interested in buying the *vivienda*, and both he and his father had gone around to talk to the Spiers, the Spiers had refused to sell. Val Spiers had said 'Don't the fools know what a contract is? They signed one with us and they're damn-well going to keep to it. Otherwise we keep their money!'

Roberto was both surprised and disappointed.

'I think it would suit them if you defaulted on the completion of contract for whatever reason,' he said. 'I think they want your deposit and the *vivienda*. In which case, all you can do is wait till December to buy it, or lose your money. There's nothing more we can do. If you don't like it after you've been living in it for a while, you can always sell it to somebody else.'

It was November now and there was no way the *vivienda* could be made into anything remotely like what it should be by the end of December. We went to see Janet.

'I can't recommend you go against the *abogado's* advice, but I wouldn't recommend you ignore a *notario's* letter either. Maybe you should see your abogado again.'

We did, and regretted it.

'This time I charge you 17,000 pesetas because you do not take my advice and waste my time. How many times do I have to tell you to forget about the *notario*..? I am the advisor here. Not you! You know nothing about Spanish law! It is very complicated.'

I had had to get out of bed with a fever to come and see this *hijo de puta* (sonofabitch) sitting in his huge luxurious office, arms folded like the president of a corporation talking to us as though we were nobodies.

It was nine o'clock at night, I was tired and could hardly think, but appointments with abogados and the likes were often in the evening because of the afternoon's siestas.

'If nothing is done until January, the house will be finished and all the gaps and mistakes covered up,' I insisted. 'At that stage would you be able to authorise an architect to drill holes into the walls to check it?'

'I most certainly could.'

'Then why not send a licensed photographer around right now? It'll be cheaper and cause less disturbance.'

'Because the house is not due to be finished until the end of December! How many times do I have to tell you that? And that is why I am not going to get a headache looking at these.' With his little puppy-fat hand, he brushed aside the pile of carefully annotated photographs we had brought him, and they scattered over his desk, some over the edge and onto the floor.

'Why don't you buy the damned bloody thing and then just flog it?' he wailed, demonstrating his superb mastery of the English language and flinging his arms up in mock despair.

'We don't want to buy the "damned bloody thing" because it's a disgrace. And wouldn't want to sell 'the damned bloody thing" for the same reason!'

'Anyway,' he said, getting out of his chair and into a most ingratiating pose, 'I don't like to prosecute. I like to defend. That's my style. Come and see me in January and we will see what we can do then.'

He was already up and around our side of the desk, hand out. I was not sure whether it was for the seventeen thousand or to shake my hand and bid me farewell, but as I reached out to take it, he deftly turned it palm upwards and I was no longer in doubt. We gave him the money which went straight into his top pocket, and he was showing us out as he tucked the notes down.

We decided to tell Edmundo of our position and see if he could suggest anything. He was really dismayed to hear we were having such a bad experience in his country and said he would ask his wife to ask around to see if she knew of any flats to let. He was now coming every Saturday and we were spending half a day swapping Spanish and English information, words, grammar and phrases. The Spanish have sayings for practically any situation, but their metaphors, which are sometimes beautiful, sometimes funny, often have meanings that are difficult to guess, such as: '*dar a luz*' (give light, i.e. give birth).

Every time Edmundo came, he insisted on bringing me a Spanish book. He read cheap English novels and thrillers because the language in them was never demanding, but the books he got me were Spanish classics or non-fiction of the highest literary standard; not because he could possibly have thought my Spanish was that good, but obviously because he hoped it would be one day. In any case, he would never bring anything that looked cheap. Unlike Humberto, who would tolerate no praise of Spain and always made a withering joke of any attempt we might make in this respect, Edmundo was not amused by anything he perceived to be criticism of Spain, no matter how mild or abstruse. Edmundo, the lifelong anglophile after a single visit to Hastings all those decades ago, which must have been momentous – I like to think he was deflowered by a Kentish girl with rosy cheeks and breasts like Cox's orange pippins – even winced at criticisms of England.

When our *residencias* came through, we immediately went to see Janet about getting an NIE number and having the ownership papers of the car transferred to our name. She told us we had never needed a *residencia* to get an NIE number, that there were several ways of getting one and she could have done it in a couple of days if we had not let Val get involved. She could not understand why the Spiers would have told us otherwise. Whatever, she would now prepare the necessary documents as soon as possible, make the arrangements for us to pay the necessary taxes, and get Val to come in and sign the papers.

Although Janet did as she said she would, and telephoned Val several times, saw her on the street outside her office on a number of occasions and beckoned her to come in, Val refused every time. We had the car and were paying all the expenses of the transfer, so it would not have cost her a peseta, but she ignored all requests.

'There's no point in her refusing to sign unless she's planning to keep it and sell it. If necessary we'll get the abogado on to it. Meanwhile I'll keep trying. To be on the safe side, be very careful where you leave it and make sure it's always locked.'

We now had no direct contact with either of the Spiers. Miguel had vanished and Lew Spiers and his English fugitives – ones without any licence to work in Spain – had ceased working on his own house and were racing to get the *vivienda* finished by themselves. Whenever Helen and I walked along the road overlooking his place to have a look, he was always there, singing obscene ditties and making crude gestures while his men looked on with expressions more of embarrassment than anything else. Sometimes he would slink along in parallel with us, swinging his arms like an ape. When we came back, he would be standing, hands on hips, leering. It was unpleasant but we made no response, carrying on with what we were doing, taking photographs inside and out of the *vivienda*, making measurements and notes, and trying to appear as though we were ignoring him.

As Janet had said, every English expatriate we met had been cheated in some way, but none had ever sought redress in court. Horrendous cases were being reported in English as well as Spanish newspapers, where, over a minor disputed debt, the courts had denied the owners a proper hearing, confiscated the whole property and the owners had lost everything. There were accounts of people unable to go home for years for a holiday in case they were suddenly called into court with only a day's notice. Then there were the fees, so high and so many: *abogados*', *procuradores*' (barristers), *notarios*', *peritos*' (experts), *intérpretes*' (interpreters'), *traductores*' (translators'), and others too obscure to have identities, who had to be paid for something or other. A single delay in payment in the manner stipulated and everything would come to a halt. And then there were the witnesses, a body so base and costly, but crucial to the Spanish system.

One day Edmundo called to say his wife had located a vacant flat in Raspeig, Muchavista, a short distance along the playa (beach) from Jemina. Helen liked it, so we arranged to take it from the 1st December. Good old Humberto was able to recommend a removals man in Alicante North who would store our belongings until we found an unfurnished house. He was a typical friend of Humberto's, a good natured fellow from the working class barrio in Alicante whom we liked immediately for his strong socialist views.

We said nothing to the Spiers as we packed everything up in the days before the move. Helen was sure that on the day he would come with his men across the little wall that separated his plot from ours, and there would then be mayhem. However, I doubted if his band of illegal English labourers would want to get mixed up in anything like that, especially since the Spanish removals men were unlikely to stand by and see their clients attacked or their belongings damaged – at least that is what I liked to think. Whatever, I knew worse things had happened in Spain, so I placed a crowbar as daintily as possible on the mantelpiece in the lounge, and my biggest eye-gouging screwdriver on the windowsill outside the kitchen. I was hoping he would not come over, because if he did, I could not see the situation being resolved amicably, or my coming out of it totally intact.

As it turned out, although Spiers and his mates were watching us all the time, they never made a move and there was never a murmur out of the man himself.

The evacuation thus took place without a hitch and we had time to leave the place clean and tidy. I think he must have been taken completely by surprise, and with Lady Macbeth out at work, did not know how to handle it. Of the two, Lew was no more than an ugly, ignorant, bullying oaf. Val was the key malefactor, and I think she manipulated him the same way she manipulated everybody else. I never saw or heard of her saying or doing anything kind to any living creature.

Our new abode was a fully furnished, four-bedroomed, rather old-fashioned apartment, probably built in the seventies, on the fourth floor of one of several tower blocks inside their own grounds, with huge windows overlooking its swimming pool and the sea. We could comfortably walk to Jemina for a small shopping trip, passing a number of restaurants along the way which Helen always stopped at to compare their *menus del dias*. These were lunches that consisted of beer or wine, salad, one or two main courses, dessert and coffee, cost a total of €10 and by law were served daily. They were so tasty that even I partook of them from time to time, and Helen opined that, as opposed to the leopard in the old adage, one day I would indeed change my spots.

    The apartment was a trifle dilapidated but clean, roomy and light, and the lock-up car-park was a bonus, especially with our soon going to Ireland for Christmas and leaving the car behind. It was such bliss to be away from the angle-grinding and hammering, bawling, jeering and pop radio that went on all day, every day, and the screaming and yelling at night as Lew and Val expressed their feelings for each other.

    Like Roberto, Edmundo was adamant we should respond to the Spiers' notary's letter, so we drafted a notification of our intention to refuse to complete the contract on the grounds that the Spiers had not complied with its terms, in that they had not built us a new house of the same design as the model, nor one that was of sound construction. We knew it was going to be next to impossible to argue all of the bad construction because by the 31st December most of it would be buried under cement on the outside, and plaster and paint on the inside, so had decided to argue mainly on the grounds of design. There was nothing they could do to conceal the gross roof and misshapen rooms. The terms, *'exactemente iguale'* and *'mismo diseño'*, which I considered critical, were those the Spiers themselves had selected for the contract they had drawn up, and all four of us – Lew, Val, Helen and I – had signed it. We had checked the definitions of these words in every dictionary in every bookstore and library in Alicante, including the university library and, most importantly of all, the irrefutable Diccionario Real Academia Española (the official state dictionary of the Spanish language) which was perfect for our purpose. On these two conditions would we hang our case.

The *notario's* office in Jemina was elegant and of minimalist design, with original, though hardly eye-popping, modern art on its walls, the kind of stuff an interior designer with no taste would select. And whilst the *notario's* young, attractive, and entirely female staff rushed about with documents, answering telephones and talking earnestly to people with strained expressions, at the crescental main desk, the capo (bossman) himself, an exceptionally handsome creature, way above estate-agent grade, suave and casually though impeccably dressed, glided through the place like a god, all heads turning and involuntarily giving a little bow.

The waiting room was crammed with grey-haired couples with pink faces, some of them overlain with a strange-looking tan; not a word of Spanish among them, smiling nervously and appealingly at anything that moved, and murmuring to each other in dialects that were very familiar to Helen and me. Property was changing hands in this place, a lot of it, and His Sartorial Elegance was helping it along with ten minutes of pure charm culminating in a flourish with a very fancy fountain pen that looked as if it might have been conquistador plunder. Outside we noticed people waiting around with little brown envelopes that would almost certainly contain a good deal of pure cash ready to be eagerly handed over to anybody with his hand out who spoke Spanish.

This would be the 'undeclared portion', *un poco de gesto* (a little gesture) which was not part of the official deal and would avoid the need to pay too much tax. It would be paid separately, out of sight, and without the tiresome documentation which was such a feature of Spanish life. This philosophy was practiced in every shop, customers being offered a 'discount' and no receipt, or a receipt which would cost them the sales tax that would otherwise have been overlooked.

After briefly looking at our photographs, the *capo* – the Grand Facilitator – who guaranteed the absolute legality of all transactions in Spain, agreed with what we proposed to send to the Spiers, now transposed into legal Spanish, and read it out aloud, his faintly official smile never once leaving his face. We signed, a witness signed and God signed. Then we were wafted away to hand over a wad of euros to one of the attractive females; though if they had the choice, Spaniards would still be dealing in doubloons. In addition to the Spiers and their *notario*, we arranged and paid for a copy to be sent by hand to Roberto Hernandez at his *inmobiliaria*. We would be away on the 31st December so were authorising Janet to act as attorney during our absence, she being, apart from anything else, the only English person we knew who seemed not to be totally cowed by the Spiers. It meant another visit to the *notario's* office but would hopefully prevent anything drastic happening while we were away.

Before we left for Ireland, we continued visiting the *vivienda* every two days, even though Miguel and his itinerant builders had vanished without a trace and Lew and his crew of illegals were doing all the construction.

Things were being dashed off in great haste: hideous blockwork was being buried under a cement rendering, floor tiles had bits cut off their edges so they could fit cock-eyed walls, splinters of others filled the numerous odd spaces that had accrued, and corrugations in the floor indicated places where the ground beneath was uneven as though the area had suffered a minor earth tremor. Because the window wall in the sun porch was so badly out of alignment, there was a difference of twelve centimetres in width between one end of the windowsill and the other, and the whole room was rhomboid. On the Saturday afternoon before we departed, we were inside, Helen holding the tape measure while I was photographing the disparities, when Lew Spiers suddenly burst in.

'You're trespassing on private property! Leave right now or I'm calling the police!'

I felt sure that sooner or later things would come to blows, but when I said we were just inspecting the parts we had paid for, he was totally nonplussed and just huffed and puffed his way from one room to another, and then went out. We knew this would not be the end of the matter and were certainly not going to be prevented from checking on a house which was being built for us to live in, so we went to the police station in Jemina to report the situation before there was any violence.

Unfortunately it was a bad time: they were watching a football match on television and would not be persuaded even to record the complaint. They said such a serious matter could only be dealt with by the *guardia* at the *juzgados* (courts) in San Vicente and we would have to go there and make a *denuncia*. This meant the Spiers would have to appear in court to answer the charge. We had never heard of such a thing, but if this was what we had to do, we would do it. So, first thing on Monday morning, we went to the courts and made a statement. It was in Spanish, not easy, and the office of the British Consulate in Alicante whom the *guardia* had told us to telephone, was totally unhelpful – as everybody we knew said they would be.

EIGHTEEN

DUBLIN WAS COLD, WET, windy and dirty, but it was wonderful to be back. We had forgotten how friendly the human species could be, how good-humoured, how modest and obliging, and we immediately felt better, albeit more like released hostages than holidaymakers. It was hard to believe that all this time we had only been three hours away. We were going to spend Christmas with Alice in Belfast where she was living and teaching at a Protestant school and doing everything she could to conceal the fact that she was a Catholic. Both the Catholics and the Protestants could tell immediately from all sorts of little pointers, like a person's first name and how they pronounced certain words. Helen and I had lived in various countries around the world where Catholics and Protestants had lived and never encountered anything like it. So here we were, being briefed by our own daughter on how to talk and behave so we would not be abused or assaulted in part of a country we had lived in for twenty-two years with scarcely an incident, apart from the odd stupid remark from a drunken idiot; if, for instance, one got into an argument with somebody in the south who assumed that because one were English, one were therefore a Protestant. Hearing about having to hide behind curtains when the 'Orangemen' – often a collection of bad-tempered women, hooligan kids, silly old men with quasi-musical instruments they could not play properly, and a few hard men putting the 'hard eye' on potential detractors – marched through the estate, or having to find an inconvenient diversion for one's car because the Queen's Highway had been temporarily but completely blocked with tractor tyres and other combustible rubbish in readiness for a huge and dangerously polluting bonfire, quite disorientating. After all, we had lived just a few miles away for a very long time and experienced none of it. Aside from the 'religious' thing – if that was what it really was – and a certain cold efficiency about the place, we found the average Belfast man or woman to be not that different from any normal and friendly English person in England. Apart from the predominantly black attire and sinister looks, they were as friendly as anybody, and certainly spoke in a refreshingly frank way, more so than their cousins below.

So, armed with sufficient information to survive a few days in what was a friendly if not lovely city, one with a lot less bullshit in the atmosphere than in some others, we prepared to mix with Lagan folk, folk not so different from those on Tyneside, and quite different from the region of the Liffey. Maybe it was the old shipbuilding culture, maybe the coal and steel and heavy industrial milieu which always produces a certain kind of people – decent, tough, comradely – everywhere in the world.

Harry was working in Dublin and Medbh attending university there, and they would be joining us for our Belfast Christmas. After that, Helen and I would be going down to Wexford to spend New Year with Walt and his family.

Belfast was colder, greyer and more blustery than Dublin and the people reassuringly working-class. After Alicante, even the grotty little lawns and privet hedges of housing estates appeared verdant and soft, but it was so humid you could feel the water in the air on your skin, in your hair and in your lungs.

Unlike the dynamic Mediterranean coast, which would have new streets of half-completed houses when we got back, nothing but the facades of the cheap and tacky shops had changed in Belfast except to have become even tackier, and it seemed inconceivable that people could be content to live out their lives in a place with so much hardship and strife. We heard of a girl from Alicante who had married a lad from Belfast and been living here for three years, now with two children, and we wondered how she survived. Here people had been tearing each other apart for so long that one could not cease to be amazed by the immense stamina prejudice possesses; stoicism, a rare sight on the Costa Blanca, was in every face, old and young. That said, Belfast was very much a city; a tiny one, but with all the necessary ingredients, including a very definite civic pride. For its size, it functioned surprisingly efficiently – briskly and without much chitchat, but efficiently, which seemed to be all that mattered.

Although it was our first family Christmas where Helen and I had not been the hosts, it was very enjoyable. The children tried to persuade us to give up the *vivienda* and Spain and return to Ireland as soon as possible. But we had unfinished business to settle.

When we returned to Spain in early January it was to find a letter from the Spiers' *notario* in Xixona stating that because we had not presented ourselves at his office on the 31st December to complete the contract, we had forfeited our deposit and all other moneys paid into the *vivienda*. There was no mention of our communication via our *notario* in Jemina, and although initial enquiries suggested it had got lost somewhere along the line, there was no explanation as to how it might have happened. Further enquiries by Janet indicated there had been a mix-up in the Xixona *notario's* office but there was not the remotest intimation of an apology from any quarter, so we had to go through the whole rigmarole again with the matinée idol and his harem, and send off another communication explaining everything, without delay. As far as I was concerned, the whole thing stank, but there was absolutely nothing we could do about it. If I had blown my top and said what I felt, we would have lost everything; of that Helen and I had not the slightest doubt.

However, *Señor Dinero* (Mr Money) was not fazed in the least. He breezed in, natty as ever, we signed, he signed, we paid and he breezed out again, proving that such a personage can be a swift facilitator when properly propitiated. Because the original notification to Roberto Hernandez had been delivered by hand, the first thing we did when we came out, was to go to Roberto's to confirm that he had received his notification on the 16th December. Yes, he had. When we asked him what he had done about it, he said he had immediately telephoned the Spiers and apprised them of the contents.

Obviously we had to get ourselves a real lawyer, as opposed to the no-win, no-fee whizz-kid who stuffed one's money into his top pocket just for asking questions, and it would not matter if he spoke English, as long as he was good; maybe Humberto or Edmundo could recommend somebody.

In between times we were trying to enjoy the Mediterranean life and determine whether or not it was indeed benefiting my health. We often swam in the sea, though in some areas tourist and canine detritus had to be seriously overlooked, went for forced marches along the beaches, took train-rides, went for drives and to interesting Saturday-night concerts at the Arts Centre and on the beach. Wonderful big jazz bands regularly came down from Valencia – originally from Cuba and other places in South America – usually to play on the beach where it cost nothing to sit and listen or dance on the sand. Never in any country we had lived in, had we experienced anything remotely like this. Superb bands with male and female vocalists, and musicians who, in typical South American style, danced as they played, and had the huge audience laughing at their self-deprecating patter. At least half the audience would be *extranjero* and it was the one time different nationalities enjoyed themselves together, ignoring the fact that many of them were once or twice, in most of their lifetimes, deadly enemies. Sadly, those whose memories were so bitter they could neither discuss nor forget them were the Spanish.

For me, Spanish history was thoroughly compelling and I could not get enough about Franco and the Civil War. Helen's fascination for it would not begin until after we had left Spain when she would spend so much time reading and reflecting on everything she could.

The literature we resorted to was mainly produced by excellent English historians like Paul Preston and Raymond Carr who were so much taken with Spain that they could almost be accused of bias. Spaniards themselves could not easily be drawn to it in conversation, especially the Civil War, which made me think a lot of shame must have survived. It was totally different to what I, as an Englishman, was used to when it came to the two World Wars, one of which I had lived right through, and indeed to any other wars I knew anything about, and I think it might have been because, like all civil wars, it was a war between families, friends and colleagues, as well as fellow countrymen and women. The Irish are similarly tight-lipped about their civil war.

Edmundo's books on Spain were always by Spaniards, and I bought any that came out in English, but there were not many of the latter that dealt with modern Spain in other than a trivial way. What passed for modern Spanish history in English tended to be part-autobiographies by expats praising a Spain we had not yet encountered: one where one drank and tapa'd in the local bar with a one-armed Basque pal on one side, and a retired *guardia* civil sergeant pal on the other, and the search for the constantly moving Holy Grail, was the location of the cheapest restaurant that served steak and chips.

But Spain was more than just a giant sunbed for the retired. It was a place for criminal refugees and Walter Mittys, a place where all kinds of people could reinvent and lose themselves, old Labour supporters could slide over to the right and talk like hangers and birchers, ex-shelf-packers could remember themselves as store managers and directors, and nursing aides and 'carers' recall careers as theatre sisters. A place in the sun where lack of familiarity with the Spanish language hardly mattered because one's compañeros all spoke English, and if you needed to say anything in Spanish, you could always pay a *gestor* to do it. No wonder those who were barely articulate in any language, boasted theirs was the best in the world for expressing oneself eloquently. The few Spanish residents – 'the Immigrants' – kept their heads down, and with their innate facility for the bon mot, called the place 'Gibraltar'

Almost all the Muchavista residents – '*ancianos*', as that wonderful Spanish word has it – were owners of their flats and, surprisingly, of quite big and flash cars. There would be very few ex-shelf-packers and nursing aides among them, most having been primary school teachers or clerks in the civil service, with a sprinkling of secretaries, predominantly widows.

Although there was ample space to park cars in the place set aside for the purpose at the back of the building, and most of their owners could get about faster than a witch on a broom when they were coming after you to inform you that you had parked your car a whole inch over 'the white line', thereby breaching a law they themselves had decreed, when it came to parking their own cars they invariably pleaded severe disability, with the consequence that their cars were so close to the only entrance, that even the millipedes had difficulty getting past. Their lives were planned in terms of sorties for shopping or restauranting, where they could get back before Major Bond in his Mercedes or Mrs O'Shaugnessy in her even more foreign make, could invade their commandeered spaces and they would have to find an alternative harbour several yards away, until the next time. There was a bus stop and railway station on the road outside the gate, so some residents hardly ever moved their cars, using their social security passes whenever they needed transport.

Because so many residents were widows, cats and dogs provided ideal company and were something they could profitably converse with as well as sleep with. Consequently there was a range of dogs, from cushion terriers – little hairy things whose front end could only be differentiated from the back end when they were sitting down or walking – and mainly belonged to the ladies, to gentlemen's golden retrievers which had never retrieved anything more hairy or bloody than *ancianos'* slippers. All of them licked old white legs whenever they got the chance, such as in the elevator, and this probably accounted as much as age for the hairlessness of old legs, though it probably improved circulation, especially of ankles which so often needed help judging by the amount of anti-hypertensive medication their owners took; in this respect their owners probably considered them working dogs.

I very much like working dogs but cannot abide those that are mere appendages of their owners, like walking sticks. Old ladies tended towards cats, many of them repulsive strays whose first experience of first aid was the removal of key parts of their reproductive organs.

Most of the community had more than enough of everything they needed, and much more than most people their age in

England, yet they were often miserly, covetous, spiteful and just as xenophobic. However radiant it made the body – and this was a subjective assessment – it seemed as though a WHO climate did little for the health of the soul. Helen maintained the English did a good job as far as saving pets who had been abandoned was concerned, but I did not think many of them worth saving given the state they were usually in and the parasites they introduced.

Our flat was comfortable in that it was roomy and light with a large balcony, appropriately tasteless décor, cheap furniture, and crockery and utensils adequate for a holiday home belonging to a stingy dentist from the English Midlands, but we would have to move out before summer when ours, like the rest of them, would be tripling the rent.

With all our photographs, pictures, books and belongings in storage in Alicante, we had little to remind us that life could still have meaning even though we were long retired from useful occupation. Apart from our family and friends being so far away – never mind being 'only three hours by plane' – my workshop, study, studio, animals, birds, fishponds, trees, apiary, St John and his colleagues, were all gone, excised from our lives as decisively and permanently as with a guillotine, it was only now, for the first time since our arrival, with the time to think, that I began to wonder what we had done, what I had persuaded Helen to do, and the children to accept, as reasonable. What madness had allowed me to presume that we could give up all those things at a stroke and start a new life elsewhere in a very foreign country. And why should I suddenly become so selfish as to think my health was so important, especially at this time of my life? We had moved many times in our lives, lived in different countries and always fitted in and appreciated the differences, but now things were different in a way we had never experienced before. Had my arteries started hardening, or little black holes started appearing in the places where my grey cells used to be? Every day we heard of people who had come here to 'reinvent themselves', as though that were an index of the potential of the place.

We felt uneasy, rather than impressed, by the thought of living among people pretending to be different from what they really were. In any case, surely they were doomed by dint of the fact that it was short-term memory that failed first and the long-term one that remained to haunt and reproach. Many seemed to be fleeing from marital, family or business commitments, escaping debts, responsibilities and troubles they had created but could not solve – things young men reputedly used to join the Foreign Legion for. Old wasters were growing yellow ponytails, toenails and droopy moustaches, covered with sloppily drawn tattoos suggesting previously epic lives; wearing the ugly single carat jewellery of the small-time crook, garnering feckless chicks that could have been their daughters except for the tell-tale daddy-cool patter, and congregating at the airport to show their incoming cronies how much they had metamorphosed. What a phase to look forward to. The fashionable lady-folk were something else. In bikinis for ancient bimbos that revealed wrinkled clefts of what looked like Moroccan leather at the top of the front, and something similarly wrinkled at the apex of the rump, they managed to get into all kinds of places they would never have been allowed in the days of the little general; in his time they would not have been allowed outdoors.

We could have returned to Ireland without giving Spain a chance to redeem itself, but it was not really Spain's fault, although the conditions they created and the laws they should have created most certainly added much colour to our problems, so to go skulking back after only six months would have been indefensible. We had a battle to fight which was going to be hard enough to win, without trying to do it from Ireland. And where would we live if we went back? House prices had increased phenomenally in the time we had been away. Perhaps we should buy somewhere else in Spain and see how things went, maybe everything would look different then.

So with the intention of bettering the situation as soon as possible, we hired Trev Hall, an English builder who came from Tyneside, had a plot for sale and had been trying to persuade us to let him have his architect draw up plans for a house for us, one where, among other things, we could go upstairs to bed at night. Then we needed to find a new abogado – one who liked the English if that were possible.

Edmundo had already got us our very satisfactory accommodation and perhaps we should not have asked for anything else, but there was nobody else we could ask. Janet was not keen on recommending an alternative to her man, and Humberto said he had only lived in Spain for fifty-five years and that was nowhere near long enough to locate a good *abogado*. Edmundo considered any *abogado* who operated on a 'no win, no fee' basis, to be of dubious worth, but offered to introduce us to an ordinary one he knew, though 'recommend' was too big a word.

'*En España es muy difícil a recuperar su dinero*' (In Spain it is nigh on impossible to get your money back) he said, shaking his head grimly. The one whose name he eventually came up with was an ex-neighbour who had worked on labour issues in the past, which impressed us, though Edmundo was not certain which side he had been on. He could not speak a word of English but Humberto agreed to come along to help with interpretation of legalese and exercise his critical faculties.

The night we met Edmundo outside Sr. Luis Quintiliano Férrer de Rossa's office in Alicante at 8 p.m., Edmundo came from one end of the street, and interpreter Humberto, scourge of the *funcionario*, from the other. They both approached at the same time and it was Edmundo, beautifully dressed in his sombre, senior-civil-servant-grey suit with executive collar and tie under a classic *abrigo* (overcoat), who suffered the greatest shock. Humberto, with hair looking as though he had cut it himself, was wearing an old pink and patched Canadian anorak, baseball boots and rucksack, with the hard attaché case weapon he always carried, in which he kept his most precious belongings and documents, including his *escritura* (title deeds) of his flat. Because he lived by translating into and from *catalán* and *valenciano*, French and English, his income was very modest and he lived in a flat in what Sr. Férrer would call a 'humble district'; hence he never left anything of value behind when he went out. It said something for the relative safety of the streets of Alicante that he, a person surely incapable of physically defending himself, should entrust himself and his possessions to the public domain; I certainly could not imagine him walking the length of any street in a relatively peaceful place like Dublin without being parted from the lot in broad daylight on any day of the week. We introduced our two friends to each other: the ambassador for central government, and the one for anarchy and natural chaos, and they politely shook hands, all parties realising they were not necessarily cut out to be bosom pals.

'What do we call him?' I asked Edmundo, as we waited for a response to my pressing the bell of a narrow but very solid teak door, three floors up: '"Señor Férrer", "Luis", "Quintiliano", or what..?'

'Oh, no no no no no..! "Señor"..! He must be called "Señor Férrer" at all times!' Humberto gulped in horror at the prospect of any chumminess coming from any of our party, especially a skinny lumberjack with a pink anorak and a gross haircut. Moments later the door was opened by the most beautiful *abogada* I had ever seen, who kissed us on both cheeks – which I thought boded well – and showed us into the waiting area. Humberto, with his various accoutrements stowed under his chair, looked pensive. He was the only one fluent in both Spanish and English, but he did not believe in small talk, so Helen and I tried to talk polyvalently in order to cement us all together into a legal team, while Edmundo looked as though he were taking his role very much to heart.

Whether the claustrophobic atmosphere of Castilian law, or the glimpses of expensive clothes and whiffs of ozone-layer-attacking perfume that were being wafted around as one partner after another slipped through a door and nodded, got to be too much for him, I could not tell, but Humberto, the contemplative, the quiet-spoken eclectic, suddenly launched into a quite venomous diatribe on the iniquities of *abogados*. He proclaimed such facts as that there were more *abogados* in Madrid than in the whole of France, and that, of all professions, they had least merit and produced nothing but stress and invoices. The more *abogados*, the more crime, as far as he was concerned. Farmers were producers, artists were producers, and teachers were producers. '*Pero* (But) *los abogados*..! Pah!'

We could only hope Señor Férrer was hard of hearing because we were soon called in and instructed, in the curt Spanish manner, to sit down. For a few moments nothing was said as we sat, one by one scrutinised by a large, partly-revolving man with cropped wiry grey hair, whose eyes twinkled when he smiled, ensconced in what at first appeared to be a chair for the handicapped, but soon proved to be a device designed to deliver maximum comfort to an important personage. His desk was impressively cluttered with documents in classy-looking files, and his walls decorated with the same kind of art as the *notario's*, though less abstract, nothing that might intimidate the average client. There was nothing reminiscent of justice either, no print of Daumier's wonderful 'Plea for the Defence', for example, but at least no portrait of any generalissimo (military commander in chief) or king either.

At first, Edmundo and I did most of the talking while our prospective legal advisor spun impatiently in his chair before suddenly braking to a halt and assuming total control. Beginning by flicking through the pages of our various documents, he slapped the contract so hard he could nearly have imprinted a copy on his palm, and then lambasted the maladroitness of its author. Eyes gleaming, teeth flashing, he declared the case to be the Spanish equivalent of a doddle. With the exception of Humberto, the rest of us looked at each other with relief and chuckled with tentative joy. He then looked at it again, said he had not realised the contract had been revised – as we had already explained – and that instead of a doddle, it would be nearer sixty:forty, which was still in our favour but not quite so much as he had initially surmised.

Por supuesto (Of course) it would cost us a lot of money if we lost, and might cost a lot of money even if we won; though less, *por supuesto*. If we wanted him to represent us, things could begin tomorrow with a cheque made out to '*El portador*' (the bearer). This, it was explained to us later by Edmundo, was the Spanish way of avoiding any embarrassing record for tax purposes. But first, he would need to know how much we were prepared to settle for.

The total amount we had paid, *por supuesto*, I told him. Plus compensation for…

'*Eso es absurdo!* (Poppycock!)' Sr. Férrer scoffed, throwing a warning hand up in the air towards Edmundo and then looking away and shaking his head as if to clear his brain of such nonsense.

'In Spain it is normal to offer half. Then we have a better chance of winning,' Edmundo explained.

'Half is losing, Edmundo,' I said. 'Not winning.'

He shrugged helplessly.

'Do your thieves only have to pay back half what they steal?' I asked Sr. Férrer in what was supposed to sound like cynical Spanish. For some reason, whenever I spoke Spanish with passion, I never seemed able to retain the upper hand.

'Hah!' our man cackled fraternally to Edmundo. 'The thinking of the Anglo-Saxon..! Latin logic is very different, tell your friend.'

With Humberto sitting at the side of the impressive desk, chin in hand, saying nothing, and Helen sitting back with her notebook and pencil trying not to miss a word in shorthand Spanish, the conference followed the format of my addressing Sr. Férrer, Sr. Férrer answering to Edmundo, and Edmundo appealing to me.

'We have been cheated on two counts. Not only is the *vivienda* very different from the one Los Señores Spiers was contracted to build for us, it is very badly constructed. And because we cannot live in it, we are having all sorts of other expenses we never expected. We therefore want all our money back. And if it takes a long time, we shall want it back with interest.'

'So far that comes to 2,500,000 pesetas for the deposit on the *vivienda*, and 1,362,100 for extras. A total of 3,862,100 pesetas. Kindly tell him that, will you, Edmundo,' I said.

'Any amount would have to be rounded down in millions,' Edmundo replied, looking directly at me. 'No *abogado* would consider arguing over a few hundreds of thousands.'

'Odd hundreds of thousands..! It isn't a matter of what's easiest for their *abogado* to deal with. We want it all back,' I insisted, in my best Merchant-of-Venice voice. Not a peseta more, not a peseta less.

Sr. Férrer flung up his hands in disgust and took another phone call. There had been so many throughout the consultation that had they been orchestrated to impress a prospective client, they had been ludicrously overdone.

Edmundo was looking at us almost beseechingly, shoulders hunched, tight-lipped, probably cursing the day he ever thought of placing an advert in Quicksave.

But our time was up. Sr. Férrer finished the call, got up from his desk, smiling graciously, arm outstretched in a farewell handshake, and we were hustled out. He probably thought Edmundo would talk some sense into us, but did not look as though he would lose any sleep either way.

When we got downstairs, I complained to Humberto that he had hardly translated anything.

'He said nothing worth putting into any language but Spanish. But I must go now. We will talk some other time.'

Under the foyer light he looked pale and weary.

'Are you all right?'

He said he had influenza and had got out of his bed to come. He must have walked all the way from his flat in San Juan, but still declined a lift back because he did not approve of cars.

We were tired going back. Communicating in another language late at night with someone who talks in conditional tenses and subjunctive moods, and trying to remember what else is being said at the same time, must sap at least as much energy as putting a man on the moon. Also, wit does not always translate well: certainly nothing like as well as the other party's self importance.

My ideal of a lawyer had not existed in England or Ireland, and so far nothing resembling him existed in Spain, but we had to have somebody, and soon, so decided to 'hire' Sr. Férrer. I love that word, 'hire'. It is so essential to keep remembering its wonderful nuances when engaging the services of somebody with airs and graces who is nevertheless only doing the job for dosh…boodle…*dinero*… and we paid this one his first advance in the discreet manner stipulated so that we could proceed in a civilised manner without cluttering up his cedar desk with grubby, much-handled notes, and returned home. From then on we set about collecting and sending in any information about our case that we thought might help. It was a tedious process, Spanish legalese not being a language for the beginner.

In February, Gilbert and Mildred Forsyth, an elderly English couple whom we had invited for coffee one night when we were living in the Spiers' villa, telephoned to see what had happened to us.

They had been next-door neighbours of the Spiers for many years and would be ours if we took the *vivienda*. We could not explain everything over the telephone, so invited them around. Previous to moving here, we had said nothing about the trouble we were having, but now when we told them, they said they understood perfectly. For years they had known the kind of people the Spiers were, and as a consequence had kept themselves to themselves. But because their house was adjacent to, and overlooked the *vivienda*, they had not been able to avoid seeing and hearing a lot of what was going on. All along there had been rows between the Spiers and Miguel, with merchant suppliers, workmen, and sooner or later virtually everybody who came near the place.

They had witnessed every stage of the *vivienda's* construction, and Gilbert, who had worked in India and the Far East as a civilian major in the British Army and been responsible for overseeing the construction of many military buildings during the Second World War, and afterwards during the rebuilding of Malaysia, had been so appalled by the way our *vivienda* was being built, that he had taken photographs and kept written records. He had noted, for instance, the way the window in the lounge had been enlarged by Lew Spiers hacking chunks off the wall with a sledge hammer, and the original lintel reused even though it was now too short and had been supported by terra cotta bricks, rather than entirely replaced. He had also sketched the way the roof and chimney had been 'flung up' without regard for symmetry or simple mathematics. And many other travesties besides. He had also noted that all of this had been done by Lew Spiers and his English oppos, rather than by anybody with a proper licence.

By this time the Spiers had abandoned the tiny caravan in which they had been living, and moved into the *vivienda*, even though the retaining wall, which was supposed to protect it from the road but had its buttresses on the wrong side and no drain holes, had collapsed and the roof over the main bedroom and garage leaked badly whenever it rained. They had taken all the tiles off the roof, put down aluminium foil, and put the tiles back, but the foil had blown off, much of it into the Forsyths' garden, and the whole of that side of the roof had to be removed and completely redone.

At this stage the Forsyths were still on speaking terms with the Spiers who boasted to them that they had our money in their bank and intended keeping it.

'The fools know nothing!' Lew Spiers had told them. 'I could buy and sell the likes of him twice before breakfast! Calls himself "Doctor". Doctor of twaddle, if you ask me!'

When Gilbert mooted the risk that we might take them to court, Lew had guffawed. 'What..? Those two..? They haven't the guts. Or the brains!'

'It makes me sick to think that somebody like Spiers could believe I would approve of his shenanigans,' Gilbert snorted. 'But I let him go on because I suspected he was up to something really dishonourable this time and I wanted to know what it was.'

When we told him we were in fact taking the matter to court, his feelings were mixed.

'Somebody should, that's for sure. They've got away with too much for too long. But going to court here is a nightmare. We've been and know.'

The next day they telephoned to say they had talked things over and decided they would do all they could to help us, including standing as witnesses, if necessary. We could hardly believe it. This was our first lucky break and we thought it would be of inestimable value. We were not only impressed by their courage, but extremely grateful. Nobody we had asked so far had agreed to give evidence or help in any way, and they had all been younger and stronger, with the support of family, friends and colleagues. Most significantly, they were all people who had previously stated they were just waiting for an opportunity to crucify Lew Spiers. 'Just give me the chance to face the bastard in court. By God, I'd see he got his comeuppance all right… the things he's done to us!'

It was not that they were afraid of Spiers, they said, but they had a wife and young children to think about and you could never tell what somebody like him would do once his dander was up.

'You're all scared of him,' Helen said bitterly when we were asked to leave the local TV satellite shop owned by one of them in case we were overheard by somebody. 'You go around bragging about how you'd do this and that, yet as soon as you get the chance, you're nothing but cowards.'

NINETEEN

THE MUSICAL ADAPTATION OF a biography I had written of my paternal grandmother the year before we went to live in Ireland, was being put on at the Customs House Theatre on Tyneside, but we could not go for the opening because the *denuncia* was being heard in court on that day.

A few days before, I had had a pain in my right eye tooth and gone to a local Dutch dentist after being warned that Spanish dentists were terrible, and had the nerve removed. He was a smug fellow who kept winking and rolling his eyes at his Spanish nurse-receptionist-wife over his mask at the same time as he was drilling through my tooth, and pursing his lips towards her in a kind of kissing gesture. But there was nothing much I could do about it: frowning from a supine position, with a canine nerve exposed to the elements, is pretty ineffectual.

The following morning during breakfast the tooth snapped off into a slice of bread and honey, so I made an appointment to see the dentist on the morning of the day before we were due in court.

An hour later Edmundo telephoned to say Sr. Férrer needed to see us about the *denuncia* on the morning of the dental appointment, and that it was urgent, so Helen telephoned to change the dental appointment after apologising and explaining why. There were a few minutes silence and then quite astonishingly the dentist himself came on the phone to say he would not be 'messed about', and if I insisted on postponing the appointment, I would have to wait at least three weeks for another. Helen told him we had no choice because we had been called into court, but he said that was none of his business and did I want the 'damned tooth fixed, or didn't I?' When she pointed out that this was Spain and one did not mess around with their courts, his response was to slam the phone down.

On the morning of the day we were to see Sr. Férrer, Edmundo rang to say Sr. Férrer could not see us until 8 o'clock that night. It was an appointment we could well have done without. My tooth had an uncapped hole that went straight to the root and I could envisage the bluish white nerve spasmodically flapping around in my mouth like a hectic little minnow while Sr. Férrer spun in his chair, first this way, then that, letting his long, labrador-like tongue loll out before coming out with some ridiculous platitude.

He had refused to do anything about Val Spiers' retaining ownership of the car, on the grounds that it would have to be a separate court case, so we had not invited him to involve himself in the matter of the *denuncia*, a matter which predated our association with him; yet he had apparently taken it upon himself to advise us how to go about it, as though it were of some importance. 'Tell them not to bring that "hombre",' he had said to Edmundo, the 'hombre' being poor Humberto, the man with probably more scholarship, humanity and a better sense of justice, than all the abogados in Alicante put together, but wore a pink anorak and carried all his belongings in a ragged rucksack.

Until late that night Helen and I tried to convey to Sr. Férrer how the *denuncia* had derived, and the point of it, which was to establish that the Spiers were highly unreasonable people. But once an opinion had formed in Sr. Férrer's head, like every Spaniard we had ever met, it was impossible to disabuse him of it.

'You have no case!' he finally announced with a triumphant smile. We now realised why we had been called in and why I had had to sacrifice my dental appointment. It had nothing at all to do with advising us as about court tactics, but to dissuade us from proceeding with the *denuncia*.

'Los Spiers *estan muy, muy trastornado*' (The Spiers are very, very upset) he sympathised.

'How do you know that?' I expostulated in an irritated amalgam of English and Spanish.

Through Edmundo we learned that the Spiers' abogado, a certain Sr. Luis Víbora-Masson had been on to him. Sr. Férrer had stopped listening to my Spanish and old Edmundo was having a hard time of it, not knowing, I suspected, whether his first loyalty should be to his ex-colleague and neighbour, or his fellow language student and new friend. Suddenly Sr. Férrer's arms were up, head shaking and chair spinning with irritation. He spoke to Edmundo for about five minutes, so rapidly that I could hardly understand a word, then stood up. Edmundo turned to us with as much excitement as he could inject into his anxious, perplexed and weary voice.

'If you cancel the *denuncia* tomorrow, Sr. Férrer thinks he can persuade their *abogado* to settle the *vivienda* case and get them to give you your money back without having to take the matter to court.

'What..!? Is he sure?'

'Si, si, si, si si!'

'How's that?'

'It sounds crazy to me,' Helen said.

'I don't like it,' I said to Edmundo. 'We came here thinking he was going to give us advice about how to go on in court tomorrow. Not to be persuaded to drop the whole thing at this late hour.'

'He's your abogado now. You chose him. He knows the

Spanish law better than me. If you pay him, it makes sense to take his advice.'

Why, as a senior civil servant who had studied law himself, Edmundo should be so in awe of this fellow, I could not understand. However, we trusted Edmundo absolutely, so with some serious misgivings, we agreed. We were to come to the office tomorrow at 9 a.m., sign a paper and leave the rest to him.

'This *buenos fe* (good faith) and *carácter razonable* (reasonable nature) of yours will be much to your advantage,' Edmundo assured us as we retreated to the lift.

When we got home, not knowing whether we had done the right thing or not, we had a few hours fretful sleep and were back in Alicante without breakfast, I still with my troublesome tooth. Sr. Férrer was not in his office; instead we were attended to by his beautiful colleague and her colleague. I could not speak for Helen, but wished someone like the beautiful colleague were handling the case. In Spain everybody is judged by their looks and she looked far better than Sr. Férrer. To our surprise and contrary to what Sr. Férrer had said would happen, we were straightaway whisked off to the court, just as we were, in the kind of clothes fit only for briefly signing a form in a pokey little side office and then popping off to relax for a day on the beach.

When we arrived at court, we hardly recognised the Spiers. Fully prepared, he was in a dark suit, white shirt and tie, with highly-polished black shoes – clobber no doubt straight out of his Freemason's wardrobe – hair cut, Brylcreamed and combed like a little boy's at Sunday School, hands clasped in front of him and head lowered as in a kind of childish supplication.

His civet of a wife was well out of the cut-away denim shorts she normally pranced about in, and looking quite homely in a plain skirt, like the little boy's Sunday-school sister. Both looked nervous. Sr. Masson was with them, plus an interpreter and several other people. Our *guapas* (beautiful women) went over and had a few words with him and all three smiled. A few minutes elapsed while he translated something to the Spiers and then there was jubilation from Lew who was patting Sr. Masson on the back and practically whooping. A few minutes later he had his sleeve rolled up and was showing him his watch.

'Guess how much I paid for this..? I could get you one next time I go to the Elephant and Castle, and I promise to keep my commission to a minimum, ha-ha-ha-ha!'

Sr. Masson's eyes were glazed as he looked at his client, glanced at his watch and grimaced before quickly turning away and disappearing.

Half an hour later Helen and I signed a beautifully printed document that we were handed by the judge, which not only withdrew all charges against the Spiers but was a declaration of good faith that barely stopped short of a grovelling apology. We knew for certain then that we had made a very big mistake. It was the first time in my life I had ever followed advice which I felt was not only wrong, but abject, and we did not know whether to feel badly let down, or thoroughly deceived. The court had not been apprised of Sr. Férrer's reasons for our withdrawal, nor of his deductive reasoning as to our generous character. As a consequence we must have appeared like time-wasters and weak, the kind who make a threat and then shrink when the time comes to carry it out. We had been hustled through like a couple of nincompoops who could not think for themselves. The way I looked could not have helped our credibility either: aside from our casual clothes, not only was I missing an eye tooth, but its opposite on the bottom had snapped on the way into Alicante. A pain similar to having two long cold needles twisted around in opposite directions in the same eyeball, was nothing; the critical thing was that nowadays anybody with even one tooth missing out of a total of thirty-two, was regarded as a down-and-out; two, and you were rated as what we used to call a 'rag-and-bone merchant'.

Ever since I had contracted my illness nearly thirty years previously, which had severely compromised my immune system long before 'immune system' become a buzz term, my teeth had been decomposing at a rate faster than a peeled apple on a warm windowsill, and I no longer had access to my dentist friend in Ireland who had used all kinds of measures to preserve them. But the Dutch winking dentist would no more give me an appointment for the second tooth, than he would for the first, though Helen did her best to persuade him while I made tortured faces in the background. I had told her that whatever she did, she was neither to beg, nor be too nice. If the blighter was in any way reluctant, she was to let him go for good; we would find somebody else, even if it meant driving to Portugal: the Portuguese were supposed to like the English.

That night the Forsyths telephoned to say the Spiers were bragging that we had funked the *denuncia* at the last minute and had had to beg the Spiers' for forgiveness. They were presently throwing a party to celebrate our cowardice and incompetence. Just what we needed.

We were so glad to get away, and it was great to be back in canny old Shields. My publisher met us at Newcastle airport in the teeming rain and took us straight to the theatre, via a brief call at a fish-and-chip shop on the way. We had had nothing to eat for hours but it was so late we just had to stuff in what we could, sitting in his car, and recycle the rest into the Tyne which flowed only a few yards behind the theatre – a tragedy given Shields' fish and chips were the best in the world.

The show was very enjoyable and it felt so good to be warmly received by relatives, friends and strangers. After nine months as *pensionistas*, which is nothing like as rebellious as it sounds to the non-Hispanic ear, it was wonderful to see a smile come on people's faces when they saw us. I had to speak to the cast and to many other people, as well as sign books, but on Tyneside my host of faults, cosmetic and otherwise, did not seem to matter, for none of the people who spoke to me or shook my hand had gold crowns or porcelain teeth. It was a busy four days which went some way towards restoring our sense of value, and even the weather was not too bad.

In two weeks we were back to Spain and out again, this time to Belfast for Alice, our eldest daughter's wedding.

'Dad! What happened?' Alice was in tears before we were through Customs. 'You look like a tramp! You can't have your photograph taken looking like that..! What's happened to him, Mam?'

Trust a daughter to see everything in terms of a wedding photo… She had me at her dentist the next day and he made a temporary repair to both teeth in less than an hour, at a fraction of the cost the Dutchman would have charged, and I kidded myself that I once again looked like an ancient matinée idol.

As soon as we returned to Spain, I went to see the Dutchman, handed him a list of typed complaints and requested he read them. As though dumbstruck, he leaned back against his treatment chair and very slowly read what I had written. On his walls were a series of framed documents which, on first glance, appeared to be certificates or diplomas testifying to his skills, but on closer examination proved to be letters, mostly in Dutch, stating he had attended various seminars, and photographs of what appeared to be dentists' garden parties.

He passed my letter to his receptionist-nurse-wife-lover without finishing.

'This is the first time anything like this has happened to me…' he said with a shattered look on his face.

'It's the first time it's ever happened to me,' I replied. 'Anyway, I'm giving you the opportunity to consider what I've said and make a reply.'

He exchanged glances with his partner who did not say a word but handed him back the letter. He resumed reading for a few minutes, then tossed it down.

'A patient can't talk to a doctor like this, bringing him a piece of paper...'

'The fact that you're not a doctor isn't the point,' I said. 'But if you were, and I were your patient and thought you had treated me badly, I'd have every right to complain. I could have gone to your association or an *abogado*, but didn't. I came straight to you, and you should appreciate that. And what I have written is a formal letter of complaint...not just a piece of paper.'

Two days later I got a letter from him saying my treatment had been terminated and under no circumstances would I ever again be given an appointment. I wrote to the Dutch Dental Association in Holland, giving details of my experience but only received a very guarded reply from its lawyers saying it was a matter for the Spanish Dental Association and refusing to tell me whether my man was still a member of their association. I then wrote to the Spanish Dental Association and it took several shots to get a reply saying they would investigate. And that was that. From then on, they never replied to anything. The Spanish had a habit of not replying to letters, often taking months before so much as acknowledging receipt, and in our experience a satisfactory outcome to a complaint was never an option. Spain has produced some wonderful writers, ones who have produced works of inordinate length and beauty, but none who could write a satisfactory letter in answer to a complaint, not about anything.

We had heard no more about the 'deal' with the Spiers' *abogado*, so assumed there had been none, and that for one reason or another, Sr. Férrer had got us to throw away an opportunity to chalk up our first mark against the Spiers and make fools of ourselves in the process. Whether he had been taken in by Víbora-Masson, was in league with him, as the Forsyths were convinced, or was simply afraid of him, as we felt was the case, we would probably never know.

Edmundo worked for his government and I had worked for mine, yet our view of public servants was very different, and our views on patriotism likewise. When I asked him if he thought we stood as much chance of getting justice in a Spanish court as a pair of Spaniards, I clearly struck a very Spanish nerve. Outwardly he reacted as though such a suggestion were an affront, yet I think the gentle soul really harboured few illusions about the judicial system in his country and probably felt the way to deal with somebody like Lew Spiers would be, as in the days of his youth during the *Franquismo*: take him to a disused quarry, shoot him a number of times in the back of the head and cover it with a few shovelfuls of lime. Nonetheless, in his solicitations on our behalf, his energy and patience were unfailing and I do not know what we would have done without him. Apart from anything else, he always had Sr. Férrer's respect, and Férrer his.

By now, sadly, the fun had gone out of our weekly Spanish-English sessions because too much time was being spent talking about Spiers and the *vivienda*, and Edmundo was becoming like a humble messenger unable or unwilling to convey the nuances that were so vital to prosecuting our case with any ingenuity. It was due to his good grace that the friendship endured because by now there must have been increasingly little in it for him. He offered himself and his services and we had no option but to use him, hoping the relationship would survive and someday continue along happier and more mutually beneficial lines. Humberto was right when he said Edmundo was not only a highly 'atypical' Spaniard, but a 'treasure'. He was most certainly different from any other Spaniard we had met. What a pity he was now stuck between us and Férrer, and what a shame we had put him there.

One night we were called to Férrer's office to answer a charge brought by the Spiers to the effect that we had not gone to Ireland at Christmas, but had instead remained in Spain to 'create mischief for the Spiers'.

We could hardly believe what we were hearing… Why should it matter to anybody whether we had gone to Ireland, Timbuctu, or stayed in Spain for Christmas? But it was soon plain that it was no laughing matter as far as our advocate was concerned, and for him the only way the allegation could be dealt with was to prove we had gone to Ireland, or let the *abogados* argue the issue in a court of law.

Incredibly, Helen, who I was always nagging at for not regularly emptying her handbag, still had the receipt for a set of three pairs of Y-Front underpants I had bought at Marks and Spencers when we were in Belfast during the critical Christmas, and flushed with triumph we thrust the receipt at Sr. Férrer with faces that must have been a tad too elated, because after briefly studying it and not being able to make head nor tail of it, he pronounced it was not serious enough to be entered as evidence in a Spanish court of law. We would have to do better, such as producing the airline ticket we bought to get there. It was now many months since and we had only managed to produce the underpants receipt by sheer fluke. However, as luck would have it, Helen even had the receipt of payment for the tickets. But that would not do either. It had to be the tickets themselves, something we did not have because they had been retained by Iberia, the airline that had carried us.

'Right, then.' Sr. Férrer clicked his tongue perversely. 'You'll have to get them back from the airline.'

Three times in one morning we went to and from our house and Sr. Férrer's office in Alicante with alternative equally unacceptable documentary bits and pieces. Finally we went to the travel agent, a really uppity so-and-so who remembered having argued with me about the flight time when we had bought the tickets. Basically, I had been claiming that 3 a.m. on the 22nd December meant it referred to the morning flight, whereas she maintained it referred to the night flight on the 21st.

We had had quite a to-do with my drawing diagrams and clocks on the backs of brochures because she said she had no spare paper, and ended with my leaving the office with my head clasped in my hands to stop it bursting. She had kept half a dozen customers waiting while, in spite of her intelligence, she demonstrated her ignorance with much flinging about of arms and tosses of the head. But she was just the person to deal with Sr. Férrer. She was absolutely perfect!. And to top it all, he thought women were useless. So I told her. And anticipating that she would almost certainly refuse to spend her priceless time telephoning a male *abogado*, I said we had tried to get him to telephone her but he would not deign to deal with a mere travel agent on such an important matter, which was true in spirit if not exactly in fact.

'Will he not..? Is that so..? Right!'

With that, she picked up the phone, got through to Férrer's office, demanded to speak to him immediately and told him that international law required head airline offices – in Spain's case, Madrid – retain all original airline tickets for a minimum of five years. Any law student would know that. And that was it. He could not have got more than an initial *'Buenas'* in before she trumped him by slamming down the phone. This time Helen and I were all smiles when we left her office, and as our unwitting gladiator tossed her hair, believing she had once again capped a couple of stupid uppity English, we waved fondly.

One afternoon in the main street of Jemina we bumped into Miguel, the boy builder; actually, he saw us, hailed, and ran up. He was effusively friendly, enquiring how we were and what we were doing. When we told him we were taking the Spiers to court, he manifested great delight, though I found it hard to believe he did not already know, since everybody else seemed to. He said he would have taken them to court himself, were it not so costly.

'What about being a witness for us, then?' I urged. 'You can tell them how you never had sufficient resources to build a proper house. Not even an architect's plan. That you weren't properly paid and everything. It's a real chance for you to say what you think. You don't need to be afraid of him because the court will protect you. And it won't cost you a peseta.'

'Huh!' he said, showing how he had picked up a fair bit of English by now. 'I not afraid of Lew Spiers! I could pick block and smash head open.' He demonstrated, making all the necessary gestures in the street, finishing up with stamping his boot on the pavement in an action indicating the dashing of Lew's brains to powder. People sitting at a nearby café with beers in their hands, looked on with apprehension.

'Yes, but now you don't need to. You've got a baby, remember... How is he, by the way?'

'*Bueno, bueno* (Fine, fine). *Gracias, Señor* (Thank you, sir.) You tell me day and I will tell judge everything. You get your money back and I get mine.'

The next time we heard from the Forsyths, it was to learn the Spiers had a 'For Sale' notice up outside the *vivienda* and a picture of it with details in the windows of several *inmobiliarias* in town. *Increíble!* (Incredible!) A court case was ensuing to determine the ownership of the property and decide if it were a place fit to live in, and we had receipts for the money we had invested in it, and here in broad daylight the Spiers were trying to sell it. This required another appointment with the great man, this time with Edmundo and Janet to make sure there were no misunderstandings. We had to get a court injunction to prevent the sale as soon as possible, or all would surely be lost. But our advocate was not only quite unruffled by our agitation, he seemed quite amused.

'There is absolutely nothing we can do,' he said, putting his hands behind his head and pushing his chair back to reveal his long legs, cashmere cardigan, beautiful watch, hairy wrists and strangely flat crotch. How he loved these negative, yielding words, sounds of pure capitulation and incompetence, of hopelessness and despair that we had heard so many times before. He beamed to all and sundry. This was the way to solve a case: cast down one's cap on a cow pat and invite one's opponent to jump on it, fall upon one's sword, get the train to Barcelona and jump off the top of the Sagrada Familia without a parachute.

'*Señores Smithwhyte deben entender. Ésta no es Irlanda. Ésta es España.*' (The Smithwhites must understand. This is not Ireland. This is Spain.)

If only we had received a pound every time we had heard those words.

'What if he flogs it, then hops it?' I snapped, no longer bothering to use words that could be easily translated.

He continued to smile after Janet's translation, and I had no idea whether or not he had understood a word; but he was out of his chair now and that meant we had to be out of ours. Exasperating and no doubt expensive meetings like this, convened quickly because of some vital piece of information we had learned, or thought we had learned, seemed to be serving no purpose. They were difficult to arrange because Sr. Férrer was often at court, teaching at the university, or out of the country; and Janet, our official interpreter, whom he demanded we always bring with us these days, was also very busy. Everything was being done totally differently from what we expected and from what we thought logical or fair. Janet thought he did not like her because he would not reply to her faxes or return her telephone calls, but neither would he reply to ours. I was forever sending him letters with information and documents, and requesting specific action or information, and he never ever – not even once – replied. By now, from talking to the many people we met, we were convinced that neither the courts nor the *abogados* shed any tears over disputes among *extranjeros*. It seemed to be a case of: 'Let them get on with it!', the way it is often said about rival gangsters, when what is intended is to let them put a bullet between each other's eyes so the rest of the world can be rid of them. At this time, the English newspapers were full of tales of miscarriages of justice involving property in Spain, with *abogados* and *jueces* (judges) buying up confiscated property for next to nothing.

Towards the end of March Humberto came to the flat to stay the weekend. It had taken some time to negotiate because although he was a 'free agent' in that he did not work for anybody and lived by selling his books and translating, he would not commit himself to anything more than a day or two in advance. He had to be allowed to 'just be', to move here or there like a zephyr, albeit one with an old pink anorak and rucksack on its back and a heavy briefcase in its hand, to contemplate or simply sit and be aware of the enzymes in his intestines digesting his last meal.

Notwithstanding his self-imposed freedom, he was always punctual, so it was a surprise he should be half an hour late, and Helen and I were just wondering what the fates had decreed, when the telephone rang to yield a voice almost speechless with pathos and indignation complaining that the *porteros* (concierges) had shooed him away from the entrance to our block. They had called him a '*vagabonda*' (tramp) and when we laughed, he thought it not the least bit funny. He needed us to come and vouch for him immediately because they were threatening to send for the police if he did not leave the ancient *extranjero* reservation immediately. The whole thing must have strained his egalitarianism to the last thread, so we got down to the *portero's* lodge as quickly as we could, gave the nod and got him in.

As soon as he was safely inside the flat, albeit feeling like a refugee, Helen showed him his room, and the first thing he did was to pull sheets out of his rucksack, explaining that he did not want water and energy to be wasted on a mere night's soiling by him; he would use his own bedding which had only been in use for a relatively short while. With anybody else, one would not know whether to feel impressed or offended, but we were always prepared for a few variations when our favourite Catalan came to tea. We knew that first of all, he would lay down a few ground rules because he always did that wherever he went. They were more exhortations than decrees and he would explain them in terms of economy, ecology and liberty, quoting the likes of the French Rousseau or Russian Bakunin. If you were out with him, and parched, and suggested going for a drink, he would say something like, 'I think in fourteen minutes it would be better.' So, trying to keep disappointment out of your voice, and cracks from opening up in your throat, you would reply 'Rightio,' as though he were of course right. Then when the fourteen minutes were up, he would take out his little bottle of well water and offer it around, and you would feel like a Philistine for saying you would prefer an iced coke.

This time, when lunch was ready and Helen called us in, he demurred with 'I think I will step out of doors to prepare myself first.' He obviously meant the balcony because there was no way he would have left the building unaccompanied. We waited for quarter of an hour while Helen tried to keep the meal hot without spoiling it, and then nosed his way in delicately, like a mouse leaving its hole, and you could almost see the faint hairs on his upper lip vibrating. Naturally he did not consume 'hot' meals, nothing hotter than normal body temperature that is, so we had to sit and wait until the food had cooled to 37ºC, something he measured with the inside of his wrist, like a nursing mother checking the temperature of a bottle of warmed milk for her baby. His diet was a rare one and each time we dined with him, we learned more of the finer points, but this time Helen just put out everything we had that she thought would appeal to a man of his taste, and let him get on with it. One thing he really liked, was apple pie, and he used to say – obviously from American movies – 'momma's home-made apple pie'. Helen always kept some for him to take away, wrapped in the minimum of paper, which was the way he liked it, but through time he started bringing an empty pot in his mochila (knapsack), ready to receive the spare pie or any other pickings.

'Have you any bread more than three days old, Helen?' he murmured.

Helen was more circumspect with him than I was, and she just stood, not knowing what to say, and wary of giving offence.

'You mean stale bread?' I said.

'That is an adjective that could be used,' the scholar mused, 'but there are others… such as "mature"… and that other wonderful old English word, "ripe".'

'We normally chuck the stale stuff out,' I persisted. 'For the birds.'

'Ah,' he said, pausing and looking up at an oblique angle, as though what I had said might carry some weight. He would do this if he thought you were being facetious, and it was quite excruciating, especially when he said no more and you gathered he thought it unworthy of an intelligent reply.

In our house he had difficulty imposing the 'no-speaking' rule during a meal that lasted twenty minutes for me, thirty for Helen, and another quarter of an hour for himself. I think he had adapted his eating habits to that of a wild animal in that he could go for days without, and then gorge when the opportunity presented itself. Yet he was such a neat and orderly eater, and because he only ate what he liked and thought was good for him, he was a pleasure to watch. If people at dinner tables and in restaurants ate like him, there would never be any wars, I thought. He had brought a gift of three apples and after the meal asked if he could have one and be allowed to choose it himself. He then got up from the table and picked the one with the biggest bruise.

Afterwards we wanted to take him to the Casa de Cultura (Art Centre) in El Jemina but he would not come in the car because cars were the bane of his life and he would only consider travelling in one if he were in extremis, such as travelling to his own funeral. That was why he wrote to the newspapers almost every week, seeking to have all private cars banned. So instead of having a shower, tea, and then being chauffeured in comfort, he set off on foot an hour and a half before us, without wasting any water on a shower. The principles by which he lived meant his life would be frugal, humble and largely intellectual. Some of them were rather anti-social because he was a very private individual, yet he had an immense number of what he called 'friendly acquaintances' in so many walks of life, and every one of them made allowances for his eccentricities and admired him for his single-mindedness. We had known him for only a short time but trusted him completely. He said Edmundo was atypically Spanish, but he was surely so himself, not least because of his utter lack of greed and genuine detestation of materialism. We would not bother hiding a useless little yuppie innovation bought from a catalogue when Edmundo came for tea, but would hide all traces of such things whenever Humberto was due to put in an appearance. He did not always complain but had more ways of showing disapproval than the Inuit reputedly had words for describing snow.

When we arrived at the theatre, he was coming up one of the side streets with an extra plastic bag: Saturday night was a good time to get a bargain on perishables and he would have combed the area looking.

The majority of concerts at the *Casa de Cultura* were free, and if a charge had to be made, it would be trifling. I did not know about Humberto, because I did not think he was much interested in the visual arts, as opposed to literature, but we thought many of them excellent and winced at the disregard shown them by members of the audience, many of whom I suspect only came because the shows were free. It was a joy to see local working-class women with their best clothes on, drenched in the all-purpose, deodorant perfume that was sold in every corner-shop supermarket, to go with their dyed and puffed, 'Jemina Nut Brown' coiffure, some always coming late, the way local two-bit dignitaries always did to be noticed. They would saunter down the aisle ten minutes after the show started, push their way into the middle of a packed row, stand and pivot a few times to see if they could see anyone to wave to, and then push their way back out of the row in the opposite direction, only to return to the main aisle and begin their performance all over again in some other part of the theatre.

Naturally, people like this would not approve of somebody who looked as though he had sneaked off an immigrant boat and was hiding from the *guardia*, and because Humberto's bags were interfering with the legs of whoever was sitting next to him, Helen and I got him to move between herself and me. But he knew why and was not altogether happy with it. They were all polite to us, but to poor Humberto, these working-class women with working-class minds would barely conceal their contempt; the last thing they wanted was to have their varicosed veins haemorrhaging beneath their seats because of a wound caused by a spear of near fossilised celery.

Once the lights were out, Humberto produced three huge fermenting pears which instantly turned to mush when we tried to pluck them from the bag. In addition he had bought a packet of Kerrygold Irish butter as a little gift for Helen. Like Edmundo, and all Spanish, he never came to the house without bringing a gift of some sort. It might be a two-weeks-old *catalán* newspaper containing an interesting article, a brochure about a Tango concert that took place a week ago, a *catalán* independence tie-pin or tinylag), but there was always something: Spaniards are very generous people.

TWENTY

Spain, a country of extremes, with superabundances in some things and dearths in as many others, produced inexhaustible quantities of truly beautiful women. Not American bimbo lookalikes, although there were plenty of those as well, but exquisite human animals. Sheer loveliness, however, was not enough for the average Spanish male. Because of his intense affinity with the mammary gland, a phenomenon found otherwise only in the true marsupial, his ideal female should have hugely accessible breasts, and it seemed he could not reach orgasm unless she also had long fair hair. The latter phenomenon arose from the notorious, reputedly free-loving Swedes who invaded Spanish tourist resorts in the 1960s. As a consequence, whereas hydrogen-peroxide-bleached hair turned a woman into a bimbo Venus, exquisite, natural and beautifully dark brown silkiness would not raise a column of mercury by a single milligram. However, instead of educating their males into becoming less dependant on the teat and more appreciative of, say, the pancreas or brain, public health programmes concentrated on teaching him how to go through the motions of reproducing himself without simultaneously creating a plague of venereal disease. According to the very explicit women's magazines, which maintained that women also had preferences, these seemed to really rile white Spanish men and was one of the reasons so many treated their women badly.

From a country which, when we first visited it in the 1950s, women were not allowed to go around bare-legged, bare-armed, bare-headed or unchaperoned, to one where males and females issued sexual challenges to each other in public, on television and in magazine interviews, was quite disorientating. Perhaps this was why the Spanish were so candid in adverts dealing with vexations like incontinence, except that they implied it only happened to women, especially attractive ones who leaked when reaching up, bending down, sneezing or laughing.

After many months, Trev Hall's men finally started digging the foundations for our new house. When we had bought the plot the previous year, our impression had been of a very loosely connected *urbanización* at the frontier of a wilderness, but now there were whole new streets with people living in them or foreign owners waiting to claim them. In every direction, as far as the eye could see, in inhospitable gullies and on the hair-raising sides of mountains, there were half and three-quarter completed houses. The summer was extraordinarily hot and because Spanish builders, like so many businesses, closed down for the whole of August, any still working charged extra.

A quarter of a mile away from where our house was going to be, in the middle of the landscape leading to the sea, a Scottish estate agent was bulldozing the tops off five hills which had almost certainly stood for millennia. He said he had no interest whatsoever in a 'few hillocks', and in just a couple of months had replaced the crests with five 'super de-luxe villas'. If the owners wanted nature and wildlife, they could put it there once they had bought his dwellings. He said that in Spain it was infinitely quicker and cheaper to go ahead and build whatever you wanted, and if some 'busybody' from the *Ayuntamiento* came poking around, you simply negotiated a fine.

In the incipient street where our plot was situated, the next plot on the lower side was vacant, the one on the upper built on and owned by a Dutch couple who lived and worked in Holland, and for most of the year rented the large house on it to badly behaved Dutch holidaymakers. By arranging their rentals in Holland they excluded both Spanish and Dutch authorities from their transactions and avoided paying tax to either. This was a common ploy with foreigners who owned property in Spain, and because the holidaymakers who came for two weeks at a time treated the area as a drunken playground and showed no consideration for anyone permanently living in the neighbourhood, they were very unpopular. For much of the summer and autumn, twice as many renters as the house could comfortably contain, packed in for a cheap holiday and spent all day yelling and screaming in and around the swimming pool, with their radios blaring.

Across the road from where we were going to be was a house occupied by a Spanish family who regarded *extranjeros* as a curse and refused to speak to us from the moment we first went over to introduce ourselves. Throughout the years we would live there, experiencing various trials and tribulations of life, they would never once greet us or respond to our greeting, even though we heard that when our house was being built, during which time we were of course living elsewhere, every day after the workmen had gone, the whole family would come over with drinks and cigars, the kids with their toys, to thoroughly scrutinise the place.

Apart from the Dutch, relatives, friends and old neighbours of English ex-pats came to spend their annual summer holidays here, but not as paying guests. They expected the full hotel treatment: being picked up from the airport, accommodated, fed and watered, taken out for day trips, including the Benidorm Palace shows and theme parks, and plied with drinks and refreshments around the swimming pool more or less all day. Many expats became so fed up they started taking holidays back in England during August, the hottest and arguably worst time in Spain. This way they would not be here to act as hosts to hordes of visitors, who, apart from anything else, proved very expensive. One constantly heard of old friendships breaking up because of too much drinking, hooligan parties, and sexual pressures.

The apartment we were staying in in Muchavista was light and airy and Helen liked it very much with its large windows and flowing, pseudo-lace curtains. It was less than a stone's throw from the beach, not much further to Jemina and the shops, and the sound of the sea at night was very soothing. Our neighbours were mostly English and could easily be heard through the thin walls, as could their nostalgic Forties dance-band music when they played their old LPs to cheer themselves up, and we would imagine them clinging together in a slow foxtrot as tears collected in wrinkles, and hankies dabbed at sniffling noses. Being in their seventies and eighties, as most of them were, and living amongst their own kind, they managed to preserve their Englishness and ignore the Spanish people, their language and their culture, and as long as they paid their dues, nobody cared. They were selfish, concerned only with their own health, security and comfort, and when one of them vanished, another would quickly replace him or her and hardly anybody notice.

Decrepit though most of them were, if any saw us washing our car in the car park, they would practically abseil from their fourth-floor flat, replaced hips and knees-waiting-for-surgery, notwithstanding, to inform us, with tart politeness, that we could get it done at a particular car-wash for 50 pesetas, and expect gratitude for the briefing. If they saw our washing drying on the balcony, they would hand us a piece of paper neatly folded, with the address of a nearby 'reliable' launderette, written in a very neat hand with a full signature, plus rank, if any, at the bottom. They thought holidaying tenants lowered the tone and were always prompting the likes of Mr Watson, our landlord's 'man in Muchavista', to report petty transgressions to the various owners. Our landlord would dispatch suggested amendments to the regulations, from his Wigan dental practice, and others likewise. The most recent instruction was that Helen and I would have to vacate our flat by the end of May so that a family of summer visitors could be netted and the tooth fairy's income hiked yet again.

Poor working-class people will often keep a little bird in a cage, especially if they do not have a dog, and in Spain it was most likely to be a canary or a mule – the cross between a native singing finch, such as a linnet or a goldfinch, and a canary. Although the Spanish canary is not only smaller than the English border variety, but smaller even than the Irish fancy, it could clearly be heard down in the street from a fifth or sixth floor apartment. It made me wonder if the bird imagined the brightly coloured washing flapping on the nearby balcony, was lush foliage.

The concierges of our block kept a budgerigar which is unusual because although budgies are easy to tame, they do not sing; but because there was no room in the dark and stifling little cubby hole they themselves lived in, they kept it in the foyer. And when the residents' committee voted to give the place a face-lift and the renovators came to chisel off the old tiles and angle-grind the walls and floor, creating clouds of dust and ear-splitting noise which the stairwell amplified like the horn of a gigantic HMV gramophone, the poor budgie was left hanging on the wall long after the grosser ornaments had been removed for their safety. The workmen hammered, drilled and sandblasted around the cage until the very last moment, when they took it off the wall, put it on the floor, and continued, occasionally shoving it along the floor with their foot. This was the same building in which diseased stray cats were being fed and encouraged into apartments by the kind of keen-eyed English ladies who could walk past starving Arabs and never see them.

Generally speaking, I have found that the greater the love for animals, the less for human beings, and with people who have dedicated their lives to animals and birds, it is almost a golden rule. Whatever the relative arguments about bullfighting and foxhunting, there was no question that cruelty towards animals was more prevalent in Spain than anywhere else in Europe. In most pet shops, birds, fish, reptiles and mammals were kept in very poor conditions, overcrowding being the worst and something we had not infrequently encountered in Ireland, although piercing human howls would go up if anyone said so.

Television programmes showed competitions where hundreds of domestic pigeons would be hand-thrown from carrier boxes, one at a time, for men, women and children with automatic shotguns to blast them out of the air; or, far more often, merely maim them and leave them to try to survive. Spears, burning darts and fireworks tied to their horns and tails, and, in the case of 'bullfights', much torture before having a sword thrust deep into their necks, all passed for 'sport'. Confining them to cages so minute they could hardly turn around was the regular way of keeping singing finches, and tame mice were treated as if they were toys, such as getting a bimbo in a scanty bikini to lie in an open coffin filled with them to see how long they could endure – the bimbo that is. Dogs without sufficient food or fresh water were frequently left to guard property. Overgrown puppies that children had lost interest in, or hunters' dogs at the end of the season, were constantly abandoned in wasteland where they became dangerous, a nuisance, or dead. Yet ask a Spaniard how they felt about animals and odds on they would declare they loved them.

TWENTY-ONE

WE HAD SEEN A self-promotional pitch in an English language newspaper, written by a Welsh dentist new to the area, who claimed to be introducing the very latest in computer-aided instruments and aseptic methodology to the Costa Blanca. He spoke of a brave, new, well-informed third-millennium patient who could and should demand all kinds of things, such as an inspection tour of the surgery to make sure everything was perfect. He sounded like the kind of virtuoso we were looking for to set about the mess inside my mouth, so we drove the length of the Costa to make an appointment. His very Spanish wife, the practice's 'manager', was buxom, vivacious, intelligent, spoke excellent English, and when she bent over, something she did a lot for some reason, a ridge of soft hair went down from the base of her spine to disappear, like a column of peace-loving ants, into the long and broad cleft above her knickers.

He was very different. Much younger, awkward, Welsh, nervous and thin, with lank sandy hair, long sticky eyelashes and a pink babyish face, he blushed so easily I reckoned it should be quite easy to read his mind, which might come in handy.

Like many dentists and other medical auxiliaries to whom governments had, for some inexplicable reason, recently granted use of the title 'Dr', although they had neither a doctoral degree, nor the customary courtesy entitlement of a qualified medical doctor, Taffy wore a huge badge with 'Dr.' in front of his name, and constantly referred to himself by the title. From his manner and patter I suspected he had only been qualified a few months, and wondered how he was faring with the natives, given his negligible Spanish and formidable wife.

A glimpse of the expensive diary hidden under the counter when we made the appointment, revealed so much empty space that we realised we were in a position to more or less pick any time and date we wished, and indeed this was the case, although Helen and I had to stand making faces at each other whilst the good 'doctor' and his wife hummed and tutted as they moved metaphorical mountains to squeeze us in.

At the first appointment, the one where a dentist does nothing that he could not do at the start of the first treatment session, he examined the inside of my mouth with a digital camera and pointed out on a screen the various tasks that lay ahead. Behind him, I presumed as a focal point, was an oil painting on the wall of him wearing a mortarboard and gown, with a scroll across his lap and a sublime expression on his face, with his wife, also gowned but looking more like a glamorous stepmother, standing behind him. I would have wagered it had been painted by his sister for her 'O-level' art exam and probably earned her a 'C-'.

Like most artisans these days, he began his critique with tuts and exhalations of shock at the 'cowboys' who had messed up – according to him, 'ridden roughshod' inside my mouth – and a rant to the effect that the Dutchman should be struck off, along with most of the Spanish and other dental chancers operating on the Costa Blanca; not that it was not refreshing to hear a bit of dog-eat-dog in professions that are traditionally tight-lipped about each other.

The following day I went for my first treatment and was told it would be necessary to cut open the gum to expose more of the tooth so it would be easier to get at. Removing gum from around the neck of the tooth would of course reveal more tooth, but it would surely hasten the natural process of gum recession, as well as rendering my mouth more like an old ewe's than it was already. But if that was the only way he could do it, so be it. However, I mentioned that because of the state of my spine I was hypersensitive to pain and my dentist in Ireland had always used a dab of topical anaesthetic before he began.

'We only use that on kids!' he scoffed, though I very much doubted that he removed rings of gum from around kids' teeth.

'Just think of me as one then,' I suggested, but he ignored the request.

While he injected, drilled, filled and prattled away with the kind of anodyne axioms I could imagine him gleaning from 'What to Tell Your Patient', a little dental chapbook his mother might well have got him when, after several attempts, he eventually qualified.

I concentrated on the situation I was in, from a bacteriologist's point of view, bearing in mind his thrift, such as his nurse's tearing the paper tissues into shreds when I asked for something to wipe my mouth with. Was he so tight he recycled the paper tissue, I wondered; did his nurse hang it up to dry on a clothes line? Did he rinse and reuse his disposable needles? Did he dilute his anaesthetic, antibiotics and antiseptics? Because if there was any phenol in the water in his carton cup, it would have to have been in homeopathic quantities, so undetectable was it to any of my senses. By entertaining myself in this way, I managed to deal with the discomfort. My old degenerative illness was notorious for its attack on teeth, as were most of the many antibiotics and opioids I had taken over the years, and I was now down to eight. Ah, what I could do in five minutes with his tools in my hand and him in his chair. For a start, I would remove a few swathes of that baby pink Welsh gum which was covered in froth.

Payment had to be made immediately after each session and the fee turned out to be almost twice as much as normal because a 'surgical procedure' had been used. When I said I thought all dental procedures were supposed to be 'surgical', he turned deep red.

'I'll have you know that what you've just had is the very latest in modern dental surgical technique,' he said, stopping just short of ending with 'laddie'.

'Pruning my gums, you mean?'

Helen says I tend to 'bait' doctors and dentists, but that is hardly fair. It is just that I do not find arrogance and incompetence endearing, or that they sit well together. And considering what these 'health providers' charge, I feel I have the right to criticise, like I would with anything else I paid for. The thing is that for some reason, it is just 'not done'.

While I was having the final rinse with what I estimated to be about one part per million phenol, he informed me that my second-last molar would need removing, and that he would probably need the support of a senior colleague, because, 'like the Titanic iceberg', as he inanely put it, 'so much of it is below the surface'. From this I gathered that despite his fancy equipment and alleged modern methodology, he was not that sure of himself.

When I was paying I asked about a receipt.

'Claiming insurance, are we?' he snickered. 'You'd better see my wife about that then. She deals with those people.'

We were well aware that Spanish shopkeepers and service people were reluctant to give receipts, but expected something different from a dentist.

A week later, I had just arrived for the 'iceberg extraction' when he received a call to say the senior colleague he was expecting could not come, and began panicking. He was looking at the tooth, humming and hahing, going in and out of the room, and looking at it again; it was as though he were contemplating the removal of a two-hundred-year-old tree stump rather than half a molar in an ageing expat's mouth.

'She's not coming,' he uttered, plainly seeking my sympathy.

'I gathered that,' I said. 'But surely you can do it yourself? You are fully qualified, aren't you?'

'Of course I am!' he snapped, face crimson. 'I've got a degree from one of the best dental schools in England.'

'England?' I asked, my voice rising in exaggerated surprise.

'Wales..! And it is every bit as good as any in England.'

'Can we get on with it, then? Or…'

'Course we can!'

Anger had given him courage and without any further delay he jumped in and sliced away the ring of surplus gum that always seemed to irritate him when he saw it around the base of a tooth, certainly around any of mine. He seemed to regard it a vestige of evolution, like the tonsil and appendix always used to be thought, and that had no right to be there. He then grabbed the tooth with his pliers and it instantly snapped off with an unpleasant crunching sound.

'Ugh!' he gasped. 'Quick, nurse! Gauze here! Now!'

Whew! Just like at the most critical juncture of a heart transplant operation.

He then pressed a minute piece of single-layered gauze on the area he had exposed, and through it I could feel shreds of gum wiggling about like the underside of a sea anemone. He then called for more gauze, pressing it down with all his might, whilst turning away and humming a tune utterly devoid of melody, to give me the impression everything was hunky dory. But the blood continued to seep out. He tried whistling but it still did not stop.

Very carefully he withdrew the gauze, but no luck. More snapping and crunching, bleeding and pain, sufficient of the latter to justify a little yelp on my part.

Leaving the nurse to staunch the bleeding, he now hurried away to phone his senior colleague and I could hear him practically imploring her to come and help. For some reason she could not or would not, so he had to settle for advice. However, what she said seemed to do the trick, for after only a quarter of an hour more of chipping and yanking, amidst some gasps of pretty foul exhaled breath, his or mine, there was the explosive sound of a tooth disintegrating, followed by a squeal of delight. Leaving his nurse once again to staunch the blood, the he charged out of his surgery and there was a whoop of joy from the office. I imagined he and his wife were hugging each other in their empty office while tears of relief streamed down his ashen face.

The next visit would be to 'tackle' the bottom incisor, a 'big 'un'; 'big' I took to mean 'really expensive procedure'. But from the moment we got out of this torture chamber, we would leave no stone unturned until we had found a substitute, even if it had to be one of Humberto's locums.

When the Forsyths heard our tale, Gilbert recommended we visit his own man, a half Scottish, half Argentinian fellow who turned out to be the gentlest torturer I would ever have the fortune to encounter. Arriving with time to spare, so eager was I to put my third dental carer to the test, we wandered into one of those 'euro-stretcher' shops that cater for customers with absolutely no taste whatsoever, places Helen hated but I found absolutely fascinating. It was run by an old Scandinavian man or woman – I honestly could not determine which – and had a strange but not altogether off-putting smell which I surmised might have come from what their slightly chipped or cracked vases of plastic flowers – a speciality – had been sprayed with, and Helen was motioning from the doorway to get me to leave, when I bumped into a huge laundry basket chock full of soiled knickers. I considered myself pretty broadminded but was nevertheless aghast.

'Come on!' Helen urged. 'We'll be late!'

'Just go back and take a look at what's in that basket behind those bags of dog biscuits,' I murmured. 'You aren't going to believe it!'

'Why? What's..?'

'Just look and let me know what you think.'

'God! You wouldn't know whether to laugh or call the police!'

'Exactly! Ask how much they cost for half a dozen.'

I was so bemused by what we had just seen, I could have done without an anaesthetic for what turned out to be the most bland dental procedure I had ever submitted to.

A month after our last contact with Sr. Férrer we got a message to say he needed to see us urgently with our *gestor* to find out if we had received a *demanda* (a detailed declaration of a lawsuit) from the Spiers. What *demanda* could the Spiers possibly be sending us.? Astonishingly they were demanding the balance of the money for the *vivienda*: 11,000,000 pesetas, because they were saying we had breached our contract with them. Férrer must have realised this was not the occasion for a great lawyer monologue, and had just sat, fingers grooming his beard, while we chuntered and spluttered. Then he leaned over and murmured something to Janet, slowly rolled back into his chair like a retreating wave, joined his long strong hands as if in prayer, and with his small eyes looking over the tips of his fingers, eyed us to see what calming effect his words might have if properly translated.

'It's a complicated case,' Janet began. 'Who knows what kind of minds we are dealing with? They might only be making a threat to see how we react. Many cat-and-mouse games are played behind the scenes in Spanish justice. On the other hand, maybe now is the time to begin to prepare our own *demanda*…'

'Begin to prepare..?!' We had assumed he had prepared and handed one in months ago… Apparently we must now go to our *notario* to have him grant power of attorney to a list of people he was about to give us. I was hardly listening to the names of people I had never heard of and could not understand why they, as total strangers, should ever have power of attorney over anything appertaining to us. But he assured us we need not worry, all we had to do right now was to carefully make out a cheque in very black ink to '*Al Portador*', sign it, pass it over, and then hop it.

When he drew up our *demanda*, it was, as always, in ornate Spanish, and we had to spend the whole of yet another weekend with dictionaries and books of Spanish verbs, translating it first into archaic English, then into something that made modern sense. After we had done the best we could, we added what we wanted to say in English, translated that into what we hoped would pass for Cervantes Castilian Spanish, and took it back first thing on the Monday morning. It would have cost a fortune to have Janet do it all. It was one thing to interpret, where grammar and spelling was irrelevant and meaning only approximate, but written translation was a different kettle of fish altogether. However, what we did seemed to have put the kibosh on the Spiers' *demanda*, because we never heard another thing about it. Maybe our translation had 'knocked them for six', as we English say in our Anglo-Saxon cricketing balderdash.

TWENTY-TWO

WHEN WE TOLD HUMBERTO we had to move out of our flat in Muchavista and find somewhere else to live because our English dental landlord was turning us out, instead of bleating 'How unfair!' or showing any other kind of pointless sympathy, he thought for a while and then asked: 'Does it have to be on the coast?'

'No.'

'Would fifty miles inland be all right?'

'Certainly.'

'And no more than, say, thirty-thousand pesetas a month?'

'Fine, yes.'

'Right.'

A few days later there was a call from someone called Valentí, who spoke not a word of English, offering us the use of his flat in Cocentaina, a town to the north east, near Alcoi, at the far side of the Carrasqueta mountains.

That weekend, when he had finished his work as a *catalán-castellano* teacher and translator, we picked up a gently smiling thirty-year-old man with thick, jet black wavy hair, from the flat he rented in Alicante, to drive him to the one he owned in Cocentaina. He sat in the back, stocky and as stiff as any of my concrete saints, exuding complete confidence, and when Helen expressed pleasure at the majestic fields of sunflowers and poppies by which we were passing, to our utter delight he began to softly sing: 'Amapola', (Pretty Little Poppy) and continued, verse after verse, until he had finished the whole song, word perfect, and for a few moments both Helen and I were bereft of speech.

Valentí did not have a car but very probably had a licence, and in any case clearly believed he could drive better than any Englishman, so kept telling me which way I should go around a roundabout, that I should stop whenever we came to a red traffic light, get going again when it turned green, and other things in the same vein. In fact, there was not a single button I pressed or lever pulled, without his first having ordered it in the manner of an army driving instructor.

'Thanks for the tips,' I said when we arrived at his hometown, and he nodded gravely.

His flat was on the third floor of the only fairly modern apartment block in an ancient square called the *Plaça de l'Església* (Church Square in *catalán*, or rather, its derivative, *valenciano*), next to the church itself, and Valentí very proudly led us up the stairs, using one key after another and explaining the purpose and idiosyncrasies of each. Inside, the flat was modest but immaculate, and older than any habitation we had been in in Spain. Because of this, it more closely matched our conception of 'Spanish' and was charmingly dour.

We inspected the rooms, checked the firmness of the bed, examined the facilities, internal and external, asked pertinent questions, alternately sniffed and frowned, had a confab in private in one of the rooms, the way one does, and then announced we would take it and move in on the 30th June. Valentí, now bespectacled and respectfully reticent, merely nodded.

'And how much will it, er, be, Valentí?' I queried on the way downstairs.

'*Lo he dicho. Nada.*' (I told you... Nothing.)

'*Nada?*'

'*Nada.*'

He was saying he had told us that when he first rang us, and indeed he had, but I had assumed I had misheard him. Now he would hear no more talk of it, and walked off, mumbling '*Hasta luego*' (See you later) and leaving us feeling very, very embarrassed.

It was a great relief to have somewhere to stay, because our new house was coming on painfully slowly, the work gang frequently deserting to sites where owners were prepared to pay more to have their houses finished first. Whenever we complained to Trev Hall about how long it was taking, he would excuse himself by saying 'They're the laziest, messiest, most contrary buggers I've ever met. They won't do a thing you tell them and always think they know better. Look at them the wrong way, and they're off to somebody else and you're left with a client threatening to sue. And they love that. There's nothing they would like better than to see you in the shit. They don't know the meaning of the word 'gratitude', let alone 'loyalty'. I've been here since before some of them were born and pay them their wages and stamps and give them all their holidays, yet underneath they despise me because I'm English. Every Friday afternoon they take off to a bar at lunchtime and I have to drive around looking for it so I can pay them their wages before they put in a complaint. Plus I have to pay for whatever refreshments they've had. Yet whenever there's a problem, no matter how small, every one of them will happily gang up on me.'

But he was no better. Every time we went to him to complain, we would come away feeling sorry for him, and half an hour later would be kicking ourselves because he was such a con merchant. He was a fairly handsome fellow with golden highlights that his hairdresser wife put in his quiff to make him look like Robert Redford who was her favourite film star, and because Trev really fancied himself. He had a way of appealing to the motherliness in women, but had not long been under contract to us before he stopped appealing to me. Like us, he came from Tyneside, and that, of course, with all of us now living in the same foreign land, was fatal for us. 'Philanderer' was too good a word for him, and he and his phony hair made me wince when he so cavalierly spouted his asides about his Saturday-night lap-club women, when he was driving us to look for tiles or bathroom accessories, as though neither his wife nor Helen, existed.

Soon after we had made arrangements with Valentí regarding moving in, Humberto left Alicante before the annual *hogueras* (bonfires and fireworks) which he abhorred, started in June. The Spanish had a fascination with fire, and in summer when the great ball of it in the sky was at its most intense, drought a severe problem and the risk of forest fires at its most dire, they would light umpteen others here on earth as a kind of homage.

Up to a hundred bonfires were lit on one night in the city of Alicante to celebrate the feast of St Juan, and hundreds of thousands of fireworks set off. It was not done on wasteland away from residential areas or historic buildings; all conflagration was planned to occur in the centre of the city. Pyres were made from collages of huge Disneyesque figures (*mazcletas*) that cost millions of euros to make, and reached almost to the roofs of the closely surrounding buildings, in *plazas* (squares) that were usually relatively small. The figures were made of papier-mâché and painted, and when they were ignited, they melted, crashed down and broke up, pouring out clouds of polluting smoke and red hot flakes of debris that filled the air over the whole city.

At some fiestas, like the Valencian Falla, enormous constructions were made out of masses of flowers, though mercifully not doused with petrol and put to the torch. No fiesta in Spain was worth a light unless it involved fireworks, and even though nothing in nature would seem to mix less well than flowers and fireworks – the yin and yang of Spanish celebrations – the Spanish were pragmatic about nature, and quite pitiless when it came to trees. From them they draped strings of fireworks, and they allowed the flames of bonfires to scorch their branches as well as consume foliage.

Little regard was likewise shown for animals and birds and old and sick people who must have dreaded the season when they could not escape from their beds in tiny rooms. The whole thing about rockets shooting up and bursting in the air above crowds of people, firemen jetting water at spectators from massive pipes, squirting gigantic sprays and shaking bottles of water over them, the way male fish inseminate females by spraying semen willy-nilly all over the place, seemed to me to be the ultimate in machismo. If I am right, the time will come when Chinese firework designers perfect the discharge of multi-coloured spermatazoan-shaped sparks.

One might have expected that with all this, plus the availability of drugs and alcohol, heat of summer and exuberance of youth, all hell would be let loose and all kinds of violence done to person and property – bonfires in Belfast and other places, for instance, were created entirely for that purpose. But in Spain that was not so, not yet anyway, and the police did not interfere with people throwing lighted fireworks at each other. If you happened to be passing by, and a banger landed on your head and exploded in your hair, or a tossed Roman candle went down inside the front of your dress, you were expected to take it in good part and just get yourself to the Cruz Roja if necessary.

Twelve years before we came to Spain, something happened outside Pryca, the stupendous supermarket taken over by Carrefour, which should have caused the enactment of a law that would have banned public access to fireworks and gunpowder forever. It was on a red hot afternoon at the height of summer that somebody carrying a car boot full of gunpowder parked his vehicle near the front entrance of Pryca's very crowded carpark, collected a trolley and blithely went in to do their shopping. When the gunpowder exploded half an hour later, many people were killed, some blown to smithereens, and an elderly English couple apparently deranged after finding a child's head on their bonnet. Yet no memorial, record or trace of any of these people having died, or how, endured. '*Bienvenidos*!' (Welcome), was how their huge sign greeted one as one entered the consumer carpark, which should have been thenceforth a logo for a graveyard, better still, a crematorium. English expats were in the forefront when it came to condemning Spain for 'oversights' like this, while little or nothing survived in memoriam regarding the countless coalminers who had died in numerous pit explosions throughout their own country.

While preparing to leave Muchavista for Cocentaina, our only problem was with Telefónica, the tele-communications corporation which more aggressively advertised its 'customer friendliness' than anybody. Granted, a few of the switchboard girls were congenial for a limited period of time, but the sales department never properly informed customers about their 'product'. If you got into a spat with any of their employees, they would not hesitate to turn rude, demand to know your age and remark upon the fact that you were an *extranjero*. Unless you knew them, Spaniards were often abrupt over the telephone, gabbling, interrupting and contradicting, and never considering the possibility that they might be wrong. Valentí had said we could install a telephone in his flat, but the girl on the Telefónica help-line in Madrid said there was no such place as 'Cocentaina', so we had to have an argument about it, caused, she said, by my pronouncing the word badly. Spaniards would readily correct one's pronunciation of Spanish words, something I considered useful; however, as with everything, there was a right way and a wrong way of doing it. Then she said there was no such place as 'Plaça de l'Església'. Maybe I should have tried her with 'Alicante' or 'Costa Blanca'.

Instead I insisted. 'There is! My wife and I rent an apartment there and…'

'You're wrong! Who told you there was a plaza called that?'

'The owner of the apartment.'

'Have you asked anybody else? Somebody in authority?'

'No.'

'Why not?'

'Because we did not think it necessary if –'

'Of course it is necessary! How do you expect us to put in a telephone if you don't even know the address.'

'We thought it was the right address.'

'Well, you must speak with somebody who knows the right name.'

I rang Valentí. According to him, the name had been changed from 'Plaça de l'Església', the *catalán* name, to 'Plaza de Cardinal Feriz', the Castilian name during the *Franquismo*, but after the monster who signed death warrants by the score in the back of his car when on his way to a concert, was finally called to plead his case before the Almighty, they changed the name back again and nobody roundabout acknowledged it ever having been the Plaza de Cardinal Feriz. I tested them and they either looked blank or hostile. When I rang Telefónica again, they knew 'Plaza de Cardinal Feriz' all right, it was still shown on their street map, so I assumed the old cardinal must have been a devout *franquista*. Mind, the Spanish have some bizarre ideas about naming streets. During the time of the *Franquismo*, because of observations by an English bacteriologist called Alexander Fleming, on the antagonistic effect of Penicillium mould on certain bacteria, the Spanish named streets after him after an antibiotic drug was developed which proved invaluable in the treatment of infections caused by the many wounds suffered in bullfights, as well as during the Civil War. Fleming was knighted by the British and awarded prizes and medals all over the world, but deserved none of them. Synthesisation of the drug, an antibiotic called Penicillin, was carried out by an Australian named Howard Florey who got next to nothing for it.

On the afternoon that we were putting the last of our things in the car outside Muchavista Towers, ready to go to Cocentaina, two old Brittania dears came tottering up.

'We've been here seven months,' I whispered to Helen, 'and nary a friendly word out of any of them. Now we're leaving, they're sorry and are coming to tell us how much they'll miss us. Typical, isn't it?'

'You do realise that because of your cramming the lift with your chattels, for the past half hour everybody else has had to use the stairs?' whinged the dumpier of the two. 'We are elderly ladies and have our own apartments here! And, I'll have you know, we most certainly didn't buy them so strangers could keep us out of our own lift!'

I knew Helen loved to see the blue of the Mediterranean when she looked through the large lace-curtained windows, and I knew she was lulled to sleep at night by the sound of its waves, but I have to say there were a few too many ancient landlubbers for my taste and I was more than delighted to be on the way out.

When, later that afternoon, we arrived in *Cocentaina*, we had our first ever lucky break as far as driving in Spain was concerned. It was a tortuous one-way system from the main road through the old part of the town, with its medieval streets, to the Plaça de l'Església, so it was a case of pausing at the junction with the main road, looking up the street, and if nobody was coming, racing up so fast and far that anybody entering from the other end would have to go back. We were especially foreign here, so I was expecting no quarter from its road-users, and it was a very deep breath I took and held when we finally made the plunge.

Ignoring Helen's pleas, I tore along, preferring a head-on collision to reversing all the way back through the winding narrow streets where the chances of making it before somebody else entered, were slim beyond calculation. But we made it! Like a bolt into the blue and into the brilliant square with the sun lighting it up like the stage of a theatre. It was the Plaça d'Església all right, and there was the church. We were so relieved, especially when we saw Valentí waiting outside his block to welcome us, that I could have gone into the church, fallen on my knees and wept with real old-fashioned English Catholic gratitude. And then while I dithered about, unloading the car and taking longer than I should have, young and fit Valentí was up the stairs with the computer and all the heavy cases. I was so glad at not having to explain about being a pathetic old weakling.

Although he and Humberto were very similar in some ways – strict *catalán* socialists with a passionate love of nature, for example – I do not think Valentí relished poverty to the same extent as Humberto. However, more in the manner of a janitor than a landlord, he showed us where things were, gave us a spare set of keys each and did everything he could to express the warmth of our welcome and let us know he wanted us to be as comfortable as possible. Humberto, kind though he undoubtedly was, would probably have preferred us to have to do at least a bit of wallowing in discomfort – good for the soul, if not the body.

The furniture was very old Spanish, the most striking item being a huge bookcase filled with wonderfully dull books in old-fashioned *catalán*. There was an eight-bulb chandelier in the lounge and another in the bedroom, and I noticed that in each case the six empty sockets had been filled since our first visit; though when Valentí switched them on, only two bulbs per chandelier lit up. 'If you need more light, just do this,' he said, reaching up and screwing several bulbs further in until they likewise lit up, and then screwing them out again.

In the bathroom gold-coloured brackets, hooks and holders had been hastily and slightly cockeyedly screwed into the wall, and there were many little clues to less than totally successful attempts at repair here and there. The bed had been beautifully made up with embroidered sheets and there were similar motherly touches in every room, including the careful placing of ornaments and cloths. Oh, for a Mam and doting sister who lived only a few doors down the street, and would, we soon found out, regularly send up delicious '*postres*' (desserts) and cakes for an ostensibly independent, though very appreciative, son.

Because the flats were next to the church, and the inland heat intense, the windows had to be open most of the day, so when the church bells rang, which they did every quarter of an hour with a full symphony on the hour, we had no difficulty hearing them. I assumed the old priest considerately turned the volume down before he got into his old BMW at the end of the day to retreat to his villa in an orange grove up country where a buxom housekeeper waited, far from the simple bong sounds that comforted pious simpletons, and once upon a time comforted me. Once there, he could switch on Messiaen's trumpets to overwhelm the cicadas, or Haydn's clarinet concertos to finally get some peace.

It was surprising how soon we got used to the bells, and they became part of our life. It was the basso disco thump of the aerobic woman's video in the flat adjoining, and her nocturnal sounds of mating, that proved difficult to ignore.

After the first night on a bed so soft it was like sleeping in a double hammock where, whenever the other person moved, one's bottom bounced off the floor, I asked Valentí if he would mind if we got a board to go under the mattress. He understood without my having to whine about having a bad back, and said he would get one. I said we would pay for it but he refused on the grounds that he was gradually putting such boards under every mattress, and to prove the claim showed us one under his own. I said that if we were not allowed to pay for one, we would not accept it. He thought for a while, then asked if we were allowed to pay for one, would we be sure to take it away with us when we left? '*Sí*,' I said, '*por supuesto!*' with the appropriate amount of mockery in my voice that the phrase requires in Spanish; meanwhile I was visualising the Seat looking like a dhow packed to the nines with our chattels inside and a huge sheet of blockboard flapping on top of it.

Delighted to be of help, Valentí immediately went to fetch a tailor's tape, measured the bed, and went off. Twenty minutes later he was back with a 6' x 4' sheet of blockboard with more holes in it than a colander. 'I got the carpenter to make a few ventilation holes,' he explained. We thanked him and he left us to make up the bed, returning a few minutes later to gingerly point out that one of the coins I had given him was an Irish halfpenny instead of a *duro* (five cents).

In the middle of our second morning, just before Valentí was about to take us on a tour of the town, there was a ring of the interior doorbell and he went to answer it. Helen and I could hear everything because we were in the sitting room getting together our bags, maps and sunglasses, pocket dictionary, pens and notebooks, calculators, cash, passports and everything else the *extranjero* needs to go out into a Spanish street to buy a loaf of bread.

Two women were speaking in profound *valenciano*, most of the time both at once, but I could understand the gist of it. They were objecting to our car being parked outside and wanted to know how long we proposed it remain there. It was to be another glimpse of how righteously stubborn was the man we had come to spend many weeks, perhaps several months, with. They would have known he had no car of his own, that he was a bachelor and very shy, and were really getting stuck into him. He listened for a while, saying nothing, and then, keeping his voice very low and controlled, said '*Momento*,' (Just a moment). Without waiting for them to say 'All right' or anything, he gently but firmly closed the door so the lock clicked shut, and went off into his bedroom. Several minutes later he was back at the door with a document that turned out to be his *residencia* (deeds and documents from the town hall pertaining to one's rights) that gave him, among other things, the right to park a car in the street outside his flat. As soon as he began fiddling with the lock to open the door, they renewed their barrage, but the papers in his hand soon halted them in their tracks, as though he had jabbed them with a taser. Quietly he began by pointing out that we were guest residents, that he had accumulated years of car-parking space credit, that they were lucky he did not have an articulated lorry, that he had no idea how long the car was going to be there and was under no obligation to tell them, even if he did. And that was that. They mumbled a bit, trying to salvage a bit of pride after being so thoroughly flattened, and departed. What was so charming about the whole thing was that he never said a word about it afterwards, never warned us to park here or not there, or to watch out for this one or that.

When, a few minutes later, we went out with him, big, awkwardly solid and always three paces ahead, there was no discussion about where we wanted to go. He just led from the start and we followed, crossing from one side of the road to the other whenever he did, going up any steps and down whatever side street he did. He took us to the railway station, showed us every bus stop, told us the times and fares to everywhere, and explained the advantages and disadvantages of the various forms of transport, including the Seat. He showed us places of architectural and archaeological interest and promised a detailed tour of the cemetery where he worked as a security guard at night, as soon as we were up for it.

In Consum, a little working-class supermarket into which Valentí led the way, whenever Helen put something in the trolley, he would immediately take it out, study the written details on the packet, and either put it back in the trolley, or put it back on the shelf and replace it with a cheaper item produced locally. 'I don't want this,' Helen kept whispering through gritted teeth when we had sneaked off to another section, leaving him to study the contents of a carton somewhere else. 'I've had it before and it's awful. You wouldn't eat it.' Valentí would then come up with a beam on his face, put something else we did not want in the trolley, pick up something we had been especially looking for and had tucked away underneath the other things where we thought he would miss it, hold it up, shake his head disapprovingly and then go off to replace it with something more politically and ecologically correct, albeit much less palatable. I am all for food grown by traditional methods, but handwritten labels with spelling mistakes always make me flinch – they equate with dirty fingernails in my finicky mind.

The return to the flat was much quicker and it was then that we realised the reason for the meandering and continual crossing over from one side of the street to the other on the outward journey had been to avoid our having to walk in the bright sunshine; even his walking in front was to create a protective shade for us. It was an example of consideration of one human being for another that we were not used to on the Costa Blanca; nor anywhere else for that matter.

Valentí was patently a dedicated *catalán* scholar and his books his most precious possession. He wrote articles, translated and edited journals mainly into or from *catalán*, and was as passionate about Cataluña (Catalonia) as Humberto. Ever since the *Franquismo*, during which all languages other than Castilian were banned, it had been disapproved of by the government of Madrid, and work teaching the language was both hard to find and poorly paid. As a consequence, he had to take whatever work he could get. He did not have a computer, essential equipment for any editor nowadays, and lived and ate simply.

I have never known anybody so proud of having their own flat. He must have moved all his papers into his bedroom to make room for us, and it was in there, in front of a tiny table, that we occasionally glimpsed him working in *catalán* with a pencil he kept as sharp as a hypodermic needle.

He had set up a little marble table in the lounge, near to an electrical socket to which he had fitted an extra adaptor so that I could use my computer, and when he saw the table was too small for the printer, had gone to the *Ayuntamiento* and borrowed two trestles to extend it. I told him we would be glad to put anything he wanted on the computer and print it out for him, but when he came back ten minutes later with a very battered floppy disk and asked me to copy its contents, it was with an over-riding feeling of mean-mindedness that I had to tell him I dare not risk putting it into the computer in case it 'infected' my material. I did have a goodly amount of stuff, personal, literary and legal, and although I had never knowingly had a 'virus' in the computer, I honestly believed that if I got one, and it was Spanish, it would be a fatal strain. Poor Valentí. He stood there with the grotty little disk in his hand, obviously embarrassed at having put me on the spot, but not quite understanding why, and there was I, sitting in his house, surrounded by all my technology, screen beautifully lit up, motor purring along, panels of different coloured lights blinking and telling me everything was 'A OK' and the equipment ready to do my bidding, trying to convey to him that his disk might be the equivalent of the black rats that once carried the Bubonic plague. I briefly considered taking a chance but felt I had to decline. If his disk fouled up the files on my computer, it would have caused me considerable angst, not merely inconvenience. If only he had asked for something reasonable, such as that I type out copies of the contents of every book in his bookcase, in *catalán*...

When we first came to look at the place, Valentí had obtained maps, time-tables, brochures, tourist guides and every relevant handout from the *Ayuntamiento*, in advance, and placed them in a neat pile on the end of the dressing table near the door. And if we now asked about any old building, pharmacy hours, forthcoming concerts – anything – within a couple of hours there would be a leaflet or something relevant very neatly written on a little piece of paper and left there. If we were in the lounge and he wanted to say something, he would stand in the doorway and wait until we looked up, rather than interrupt us. One morning, after we had been staying with him for nearly a week, and were sitting reading, I was aware of a darkening of the threshold.

'*Holá*, (Hello) Valentí.'

Without his usual greeting, or saying a word, he curled his forefinger towards me, commanding '*Venga!*' Come!) and disappeared into the kitchen. I had never been enamoured of a beckoning finger coiled in my direction, and remained sitting, rather taken aback. Helen looked at me demurely and smiled.

'You had better see what he wants,' she whispered.

I shrugged in a nonchalant manner, and got up. Valentí was standing facing the doorway, arms by his sides, feet planted in the middle of the floor, waiting. To avoid any misunderstanding, he must have decided to dispense with the spoken word and rely entirely on hand signals and facial expressions, and beginning with the already proven effective curling finger, drew me out to the *galeria*, the tiny utility-room area in front of the main window, which contained the washing machine and cleaning implements, all arranged in logical order, and seemingly doubled as the Bollocking Room.

Spaniards do not use gestures the way they used to, such as touching the lower lid of their eye with their finger when they want you to look at something, or pulling their earlobe down when they want you to listen – and never the younger ones – but if and when they do, the gestures are large, theatrical and unambiguous. Valentí pointed to a little *basura* (rubbish) bin and plucked an orange juice carton from it. Holding it at arm's length, as though it were a dead rat, he carried it to the kitchen sink, turned it upside down to drain every last imaginary drop, and laid it on its side on the draining board. Then he straightened it out, flattened it with his steam-iron like hand, and folded it exactly into what it must have been when it arrived at the bottling plant with a million companions. He should now have done a bit of origami with it, I thought. He was probably well able to turn it into a cardboard stealth bomber and send it out through the window where it could have done a couple of circuits of the plaza, gone in through the door of the church and made a perfect landing on the altar. But he simply put it carefully back in the *basura* bin, took out another carton and mercilessly did the same with that, while

I tried to remember how many more there might be. Then he curled his finger at me again, this time more tightly, as though this next lesson were rather more serious, and pointed to the food cupboard. He looked at me querulously as much as to say 'Come on, now! You've already been told about this one!' But I had my nonplussed expression on and was keeping it on.

Undaunted, he opened the door, pointed to an open bag of sugar, brought it out and set it down on the bench, pointed to a jar with minute coloured pegs in it, selected three greens, carefully folded the top of the bag over and over and then pegged it at equidistant intervals with tiny meant-to-be-disposable plastic pegs. While I was trying to divine the connection between sugar and green, he deftly made his hand look like an ant – actually, it was more like a tarantula because of his amazingly hairy skin – and made it crawl along the bench towards the bag while he shook the finger of his other hand and said 'No, no, no, no, no!' He then put the bag back, I sighed in English, and he must have been satisfied with my level of comprehension because I was then dismissed and allowed to return to Helen in the sitting room.

Because he could not understand English, Helen and I rarely spoke it in front of him, and I winked at Helen to assure her I would tell all later. However, after a few minutes, he went out, so I decided that for a joke I would take her into the kitchen and do to her what he had done to me; after all, she was the one who had chucked fully expanded cartons into the *basura* and left the sugar bag open with a kind of ramp for the ants to embark.

We had only just returned to the lounge after rather making fools of ourselves, and I was meditating on the bollocking I had had on this, my sixty-second birthday, for our jointly failing to empty our fruit-drink cartons properly, and not closing sugar bags designed without regard for the predations of the ant, by a Spaniard I hardly knew, who was only half my age but whose rules now governed my life, when Helen nudged me. He was back again.

Up came his arm and slowly his forefinger began to curl, but this time, instead of briskly clicking my heels and leaping to attention, I just hauled myself to my feet and traipsed after him like an old man of sixty-two, this time into the bathroom, the place where the 'dropper thing' in the middle of the ancient cistern had to be centred properly at the end of every flush, otherwise the water would run continuously. Helen again. She would never get the hang of it. More tactlessly, the shower curtain he had got especially for our coming, was lying in the bath. Worst of all, the door lock was bust, but I think he had been half expecting that to happen. With a series of gestures that included his sitting on the pedestal, he indicated that from now on, if the bathroom door were closed, it would mean somebody was in; if open, that it was vacant. I knew, and I suppose he knew, that this would not be foolproof, but that it was probably enough to be going on with until he could locate a *catalán* plumber or joiner who would be grateful for such a commission. Later we were to learn that most Spanish people do not have locks on bathroom or toilet doors; but if they do, they do not use them religiously the way we English do.

For us, and for today at any rate, enough was enough, so Helen and I went out to sit in the car in the plaza and listen to the radio before he discovered my slippers had perhaps not been left perfectly adjacent – 'heel to heel and toe to toe' as they say in Scotland – or that the bristles of our toothbrushes were not pointing in the same direction. There was no house television or radio, and although on the first day we had brought our radio in and set it on the sideboard, the look on Valentí's face had been sufficient to fuse internal metal parts and melt the plastic, so we had taken it away and put it facing the wall on top of the wardrobe in the bedroom, to show it was temporarily obsolete. Normally Helen and I never let a day pass without listening to Radio Clasica, and had sorely missed it since coming to Cocentaina.

Now, with peeved neighbours straining their eyes at us from behind their blinds, we sat for a blissful hour in the sunny mediaeval square in front of the church, listening to Renaissance music and saying nothing. It was lovely. Life here was so detached from the shenanigans in Los Pajaros Rojos, Jemina and Alicante, that it was like being in a different world. Cocentaina more reminded us of the Spain of Laurie Lee, Gerald Brenan and our own impressions forty years previously, than in any place or experience on holiday in subsequent years, or in the year since we had come here to live. The buildings in the old quarter where we were living were mostly houses divided into flats, and so old and badly built that they were cracking and crumbling, though they would no doubt see us out. All around the plaza, skilled restoration work was being carried out by builders of a kind we had not seen anywhere near Los Pajaros Rojos. They not only worked hard, with hardly a break, but were quiet, quick and tidy. There are few sights on earth more pleasing to me than skilled men working hard on something for the common good, and it was a delight to see how they worked in cramped and difficult conditions, the ingenious methods they used with ropes and minimal scaffolding, and the way they utilised sun and shade.

Like nearby Alcoi, Cocentaina was no tourist or dormitory resort, but a town inhabited by a population that had to live with itself and by itself, and as a consequence had great working-class traditions. People in shops and out of them were everywhere friendlier and better humoured than their more cynical counterparts on the coast. They had relatively little experience of the *extranjero*, and as a consequence rarely resorted to the cynicism of the coast. The girls on the checkout in the little Consum supermarket were all sweet-natured, the woman in the bread shop who was amused by my addiction to *calabazate* (sugared pumpkin) was always ready for a joke, and the one with the big bust and prima-donna hair, who owned the newsagency, was delighted when I went in for my specially ordered copy of *El Jueves*, the political comic, which, because of its bawdy humour, was regarded as very risqué for an Englishman. When I had first asked for it, having been given the name by Valentí, she had been really taken aback and spent at least five minutes beneath the counter, terrified in case she should bring out the wrong item. Eventually she produced *The Financial Times*.

'No, no,' I said. '*Más grosero*.' (It's ruder than that).

'*Más grosero?*'

'*Si. Un poco más*. (A little).

She did not have the comic in stock but said she would order it, and did so. However, a few days later when I went in to collect it, she was astonished Helen was with me and should be seeing what I was buying, which was only a satirical political comic and by no means pornographic. But when she bent down to get it from under the counter, acres of breast were displayed, and as she handed it to me, the words, '*Señor!*' came out of her as out of the huge woman in Fellini's *La Dolci Vita*, when she was pretending she was seducing the boy.

'*El Jueves*' was very contemporary in its material. '*Jueves*' meant 'Thursday', but it came out on a Wednesday, something *aficionados* seemed to find hilarious, and I became a fan. The standard of draughtsmanship was very good, the humour, like all Spanish humour, cynical, personal, ribald, and dead on. Nothing was beyond the pale: not the Government, the Pope, fraternities or anybody's royalty. '*El Jueves*' maintained Spanish television decerebrated the viewer. So did British television, of course, but it would pretty much constitute an indefensible libel to say the BBC contributed to it. However, Helen and I very much liked *Radio Clasica* (Classic Spanish Radio), which was exceptional for the variety and quality of its programmes, as well as for presenters who spoke the most excellent Spanish, a claim the BBC could no longer make for its pronunciation of English. Our only quibble with it was that applause for Spanish classical musicians went on for far too long and was too frequently punctuated by effeminate little yelps from males in the audience, yelps doubtless intended to sound like the gasps of someone in thrall to art, which came out more like the whimpering of someone riveted by his own zipper.

TWENTY-THREE

The library and tourist office were housed in the beautiful old Palau Comtal, a small Renaissance palace which purportedly belonged to the people of Cocentaina. The staff were exceptionally friendly and helpful and such was the librarian's wish to please and encourage local history studies, that we were able to borrow original books of considerable value that really should not have been allowed out to anyone, let alone a *turista* (tourist) It was an example of the great wealth of antique things in Spain, which included so many wonderful, often abandoned, buildings that people were blasé about their conservation.

At least twice a week we drove into Jemina, and sometimes Alicante. Cocentaina was about one third of the way inland between Alicante and Valencia, and a wonderful drive through the quite perilous Carrasqueta mountains. After the province of Alicante, where the relative humidity often registered in single digits and the overall expanse was a drab ochre-grey, to suddenly enter a terrain of golden sunflowers, yellow oilseed rape and russet cereals, green grass and black-trunked tall trees, was like taking a journey over a rainbow. The verdure was so strong one could have sensed it with one's eyes closed.

Afterwards, returning to our virtuous landlord, church bells, busty newsagent and check-out girls who reminded us of our own daughters working at Dunnes Stores in Ireland during their holidays, was more like retreating to a place of refuge than Los Pajaros Rojos or Muchavista had ever been. It felt like a thousand miles from expats, English shops and English breakfast cafes, from *notarios*, *gestors*, *alcaldes* (mayors), *banqueros* (bankers), *dentistas* and all the other swindlers that surfeited, like vultures, off the feckless carcases of *extranjeros* that stretched all along the coast. It was possibly a place to start to get to know the Spain one had dreamed about, a place where one could imagine republicanism having been a reality and anarchy essayed several times.

One day in August, hot enough for an expat to germinate half a dozen malignant moles on the most fertile parts of his body, and produce a migraine that would last a week, we were returning from visiting our new house – or rather, the building site – and were almost atop the Carrasquetas, after a long, winding and climbing stretch, when the engine suddenly quit and could not be restarted. I opened the bonnet to let it cool down, admired the view, the way one disingenuously does when cursing over a conked-out car on a busy road, and every few minutes got back in and tried a few more obscenities.

Years ago in England when one suffered a roadside breakdown, a not uncommon experience, one felt something of a pioneer and invariably received sympathy; nowadays it was to feel like a proper fool.

After a while, when all recriminations were exhausted, who it was that had insisted we travel on such a blistering day, who had insisted on the punishing scenic route, who was driving too fast when the car was obviously labouring, and the likes, it was time to consider something positive. We knew there was no garage ahead or behind that either of us could have walked to in less than a week, but I remembered seeing a group of six *guardia*, ancient enemy of the working class and now an armed highway police force much vaunted in travel guides as Samaritans who travelled as motorcycling duos – one a trained mechanic, the other a paramedic, so that travellers could theoretically have their blood pressure checked while their fan belt was being adjusted, sort of thing. They had been halfway up the mountain, standing by their vehicles, having a laugh and a smoke. Granted, none had saluted the way the RAC and AA patrolmen in England used to do, but I was prepared to overlook that, considering they did not have their hats on, and that even the English patrolmen might have dropped the habit by now. Incidentally, during the forty minutes we had been stuck and clearly in need of help, not a single vehicle of any kind had slowed or head turned, as though we were completely invisible.

I had given Helen some basic survival instructions and was about to head down towards the 'patent-leather men', as Lorca called them, when a sports car containing a German with a handlebar moustache and an under-age companion, pulled up to ask if they could be of assistance. I told him there was a group of *guardia* in the direction he was headed and asked if he would mind sending a duo up. He looked surprised. '*Guardia Civil*..? Come to help..?' He was grinning. 'No, no!'

'Yes, yes,' I assured him. 'They do nowadays.'

'Rightio, old chap,' he said in pseudo-Wimbledon English, while winking at his pretty companion.

He was right, but Helen suddenly remembered the mobile phone we had bought two days ago from Eroski's and not yet taken out of its box. Miraculously, or so it seemed to us, we got through to the insurance breakdown service and inside an hour were in Cocentaina, and our car, only just still inside its guarantee, was in a Seat garage waiting for a new thermostat from Alicante.

'*No Italianos?*' the breakdown mechanic had asked when we climbed into his cabin with the Seat suspended on the back of his truck.

'No,' I said, not knowing whether I should be affirming it with relief, or apologising.

'*Me gustan los italianos.*' (I like Italians).

'*Lo siento, pero somos ingleses.*' (Sorry, but we're English.)

'Ah…' he said. Then, obviously thinking there was nothing to do but sing under the circumstances, he good-humouredly started on a medley of Italian oldies and we joined in the refrains where we knew them. Helen reckoned he fancied me but I think she was a bit lightheaded from the altitude.

Nowadays police in Spain tend to be more conspicuous by their absence. After thirty-five years of the *Guardia Civil* behaving like vengeful occupying troops, and a hundred years of exercising routine barbarity before that, it would take a lot of penitent history to convince the Spanish people – and the *extranjeros*, who certainly got it in the neck as much as any in Ireland got from Customs – that police can be a force for good. You might see a Spaniard arguing with a policeman over a traffic offence, but not if he is a member of the *Guardia Civil*.

One day we were waiting for the bus in Muxtamel, at the stop next to the *Guardia* barracks, and I was looking through the open arch into their courtyard, always fascinating places in Spain, and like so many enclosed buildings in sunny countries, wonderful in the way they catch the light, when a slovenly little man in green, with a legionnaire's forage cap, black leather belt and straps, pistol hanging loosely out of his holster, sloppy sunglasses and arms folded, sauntered up to within a few inches of my nose and asked what I was doing. Had I been staring across the road at the crumbling façade of the derelict building opposite, innocently trying to figure out how long the decaying electrical cables were likely to continue drooping before they fell and zapped half the people in the street, he probably would not have taken umbrage; but because I happened to be looking in the direction of his stronghold, he did not like it at all and kept looking at my feet as though resenting my trespassing on the shadow cast by the arch over the gate. I told him I was interested in old buildings and he looked at me hard to make sure I was not being sarcastic, then said there was a museum up the road, and that was where I should go if I wanted to see old buildings. I could have said 'Excuse me, but is that the yard you used to shoot Republicans without blindfolds every morning?' because that was certainly what I had been thinking. These military police have always been thug enforcers of unpopular government measures against the poor, and are unique in their absolute unfriendliness and detachment, suspiciousness and arrogance.

The first time Helen and I came to Spain, which was on our Triumph 650cc twin motorbike in 1960, I had parked the bike outside a garage to let the engine cool down; it was only a few weeks old and still being run in, and because it was my pride and joy, like any other young man with a new motorbike, I took the utmost care of it. So when we had gone into the café for some refreshment and I suddenly heard the engine roaring, I rushed out, astounded to see three *guardia* at my bike: two sitting on it and one alternately wrenching open and slamming closed the throttle. I dashed over and started pulling them off, whereupon they began shouting and poking me with their rifles; I was lucky they did not have bayonets fitted. I was furious and yelled back but several men from the cafe advised me to beat it before they kicked the shit out of both me and the bike. It was a long time ago, more than fifty years, but I would take some convincing that today's lot are not governed by the same DNA.

We had a Spanish friend who had a relative in the *Guardia Civil*, a woman, and that might have made a difference, but we certainly did not have any relatives or friends among them; that would have been like saying our best pal was in the Gestapo. I had no doubt there were ordinary human beings who had familial or other relationships with members of the G*uardia Civil*, but when I heard of yet another book written by an expat whose drinking buddies consisted of a one-armed Basque, on one hand, if I could so insensitively put it, and a sergeant on the other, it felt as though someone were trying to stretch my credulity beyond breaking point.

Like so many English expats who had never in their lives been stopped by a police officer, we had a number of run-ins with the *guardia* – though rarely with the other police corps – over the most minor and sometimes imagined transgressions, such as when they claimed we had been telephoning while driving, when we had done nothing of the sort. Veterans would tell you that the way to deal with the charge of driving under the influence of a mobile phone, a common allegation, even though you might not even possess one, was to pay the on-the-spot fine, rather than end up in court paying twice as much and suffering a lot of hassle. Suggesting they search your car for the phone would be seen as provocation.

Mildred Forsyth told us about a woman who had lived in Nigeria for years, and on retirement had bought an apartment in San Juan. She had kept horses in her previous life and could not bear to get rid of them all, so at great expense and after much faff-on with both African and Spanish authorities, she arranged to bring the best one, one to which she was very much attached.

Not wishing to leave the horse in the hands of the Nigerians who she said were very fond of horsemeat, she arranged stabling near Alicante, hired a private plane and had the horse flown over in advance. On its arrival at Alicante airport Customs decided there was insufficient documentation accompanying it, and nowhere to put it until transport to the stables had been arranged, so they contacted the ultimate authority for everything in Spain, the *Guardia Civil*, and sure enough they showed why people held them in such respect. After deliberating for several hours a solution was arrived at: a butcher from the catering division was summoned, a corporal shot the horse, and the butcher dealt with the carcase.

Naturally the local expat community were aghast, such a crime being far more likely to exercise the dudgeon of an English expat than if the horse had been, say, an illegal Moroccan immigrant. Significantly, nobody I knew in Spain, on hearing the tale, expat or native, was in the least surprised.

The owner of the horse apparently entered a long spell of depression but people were very supportive and she stayed on, ending her days in a home for disenchanted old expats.

Expats are a cranky assortment, wherever they come from, and usually evolve similar foibles wherever they go. Many, especially if they are English, have always regarded themselves as a welcome, civilising and peerless force for good, and always ready to demonstrate to their hosts how to do things properly. In Spain the huge readers' letters columns of the English language newspapers were the most dynamic sections, and most of the writers of the various other columns derived from capitalist, quasi-Christian stock of thoroughly decent hypocrites.

The '*Cost Blanca News*' was the essential organ for expats in our region, and its sister paper, the '*Costa del Sol News*', and various cousins were always coming out somewhere. They were read by almost all of the British and Irish, plus Spanish business people, because they were virtual floating bulletin boards providing expats and Spaniards servicing expats, with vital local and national information, and expats depended on them for information about the constantly changing laws and regulations that were difficult for *extranjeros* to comprehend. There were regular columns devoted to common interests, such as health, law, finance, housing, pets, sport for the aged, DIY, gardening, swimming-pool maintenance, clubs, English hobbies, clubs, eating out, cultural activities, local news in various towns along the coast, details of events such as market days, the need for updating licences for all sorts of things, advice about whether to have a will made in Britain or in Spain, whether to bring one's vehicle to Spain or buy one when one arrives, whether to be buried or cremated in Spain or back in one's homeland, a crash course in juvenile Spanish, and an infinite series on the adventures of new ex-pats, all of whom experience the very same trials and tribulations but do so as though they were the first and only.

All manner of amateur experts advised, and although frequently derided for opinionated opinions and repeated gaffes, were sorely missed when they ceased to exist. Some who had contributed columns for years before retiring, not infrequently fed up with Spain, returned to Blighty where they bored relatives and friends with their encomiums about what a wonderful place Spain was. Others stayed the course and friends made sure their selfie obituaries were published when the time came. These, the stalwart expats, for whom a special category should be created, were unquestionably different to those who just came for a very long holiday and eventually tucked their tails – docked stumps or road-sweepers – between their legs and slunk back to their real home. In the ludicrously self-deceiving words of the great crooner who was rarely let down by the melody makers but tragically often by slobbering wordsmiths, the stoics had always done things their way. If royalties had been paid every time an old beachcomber who finally hit the deck had arranged for the record, with its maudlin but boastful sentiments, to be played at his funeral, fortunes would have been made.

By far the most popular item in these papers was the Letters to the Editor, which consisted primarily of personal complaints by English curmudgeons of whom the *costas* (coasts, mainly the Costa Blanca and Costa del Sol) sported many. Sometimes, though rarely, letters might be enlightening, but when they degenerated into dialectics between two notorious soap-boxers, they could become excruciating. Week after week an eighty-eight-year-old Luftwaffe pilot would rehash the Battle of Britain with an eighty-seven-year-old RAF dam-busting rear gunner, often with old friends and enemies joining in, and the battle broadened through the pages of the German expats' paper.

There were letters praising the Spanish, and letters criticising them, the latter invariably referring to authorities, though few expats were interested in national topics except where they adverted to their welfare, security or enjoyment. Few knew or cared about contemporary Spain, its history, sport, art or politics, most still being much more interested in life in Britain even though they might have been long out of it.

Charity, particularly where it applied to animals, was a popular topic and information gladly provided on fund-raising events for abandoned cats and dogs. It was amazing how much money was spent on very expensive veterinary investigations and treatment like scans, chemotherapy and micro-surgery, even on the very old, the fatally sick, the badly handicapped, and filthy old strays.

For the Anglophobes, who consisted mainly of the relatively few envious Spaniards and the many petty, egocentric Dutch who constantly looked for flaws in everybody else's character, the 'CBN' was a valuable source of enlightenment and entertainment.

There were also local, very amateurish, name-dropping radio programmes in English, but these were Citizen Band-like stuff and could not compare with the newspapers. Media entertainment for older people meant television, and television meant Murdoch's Sky, which in turn meant continual problems with satellite dishes and recent modifications to reception. There were plenty of chancers advertising their capability to set viewers up with Sky because, unlike in Britain and Ireland, the Spanish had no interest in supporting Murdoch, and threats about getting the FBI over to beat one up viewers watching his Disneyesque drivel without paying, fell on pretty deaf ears.

The Spanish loved their television, and 'opium for the people' these days consisted of one or more of the many Spanish channels. Bullfighting, sport – particularly football – and gossip shops that went into infinite details about celebrities' misdemeanours, especially when of a sexual or fiscal nature, meant televisions were on all day in Spanish homes. Even in summer, when it was sweltering hot and everyone sitting out on the veranda, the television would either be outside also, or if inside, placed where it could be seen through the window.

Because the English had always been great 'clubbers', it was inevitable that the English Speaking Club, an association which had staunch supporters and equally staunch traducers, would come into being. Some regarded it as a poor man's gentleman's club, others saw it as a sanctuary from all things Spanish. I thought it primarily a jingoistic haven for expats who could not speak Spanish, but Helen went there from time to time with friends and considered it contained the best and worst of our race. It had its own bar whose wares were cheaper than in many Spanish bars', and for this reason was blamed for contributing to the unquestionably high rate of alcoholism among expats. Drink was cheap and readily available in Spain anyway, and what with the heat and common social problems, many people became alcoholic within a short time of arriving; thus, depression, financial hardship and marital break-up were also common.

In countries like Australia, Canada and New Zealand, places to where English people had always emigrated, apart from English clubs and associations there were always good book clubs, but in Spain it was not the case; the kind of English trash available would hardly merit a discussion. There was Bingo, of course, but… And some good bookstores, though not nearly as many as the Spanish seemed to think, and few had more than a couple of books in English.

The U3A (University of the Third Age) started up after we had been in Spain a few years, but it was slow to get off the ground and tended to be very autocratic. A sexist but artless observation might hold that because male expats died off sooner than females, and older females enjoyed better health and were more independent, associations like this tended to be orientated around elderly women and were the worse for it.

Nothing seemed to be happening with the case. This being August, nothing seemed to be happening to anything anywhere except for fireworks exploding and dogs barking. Many shops and businesses were shut and most Spanish people devoting their energies to eating, drinking, smoking and gossiping with extended families. We were waiting to be called to court for a trial in public where everybody's character would be exposed, evidence minutely examined, and I got to make an impassioned speech about property scams and the awful judicial system where lawyers and judges seemed to decide legal matters among themselves. What we really needed was a first-rate Scottish trade union steward fluent in Spanish, were there such an animal; but failing that, I felt confident my bile alone would carry us.

From the outset we had always, however laboriously, translated everything we had been given, ourselves, delivered documents or information requested without delay, postponed conflicting dental and medical appointments, and changed any other arrangements where necessary, all in order to propitiate Sr. Férrer. When he whistled, even though on every occasion without exception we were given minimal or no notice, we obliged. But to what avail..? The Spiers had, if anything, increased their advantage: they had our money, the ownership and occupancy of the *vivienda*, the ownership of the car, and all the time in the world. And in Cocentaina we felt more out of it than ever.

One night I telephoned Edmundo on the mobile telephone and our gentle friend nearly blew up. Months of frustration and thanklessness had finally had their effect on the gentle human being who had become a sublimely patient, sometimes scapegoat, emissary, and poor reception and failing batteries mercifully closed him down before he could get around to calling me a '*hijo de puta*' and making it impossible for two elderly gentlemen to ever again get back to their former urbanities. Next day, quite independently, we telephoned each other, on both occasions hampered by faulty transmission, to try to say things that would have been difficult under any circumstances. Plainly there was a breakdown in comprehension all around. Edmundo let out that Sr. Férrer had told him he believed we had got another *abogado*. At this point I had had enough of Férrer and decided to write him a real letter, rather than a selection of mannered archaisms. I would write in the plainest Spanish I could devise and be candid to a fault about things from Helen's and my point of view. I would tell him something of the kind of people we were before we came to Spain, and what I felt we had a right to expect as citizens of the EU. And I would tell him what I thought of his attitude to Janet just because she was a woman and English. Most importantly, I would tell him what I thought of his attitude and lack of action on our behalf. After he read it, he would either have more respect for us and show greater commitment to our suit, or would withdraw and tell us to go elsewhere, perhaps somewhere even hotter than Spain. Whatever, that was the way it had to be now. First, however, I would write an equally passionate letter to Edmundo, apologising for the way we had put upon him for so long and telling him we wanted very much to continue having him as a friend. I got no reply from either of them.

Some Wednesdays we would go to the new house to find next to nothing done since our previous visit, except for an increase in the piles of fag ends and beer bottles, and we would not know whether the *albañiles* (blocklayers) had been having a conference, or the local youth partying. We would stand on the few square metres of baked-hard barren ground surrounded by half-built walls that looked too short to contain bedrooms and bathrooms, a lounge and all our furniture, art, books and whatnot. Bales of concrete blocks, heaps of sand and half-used bags of cement, were scattered all over; ragged sheets of dirty polythene flapped listlessly; plastic bottles, faeces, rusty bent rods and broken glass littered the ground underfoot, and polystyrene flakes with their defiant little beads signifying the artificial and ephemeral nature of everything, coated whole areas as though in the aftermath of a blizzard. It was nigh on impossible to visualise sleeping soundly and safely a few feet above this spot in less than four weeks – the completion date – or imagine a garden with fishpond, flowers and trees, and family or friends sitting with refreshments, chatting and chuckling.

The Dutch next door, with their two-storeyed villa sitting on the highest ground in the estate, had managed to find functioning builders who were perfect and the best there was, i.e., Dutch, because they were now excavating a swimming pool close to our plot. Theirs was a holiday habitation, not a real home by either their or our standards, and quite different to the Spanish concept of a home. As Roberto said, as long as the Spanish have a terrace, a barbecue and table with a few chairs and a swimming pool big enough to get wet in, access to a television with a sports channel, plus a few beds, they were quite content.

What we called a 'home' had thick walls and an upstairs, a fireside, armchairs, meals indoors, lined curtains, carpets, eiderdowns and neither a chandelier or bidet – although I must say that the practicality of the latter became increasingly obvious after a certain age. Incidentally our first encounter with the latter was in the villa we had rented from the Spiers when we first came, but had not been able to get to work. I mentioned it to Lew and to our horror, he had reached into the basin, unscrewed the faucet with his bare hands, put it to his lips after filling his mouth with water, and blew a jet through it. Then he screwed it back, turned it on to show that whatever had been blocking it had now been dislodged, possibly even swallowed – grinned when we pulled faces, and swallowed the rest. Even now, years later, I cannot hear the word, 'bidet', without an image of Lew Spiers blowing through the bidet faucet, as though it were the reed of a clarinet and he was clearing it so he could play 'Momma Don't Allow No Bidets Blocked In Here!' or something similar.

For Western Europeans like us, gloominess was next to homeliness, and after more than a quarter of a century in a lousy climate, even an old, unbeautiful farmhouse could become a wonderful home, and the neighbours predominantly friendly. Quite a few English and Irish returned home. Some because they had lost their partners, some because they would rather their remains be dispersed on home ground when their time came, and they wanted to be prepared for it; others because they had had enough of the foreign life and realised it was not for them. Not a few then came back to Spain.

Apart from the family, hawthorns, traditional music, sparrowhawks and other treasures redolent of Ireland, I must confess to increasingly missing God, missed saying my prayers and communing with Somebody who never interrupted and never said anything disingenuous; and if at times He was conservative or a tad reactionary, I should not have minded too much, I was becoming that way myself. Unfortunately God left my life some years before we left Ireland, he had been slipping away to some other dimension and in His absence His staff had messed up rather badly.

TWENTY-FOUR

On our first ever trip to Spain, which was in 1960, we had gone to a bullfight in Madrid and observed, in those few hours on that brilliant late Sunday afternoon that simmered into garish early evening, how different Spaniards were to us and to any other people we had ever been among. We did not know that Spanish manhood was obsessed with young blonde women because of the statuesque, reputedly 'free-loving' Swedes who had started coming to the Mediterranean for holidays. Had we done so, it would have explained why gangs of them kept following us all over, just a few paces behind Helen who, alas, almost fitted the bill, physically at least, and irked me so much. They were far worse than flies, and when I bought a couple of ice-creams from a vendor outside the main gate, a crowd instantly gathered around to make sure the poor fellow did not cheat us. As he counted the change into my hand, they were all loudly chorusing the value of each coin. As a consequence, he got himself into a dither and made mistakes and then they really let him have it, with the consequence that what should have been good for his business turned out to be the very opposite.

There was a tremendous atmosphere outside the stadium before the corrida (bullfight) began, with touts selling seats in the shade, partial shade, or full sun, and tiny portable stalls with rapidly speaking sharps doing card tricks and making marbles disappear under little glasses, while lookouts 'kept toot'. Once inside the stadium the excitement was fantastic, and when a ferocious bull came tearing into the ring, before suddenly halting, snorting, glaring, and daring anybody and anything to enter its territory, something more than the wonderful blend of sweat, sand, blood, perfume, flowers and bull, filled the air, something one could feel with one's skin.

In the forty years since that incredible day, the sport, art, semi-religious sacrifice, or whatever it was, had very much dwindled in popularity, but for some reason it had recently begun to regain it, and the new heroes of the corrida were like movie stars, their effect on young women like nothing we had ever seen before. Not only were the young bullfighters physically handsome, but in their gorgeous costumes there was little to distinguish them from gods. No pop star, however eccentric his get-up and brilliant his lighting effects, was a patch on these chaps: they were magnificent.

Every city had its bullfights and every Sunday afternoon one or another would be shown on television. When we lived in Muchavista, whenever we were not going out we would always watch one on the huge screen that everybody had, no matter the size of the room. A bullfight was so unlike anything we had ever seen on television, and being live seemed so much bloodier and more lethal than any film, that it was absolutely compelling: the noise, the colour, the crowd, the band, the beauty, the style – and the horror. We felt we were party to something terrifyingly primitive that could not go on much longer, it would not be allowed. I had once mentioned my impressions to Edmundo and the result was the gift of yet another book. But it was no ordinary bullfight book, of which there were numerous intended for the easily pleased who liked plenty of gory pictures with no demanding text. Edmundo's was a classic, a study, an academic treatise wonderfully illustrated with everything from line drawings and paintings, to superb photographs, beautifully printed and bound, on the history and art of *tauromania* (bullfighting craze). There was no aspect of bullfighting that was not covered brilliantly in this book. As a gift, it was financially way beyond our usual exchanges, and as far as the relationship was concerned, clearly intended to be a long, deep puff from a peace-pipe charged with the most exquisite tobacco. I read it in a week.

It was fascinating to learn how bull hunting – the origin of the *corrida* – had gradually become a staged event where the audience played a role in the assessment of both man and bull, so interesting to be apprised of the different types and temperaments of *toro* (bull) and torero (bullfighter) – the American word, 'toreador', is deplored by the Spanish – to learn about the *ganaderos* (breeders) and their ranches, the various famous plazas de *toros* (stadiums), and most of all, to read about the chicanery and paraphernalia that went into the making of a first-class *corrida*.

The *espectáculo* (show) comprised three separate teams of toreros, each headed by a matador who would eventually kill the bull, and each team would do the whole thing twice. One of the *matadores* would be chosen to be the principal and it was his duty to take over and finish a bull which, for reasons of injury or otherwise, a colleague had become incapable of doing, in which case it would be dispatched quickly as possible without any acclaim.

In addition to the *matador*, each team had five toreros: two were *picadores* mounted on horses, one of whom would make the initial wound between the shoulders of the bull with a lance, and the other three were banderilleros (darters) who, each in turn, thrust a pair of darts in much the same place. During the early stage of the contest – to call it something it really was not, because the bull was not a contestant but merely defending itself – the banderilleros played an important part, with the aid of capes, in drawing the bull into areas of the ring that suited the matador, and when necessary, such as when he repeatedly failed to kill it with his sword, to dispatch it by plunging a dagger into the top of its neck. That was the basic format but it varied considerably depending on the character, personality and skill of the matador, on whose whim and, to a lesser extent, that of the bull, everything depended.

There were pretty bullfighters with sleek hair and white teeth who were matinée idols, crazy young bullfighters who made up for their lack of natural charm with wild and dangerous moves; and older stolid reliable men who always got the job done but did not get half as many young women; and every spectator knew and appreciated the difference. Consequently, if the corrida had been arranged so that there were one of each kind performing during an *espectáculo*, the crowd was well served.

When I first perused the book, I was enthralled to think that perhaps many of the things that puzzled me, and darker things that bothered me, about Spain and the Spanish, might gradually unravel, and I could end up respecting some of the things I disliked when I knew the reasons for them. But instead, as I read, all that happened was that I became increasingly disenchanted with the fight, and by the time I had finished, I did not want to see men gored and I did not want to see bulls brutally treated. Blunting the bull's horns might reduce the danger to the *torero*, but it reduced the bull's sense of balance, and having to watch a so-called 'fighting sportsman' yanking the tail of an animal that had collapsed, in an effort to get it to its feet so the mime of a life-and-death tussle could continue in order for the fighting sportsman to win applause, was not only unedifying but sickening. In situations such as this, because bullfights lacked a referee, it seemed to me that the president of the *corrida*, whose power was absolute, should call an end to the farce and order the bull humanely destroyed.

Now I knew why the *picador*, usually an older, much brawnier and more pugnacious individual on a massive, very heavily-padded draft horse, was always booed. His job was not merely to break the tough skin between the bull's shoulders so that the matador could deliver the coup de grâce, straight down into the bull's heart with his rapier-like sword, as I had always thought. It was also to weaken the animal so as to make the job of the matador and his assistants easier, and it explained why, after the initial encounter between *picador* and bull, which is often so protracted and contentious that an animal which had charged straight into the ring ten minutes previously, was now staggering about, dazed and bleeding profusely, even though the *matador* had not touched him yet. Quite often it would drop to its knees and somersault, sticking into the ground like a dagger, by its horns, so that for an instant it was perpendicular, a sight incongruously awful. After a scene like this, for the matador to drag out the death scene by provoking, wheedling and almost imploring the animal to stagger a few steps in his direction, while he claimed valour for himself with flourishes of the cape and thrusts of his prominently stacked genitals in the direction of its dazed head, while its eyes rolled around in its head, was too much.

When the *matador* then strutted, head high, back to the bull but never letting it out of his sight, the backside of his trousers pouting falsie buttocks, was to perform nothing but a cruel travesty. If he then made a hash of inserting his sword, so that instead of going in to the hilt and down into the heart, it waggled about, half in, half out, and he then tried half a dozen more times with a new sword before asking for a dagger to sever its cervical cord, which might require a further half-dozen stabs, it was appalling. The crowd might show displeasure by whistling and hooting, but this was for incompetence, cowardice or clumsiness, not cruelty. Some time after I read the book, I elsewhere read of allegations regarding horrific cruelties perpetrated against the bull and the horse, but had reservations about some of them. They were mostly in English publications, and as is usually the case with English animal rights protestors, some of the claims sounded widely exaggerated.

In English we have several similes to denote strength: 'as strong as a horse', and 'strong as a bull', are two of them, and when working, both animals can display enormous strength; but to see the two in a corrida leaves one in no doubt about which is truly the stronger. As for the *picador*, the undisputed brute of the *corrida*, we once saw a particularly big fellow and his horse, with all the huge trappings and mattress-like cover meant to protect the horse from being pierced, gored and tossed so that both horse and mount were flung into the air and turned upside down, horse and trappings landing on top of the man, crushing him and breaking the horse's neck. An uglier scene would be difficult to imagine, especially in a Sunday afternoon show for the family, yet in a matter of minutes the various carcases were removed from the ring on litters while the band played movingly, if a mite too hastily, and a clumsy slaughter was transformed into a scene of quite stirring nobility.

From Edmundo's book, and subsequently shortly afterwards in the flesh, I learned of something almost magical that I was totally unprepared for, became almost obsessed with, and of which I thereafter time and again saw further examples.

When a bull entered the ring, whether cautiously and thoughtfully, or angrily and challengingly, it very quickly detected an invisible spot, not necessarily in the shade or with any perceptible advantage, but somewhere that has a quality of comfort and security that only the bull senses, and it will stay in that spot until drawn or forced out or off it, and return to it again and again. If anything happens to the spot to render it no longer attractive, the bull will find another, inferior, one; and if necessary, another and then another, so it is never without one. In this spot, its *'querencia'*, an invisible refuge, the bull feels relatively safe and comfortable. The matador is very much aware of all of this and he and his assistants will try to eliminate the advantage by enticing the bull away. The moment I learned of this, it instantly became clear why all the dogs, goats, hens, rabbits, birds, fish, reptiles, insects and every other creature I had ever kept or studied, had at some time sought to stand or lie in a particular place that had no manifest advantage in terms of shelter or comfort overhead or underfoot. And human beings were just the same, whether in a school playground or prison cell, although I never met anyone, before or since, who knew what they were doing when obeying the instinct. It was certainly a revelation to Helen and she was equally enchanted and identified her local *querencia* as the *fuente* (spring) in a tiny grassed area surrounded by a few trees and seats in Cocentaina. Whether or not this had anything to do with it, I could not say, but the water was delicious and tasted just like that from our old well in Ireland had done before the farmer with the field above the road and across from our farm, started using all manner of fertilizers and insecticides on it.

Old people sat chatting or dreaming on seats nearby and kids with a ball were surprisingly considerate. Valentí had introduced us to the fountain, though not as a *querencia*. It was free and people came from all around to fill their flagons and bottles, passersby frequently stopping for a drink. Apparently all villages in Spain not only had their own *fuentes*, they had areas for washing under a shade, and many poor locals without water at home, used them. Such places were ideal for gossiping and the women behaved just like washerwomen fabled the world over for their banter and behaviour.

Locals insisted the water was blessed, but I had my doubts. As a microbiologist who often had to examine samples of public water to test for contamination, I never detected any holy component.

After reading everything I could find on the subject of *querencias*, we spent more time around the fountain, sitting among the old Spaniards, watching the poor people coming for their water and the little ones playing with their ball. It seemed to help wondrously to banish homesickness and I could always see the difference in Helen after a spell under its influence: she would be calmer and more confident and say that she felt much better.

Whenever I mentioned the word, '*querencia*', to Spanish friends, although every one would say they knew the word – none being so humble as to admit to not knowing a Spanish word that an Englishman knew – I was sure many did not, because they would often say, '*¿Usted significa carencia?*' (You mean "*carencia*"?) which means 'a lack of something'. When I would then say '*No, "querencia"*,' and spell it out, they would affirm '*Si, claro..! ¿Tan qué?*' ('But of course..! So what?') But I knew they were bluffing. The only reference I ever again heard to the word was much later when I read that Edward Said had said his sister told him of a spot in her New York kitchen which she claimed was her *querencia*. It seems a pity to use Professor Said to substantiate a long drawn-out explanation like this, but 'needs must' and good evidence is sometimes hard to find.

Two months after my letters, there was still no reply from Sr. Férrer, so we had no idea how my chastener had gone down: was he doing penance in an *abogado* monastery, or had he simply wiped us from his books? One night, after a moderately severe bollocking, again largely on Helen's behalf because of some old English magazines she had left out for Valentí in case he wanted to look at the pictures and he had mistaken them for rubbish dumped in the wrong place, I nodded to her and we went out. It had been a bad day: no work had been done on the house for ages, nothing presumably done about the Spiers for ages, yet we always seemed to be paying Janet for something or other. The Spanish always wanted money before they would do anything, and if they made a mistake and one were due something back, one might as well whistle – or whatever it was one did – into the wind. Even the *querencia* did not seem to be much use in situations like this.

When we got back, Valentí was sitting typing in his room and it was quite a while before he came out. Eventually I heard his huge bare feet padding along the passage and was suddenly aware of him tentatively eclipsing the threshold. But I did not look up. He was a very patient fellow in some ways and waited quite a long time before giving a tiny cough.

'*Holá, Valentí,*' I said wearily, half raising my hand.

He could not say 'Sorry for before,' or anything like that, because although he was a proud *catalán*, he was still very Spanish and yielding an apology was about as difficult as handing money back. I was already acquainted with the problem, the Irish had been just the same. But his attitude had definitely changed and I suspected he realised he had gone a bit too far this time, gone down to tell his mother, and in rich *valenciano* she had said something like: 'They're English, son, and you mustn't forget it. On top of that, they're an old married couple, and an old married couple doesn't always think the way a thirty-year-old boy does. And if you're going to make a habit of bringing the likes of them into your lovely little flat, you're going to have to come to terms with it.'

'Right, Mama,' I like to think he answered, giving her a big hug.

He now took a short step towards us and volunteered 'I found out what time Eroski's close on Saturday.'

How could anybody not like him..? Earlier in the day I had been asking him where I could get a new phone, and he had been making inquiries – as always, *por supuesto*, without the aid of anybody's worldwide web. I thanked him and asked him to sit down if he had five minutes to spare, because I wanted to ask him certain things about Cataluña and Spain, particularly the politics.

He was so eager to oblige that he accidentally smiled. But before he sat down, he went into the kitchen and brought back three tiny wine glasses into which he poured a measure from a decanter we had never seen before, nor ever again. I realised we were celebrating, and it was friendship we were celebrating. We talked for about an hour and he listened attentively to every question before answering in his quiet, firm, irrefutably pragmatic way. Suddenly he got up because it was time to do his night shift. The scholar was off to the cemetery to make sure nobody disturbed anybody's eternal rest. This was the Spain of yet another little man who wanted the world to mistake him for a giant, this one with a say in the economy of Europe and the internal problems of countries far outside it: Aznar, ghost of the Generalissimo, a prime-minister prepared to do no more for one of his decent, intelligent, hardworking, scholarly citizens, than have him keep toot for the dead.

The next night at exactly the same time, he reappeared, this time with a look of anticipation on his face. '*Continuamos?*' he asked, meaning 'Shall we continue our little chat?' And every night from then on, he would come in and for quarter of an hour delineate the differences between things *catalán* and things Spanish, some of which seemed almost immaterial to me; though no doubt if we had immigrated to Ulster instead of Leinster, they would have been more apparent. At the end

I would say 'Is there anything you would like to know about England or Ireland?' and he would unhesitatingly shake his head.

'Nada?' (Nothing at all?)

'Nada,' he would confirm.

Was it him or was it us? Surely there was something or somebody of at least momentary interest during the last couple of millennia of British Isles history. I pressed him hard on the last occasion we had together and I could see he was really straining to accommodate me. But no, there was nothing and I could see he was perfectly sincere; he was not the sort of person who would want us to invent something or somebody just to appease him. The war? Which war?

He slowly rose to his feet, paused, and then asked wearily, '*¿El Loch Ness monstruo aún está vivo?*' (Is the Loch Ness Monster still alive?)

'Only for the Americans.'

We had heard that the fabled monster of the Scottish Loch captured the imagination of Spaniards and they were even taught about it in school; presumably they found him or her more interesting than the innumerable human monsters over there.

Valentí was one of the handful of men I had met in my life who would have made perfect comrades in battle, or marrers down a pit. The day we left to take occupancy of our house, he insisted we retain the two sets of keys to his flat that we had been using, so that if at any time we needed somewhere to stay, we could come back to Cocentaina, let ourselves in and make ourselves at home. And it was only because he was upset that I was able to coerce him into accepting something for rent by saying it was a gift to buy a few more of his wonderful books.

Driving back to the problems in Jemina, to live among the expats and *extranjeros*, leave behind the lovely town of Cocentaina and its friendly people, and most of all, our generous and trusting host, was a melancholy experience. Wanderers like Humberto, rare enough though they are, could be encountered in the outer reaches of the greater world; people like Valentí, only in lost worlds like Cocentaina.

Inside and out, work still had to be done on the house, but in the few days before we moved in, enough was done to make it habitable. We had arranged for our furniture and effects to be brought from Alicante and it was good to be reunited with photographs, music, books, paintings and so many other personal things, some of which we had nearly forgotten. It did not take us long to get the pictures up and put things where we wanted, because we needed to create a semblance of a home of our own as quickly as possible.

The house had a balcony upstairs and veranda downstairs, a lounge, hall, kitchen, bedroom upstairs and downstairs, office, bathroom upstairs and downstairs, utility room, working area at the top of the marble staircase, and a fully tiled and plastered double garage which could easily be converted into another bedroom. The main snags were that it had no fireplace to join with the chimney, one being in one room, the other in another; one room had been plastered before the electric wiring had been put in, and the dividing wall between our neighbours and ourselves had the buttresses on the wrong side. We would soon discover others. Telefónica, for instance, had disregarded the pipe that had been laid in readiness under the garden, and had instead strung a cable overhead, crudely connecting it to an upstairs room instead of to the wall in the front hall downstairs where fittings to receive it were already in place.

Outside were 1200 square metres of garden, comprising wasteland split into two areas on different levels, both ample enough to accommodate a swimming pool had we wanted one. The fact that we did not want a swimming pool seemed to everybody – Spanish, English and Dutch – to be a perversity beyond all understanding.

Because it was against the law to drain heavily chemicalised swimming-pool water into the street where it would erode the surface, some swimming pool owners boasted they had retained the original body of water from the time it was built, perhaps ten or twenty years before. Of course it collected rainwater and occasionally needed topping up during a drought, but that was hardly enough to deal with decades of sweat, urine and worse, discharged by a large variety of people in the case of properties regularly rented to many different holidaymakers.

Letters in the expat newspaper were always complaining about swimming pool problems. Helen and I had enjoyed swimming in the days when we had the agility and energy to enjoy it, and bodies that were less offensive than they were now, and if we wished, we could get into the car and within ten minutes be on the beach, in the mother of all swimming pools. Neither of us were enamoured of artificial swimming pools and preferred giving the space to trees, though the difficulty with planting anything more organic than an iron rod, was that our garden contained little real soil, only a substrate of stones, dust, clay, cement, plaster, crushed terra cotta, particles of polystyrene, shreds of polythene, shards of glass, rusting wire, plastic cable, dried paint tins, solvents and cigarette butts, the longevity of the latter to be compared only with certain kinds of radioactivity, and dirt. The nature of the ground had been created not only by carelessness and negligence during the construction of the house, but by wilfully ploughing in everything of no value to the builder, as soon as the house was finished, to save him having to take it to the dump. Wire, plastic, glass and stones could be laboriously picked out over a period of time, but there was nothing to be done about the cement, plaster and other fine catalysts and adhesive powders that were far more deleterious and blended so irreversibly with soil.

We had long since determined to dispense with the *bandera* (flag) party that Spanish builders traditionally organized for themselves at the owner's expense. This took place when the roof was on, and then again when the whole house was more or less finished. We had heard about these builders' bacchanals and for us they had no appeal whatsoever. Anybody who had had anything to do with the construction of the house at any time would be invited by the *albaniles* to a booze-up where they could drink themselves silly, stuff themselves with food supplied by professional caterers, throw the surplus at each other and the bemused owners, toss each other into the pool, and leave all the mess behind. Thus all kinds of tales circulated about the expense, damage, humiliation and revenge visited on owners who had been less than absurdly generous and tolerant during the period of construction.

Apart from anything else, we had no time for flags.

We had decided to plant undemanding species of tree and bush, manure and mulch them with kitchen waste, give them only potable water and maintain the pH as near to neutral as possible. Notwithstanding, some plants failed almost immediately and all of the expensive trees, such as the Ficus, had to be replaced several times. The Jacarandas fought hard but no matter how we pampered them, never looked other than tortured. Proof of the devastation done to our earth by the builders was that any kind of plant we threw on the wasteland beyond our wall, which had been untouched by the builders, grew luxuriantly with no attention at all.

Cacti were something neither Helen nor I had ever been keen on, but in our region they grew huge and wild everywhere, so we went into the *campo* with a machete and tomahawk, cut pieces off plants that had been dumped but had regenerated, brought them home and stuck them in the ground; same with succulent ground cover like Witch's Nail. We also planted Bougainvillea and Oleander which, like the cacti, were tough, opportunist and colourful. Aloe Vera grew well and the sap had healing qualities of which we availed ourselves for a number of minor ailments, to no benefit.

Succulents, even more than cacti, would almost burst with sap in terrain where there was not enough water to support the growth of a blade of grass. Both were amazing and would have been a godsend had they not been so fiercely intrusive, and the cactii not so hostile to man and dog. They grew alarmingly on any ground, needed no special care, feeding, staking, watering or watching over, apart from making sure they did not grow overnight to any inhospitable giant's castle in the sky.

European deciduous forest trees did not grow well at all in our area, but certain pines did well and we planted a dozen of them to give our very exposed garden some privacy. However, come December, nearly every pine in Spain was infested with the 'procession caterpillar', and although it sounds like an entertaining creature, it is in fact a nasty little beast. From almost indestructible communal cocoons in various parts of the tree, where it lives alongside hundreds of companions, it drips corrosive liquid that can severely burn mammalian skin, blind humans and occasionally kill cats and dogs. The best way to eliminate it is to soak its cocoons in paraffin and set fire to them, and even then they will twist and crackle for quite a while before expiring. The trouble is that if you are not very careful, you can burn the tree to the ground in minutes, while hundreds of the vile things make their way out of the pyre, fall to the ground, and 'process off', steaming and trailing smoke but still alive – a horrendous sight.

They are called 'Procession Caterpillars' because they follow each other in long columns, rather like ants, until they find a hole in the ground in which to hibernate and metamorphose into the adult insect which is a very ordinary-looking moth. When the female emerges from her chrysalis, she mates, finds a pine in which to lay her eggs, and the whole process begins again. The silky cocoon which the tiny larvae manufacture as soon as they hatch, and continue to enlarge as they grow, is remarkably tough and almost impenetrable. Poking a cocoon with, say, a hoe, will merely cause it to bend without breaking, and a swipe with a spade will nowhere near dislodge it.

One year in the south of France campsites had to be closed because of the things which, because of bizarre weather conditions, had become a real menace outside of their usual season which was winter, but I never saw or heard of any action taken, or warnings given, in Spain. Even where there were huge, massively infested pines by the road along which people frequently walked, the Ayuntamiento never saw fit to do anything; not even giving out information in newsletters or on the radio. Not surprisingly, it was the unwary *extranjero* on whom the caterpillars more often dropped, and his or her dogs who suffered the worst injuries, especially to their eyes.

When we bought trees, we could never get the advice we needed from the *viveros* (nurserymen); all we could get was the standard spiel that their plants grew rapidly anywhere, needed very little water, produced plentiful fragrant blooms over a long period, then delicious nutritious fruits that were resilient in inclement weather and resistant to parasites: the perfect plant, in other words. But nobody had the kind that fared well in 'builder's soil', the stuff of our garden.

One afternoon we went to a nursery and bought a set of plant pots, a bottle of rooting compound, a couple of bags of rooting peat mixture and pair of special secateurs, in order to take cuttings from variously coloured bougainvillea that we had bought from this same *vivero* a couple of weeks previously. When I asked the *jefe* whether the cuttings should be kept in a dark or light place, he looked at his wife as though he could hardly believe what he was hearing, but made no reply. I knew exactly what he was thinking: 'Why the hell should I tell this mingy blighter how to propagate his cuttings? What does he think all those lovely little things waiting to be bought in the big tent over there, are for?'

So I asked his wife.

'*En oscuro,*' (in the dark) she mumbled.

'Pardon..? Sorry, I mean "*Perdoneme?*"'

'*Oscuro, por supuesto!*' the bossman spluttered, pushing her away to do some more backbreaking potting before she could spill any more free-information beans.

'Do you have any *triturata caleza* (lime) ?

At first he pretended there were no such words in Spanish. Then he corrected my pronunciation but said I would not be able to get it because such chemicals were only for professionals like him to use.

'You mean to tell me I can buy a hundredweight of gunpowder at a hardware store, but can't buy a kilogram of calcium carbonate from a garden centre?' I expostulated in my native tongue, it being the perfect one for outrage. He grinned. He had not the faintest idea what I had said but was enormously gratified to see I was so exasperated. I asked again…

What did I want it for… Perhaps he was thinking of reporting it to the *guardia*.

When I told him it was to neutralise the pH of the soil, he said stale tap water would do the job. I asked if he had any other alkali but he was shaking his head before I had the question out. That was what the Spanish did when they did not wish to tell the truth without telling a lie, not that they had any trouble with telling lies. But I was not going to say '*Muchísimo gracias,*' like any polite English *extranjero*, and then slink away, so I repeated the question slowly with emphasis on my BBC Castilian pronunciation. He continued standing there for a few moments on one leg, leaning against the doorway of his tiny shop, with me standing in front of him, and then he suddenly brushed past me with his brawny brown arm held out, growling '*Cuanto, cuanto, cuanto?* (How much)?'

'*Tienen caleza pues?*' (You mean you've got some, after all?)

'*No, no, no, no, no! Caleza no… Calcio Carbonate!*'

'Great!' I said. 'About a kilo.' I showed him with my hands.

'*Eso no es un kilo!*' (That's not a kilo!) he scoffed, grabbing my hands and pulling them further apart so they could have encompassed a real kilo had one been suspended in mid air. But I did not mind him having the last word, as long as I got the lime. Suddenly he went off without my knowing whether he had gone for some, or had just decided he had had enough and terminated the enquiry. Five minutes later, when we were looking at something else, he came back with a plastic bag containing white powder and thrust it at me, as much as to say, 'Here, you bloody old twat. Take it and give me nine hundred pesetas. Then get back to your silly little garden!'

Both our fronts were already covered in calcium carbonate, the only difference being that whereas I had on one of the expensive new microfibre T-shirts and a fairly classy pair of trousers, he was in scruffy overalls, this obviously being what he had intended by giving me an unwiped bag with holes in it. For him it would be worth breaking the law – if there were such a one, which I very much doubted – to think of me walking around, looking like an idiot and messing up my car; then when he and his staff were having their coffee break, for him to be telling them how he had so wittily played his hand against an old *idiota inglés*.

A plant we had always taken for granted in Ireland, was grass, and we had many varieties of it. Almost every animal we had thrived on it, from goose to donkey and rabbit to sheep; even the hens and dog occasionally ate it. It was just as well, for no matter what we did, we could never deter it for long; it was the classic weed. In Spain it was a rare plant, taking a long time to germinate and grow, and a great deal of water and care to sustain. Neither lawns or fields were a feature of the territory where we lived now, so, from having to mow it twice a week in Ireland if one wanted a lawn, one now had to learn to do without it altogether.

TWENTY-FIVE

IN EVERY STREET ON our *urbanización*, on every road leading from Jemina to the *urbanización*, and everywhere within a few metres of the beaches up and down the coast, habitation of every shape and size was continuously being erected. Every other vehicle that passed was an earth-moving machine, a churning cement lorry, a huge waggon packed full of building materials, or one of the countless tradesman's white vans with a little middle-aged man inside. No wonder the roads leading to *urbanizaciónes* were always cracked and full of potholes.

The swimming pool installers next door had now finished, and renting Dutch holidaymakers for whom heavy rain and North Sea inundations were their natural enemy, were already jumping in and out of the water, males roaring and guffawing, and females screaming and squealing, as though none of them had ever seen anything like it.

On the plot to our left, a new house was being built for a family of Walloons by a gang who managed to make even more noise than Lew Spiers ever had. Machines screeched and scraped, the highly irritating alarm peeps warning of impending accidents went on almost nonstop, and radios blared Hispano-American pop – nobody seemed to have heard of *flamenco* or *fardo* (type of Portuguese music) let alone Segovia or Peña (both famous guitarists). Workmen shouted, argued and bawled meaningless profanities and obscenities, and lorries with all kinds of contraptions and building impedimenta constantly came and went, each creating more chaos, mess, and noise. Noise was not the only noisome thing, however.

First thing every morning, without fail, immediately yon side the boundary wall they had built, a line of defecators could be seen squatting, adamant, according to Trev Hall, that all bowel movements be made during working hours, and the volume of accumulated material was such that every Friday Trev had to send a JCB digger to bury it. Urination was carried out from the roof, and young ones would compete from the edge, arms akimbo, legs apart, like rodeo riders minus hat and horse, while they sprayed or dribbled on anything and anyone underneath. Chic Mrs Hall once got caught in one of their showers when she called to see her husband on her way to the bank, and they had all laughed their heads off, which made one wonder what the grandees did for a living. When I asked Trev why he put up with it when he was the boss, he shrugged despairingly and said that if he were to criticise any of them for anything, every man jack of them would pack up and leave; they could find other work a lot easier than he could find other workers.

Apart from the less than appealing sights and sounds that enveloped us, we also had to endure the continual poaching of our water and electricity and repeated blowing of fuses from far too highly demanding equipment, which began as a favour to Trev and ended in umbrage. The *albañiles* did not care who was paying for the usage, wastage, damage and mess as their cables and hoses dragged our plants out of the ground, and as soon as Trev had got them started, he was in his sports car and off somewhere else, somewhere supposedly beyond the reach of his mobile telephone.

In every *urbanización* there were always blaring radios and circulating loudspeaker vans advertising fiestas, touting for scrap or campaigning for politicians, that would come around again and again in case somebody might have missed a syllable on the previous loop. And numerous dogs barking. Such was the Spaniard's infatuation with noise, that two-stroke motorbike owners removed their exhaust pipes to amplify what their engines ordinarily generated. They loved cacophony. The more there was, the happier and more secure they felt. After numerous complaints to the authorities in Brussels by foreign residents in Spain, in a move as ingenious as the Irish solution to the driving test backlog when the government had granted its 'driving test amnesty', the Spanish passed a law whereby every house was to soundproof its windows. How religiously this was obeyed by the least law-abiding, most insurgent people in Europe, if not the whole world, could easily be conjectured.

I had never known dogs to bark the way they did in Spain. Most were Alsations because Alsations looked as aggressive as they sounded, but they would always have two or three mongrels equally capable of shattering the peace, as companions. Left on their own during the week while their owners were away, they were fed and watered from automatic devices. Trained to do nothing else, and failing to obey a command from anybody, all they did was roam the property, eat, drink, defecate and bark at any human being that passed, plus all dogs, and at night the noise was horrendous. It took one cur to start things off, and the whole lot of them would be at it, night after night, like a well rehearsed mind-blowingly atrocious canine choir. Most of the time when their animals were causing the din, the owners were either miles away, or inside watching television and feigning not to be able to hear a sound outside. Any complaint – and it could only come from an *extranjero* – would be met with fury, and nothing at all done by anyone to control them. Dogs in Spain were supposed to be licensed, but because the head of the Spanish Alsation Association was also head of the country's Dog Owners Association, Alsations were exempt from licensing.

So these most unpredictable of dogs, capable of inflicting serious wounds and making more noise than any Rottweiler, went virtually unhampered while the Rottweilers and other big dogs which were usually licensed, were treated as if they were pet lions or tigers instead of the mild-natured creatures they usually were.

At first when we went to live in our new house, we took to walking around the *urbanización* at night; it was warm, the streets were empty and the fragrance of oleanders and bougainvillea was delightful. But nobody else did it and after a week we gave it up. The numbers of times we had been passing a wall when two or three large dogs had suddenly hurled themselves at the wire netting that separated them from us by only a matter of inches, barking like Dogs of War and splattering us with streams of steaming saliva, was more than enough to outweigh the pleasure one would normally have expected from such a stroll. And by the time we returned to the house, we would be shook up and annoyed and Helen would be trembling, even though she was well used to dogs and other animals. Whether dogs were on the loose in the streets, or tearing around their premises, they were no joy to anybody, and whenever they were seen attached to a leash, ninety percent of the time the other end would be attached to an expat, English or German.

The situation was so bad that expats would move house and sometimes country, to get away from it. The trouble was that when one was buying a house from abroad, it would not be until the day after they came to occupy it that they would find they had neighbours who behaved like hyenas and had dogs like jackals. One could go to the airport to meet a visitor and have half a dozen silly, yapping little toy-dogs on leashes so long they wrapped themselves around one's legs, and often somebody else's as well, whilst they tried to mate with or kill, each other. Or mate with one's leg. And all the time their ingratiatingly smiling owners would be looking at one with such an appealing expression on their face, one which conveyed a sentiment like, 'Isn't she sweet?' or 'Isn't he a lovely little boy? Go on, you can lift his tail and kiss his bottom, if you want. Everybody does it and he loves it.'

One day we got our first communication from Edmundo in a long time, a very embarrassed telephone call in which his English showed it had gone seriously downhill and would need a lot of Saturday mornings to restore. He was very formal and said we had to go to Sr. Férrrer's office immediately. Helen had to tell him I was ill in bed.

'In that case you must both come to see Sr. Férrer at 7 o'clock this evening.'

Edmundo always spoke to Helen in English, but speaking another language is always difficult over the phone and he was expressing himself via a mixture of formality and informality: half *funcionario*, half old *amigo*.

'If it's important, Edmundo, I'll come,' Helen told him. 'But Jack cannot.'

An hour later Edmundo rang back to say Sr. Férrer would come to see us at our house that night, and he, Edmundo, would accompany him. Could Helen meet them in Jemina to show them the way?

That night was the first time we had ever known fog in Spain and it was pure pea soup by the time Helen reached the main road between Jemina and Alicante. She was hurrying to keep the rendezvous with the great man and hoping our friend would be placating him and thanking him over and over on our behalf for doing the mountain going to meet Mohammed thing. Hard though it was, she managed to meet up with them, recognising the anxious white face of our friend next to a large, darkly dressed figure in a kick-ass jeep, rather like Faust and Mephisto on their way to some assignation that did not bode well for poor Faust.

For a few moments Helen and Edmundo had waved at each other in recognition and relief, until the powerful arm of justice had come chopping down out of the window, like a railway signal, to halt the maudlinism and indicate that Helen was to go on ahead so that the jeep could follow.

Alas, there was a *Moros y Christianos* (Moors and Christians) procession rehearsal that night, so because the roads were closed off, Helen could not take the normal route and had instead to drive out of town in a northerly direction, in a state of near panic, imagining the Spanish pejoratives being used about her by the occupants of the pursuing vehicle, one of them, at least, a twenty-four carat misogynist. They were trying to signal her to stop but she had decided she would be unable to muster the necessary Spanish to explain the situation under the circumstances, so when they tried to draw alongside to point out that they were all heading for Valencia, she merely accelerated into the fog. However, Edmundo was fairly well acquainted with the area, so, one way or another, the two vehicles and their three occupants eventually all arrived at the house.

'How am I going to take them back?' Helen whispered to me in the kitchen as soon as we were alone. 'The fog's getting worse.'

But I knew better. There was no way our guest would deign to be shown anything twice by anybody, whether or not it was back to front, let alone by a woman, English at that; he would sooner have driven off into the twilight zone and take Edmundo with him.

Sr. Férrer would not accept any refreshment, so poor Edmundo who looked as though he were dying for a cup of tea and a biscuit, declined likewise; for a Spaniard, Edmundo loved his cup of tea and biscuit – which he pronounced 'bisquit' – when he used to come for our lesson, delighted to be partaking in what he considered to be a typical English ceremony. But both were extremely considerate and polite, Férrer more than ever before, and Edmundo, despite no sustenance, did everything he could to facilitate things. The reason for the visit was to sort out the photographs of the *vivienda*, and comparative ones of the villa. We had taken dozens, and so had other people, and Sr. Férrer now had all the best ones. Sometimes photographs had been taken, developed quickly and sent to his office with a written explanation; at other times we had taken them in and explained them. Now they had all come back, or many of them, and Sr. Férrer wanted them identified and dated. This had been done initially, of course, but many of the labels had come adrift and markings rubbed off the backs; in certain cases the business sides had been permanently written on and the marking could not be removed without removing key parts of the picture, but that certainly had nothing to do with me.

All the time we had known him, Sr. Férrer had never uttered a single word of encouragement or optimism about our prospects. It would not have cost him anything to have once or twice murmured, 'Don't worry, dears, I'll do what I can to extricate you from this mess,' or something like it, particularly on occasions when things had been especially fractious – and, let's face it, there had been quite a few of them. Helen would certainly have appreciated it. But this warrior for justice was not an allayer of anxiety, he was a defeatist, and, I believe, a closet depressive. He had plenty of physical presence but often appeared on the brink of floundering and I could not avoid the suspicion that he was afraid of Víbora-Masson, the Spiers' *abogado*. Too often he kept saying 'Sr. Víbora-Masson *es muy, muy intelligente*', and we would be wondering where that was supposed to leave us.

Apparently the Forsyths had once used Víbora-Masson themselves and had no doubt he was the better abogado. Repeatedly they urged us to sack Férrer and get somebody else, somebody with a reputation in property cases, most importantly one who spoke good English and would not be intimidated by the likes of Víbora-Masson. But it was too late. We had spent too much time and money on Férrer and invested too much sweat and too many T-cells. Besides, it would have caused Edmundo great embarrassment. Anyway, we knew much more about abogados now, and had no faith in any of them. Whatever their individual character, everybody said the judicial system itself was appalling: antediluvian, dead slow and hopelessly corrupt.

At least Sr. Férrer had come out to us, something people, including Janet, said no *abogado* would ever do; though it was a pity he had not hired a coach and brought the judge and the rest of the shebang.

TWENTY-SIX

GILBERT WAS NEARLY EIGHTY and in poor health, yet had expended much of his time and energy on his computer writing letters and seeking information on our behalf and passing it on to us in the form of faxes; so much so, that on some days our hall must have looked like Reuter's. He was an Englishman of the old school, having spent most of his life in the colonial service, and although long since retired, was peremptory about getting things done and not suffering fools gladly. Mildred said that all his life he had raged against injustice and helped many Spanish and English people who had sought his help when they could not get it anywhere else, and everybody who knew him respected him for his generosity, ability and integrity.

In England, at least, it used to be that when you were over eighty you could rant and rave, slander and clamour for floggings and executions, and people just smiled; but I had a hunch that if we raced down to Sr. Férrer's, burst into his office and demanded he do this or that immediately, or that we issue some challenge to his knowledge of Spanish and EU law, it would not have advanced our case one whit; more likely than not we would have ended up on the street, having paid an awful lot of money into the 'Férrer Charity for Useless Abogados' box. Sometimes I was so exasperated with something he had said or not said, done or not done, that I could have gladly stabbed him in the eye with my nail file and watched him weep as the vitreous humour dribbled down his beautiful tie, though I never shared that particular thought with anybody but Helen, and even she was absolutely disgusted. Anyway he was not the type to have been impressed by such a show of English high dudgeon; only Edmundo would have appreciated such a thing.

The good news was that Edmundo and I had resumed our former Saturday conversation classes for two, and our relationship was almost as good as it had been, '*A las cinco de la tarde*' (At five in the afternoon) becoming part of our language in keeping with our new timetable – afternoons by arrangement: it was our parting adieu, like Hemingway's reputedly was, signifying the critical time of day when the bullfights began, and it made us feel very much like true *compañeros*. It was inevitable that we would return to the court case, although we had tried to eschew it as the cause of our previous rupture, and whenever there was any suggestion of our intervening on our own behalf, he would invariably counsel, 'Remember, things are done differently in Spain, my friend.'

So many times what we saw as valuable collaboration, he saw as unacceptable interference and Sr. Férrer saw as pretty much standard English ignorance: 'Forgive them, for they know not what they do'.

'Try to be patient, my friend. Señor Férrer is a clever man. Who knows what he has up his trouser leg?'

To have let that pass would have contravened one of our principal literary rules, which was that we would never hesitate to correct a major faux pas.

'"Up his sleeve", Edmundo... "Up his sleeve".'

'Ah, yes. Of course. "Up the sleeve".'

'Pardon me for asking something I feel I must ask, Edmundo, but for how much longer are we supposed to be patient? At our age we haven't a whole lot of time.'

He shook his head sorrowfully and lamented: 'I think Alicante is very different from Hastings, my friend.'

'Mmmm,' I replied, but I was not exactly sure what he meant.

Christmas would soon be upon us again and the Forsyths were convinced we should cancel our trip to Ireland because, they said, notice to appear in court would be three days at most, and if we did not attend, for whatever reason, we would not only lose the case but would very likely be had up for contempt. But some things were more important than righting material wrongs – certainly a lot more than fiddling about, which is what we were having to do, and going to see our family was one of them. In any case, the likelihood of our suit being heard immediately before or after a Spanish Christmas, was patently slim. *El Pais*, the Spanish paper we took a week to read, was always reporting delays in the courts, not least because the judges were going on strike. So I wrote to Sr. Férrer and told him our tickets were booked, gave him the dates we would be away, gave him our telephone numbers in Ireland, wished him '*Feliz Navidad*' (Happy Christmas) and off we went, bearing in mind that this time we might need to return with rather more substantial evidence as to our absence, than a receipt for a couple of pairs of Irish Y-fronts.

We went, had a wonderful time – although the family all hoped we would come back forever – and returned to Spain on New Year's Eve to find Telefónica had lopped us off and it would be five days at the very least before we could be reconnected. They had made a mistake in our bill, charging us twice for a bill we had already paid in Muchavista more than six months previously, and unless we paid immediately and then disputed it, should a dispute be our wish, we would have to pay the full cost of re-installation: new cables, new poles, new telephone, new everything down to the galvanised tacks.

Not only could Telefónica be extremely rude to *extranjero* complainants, especially if one were elderly and English, but they could be incredibly smug because they knew the complainant would realise their future as a troublemaker would be assured: their name would already be down in their black book and forever after they would have no end of trouble sorting out bills and utterly bogus claims, such as the commonest which was that the last thing one did before going on holiday was to instruct Telefónica to close one's account. This was how they dealt with notice to the effect that one would be away from such and such a date until such and such a date, in case they wondered why there were no calls during that time, a courteous but fatuous message as it turned out, but I managed to get someone on the helpline who said they spoke English.

'What a load of utter tripe..!' I replied after she had repeatedly repeated Telefónica's claim that we had cancelled our account. It was a good test of her proficiency in English and although it might sound a trifle haughty, surely it could not have caused offence.

She then came out with the hardy Spanish interrogator's standby: 'How old are you?'

'What's that got to do with it?'

'*Que..?* (What?)'

'Why do you want to know..? How old are you?'

'I need to know because I think you might be going senile.'

'Is this conversation being recorded?

'*Por supuesto!*'

'Can I have a copy?'

'*No, no, no, no, no! Pertenece a Telefónica.*' (It belongs to Telefónica).

Naturally, no good ever came of conversations like this. Even our female bank manager, with whom Helen was on good terms, had no authority when it came to dealing with the probationers on the Telefónica helpline, and Helen was so upset about being unable to contact the children, that the bank manager had argued with them for twenty minutes before having to give up to get on with her duties. In the end, after deductions for 'administrative costs', we paid the unjustified charge, disputed the need for it in writing, and had the telephone reconnected. Somebody had to pay for the mistake…

Late in January Humberto came back to his little flat on the outskirts of Alicante. No postcards had been sent out – he always hand-delivered postcards on his return from his trips into wilderness where he visited all kinds of old friends – and there was no celebration, no 'Cooee, I'm back, folks!' People said his friends were ipso facto as dotty as he was. We just happened to ring one night, and he was back, like a swallow that had returned from its epic journey to foreign lands, to its dilapidated little nest on the same rafter of the same dusty old barn of a neglected little farm on a patch of land long since re-zoned for the building of huge and awful apartment blocks that resembled prisons of the future.

Despite living like a hermit and refusing to make phone calls, an economy resolution, Humberto was a very sociable creature in a quiet and polite way, and nobody could sit or stand near him for more than a couple of minutes without learning of several of his strongly held opinions. He was self-righteous and pathologically stubborn, always ready to challenge anybody or anything he considered unreasonable, yet totally unaggressive.

We had not seen him since going to Cocentaina, so had lots to talk about and arranged to meet him in L'indret, the vegetarian restaurant where he held court in Alicante, not too unlike Dr Johnson in his London tavern, except for their comparative midriffs and a few other trivia, and the menu which in Humberto's case consisted of stewed broccoli and water that had never been exposed to the inside of a plastic container, rather than the 'good doctor's cold beef and warm sour ale; but the patter would probably have been remarkably similar given that the good doctor would not have belonged to a socialist party.

L'Indret was an easy-going anarchist's vegetarian restaurant in the northern part of the city, run by two friendly ex-Hare Krishnas whose customers were predominantly unattractive intellectual females. Seventy-four percent female was the interesting statistic Humberto came out with and I could imagine him apparently deep in thought, ruminating on metaphysics as well as kale, but carefully computing the women, including those who had gone into the toilet. I had never seen him make a pass at a female, or refer to any woman in any way other than with maximum gallantry, but I had a feeling they nevertheless appealed to him in as fundamental a way as they did any ordinary alpha male.

Because he ate little cooked food and never meat, few restaurants suited him. At L'indret not only were staff and customers liberal in the best sense of the word, but the management would go to considerable lengths to accommodate individual customer's whims. In Humberto's case, because he ate little that would cost them much, they allowed him to repeatedly circumnavigate the buffet counter, where he loaded up his plate again and again with mainly raw, vividly green vegetables and greasy nuts, smiling at this fellow diner and having a pleasant word with that. Depending on a proprietor's point of view, he must have been either the world's most perfect client or most aggravating customer. As a friend, he could be extraordinarily obliging and incredibly awkward in the same breath. As a pragmatic ecologist – and he was certainly one of those – he cherished migration but deplored the introduction of foreign species, no matter how fascinating, lovely or valuable – and that certainly included homo sapiens. When I wanted to show him some exotic rice fish that were tremendous gorgers of the mosquito and other troublesome vectors, that I had ordered from Thailand, he was so disgusted by my interfering with the 'balance of nature' that he refused to walk the mere eight or nine paces it would have taken him to reach the pond; and so he did his bit towards maintaining the purity of the species, and to hell with the hybrid and evolution. Fortunately for him and his ilk, he had the ability to so eloquently argue the case for contradiction and the oxymoron, that he got away with what would have made a cropper out of many a renowned scientist or philosopher, and I came to think it was the argument, rather than the principle, that mattered to him most.

He was delighted to hear how we had enjoyed Cocentaina and our stay with Valentí, and his face lit up when we recounted various experiences. He was 'deeply gratified' to read a piece I had written for a Valencian journal about our time there, which had been translated into *catalán*, and only suggested four or five improvements should I be seeking to have it published elsewhere. I had probably overdone the praise, a far greater lapse than skimping on it, as far as Humberto was concerned, plus it should have been done in *valenciano*. He hated flattery, so even mild approval from him was praise indeed, and when he went so far as to quote sentiments or sentences from a book about coalminers that I had written, I have to say I was as proud as I would have been had it come from any English literary icon.

Unlike the majority of Spaniards, who loved to, Humberto would never flatly contradict what one said, no matter how strongly he might disagree, and this was one of his endearing qualities. He would just put his finger to his lips, lower his head and keep it lowered, and you would realise he had literally bowed out. The one thing he did not expound about with the usual self assurance that could make a listener feel like an ignoramus, was sex, and I cannot imagine him ever having delved into it apart from between the covers of a book. By virtue of his age, his life had straddled both extreme epochs when it came to this particular chestnut. In the first, it was virtually illegal – though indoors, far from it – and in the second, the present, it was anything but. Whether or not the current attitude was a form of moral anarchy, or plain and simple machismo, it surely said something for the culture when a popular magazine could give away a free tampon one week, and a free condom the next, rather than yet another CD to enable the recipient to clamber aboard the Internet via a trashy pop song. And when, in a small town like Cocentaina, the old and young could similarly and without the slightest sign of embarrassment, stroll past huge Ministry of Health posters showing graphic details of male erectile dysfunction and its treatment – even though Humberto dismissed it as a not very subtle attempt to reverse the falling birth rate – I felt credit was due somewhere. Were such a poster to have been put up in England or Ireland, half the population would have been scandalised, and nine-tenths of the other spray-painting something smutty on it after dark. Yet England could put up posters just as big, declaring 'Greed is Good', and people would respect them. In Ireland, while the Catholic Church was still doing its damnedest to prevent the prevention of Aids by using condoms, two nuns in Spain could stand in a bus shelter plastered with the Ministry of Health's luridly coloured diagrams and a spiel indicating how such items might be fitted, by showing a pair of disturbingly delicate female hands, a condom, and a quarterback's penis, step by step. I know, I witnessed it in Muxtamiel myself, several times.

The Spanish had a board game with pieces representing pimps, whores and transvestites, where those unlucky enough to catch a venereal disease had to go to the 'Clinic', instead of 'Jail'. Imagine such a divertissement in Ireland..! They also had games and adverts for sanitary towels, that celebrated every kind of heinous American violence, but nothing as evil as a game about venereal disease. Humberto said that when the world's first test tube baby was born, Spanish newspaper and television headlines blared: 'Born Without Stain of Original Sin!'.

Although his family were bankers, Humberto considered himself a devout socialist, and things *catalán* were an obsession with him. It was difficult for a non-Spaniard to understand the attitude of Catalans, and, I think, for a non-Catalan Spaniard, really difficult. Because of the little I understood of Catalonia's quest for independence, my sympathy was limited. It seemed to me that there was much that was selfish in the Catalan, and I felt the same about the Scots and Northern Irish; maybe the gaelic Irish were not that different either.

Humberto liked the northern district of Alicante because it was largely where the working class lived. It was full of little shops: cobblers and haberdashers, tobacconists, cheap bars, cafes, confectioners and ice-cream shops, small newsagents and stationers, photocopiers and photographers, pet shops, hairdressers, shoe shops, dimly lit and perpetually empty purveyors of dusty religious statues, ancient outfits and medallions; little groceries with most of their ware outside on racks or on the pavement, and most important of all, tiny little shops that out in the back trafficked water that had never been in contact with plastic, an esoteric element the naively trusting skeptic, Humberto, walked miles for, several times a week.

There was also a little jewellers-cum-watchmaker's owned by two brothers who dealt in pre-digital clocks and watches, gave a very modestly priced and amazingly quick service, and clowned with any customer who would put up with it. Imagine a friendly – or even faintly affable – watchmaker with a sense of humour! It is quite disorientating. Humberto introduced us to these two the way he had introduced us to so many other people who provided special services at very reasonable prices – though nothing *outre*. These brothers had arranged the repair of my old factory 'clock-inner' whose pendulum had got broken during its journey from Ireland when we first came over and had not been lucky enough to find anybody to fix it. They had ordered a part to be specially fashioned, and the task was done perfectly, even though the device had been made on Tyneside in the 1930s. The workshop, which was directly above their business premises, was a tiny room absolutely full from wall to wall and floor to ceiling, with all kinds and bits and pieces of clocks and watches, occupied and worked in by their uncle, a very old dwarf who could hardly move and was almost indistinguishable from the innumerable eccentric but charming clockwork figures who bowed, waved, raised their hats and to whom he chatted non-stop and treated as *compañeros*.

It made me wonder why writers of 'health' columns in magazines recommended sedentary workers get up every forty-five minutes, jog around the room and do a couple of dozen aerobic exercises, should not advise their readers to spend their teabreaks and lunch – times on treadmills attached to a generator.

Geniuses like this diminutive watchmaker would never be replaced. Like many a venerable artisan in the area, he had come into being before the Civil War, but now that Spaniards were much bigger than they used to be – he could not find apprentices to work for him under such appalling, claustrophobic and impecunious conditions, the art and trade would expire with him, and many exquisite, sophisticated little artefacts would no longer survive more eighteen months, let alone three or four generations. The sad thing was that not only was this already coming to pass with his nephews' – the two of them had already taken the first step in the 'devolution' of the craft by confining themselves to sales, but in all the other master craft shops as well, and except for a few in hiding, the wonderfully clever wild-birdtrap-makers had already gone, forced out by the RSPB and other conservationist blackshirts. The latter had long gone from England, *por supuesto*, and scarcely existed in Ireland, so all that the bird-fanciers could do was wait to see if the Chinese decided it was worth rekindling the magic.

In the past, along with utility went beauty, whether in the form of a pocket watch or a steam engine, and along with those features went durability. Nowadays obsolescence was a side-effect of speedy manufacture, poor design and progress, and was present in all things, including art. But the Spanish, unlike the English and Irish, maintained that durability and thrift were still virtues, and in this, perhaps by coincidence, perhaps due to DNA, they were evident in other Hispanic countries, such as the Philippines, Africa and most especially in Cuba where the extremely visual motor vehicles might be ancient but were still capable of moving people and goods from one place to another. I loved the art and morality of restoration, and the sureness that one could have almost anything repaired if one looked hard enough for the right virtuoso. They exuded a wonderful feeling of selflessness. I could remember a time, such as at the end of the Second World War, when because of the urgent need for repair and improvisation, all sorts of things that had become so vital throughout the years of conflict and destruction, and of poverty and industrial strife before that, were recycled long before the word was coined.

The first time we saw the extraordinary Moros y Cristianos, an unashamedly racist fashion parade commemorating the expulsion of the Moors from otherwise Christian Spain, was in Mutxamel (Muchamiel) at the end of our first summer. The event was held annually, but at different times, by every town in the Valencian region, though some had only been on the bandwagon for the last couple of years, and every week somewhere was in its throes. Nobody seemed to object to the basic sentiment, though if they had celebrated the expulsion of the Jews – who the Spanish also ejected – there would have been hell to pay.

It began with a procession led by local dignitaries dressed as Moorish warriors, in phalanxes of about a dozen – mixed gender, if short of males – and attired like half-transvestite, half-beasts, with weapons that looked as though they had come from the inside of a gigantic plastic wristwatch and were incapable of inflicting a wound on anyone but the bearer. The headgear was the most elaborate part of the uniform and the eye shields so huge that were the wearers not linked together, they would hardly have been able to find their way to the pavement, let alone the other end of the street. Costumes were as lurid in colour as they were outrageous in design, and many so cumbersome their wearers could hardly walk, as each succeeding phalanx tried to outdo in Hollywood splendour what had preceded it, and Africans were shamelessly represented as a kind of nigger minstrel without the banjo.

Although the Moors always got the best outfits, they did not necessarily get the best girls, and when the austere Christians come along, dressed like lepers in comparison, they were as coquettish and pretty a bunch of soldiers as one might have hoped to encounter in any army. When we visited the Moros y Cristianos museum and I asked the curator how frequently the costumes changed, without winking or turning a hair, he replied that researchers were forever abroad studying the ancient Moorish culture and garb. I would have wagered that first-year students from the local college of Art and Design, high on Moroccan hash and with a better sense of humour than an appreciation of military ordnance, had more to do with it.

Every phalanx was led by an officer, usually smoking a cigar, whose main task was to whip up enthusiasm in both his or her squad, plus the crowd of relatives and friends standing or sitting on rows of chairs along the sides of the road, by waving his or her weapon in their faces. The few who were sober, swaggered like fools but still endeavoured to stay in formation, whereas the many who were not, staggered into the crowd, cackling, puking and collapsing into the arms of spectators.

Most of the men relied on beards to give them credibility, but with the exception of the few to whom Nature had been less than generous, the women steered away from anything that rendered them less than gorgeous. The ineffable loveliness of young Spanish women and many of the middle-aged, was such and so varied that one was constantly having to redefine the parameters: 'Ah, this is the way the perfect nose should be: long, with comma nostrils' or: 'Perhaps this one, short and soft with the orifices round and transparent'; or again: 'This must surely be the most exquisite shape for an ear, and set close to the head with the whorls perfectly symmetrical'; or: 'Just look at the way hers are so perfectly attached and the mouth remarkably curvilinear…' And that was just the face.

After hurrying down dirty, litter-strewn streets in cold and blustery weather almost every day of one's life among fellow depressives, to now be strolling every afternoon and evening in glorious warm sunshine down spotless boulevards among such creatures as the Spanish women who graced every one, was an unbelievable delight. They were also in every café, on every bus, crossing every road, chattering or totally preoccupied with themselves, while even little boys gaped and their wide, protuberant eyes rolled.

After being subjected to generations of images of the universal American deadheaded bimbo ideal, to be swarmed all around by Spanish girls in their late teens, mid-twenties and early thirties, was to forget for a while even the magnificent proboscises and thighs of the *bella* Italians in their late thirties and early forties. Apart from a nanogram or two of extra special DNA, I think the supreme natural confidence of the Spanish female had a lot to do with it. If for anthropological or freakish reasons one wanted to recollect the much shorter, though not necessarily squat, physiques of the women of the past, one would have had to confine one's search to the over-seventies whose diet, for generations, was chiefly of snails and dune grass with chick peas on a Friday. Today, with their much better diet, the men and women were as tall as the average European, and most certainly infinitely lovelier. The English rose might be more than a myth but was harder to find than any legendary black tulip.

To return to more martial matters, instead of marching or dancing, both Moor and Christian moved in a strange, part shuffle, part rhythmic sidestep, carried out to the monotonous beat produced by the white-shirted, undisciplined brass band which followed behind.

The men were remarkably quiet and all the women did was to murmur 'Ba-ba, ba-ba', a sound more derivative of a herbivore covered in wool, than any Arab in leather, and it made me wonder how favourably the English and Irish women would compare if singing carried the same value as looks, as indeed it might to an old fogey.

Really tiny children dressed identically to their parents, toddled in the procession, and not a few processioners carried babes in their arms. Plainly overwhelmed, these frequently disorientated and tired-out extensions of parents who seemed to have more money than sense, and never knew when enough is enough, had to endure the ordeal for hours, night after night, because the processions were repeated several times during the week to make sure no relatives or family friends had an excuse to avoid coming to seeing them.

On the Saturday things took on a more serious turn and an inane dialogue began between the leader of the Christians and the leader of the Moors. This was a kind of peace initiative, but after a quarter of an hour of abuse and several long intervals of silence while the parties worked out what they were going to say next, what the crowd was waiting for happened and the participants resorted to force to resolve the matter. A battle that once created divine reputations for Spanish Catholic monarchs was now enacted where two local dignitaries, such as the manager of a bank and the owner of a Memorex bedding store, attempted to achieve the same thing, as dozens of males, from old men down to young boys, wandered through the crowded streets of the town, willy-nilly firing harquebuses (ancient blunderbusses charged with real gunpowder) sometimes pointed at the ground, sometimes in the air, and sometimes at nowhere in particular. No sooner had they been fired, than the snipers moved on a few yards with their underdogs who reloaded the weapons from bags of gunpowder, and massacred the cobbles and any feet that got in the way.

Many of the infantry wore earplugs which rendered communication between them virtually impossible, and every year there were injuries, some horrific, from the unbelievably primitive muskets, fireworks and *hogueras* which were nearly always a feature of Spanish celebrations. An unpopular law to regulate the wide use of gunpowder and fireworks had recently been enacted prohibiting the sale of same to children under eight years of age, but so far it had not made much difference.

The ultimate event of the Moros y Cristianos was perfect for a materialistic society with no regard for the environment.

Lorries piled high with the kind of dross that even the most desperate pavement stall-holder would have rejected as tasteless, brought up the vanguard, and energetic youths, who would have been more gainfully employed cleaning up the countryside and putting the dross into these lorries, instead of throwing it out, were tossing it into the crowds who were grabbing it as though it were crusts of vitamin-and-mineral-supplemented bread, and they long-term POWs. I would not have cared except that the majority of them were well-nourished, well-dressed, middle-class adults with large bags into which they stuffed their trophy, and looked as though they would have readily trampled to death anybody who got in the way of their seizing a sticky lollipop concocted from an alphabet of banned EU substances.

Alcoi's was the most famous Moros y Cristianos, and definitely the most preposterous we ever saw, though the format everywhere was pretty much the same, lacking, as they all did, any imagination or diversity. When one saw the New Orleans Mardi Gras or Rio de Janeiro Carnival on television, one could not help wondering why the Spanish never sent somebody over there to pick up a few tips, except that after living among the Spanish for a while, one soon learnt that they were not generally given to following the examples of any but their own antecedents.

TWENTY-SEVEN

When the Forsyths telephoned one day to tell us a lot of building materials had arrived in the drive of the *vivienda* – our *vivienda* – and Lew Spiers and his gang were digging a trench around the front, Helen and I drove over to see what was going on; it was obvious that major alterations were being made to the side that had the badly slewed sun-lounge wall, and the main window had been modified with a sledgehammer. The window had been enlarged but the original lintel retained, with the consequence that it failed to support the wall above.

Because it no longer reached from one side of the window to the other, the spaces between the ends of the lintel and edge of the wall had been packed with pieces of broken concrete, and Lew and his buddies were plastering over everything in order to cover up the dangerous, unholy and slaphappy mess.

We were in the middle of a court case that depended, among other things, on the state of the wall being preserved as evidence, and here in broad daylight the *demandados* (defendants) were erasing it. As soon as we saw what was going on, we contacted Sr. Férrer to urge him to come and see the situation for himself, then seek a court injunction to prevent any further interference with evidence. His reply was that such a thing was pointless because the judge was a woman and therefore would not understand anything about building, notwithstanding the fact that the council building inspector was a woman. I then telephoned Edmundo to ask if he could come and see what was going on, so that he could act as a witness if necessary; otherwise it would be too late to do anything. He was so congenial and obliging that I felt heartily ashamed to be using him in this way, particularly after all that had happened, or, rather, not happened; yet here I was, asking him to leave his important job as deputy head of the Spanish Social Security in Alicante, at a few minutes notice, to involve himself in our petty affairs. But I could not think what else to do, and in some absurdly unfair way, felt he must share the blame, even if it was just because he was Spanish, a *funcionario*, and therefore, by association, one of them.

His position was wholly untenable, and if he was trying to be all things to all men, it was something Férrer and I both required of him. He had come late into my life, and from a very different background, but I had very real affection for him. For this reason, if for no other, I should never have involved him in the affair. Not once, for instance, had I paused to consider how he might have felt compromised or how I might have been expecting too much of him. Because I was his friend he had done his best to oblige me and I had let him and asked for even more, and it had just gone on and on. Anybody else would almost certainly have objected long before. It had very nearly come to that the time we were in Cocentaina. Instead, he had forgiven me, we had become reconciled and we had moved on together. That he had got upset because of a misunderstanding by Férrer where he had accepted what Férrer had told him about our getting another lawyer, instead of first asking me if it were true, was irrelevant. I really hoped our friendship would survive, but only time would tell.

It was easy enough to stand on the road and view all the relevant dwellings, but the individual who should have been there, observing, taking photographs and notes, or at least arranging for somebody else to do it, could not be persuaded to get that involved. So all we could do was to take photographs ourselves and deliver them to him in person, accompanied by Janet to ensure a minimum of misunderstanding, for there would always be some.

'I have told Señores Smithwhyte many times that neither English nor Irish laws apply here. It isn't a case of what is fair or reasonable, but what is law. We are Latins, not Anglo-Saxons. There is nothing to prevent Señores Spiers pulling the *vivienda* down if they want to. In any case, the Smithwhytes' photographs are invalid because they have not been witnessed by a *notario*.'

He then suggested we hire a private detective with a camcorder, and a court-approved witness. Janet rolled her eyes and made the Spanish shaking-hot-hand gesture that indicated such a thing would cost at least half a dozen arms and legs. If we had had every shred of evidence, and everything we had said and done from the start witnessed by a *notario*, we would have run out of money long since. But it was his smile – or rather, rictus – that got to me.

The next day, with a friend who was sufficiently smartly dressed to have passed for an *abogado* or some such figure of authority, to act as witness, I returned to the *vivienda*. He did not say anything but took notes and photographs of the state of the *vivienda*, and of me with an expression of utter disgust, photographing it. Spiers clearly did not know what to do as he scurried back and forth, shouting to his men before eventually herding them all inside. There they remained, with Spiers hiding behind the building, popping his head around a corner every so often, while we took a couple of dozen photographs. It was obvious that extensive alterations were going on.

'I no want my picture in camera!' a German worker called out.

'Move away from my house, then!' I called back.

We had no idea how much Spiers's accomplices knew about the situation between the Spiers and us, but no matter how badly we had been painted, they must have realised he was up to no good.

When I went back by myself the following day, it was to find they had erected a huge curtain of black polythene over the areas they were working on, to hide themselves and what they were doing. It was a windy area and the plastic kept lifting up, ripping and blowing all over the place, so anybody could have seen what they were up to: basically knocking down and replacing faulty parts. And this was the way things continued until one day Spiers yelled 'You're too late, matey! We're finished! Ha ha ha!'

It was so blatant. But what else could we do except complain to Férrer about the plan which had been drawn by Spiers' architect a year after the *vivienda* had been completed, and appeal to him once and for all to come and bring the judge with him.

'Surely she can see what's going on, if you explain it to her?' I protested. 'It doesn't need an architect. She could look at the villa at the same time and see the difference between the two roofs from outside. It'll save photographs, expert opinions and everything else. Surely, if she's to judge the case, she has to be able to appreciate what's going on.'

A week later Férrer sent an architect inspector to make a report, but Spiers refused to allow him on the premises and would not co-operate with him in any way. Photographs taken by Spiers of the house we were now living in, had been submitted by their abogado to support their current allegation which was that we had failed to honour the contract on the *vivienda* because we had decided to buy another property instead. Despite all that had passed between ourselves and Férrer, both the judge and all the rest of them seemed to accept every absurd contention the Spiers made, whilst rejecting out of hand every reasonable contention we made. No wonder the Forsyths doubted Férrer was on our side. Maybe they were right and Férrer was a freemason, along with Spiers and Vibóra. They reckoned Spiers held some rank within the freemasonry and had had Vibóra enrolled.

'Maybe if they knew about him, they would kick him out,' Mildred suggested. But I was sure the masons already knew all about it.

The villa Helen and I were initially going to buy had long since been sold, altered, extended and occupied by a French couple, and the plan of the *vivienda* drawn by the Spiers' architect a year after construction, was being waved about by Lew Spiers who was claiming it was the plan Miguel had built the *vivienda* from. There was another drawing of the *vivienda*, done by the same architect, which nowhere near matched his own first drawing, and another, done by Gilbert, which showed considerable external differences between the supposedly identical villas. In addition, the numbers of the various residences were all mixed up in the 'official' drawings. If the purpose of the Spiers and their architect was to utterly confuse the similarities and differences between 'villa 1' (the house we were initially going to purchase) and 'Villa 2' (the *vivienda* presently being constructed, which was contracted to be of *'mismo diseño'* and *'exactemente iguale'* to 'Villa 1'), they could hardly have done a better job of it.

Over a copy of the Spiers' architect's drawing of 'Villa 2', the supposedly completed *vivienda*, I had drawn a representation of the *vivienda* as it currently existed, and then shaded in bright red where it departed from the original model, 'Villa 1'. It was a very graphic illustration of the difference between the two, and although I had not hired a *notario* to look over my shoulder, if Víbora-Masson had got the court to accept Spiers's photographs without their being 'legitimised', which he obviously had, Sr. Férrer should have been able to have it accept my drawing alongside photographs I had taken to substantiate it; or, if they wished, they could have a drawing done by a court appointed draughtsman. Surprisingly, my drawing showing the two totally different buildings, proved to be the turning point for Sr. Férrer. At last, as though a magic wand with our name on it had been waved over everything, he suddenly began wondering if we might have a case after all, and decided to come to see for himself.

As soon as he saw the two houses with their currently very different roofs, plus the underhanded attempts still being made to alter the *vivienda* and remove some of the faults, he understood. Finally, he knew what we were talking about and affirmed that the *vivienda* was exactly as I had photographed and drawn it, and not at all as Spiers' architect had depicted it in his drawing, or as it had been detailed in the contract. He was also very congenial towards the Forsyths, assuring them that things would soon be over.

The Forsyths had declared themselves to be on our side by inviting Sr. Férrer into their house, and the gesture was soon acknowledged by the Spiers. Within hours of Férrer leaving, both he and she began harassing Gilbert and Mildred and, from then on, insulting and menacing them whenever they came out of their house. Gilbert had a broken shoulder from a recent fall and the Spiers guffawed whenever they saw him struggling to carry anything heavy from his car, as well as shouting insults at Mildred whenever they saw her toiling in their garden.

Whenever the Forsyths had friends visiting, Lew Spiers would wait until they were leaving, then jump out from behind the fence with a camera and shout 'Gotcha!' If they came after dark, he would get a torch and go around their cars, purportedly inspecting them, until the Forsyths' friends became so upset by the harassment that they stopped visiting. Unfortunately, Lew Spiers was so much bigger than everybody that they were all afraid of him.

When we complained to Sr. Férrer that our witnesses were being intimidated, and urged him to inform the judge, we got no response. When we repeated our complaints, and the Forsyths did likewise, still nothing. Then they went to complain to the judge themselves, but his answer was to say that in Spain people used insulting language all of the time and no judge would consider insults to an *extranjero* to be of any import. Children often called their mother a '*puta*' (whore), for instance. I then wrote several letters protesting to the court and others, but every one went unanswered.

The Forsyths were typical of what decent, fair-minded and courageous English people used to be like, and although they were elderly and Gilbert quite infirm, they always did what they thought was the right thing, even when the odds were totally against them. Both were very strong-willed, and instead of going to the police, as we advised, they went to the *Ayuntamiento* to ask what the Spiers were building, because, as next-door neighbours, they considered they had a right to know. The *Ayuntamiento*, for whom the Spiers' architect worked, told the Forsyths they had no such right, and whatever the Spiers were doing was their own business.

One day Sr. Férrer telephoned to say he had contacted Miguel about giving evidence in court, following our telling him we had met him in the street, and he told us Miguel would be willing to testify against the Spiers. Férrer wanted Miguel to tell the court that he had never been paid a sufficient amount to build our *vivienda* properly, and had never been given a proper plan to work from, apart from an infantile drawing done by Sra. Spiers on a single page of a child's school exercise book.

Miguel had told Sr. Férrer he would be glad to tell this to the court because the Spiers were bad people, but we would need to pay him 625,000 pesetas for the favour. Férrer replied that he did not think we would be prepared to pay any witness. Miguel said he had already been offered this much by the Spiers because it was the amount they owed him and they had told him that witnessing for them was the only way he would get it. He only had to deny our claim that he had never had access to proper building plans to work from, deny there were any building flaws or that anybody had ever said there were any, and deny there had ever been any trouble between him and the Spiers.

'Great!' I said. 'Now we can have him and them for perjury and bribery!'

Férrer smiled. 'It would be his word against mine.'

'But you're an *abogado*!'

'Everybody lies in Spain. Especially in court. We aren't Anglo-Saxons. Judges don't expect anybody to tell the truth. They know that if you pay a witness enough, he will say anything.'

'What if everybody lies all the time?'

'Ah,' he said, grinning, as though things were obviously at last becoming clear to us. 'That's where the cunning of the witness comes in…the skill of the liar.'

I looked at him, expecting him to curse or laugh or exhibit some expression of thorough cynicism. But he did nothing of the sort. All he did was remind me that his next 200,000 pesetas were due, and ask if we needed a pen with which to write him a cheque before we left.

Both of the Forsyths needed hospital treatment that they had been postponing so that they would not be indisposed when the judge called them to give evidence. But they had never mentioned anything of it to us, nor said one word to make us think they regretted having got involved, so we were naturally very embarrassed when we found out. On top of this, they had had to suffer continual intimidation from the Spiers. They had complained directly to Sr. Víbora-Masson, who they knew, as well as to Sr. Férrer, but nothing had been done. They were very independent and remarkably capable, but the attrition was definitely beginning to tell. Gilbert kept nagging on at me to make Férrer do this and do that, and was becoming very impatient with me for not following his advice. But we were hamstrung by the fact that this was Spain, and at times I became exasperated with him for not bearing that in mind; after all, they had been in Spain much longer than we had. I once remarked that I felt we had better rapport with Sr. Férrer than we used to, and did not wish to alienate him by losing my temper and saying something I might regret, and he got really upset at this. They were doing their best to help, but in their own way, and we were grateful, but alone responsible for everything.

I regularly sent Férrer strong memos, and the letter I wrote him when we were in Cocentaina was his rite of passage as far as we were concerned. It was all very well Gilbert saying he must be corrupt, the judge corrupt, everybody connected with the case corrupt and the whole Spanish judicial system corrupt. We agreed and were always saying so ourselves, but where was it getting us.

Gilbert had been a close friend of Víbora-Masson's father, also an *abogado*, and as members of the Royal Yacht Club they used to go sailing and socialising together. Víbora-Masson junior, then the fat, spoilt, boarding-school boy that Gilbert, somewhat of a polymath, had helped with his English, history and other subjects required of university applicants, and now sole inheritor of his parents' estate and yacht, was the much pampered and highly arrogant playboy lawyer and scourge of Alicante's defence lawyers.

When he had finished university – always a very long undertaking in Spain, whatever the subject – and emerged with a law degree a few years before his father's death, Gilbert had assumed he would have continued his father's friendship. Generously started, thanks to his father, and now with a practice of his own, the son quickly established himself as a shrewd and cunning practitioner specialising in fiscal issues. Unpopular, though respected for his skill, and in appearance an almost exact adult version of the schoolboy, Luis never fulfilled Gilbert's hopes. He lacked – or rather, disregarded – the style and dress sense of most wealthy professional Spaniards and looked more like an American Jewish ambulance chaser than a successful Spanish lawyer. I think it was arrogance that did it, that allowed him to go around with a jacket too small for his belly and pocket flaps that were half inside the pocket, half out, a handkerchief that never seemed fresh, and a brow that always glistened under a head of hair that was wavy but long and greasy. Completing the portrait with a pair of lips that did not match, he was sexually unattractive – or so I thought, and could not understand how or why Helen could possibly think otherwise. Compared with him, our man was a gentleman even in one of the pullover-and-tie combinations he usually wore for a late evening session. Plus he was handsome in a kind of Harrison Ford way.

However accurate or otherwise my thumbnail portraits, Helen and I were convinced that justice must have been irrelevant to most *abogados*, as it probably was to lawyers everywhere, and jurisprudence a game they played but never personally lost.

It was so good when Humberto came, as he did one Saturday in the middle of all this; he was just what we needed. His submersion in a world both too small and too big for the one we were living in, was the perfect way to escape back to humanity, if not reality. We were telling him the tale about how we had been to the local tourist bureau to confirm the time of a tango concert at the Teatro Principal in Alicante that he himself had told us about, and he was listening intently with his finger to his lips as though to shush himself.

'…And when she said there was no such show in Alicante within the coming month, Helen said 'We already know that there is'.

'I have already told you there is not. It is my job to know these things!'

'I am sorry, but there is. Definitely.'

'You don't know. I do. And there is definitely not!'

'Would you mind looking in your computer?'

'There is no need. You have made a mistake. You mean the cinema. "*New York, New York*" is on with subtitles…although they are not in English.'

'No, no! We mean the tango concert at the Teatro Principal… Would you please be so kind as to check your computer?'

Impatiently she hammered the keys and details of it instantly came up.

Without faltering or fluttering a single eyelash, she said 'Yes… 2000 hours for the tango. That's eight o'clock in the evening. Shall I write it down for you?'

'Was this all in English?' Humberto interrupted, something he very rarely did.

I nodded.

'Anyway, as I was saying… "No, thanks," I said to her. "That won't be necessary. A friend of ours told us it was on, and he is always reliable about things like this."

'"We are very reliable too!" she said.'

Humberto was rubbing his eyes but still a tear rolled down his cheeks.

'I knew exactly what was coming from the second line… Now that is the real Spain..! Not Lorca or Cortes. Or Cervantes even. But that woman!'

The previous time we had seen Humberto, he had happened to mention that he did not possess a radio, so the next time we went to Ireland, we had bought him one and Helen now presented it, gift wrapped. We knew he had an aversion from gift paper, so I had told her to just wrap it up in an old newspaper. She would not, of course, but he simply nodded when she put it down, wrapped in the kind of fancy paper he abhorred. Now and then, as he ate with his usual attention to every detail on his plate, he glanced at the parcel out of the corner of his eye, as though there might be a large, particularly bad-tempered scorpion inside, waiting, bayonet extended, ready to shoot out.

Humberto sat there, picking up minute pieces of food that had not yet been cleared away: a soft celery top with yellow leaves, the end of a crust of bread dampened with oil, and the blackened skin of a grape, pecking at everything but the package. Normally I enjoyed seeing him scavenging like a chook mopping up morsels: a brief examination with the eye, a quick movement, and then…gone. But I wanted to see his reaction to the radio, so I made the mistake of asking him if he were going to open it, something I would never normally do when making a gift of anything to anybody.

'What is it?' he asked, without looking.

'A radio. We remembered you said… So…'

'Mmmmm.' He continued cleaning up, now more like a wren than a sparrow.

'It has a mains option, so you don't need to use batteries.'

He loathed batteries because of their price and destruction of the environment.

'Mmmmm.'

'Last time you were here it seemed as if you would have liked one.'

'Oh..? I must have given that impression?'

I felt like picking it up and flinging it out of the window, but he gingerly moved it, as though with the tip of a beak.

'You do like listening to the radio, don't you?'

'Well, the trouble is that there is as much contamination of the airwaves, as of the gases we breathe. Already I have too much sound coming into my head that I cannot filter out.' He waved his hand in the vicinity of his ears and screwed up his eyes as though trying to ward off shafts of pain.

'One switches on a commercial device like this in the hope of hearing good things, and instead hears things one would rather not: people being praised who should be shot…monsters being decorated…the inarticulate being paid fortunes for playing with various balls…'

'Does that mean you don't…want it?' It was childish but I could not help a gulp coming into my voice.

'What about Mozart?'

'Mmmmm. "Want" is such an ambivalent word. And I'm not sure one could blame Mozart for such things.'

'Do you not want to bother opening it, then?'

'Not if you might wish to give it to someone who might appreciate it even more than myself. Helen has clearly taken the patience to wrap it up so well that it would be a shame to…'

The matter was dropped, there was no point in torturing him to elicit appreciation or gratitude for something he so obviously and genuinely did not want, so we just took it away so that the sight of it would not bother him any more. A few days later an Algerian who was desperately poor and without work came to the house; we had been helping him get a residencia so he could get into Ireland which he was convinced was Heaven on Earth.

Helen gave him the radio and he was delighted. He was dying to see his wife and daughter, but they could not get into Spain, and if he went back to visit them, he was afraid he would not be able to get back into Spain. She would be delighted when he told her about the radio, it would be another reason for her and the daughter coming.

TWENTY-EIGHT

The campo I used to go walking in an hour before sunset, was the wild area which began at the bottom of our garden and extended all the way to Los Pajaros Rojos and beyond. It was a hard, rough, almost treeless terrain covered with patches of scrub and occasional badly neglected little plantations of olives consisting of half a dozen rows of mainly cracked and broken trunks, with here and there ragged little replacements that served as stakes to prove a claim. That said, there was a surprising quantity and variety of herbs of all kinds, both medicinal and culinary, and poor locals collected them in sacks and sold them in the market. An odd thing, amounting almost to a phenomenon, was that given the variety of cacti that grew so prolifically in almost every garden in the region, comparatively few grew wild in the campo, an area in which they would have thrived, and sometimes did, to produce huge luxuriant structures which surely must have been models for Gaudi.

Every public holiday was an excuse for young people and kids abandoned for the duration, to pitch their tents, cut branches off trees, light fires, dig holes, leave behind badly behaved dogs as well as every item of their litter, and all wildlife in the area would have been exorcised by their 'scorched earth' policy'.

The arthritis in Helen's knees prevented her from accompanying me, so I mostly went on my own, which I preferred anyway. When she did come, like most companions on nature walks, she wanted to chat about anything but nature, whereas I wanted to be able to stop, look and listen, smell, and think to myself. If I was not engaged by the ground immediately in front of me, with its tripping burrows and twisting roots, mounds and cavities, tiny cadavers and tough little plants, I would be thinking about the family, about the court case, or about ideas for art, and rarely encountered anybody. Anyone out with their dog or companion would hide or make a detour when they saw me from a distance, and I liked that, seeing it as a mark of respect for solitariness, even though it was more likely a demonstration of genuine unsociability or fear of the dog.

It was a surprise to me how in Spain so few fauna were evident by day when so much came out at night. Then there would be legions of insects, rabbits and raptors, even amphibians like frogs and grass snakes, although there was no water anywhere apart from the occasional damp patch in an old aquaduct. As I would come towards the end of my ramble and the sun disappearing, I would imagine the ground heaving as various creatures just below the surface, within the foliage of a plant, or just over a hill, waited for the moment when they would emerge to fill the air, or swarm the terrain that had seemed such an arid, almost lifeless desert a short while before.

There were never any domestic animals tethered or corralled – apart from those that were being abandoned – but a large flock of goats would appear once a week herded by a goatherd and his two or three raggy mongrels that were surprisingly good at keeping control, especially given that goats were so difficult for dogs.

Goats, of course, were proud independent animals that did not mind being led, but hated being herded from behind, so it took a damned good sheepdog to make them go exactly where the keeper wanted. Very much browsers rather than grazers, goats moved fast and constantly, and were very different from sheep. This flock consisted of several hundred animals of mixed breeds, one or two of the bucks being magnificent beasts, powerful and aggressive like small bulls, and not a few ancient or runty animals that should have been culled. It was impossible to identify the breed because they were a mixture of so many, this being reflected in their colours which varied from cream to beige, mahogany to black, white to pied and some of the pieds quite blue. Some had the long droopy ears of the Nubian, others the thick winding horns of the mountain species. There were those with large elephantine hooves, and those with feet more like paws; ones as hairy as Highland cattle, others smooth and almost hairless. Young ones pranced about from one side of the herd to the other, whilst oldsters dragged their weary bodies as they trailed behind. These were the sort of creatures that a loving parent like their keeper would not want to put out of their misery.

The goatherd, a very solitary figure, was the personification of rural poverty, plodding along with his head lowered, looking at the ground as though deep in thought, and very reluctant to cross anyone's path or have them cross his. But we had kept goats for many years in Ireland and had great affection for such intelligent, interesting and independent animals, and I simply had to make contact with their *seigneur*. I am sure he realised, even from the considerable distance he had always maintained between us, that for a long time I had wanted to meet him, so adjusted his direction ever so slightly so it would never come to pass. No matter, I was determined to share something of our experience, at the very least to let him know I was a goat man myself, a fellow human who appreciated the qualities of this fascinating creature, and I plotted one path after another until, as in some sophisticated board game, I cornered him, albeit out in the open, and gently but firmly pounced.

Addressing him in Spanish, though unsurprisingly he proved to be a *valenciano* and reacted more like an animal than a man, I kept our first encounter to a minimum so as not to unseat him or cause his stock to stampede, and it worked. The next time I would introduce the topic of dogs; after that, the vegetation and supply of minerals, until, without behaving as though we were necessarily amigos, I would have established a degree of acquaintance such that whenever we passed each other in future, even at a distance, we would always acknowledge it and he would know he had a friend among the settled community, a *compañero* of the *cabra* (goat) and an Englishman at that.

I always heard him before I saw him; not because his dogs were barking, because good herding dogs never bark, but because of the tinkling of the winsome bronze bells that hung around the necks of the lead goats and could be heard for miles. Every now and then there would be new bleating when more kids had arrived to join the flock, but never a call from the man himself who preferred to go about his business with the utmost discretion. Whether this was because of his nature, out of consideration for the fact that his animals were of a nervous disposition, or simply because he did not want to alert any landowner to the presence of his hundreds of poachers and vacuum cleaners, I never ascertained.

When he and his charges descended on an area, they never stayed longer than it took to snatch the tops off anything ripe and nutritious, before moving on; never devastating an area like certain throngs of opportunist creatures that feed on the move, and never leaving more than a scattering of pelleted droppings that would mostly disappear before dawn. So orderly were they, that it would nearly have taken a scout to track where they had come from or gone to.

Eventually I discovered his abode, far from the campo near where Helen and I lived, and I was thoroughly dismayed to see it was just a rusted corrugated metal and wooden packing-case shack among other corrugated and packing-case shacks and lean-tos, and I wondered, but never found out and very much doubted, if he had a family living there. Helen was quite upset when one day we were driving along the highway past where he dwelt among his animals, and I pointed out his home. Like all of our family, Helen loved goats and had warm feelings for those who linked their lives with them.

Before we left the area, the goatherd and his goats had disappeared. It was impossible to tell whether the ruins he had lived in for many years, according to Humberto, were now deserted, or whether he had moved on in a different direction, but the land over which he had walked so many thousands of aggregate miles was eventually turned over to the JCBs.

All the time we had been in Spain we had kept a close watch on the situation in Ireland. We read their papers every day over the internet, went back for holidays several times a year, had visits from our children, and were in regular contact with them by telephone. Disturbing political and financial upheavals had begun within months of our departure, when the so-called 'Celtic Tiger' boom began, a sickeningly greedy state of affairs brought about by the banks, property dealers and politicians, and enthusiastically supported by ordinary greedy people, that gave a totally disingenuous impression to the world to the effect that Ireland had suddenly become economically acutely successful. It was as though the nation had discovered some new way of becoming collectively rich, like the lucky prospectors of the gold and land rushes of the nineteenth-century elsewhere.

We watched and listened while week by week prices of everything, especially the sale and rent of property, went sky high. Regulations that could have prevented or controlled the situation were removed or relaxed and standards of services and manufacture subsequently plummeted. Government policy was to interpret the apparent flood of money as the concomitant of superior Irish intelligence, and ludicrously and embarrassingly advertised the setting up of 'think tanks' into which the rest of the world could dip, for a fee.

Whenever we went back to see our children, all anybody talked about was of getting rich, of selling the mortgaged house they lived in and buying others – sometimes several – whose mortgages the banks would facilitate. Ordinary people were changing their spectacles to match new clothes, having every tooth straightened and bleached an ungodly white, and silly men were going abroad for facial tucks and botox injections.

With narcissism this rife, every other person considered him or herself to be a kind of celebrity, parties were thrown at the slightest excuse, and expensive play equipment hired for toddlers too young to understand what a birthday was, and broke limbs and drowned in hired temporary swimming pools and the likes.

Dublin and Newry were no longer adequate shopping destinations, serious shoppers were flying to New York and Dubai for 'learn to spoil yourself' sprees. Stinking rich young farmers hired managers to look after their enhanced acres with elaborate machines, while they themselves went to check on hotels and bars they now owned in Spain. Those with more than 'modest resources' bought apartments in Florida, while those of modest means settled for a pair of apartments to do up cheaply and sell to investors or rent out to much less well-lined Bulgarians.

Sadly, the soft spot Europe had always had for the Irish, began to diminish in the face of so much avarice, arrogance and, inevitably, incompetence, though the Government obstinately refused to consider revising its attitude. Politically the country was a disaster, and Helen and I realised that if we returned, it would only be for the children. The only thing that seemed not to have notably changed for the worse, was the friendliness of ordinary people.

TWENTY-NINE

Because of the increase in burglaries in the *urbanización*, coupled with missing having any animals after all this time, I fancied getting a dog. Apart from acting as a deterrent – I knew few dogs made good guards – it would be company for me on my evening walks in the campo. So we decided to get a young mature male Rottweiler: Rottweilers did not require much exercise, were not fussy or excitable, and would deter most miscreants. An animal of nine to twelve months meant we would not have to tolerate the destructive puppy stage and would have something old enough to start training.

Thanks to the computer, within a couple of days we had located someone who not only bred Rottweilers and other breeds of dog, but poultry and goats as well, making our visit to their farmstead in the salt flats seventy miles away, a most interesting one. The breeders, two typical rural brothers, had a ten-months-old male which had been rejected by previous prospective buyers because of his rather 'houndlike' features. Some Rottweilers had a tendency towards elongated faces, instead of the blunt form preferred by German and Spanish breeders, but English and Irish breeders often preferred the hound type, and I did. After all her years of close association with all kinds of animals, from goats to snakes, and hawks to guinea fowl, Helen did not mind either way, 'as long as it has nice eyes'. I was well aware that with dogs in particular, it was the breed that determined the character, and only the personality varied between individuals. His name was 'Nero' but I thought this a tad noble for somewhat of a slouch, and I wanted to make a complete change to his upbringing, so decided on 'Ned', which went with his eyes.

Big and strong, with a back end as broad as his shoulders and showing no indication of a tendency to tapering, leonine paws and a docked tail, he was absolutely unfussy – which I insist on in a dog – and having had all the recommended immunisations, we bought him. The two brothers were obviously poor, trying to supplement their sparse livelihood from a couple of acres of rough ground, with their dogs, goatsmilk and a few poultry, but all the dogs were in good condition and I had no doubt that the vet would more often be consulted than the doctor.

As soon as we got him home I began with his training, and fortunately he was keen to learn. Compared with the gentle and courteous collie, although the Rottweiler male was, like all intelligent animals, sensitive and sentimental, he was bad mannered and very clumsy. A collie would stand back to let you through a narrow gateway, whereas a Rottweiler would practically knock you flat on your back to get through first. And when it came to security, a male Rottweiler would apply itself more to chasing away pansy little dogs with waterproof waistcoats supplied by over-indulgent owners, than humans with the demeanour of ne'er-do-wells. But for a couple of humans past their prime, a mature Rottweiler was an ideal companion who did not want more than minimal exercise, had a relatively small and unfussy appetite, was unimaginative and incurious, never dribbled, rarely barked, and his value as a 'guard' dog definitely resided in his appearance.

Ned, whose working-class name definitely suited him better than any Roman emperor's, had been with us about six months when a pack of Hollander holidaymaker's mixed breeds from next door – there were five, all female and three of them flagrantly in season – were, on arrival, immediately let loose into the street, and likewise every day thereafter. It was a perversity that people from pedantically regulated countries like Holland, where by-laws were strictly enforced, should so readily abuse the laws in Spain, yet it happened all the time.

One particularly hot afternoon, when Ned was acting like most male mammals whose gonads were heftier than their cerebral lobes, jumped clear over the garden wall into the street. It was only three feet high on our side, but eight on the other, and a miracle the bozo did not crush both testicles and break all four legs. Nowadays large dogs went through all kinds of veterinary tests to try to eliminate hip dysplasia, and ours had to voluntarily make a ball-busting leap like that. Amazingly he survived to chase the holidaying Dutch bitches back to their temporary premises, but a party of Spanish women – a rather rougher analogue of the Irish biddy – coming up the street on their daily *paseo* (walkabout), witnessed Ned's steeplechasing and complained to the local police that they had all suffered minor heart attacks because they thought Ned was going to attack them.

I had been in the garden when it happened, so was able to tell the policeman exactly what Ned had done and not done. Being a young fellow with somewhat of a gigolo reputation himself, when he saw the size of Ned's pudenda, he guffawed and said Ned was '*obviamente un macho. No es gay, eh? Gusta las putas!*' (He's obviously a man. Not a gay, eh? He likes the whores!')

After I had produced Ned's licence and got him to give a demonstration of how well disciplined he was, the policeman said I should not worry about the women, who were always complaining about *los extranjeros* and seeking financial compensation for one thing or another.

Notwithstanding, I put up an electric fence: electricity is something dogs' scrota have an infallible memory for, and it was not right to have any dog loose on the street.

One time I was out with him in the hills at the back of the house, when I heard whistles being blown and dogs barking. Wherever I went, I would hear it, and after a while realised whoever it was following me. Then I saw them: a gang of young lads blowing whistles at a pack of dogs who were barking their heads off amidst a lot of exasperated shouting. None of them came anywhere near me, and were no bother, so I just ignored them and eventually returned home. But the next day, and for several days after that, the same thing happened.

After about a week, several Spanish lads came to the door to ask me to show them the whistle I was using with Ned. I realised then what they were up to, so got my whistle and showed them. Immediately they pulled their own whistles out of pockets, off belts or from around their necks, and compared them with mine. Some were huge fancy things, more like trumpets than whistles; others tiny, like a toddler's toy; still others, police issue. They asked me to get Ned and show them how I used mine, so I did, giving Ned various quite complicated commands which he obeyed instantly, to their great amazement. Two of them had brought their own dogs with them and insisted I blow my whistle at them, even though I said it would be pointless.

'If they were going to obey, they would have obeyed when I blew for Ned,' I told them, and sure enough their dogs took no notice at all.

'*Es su perro!*' (It's his dog!) one of them shouted excitedly, convinced he had solved the mystery. '*Dile que intente soplar nuestros silbatos.*' (Tell him to try blowing our whistles).

I was not too keen on that, and explained that it was neither the whistle, nor the dog. It was the trainer. I told them they would have to train their dogs to obey the commands they wanted him to obey, and then link the whistle to the same commands. But it took a lot of time and a great deal of *paciencia* (patience) to get this across.

They were most disheartened to hear this, *paciencia* being so scarce in Spain, so instead of going through all that faff, they decided to have another go at their dogs in my and Ned's presence, as though that might make a difference. So they blew and they blew, and all at the same time, trying to outdo each other in sheer decibels. There was pandemonium as they nearly blasted peas out of barrels and lungs out of chests, all the while cursing their own version of man's best friend, none of whom took the slightest notice of their would-be masters. They then asked to borrow my whistle, so I told them that not only would it not work with their dogs, but that it was bad karma for them to put into their mouths what had been in mine, and they readily accepted this.

No doubt they regarded my dog-whistle explanation as the sort of 'twaddle' one would expect from a *jubilado* (old retired person), and my concerns about hygiene proof of the wimpishness of an old 'wrinkly' – as the Spanish press was increasingly given to refer to us expat *ancianos*. Anyway, the reality was that these lads would have been brought up on gigantic communal paellas where nobody flinched when a few bluebottles dropped in, and every one of them probably had an immune system for which I would have given an arm and a leg.

With more patience than Helen generally gave me credit for, I spent a good half hour explaining in detail how to train a dog properly, by voice, hand and whistle, and by the time I had finished, every last one of them had completely lost all interest in dogs, whistles and all the rest of it. Why go to all the trouble every day of trying to make a *perro estúpido* (stupid pooch) do what it patently does not want to, when a curse coupled with a *golpéelo para arriba el culo con el pie* (good kick up the arse), was far more satisfying?

One evening Sr. Férrer telephoned to say the Forsyths had to appear in the main court of Alicante in two days' time. I immediately contacted them with the news and they went straight into action, Gilbert collating his large and lovely architectural drawings done on special architect's paper, making copies of letters, faxes and phone calls, getting himself an especially fine haircut and wearing an academic tie from his architectural past; and Mildred a new dress and hairdo; plus much rehearsing of speeches in Spanish between the two of them, as they each in turn played *abogado*, juez and *testigo* (witness). And when they arrived at court on the day appointed, they were perfectly prepared in mind and body, and in a state of high excitement.

After a two-and-a-half-hour wait, they were told the judge would not be coming and they would have to return the following week at a time not yet determined. They were highly annoyed and very disappointed when they called on us on their way home.

'Even so, we had to pay the court interpreter,' Mildred said as soon as she came in the door. 'She charges from the moment she shuts her front door behind her, and the rate is just the same for sitting around or driving, as it is for actual interpreting. I wouldn't care, but I can speak Spanish as well as she can. It's just that the court insists you have one of their licensed *funcionarios*.'

'Maybe she should go around with a meter on a gold chain around her neck.'

'Even taxis have standing rates,' Gilbert grumbled.

When they were next called, which was ten days later, Roberto Hernandez was there, Miguel Diego was there, people the Forsyths did not know were there, and Lew Spiers was there. The way the court had decided to do things, was to first hear evidence from the Spiers' witnesses, then ours, then us, and then the Spiers – though not necessarily all on the same day. Helen and I stayed away because neither Férrer, nor the Forsyths thought it would have been a good idea to show our irritating expat visages too early.

While everybody was waiting, Lew Spiers had got himself really worked up, stomping up and down the corridor, leering at Gilbert and Mildred, waving his arms about, and declaring that our *abogado* had not turned up because he was afraid of theirs, and had sent a junior – a woman – instead. When Sr. Férrer did appear, Mildred straightaway told him about Lew Spiers' behaviour which she said was obviously meant to intimidate them. Férrer complained to Víbora-Masson, pointing out that the Spiers were not supposed to be there, but Víbora-Masson retorted that it was a public area and Lew Spiers had only come to give his witnesses moral support. Bolstered, Spiers continued with his behaviour until Férrer complained to the clerk of the court and Spiers was eventually told to leave and not come back until the day he was called to give evidence. An hour later everybody was told the judge had been delayed and they would have to come back the following day.

'Do you know that builder laddie had the nerve to come up and say '*Holá*,' Gilbert spluttered. 'He said he was sorry to have to give evidence for the Spiers, because they were such bad people. And that he liked you two and would much rather testify for you. "Why the hell don't you, then?" I practically shouted at him. "Because I've a wife and *bambino* to look after," he said, "and the Spiers are paying me 650,000 pesetas. The Smithwhytes expected me to do it for nothing. They don't realise I'd be doing them a favour."'

We did our best to cheer up the Forsyths. They were

obviously thinking that if Lew Spiers was crazy enough to intimidate them in broad daylight at court, what was he likely to do in the privacy of night, if things went against them.

The following day the Forsyths were back in court and so was Lew Spiers, striding back and forth, making his physical presence felt and cracking jokes about them and us. There was a security guard complete with truncheon and pistol, but he just sat dozing on the end of the bench. Sr. Férrer did not even turn up, he had told the Forsyths he would be giving them subtle signals with his fingers to indicate how they should answer if they were in doubt – something they considered utterly galling – but even then sent somebody else in his place.

When they were called, the Forsyths were first questioned as to their relationship with us. Realising the implication of the question and not liking it one bit, they had endeavoured to say that although they had only known us a relatively short time, they had known the Spiers for many years and those years were very significant; but they were not given the opportunity to qualify any of their answers.

The judge gobsmacked them by announcing there were three – and only three – categories of friendship recognised by Spanish law: a weekly friend you saw once a week, a monthly friend you saw once a month, and an occasional one you saw less often than once a month. To which category did Helen and I belong?

Gilbert, a gentleman and normally very polite, snapped that they had never classified friendships on such a basis, and the issue of friendship in this instance was irrelevant as far as they were concerned, because in the matter before the court they were acting out of a sense of public duty, a matter of right and wrong, pure and simple. The judge said he must inform us that Spanish law was not handicapped with the discombobulations – a word he had plainly researched – of an Anglo-Saxon court, and that the *testigos* must answer according to the categorisation stipulated, or be held in contempt.

Gilbert had spent months working on his drawings of the *vivienda* at various stages of its construction, and they were a work of art: accurate and finely drawn, clearly labelled in Spanish, and pinned to an architect's board he had especially obtained. He was determined to have them recognised and recorded, but as soon as he started to produce them from his large and officious briefcase, the judge told him to put them away because they could not be treated as evidence. Gilbert said they were copies of what had already been entered as evidence, and he needed them to illustrate his answers to any technical questions he might be asked. He was brusquely told they had not been entered in evidence and to put them away immediately or be prepared to suffer penalisation. He was then directed to say nothing further except in answer to what he was asked, so when he tried to raise the matter of their intimidation by the Spiers, the judge cut him short, telling him it was inadmissible. He then rubbished the value of Gilbert's testimony by obliging him to declare he had no specifically Spanish qualifications in architecture or any other profession recognised by the Spanish state. This was a common ploy in so many contentions in Spain where foreigners were involved, qualifications in anything from anywhere in the world being automatically considered inferior to anything awarded in Spain. Thus when Gilbert began drawing a simple diagram on a piece of paper, because the interpreter could not explain some of the building terms, he was halted again.

At this point, though a person of considerable character, Gilbert felt humiliated. Not only had he and Mildred expended a great deal of time and exhausted themselves physically and mentally going through their daily journals, preparing documents and illustrations, writing statements, doing translations and studying the law process in Spain, but their health and general wellbeing were clearly suffering from being in such close proximal contact with the Spiers all this time, day in, day out, having to endure their harassment. They could not go into their garden, take their dog for a walk, or go shopping, without passing Lew Spiers who was always hanging about, looking for an opportunity to cause trouble. To the Forsyths, at their age and because of the way they had been brought up, the Spiers must have seemed like crooks and thugs.

When Mildred's turn came and she tried to raise the matter of intimidation, thinking the judge would at least listen to her, she also was abruptly cut short. And when it was over and they came to tell us what happened, they were both very bitter at the way things had gone. The judge, they said, was well-mannered but sarcastic, and had clearly made up his mind before they were called in. The fact that the intimidation – which indicated the Spiers' guilt as clearly as anything, as far as we were concerned – had been considered irrelevant, appalled them more than anything.

'It's like going to court against the devil, with the courthouse in hell,' grouched Gilbert, quoting an old Irish saying. 'The way things are being done not only establishes beyond doubt that Férrer hasn't the stomach for a battle with somebody like Víbora-Masson, but, what is more important, that he just isn't smart enough. The only reason he could have had for persuading you to drop the *denuncia* against Spiers was because he was in cahoots with Víbora-Masson, and your dropping it was interpreted as an indication of how weak you…all of us…were.'

It was niggling how Gilbert and Mildred remained in awe of 'Víbora-Masson' and smarted when I referred to him as deceitful and disloyal to them. As far as they were concerned, the problem was with Férrer, when as far as we were concerned, it was more Masson, whom they would not have criticised for anything, especially as untrustworthy.

We also thought Férrer a defeatist and overwhelmed by Masson, but insisted he was honest and basically decent. We knew he had little respect for us, our nationality, my qualifications, or anything that spoke to possible attributes, so although at times I could have hit him, neither Helen nor I truly disliked him. In any case, there was no question of getting anybody else now, so there was no point in Gilbert continually bemoaning the fact that we had the wrong lawyer.

Out of the blue through Masson, the Spiers now had the neck to offer us official ownership of our car. Val Spiers would sign the papers if we would drop the case. We thought it incredible neck but Férrer just shrugged, this was the sort of thing Spanish justice was about, this and the 'witness auction'. We told Férrer we refused to dignify it with a response, though I had no doubt he went ahead with it anyway, never failing to reply respectfully to even the most terse communication from Sebastián Víbora-Masson.

Almost all expats had cars. If one lived out of town, they were essential because there was no public transport, though buses, when one could get them, were the best we had ever known: cheap, punctual, comfortable, and the drivers well groomed and good at their job. Mind, they would happily take great risks driving down narrow streets and in between other vehicles, and several times we had been sitting near the front when the driver, after greeting some colleague driving another bus, or while adjusting the radio, had shaved quite a hefty chunk of stone off the corner of a wall in a narrow street, or applied a dent or scrape to a parked rival.

They were friendly and appreciated being thanked, something most expats did and most Spaniards did not. Humberto was right: it was not Spanish policy to thank people who had served them, whether in a shop, office, or bar, and it seemed a pity, given their 'grandee' reputation and readiness to automatically greet anyone who spoke to them, even if it were just a silly old *pensionista inglés* asking where the post office was, or the nearest public convenience – something which did not even exist. Apart from the drivers themselves, their vehicles were always clean and tidy; like chauffeurs', it was something they took pride in.

Although Spaniards were convinced of their superiority to other races in virtually every walk of life, football being merely one example, when expatriates needed plumbing or electrical work done, they would invariably seek someone of their own nationality, at least until they had had such work done by a native and found him to be no worse.

Many expats of working age, with a family to support, found they had grossly miscalculated the cost of living in Spain. Things did tend to be cheaper, some much cheaper, but not if one squandered on non-essentials, as many did, and in a dismayingly short time many expats found they had run out of any savings and would have to get back to working for a living. This might have meant learning to do something for which the disillusioned expat, who had intended to be only a playboy, had neither the skills or experience; and things were often done differently in Spain. The sun, *por ejemplo* (for instance), could make a huge difference. Cement needed to dry slowly to cure properly, and much of the work in Spain involved the use of cement. Unless it were covered with plastic sheeting and periodically sprayed, it would crack up and there would be nothing for it other than to clear it away and start all over again.

Because the buttresses had been put against the wrong side of the wall between our *parcela* (plot) and our Dutch neighbour's – a common mistake – and the *gota fria* (a seasonal, much needed but dreaded inundation) had washed the wall down, we hired a Spanish builder who never laid a finger on the job himself but hired an Argentinian labourer who was strong, amiable and always ready to stop and chat, but absolutely useless, never having had any prior building experience. Instead of laying three rows of blocks at the most, allowing these to harden overnight and then laying a further couple of rows the following day, he would lay ten rows in a day, and all the mortar would be squeezed out, leaving the whole wall in a perilous state. The labourer thought he was pretty cute and spent most of the day astride the wall, chatting up the female Dutch holiday-makers next door, one of whom was attractive but paralysed and spent all day sunbathing topless, and while he spent the greater part of his day ogling her breasts, the cement rapidly dried out and the wall got worse. His boss was elsewhere in a white sports coat and pink carnation with a chic *puta* setting other very low-paid immigrants to work on jobs they likewise knew nothing about, and making himself another little pile of *dinero* for doing nothing bar *toro*-shitting.

After two days I checked the mortar between the blocks and found it hardly thick enough to get a screwdriver between, so called the 'builder' and told him to come to the house pronto. When he arrived, I showed him the travesty and told him the whole lot would have to be redone. He retorted that it was '*muy duro*' (very strong), so I took the screwdriver and drew the point between the blocks, from one end of the wall to the other, leaving a gouge an inch or so deep with soggy sandy cement leaking out. Sand being much cheaper than cement, the two of them were clearly intending to leave us with a long high wall held together with dry sand, a sprinkling of dead cement, and a lot of hot air.

'Who was that speaking to me on the phone?" *el jefe* snarled in very poor Spanglish.

'*Yo,*' (Me) I said. '*Por qué?*' (Why).'

'*No puedes hablar español!*' (You can't speak Spanish!)'

'*Estoy hablando ahora, ¿verdad?*' I'm speaking it now, aren't I?)

That really threw him and he stood there, gobsmacked. Then he angrily screeched, '*Nadie me dijo que podías hablar español.* (Nobody told me you could speak Spanish!)'

Nobody had asked, I told him, but he seemed more concerned about this than anything. He considered he had been deceived but it was a useful strategy when dealing with somebody one did not know and had doubts about, and I could see from his face that he was scrolling back through his memory to see if he could recall saying anything to his man in my presence that might have compromised him.

In Spanish I told him I wanted the whole wall redone or I would knock it down myself there and then and get somebody else to do it again, properly.

The following morning, even though I had told him we did not rise early, he came to the door at 8 a.m. with his Argentinian labourer and a couple of other 'hard men', to tell me he needed to be paid in full for the work he had done. He was making out he could not understand my bad Spanish and therefore could not understand what I was complaining about.

I told him to beat it. We would pay him for the cost of the blocks, and that was it. We did not want to see him or his Argentinian labourer again. He returned several times, humming and hahing but I felt I had more reason to feel aggrieved at how things had ended, than he did, and his threats of taking me to court were like water off a duck's back; we had had sufficient experience of Spanish justice by now not to be too easily bullied into parting with our *dinero*.

The following week Férrer called for Helen and I to go to his office because we were summoned to attend court the day after. The first thing he said when we arrived was that the experience would be completely different to anything we had ever experienced, and that much he was dead right about. Everybody would be telling lies, he assured us: not only the Spiers and their witnesses, but the *abogados* and *procuradores* (barristers) who would be prepared to say anything to win.

When he had previously warned us of this, we assumed he was talking tongue in cheek, but now realised he had been serious, and it made us feel sick. What kind of court was this? How could there be any pretence of justice if this was the norm? Perhaps this was why all along he had been so lacking in enthusiasm, because he knew he/we could never win. If he knew he was going to be up against paid witnesses and knaves who would lie through their teeth, fabricate false documents and say whatever was called for, he must have seen us as a dead loss.

'The curse of a successful *abogado* is the honest client,' he must have moaned to his wife over breakfast. 'And I'm stuck with four of them. *Hostia*! (Jesus!), they're too mean to tip their own witnesses!'

If the male judge we now had was a freemason – and there seemed little doubt about it from what we were hearing from Férrer and everybody – why had he not told us when he found out, and said something like, 'Sorry, folks, but I'm out of my depth here. I'm totally outclassed in roguery, fraternity, ability, fate and everything else. I've never had an honest client before, and wouldn't know where to start with one. At law school we were never taught how to deal with such a contingency'.

'Do you mean to say that when my wife and I go in there to tell the truth, the *jueces*, *abogados* and everybody else are going to assume that whatever we say will be lies..? In which case, why don't they just set up a roulette wheel in the middle of the room..? At least that would be fair. That way the other party might lose…'

But I was talking to myself; he was busy dishing papers out; he never listened to anything he thought jocular or trite. And whatever an Englishman said would surely be trite, even if it were the truth.

'These are a list of questions for Los Spiers. Take them away and read them and suggest others if you like. The hearing has been postponed for a week.'

We were actually being invited to do something, to contribute something other than *dinero*..? One could hardly believe it.

'You will be asked a list of written questions by Sr. Víbora-Masson, that the judge has already approved. You must never say anything but "*Sí*" or *No*". When you are asked a question. Instead, you must look at me. I will be standing at your side. If I rub my nose with my finger like this' – he demonstrated – 'you say "*No*". And if I touch my glasses like this' – another demonstration – you say "*Sí*".'

'You mean if the proper honest answer to a question is "*Sí*", and we know it is "*Sí*", we are to tell a lie and say "*No*", if your nose appears to itch?'

'No, no, no, no, no..! Not because my nose itches, because it won't! You only say "No" if I give the signal to say "No". Otherwise you won't know how to answer and could say the wrong thing.'

'Look, César, I'm not trying to be funny, or awkward, or unhelpful in any way…and we very much want to win this case…but I'm afraid my wife and I will be telling the truth from start to finish. That's what all this is for, as far as we are concerned. We don't tell lies. You must have realised by now that Mr and Mrs Forsyth don't, either.'

'Janet,' he said, turning to Janet and leaning right into her face, '*Háble con ellos! Explique!*' (Talk to them! Explain!).

'Ask him what if their *abogado* asks me a "Have you stopped beating your wife?" question, will you, Janet?'

'What do you mean?' she asked, puzzled.

'It's a question where you commit yourself however you answer.'

'You should be very careful about saying anything about anybody beating anybody's wife up in this country, or you could get yourself into serious trouble. I don't think he has a great sense of humour.'

Férrer could see we were very perturbed and as if to reassure us, came out with the most extraordinary thing: 'Don't worry. It does not matter what any of you say. All that really matters is what the report of the *perita* (expert) says. Everything depends on her. If that is not in your favour, you will lose, no matter what you say.'

I was gobsmacked.

'The "*perita*"..? Are you saying that all the Forsyths have been through has been for nothing...their intimidation and everything? That the Spiers are paying Miguel Diego and God knows who else to lie for them, for nothing?'

'The *perita's* evidence is by far the most important.'

'What if she says that all the things we said about the house are right? Does that mean we win and get our money back?'

'You can never tell the way these things will go. If I knew the answer to that I would be a rich man,' he laughed.

'So we pay for the *perita*, but if she gives evidence in our favour, we don't necessarily win?'

He shrugged.

'But all the evidence showing the faulty construction has vanished..! The two walls have gone forever and been replaced... presumably properly...by a German builder! Same with the chimney… You saw all that going on yourself. Why didn't the *perita* come then..? Why didn't we just pay her and forget about all the rest?'

'Because their *perita* will deny it all.'

'Their *perita*? You mean they have one as well..? Bloody hell..! Can't she use our photographs? The ones you have that show everything we told you?'

He waved his hands in the air.

'*Imposible. El juez no ha dado permiso*. (Impossible. The judge has not given permission).

'But there's only the roofs left… Will she be able to use our photographs of them?'

'No, no, no, no, no! She has her own special camera.'

'It would have to be very special to take photographs now that show what ours showed two years ago, before all the changes were made… Who is she? Is she an architect? Or maybe an archaeologist?'

Finally, as though he were releasing state secrets, he told us that our *perita*, whom we did not have yet, would be an *aparejador* (building inspector), a young woman just out of college, and would want 150,000 pesetas. But because we were *pensionistas* and she had an old grandfather and grandmother herself, who looked like us, she would reduce her fees by 50,000 if we lost. We would have to hope she was more honest than the other female *aparejador* and *arquitecto* who were giving evidence, the ones who had got their college of architects to stamp the building plans that the Spiers' architect had drawn up long after the *vivienda* was built – and not until – with a false date. But we were now being ushered out. We had agreed to return with a cheque next morning, and that was the most important thing at this stage.

Now that I knew – or thought I might know – how things were going to be conducted, I would spend every waking hour of the next few days preparing an exhaustive list of questions; not only for both of the Spiers and Miguel Diego, but for their architect and building inspector. Then I would fax it to Sr. Férrer.

Helen had kept a journal ever since we came to Spain, so we had a record of virtually everything that had happened from the very first morning. In addition, we had both spent a great deal of time over the past three years getting and checking information, preparing documents and copying others, making arguments, refutations, and anything else we could think of to make things easy for Abogado Férrer. From the very first, I had insisted on building our case on the fact that the contract stated the *vivienda* had to be of *mismo diseño* (the same design) and *exactemente iguale* (exactly the same) as the model villa, and I had submitted details of departures from this stipulation to Sr. Férrer over the years. He had continually retorted Spiers' old chestnut to the effect that no comparison could be made until the first of January next when the *vivienda* was contracted to be complete, but my argument was that because most of the bad construction was being retained – though hidden under subsequent work – it would never be verifiable. Férrer said we would have to pursue a different tack, but on this, come hell or high water I refused to budge.

Gilbert and Mildred, the only English with sufficient backbone to stand up in court against the Spiers, were almost past themselves with anxiety and exasperation, and kept ringing up and faxing us with last minute advice and more tales they had heard regarding miscarriages of justice in Spain. But we did not want to hear any more now, we just wanted to be left to conduct things ourselves in our own way when our time came. One thing we were certain about was that we were not going to allow ourselves to be cut dead in mid-speech when we needed to explain ourselves. We had paid for this show, waited two and a half years for it, and cancelled an important hospital appointment scheduled for the same date, and we would be proverbial dogs having our day.

THIRTY

When we got to the court, which was in Alicante, we were put in a narrow unventilated corridor with a tiny office at the end of it. There were two benches: one right outside the door of the office, which was occupied by the Spiers and their party, and another halfway up the corridor, on which we sat. There were no toilet or ablution facilities. This was quite an anomaly because in the majority of public buildings there were always toilets – more so even than in England or Ireland. So, in a place such as this, where angst could easily assume control of one's bowels, it would be necessary to go outside of the building to one of the numerous bars nearby and avail oneself of their '*servicios*'.

There were tiny rooms that looked as though they might have once been used for the purpose, because truncated parts of ancient pipes could be seen, but all space was now taken up with boxes and files in total disarray.

Férrer looked different to how we had ever seen him: limp, mute, unimposing, and at first we did not recognise him. When I enquired about the *perita's* report, which I did immediately, he said she was very busy and had not started on it yet. I said I thought it was essential it be presented as soon as possible.

'*No problema*'. Sr. Férrer would explain things to the judge.

I asked who had been in so far and how they had performed. He shrugged. Only Miguel Diego had been in and he had lied without faltering for a whole hour.

Where were the Spiers' *arquitecto* and his *aparajedor de facto* wife..? Them..? Oh, they were not here. They were professionals and professionals never gave evidence alongside ordinary witnesses. This was a matter of respect. They had seen the judge months ago. The two of them bore much of the responsibility for the shocking construction of the *vivienda* by not supervising it properly, and issuing false certificates which they had both signed and had had stamped by the College de Arquitectos, yet they were worthy of more respect than the rest of us put together.

I had a doctoral degree in medical science, but that was not recognised by anybody here because it was just an English qualification, not a Spanish one. Here my only rank was *pensionista, anciano, extranjero jubilado* – a retired foreign pensioner and therefore just about the lowest creature crawling in Spain – and when '*inglés*' was tagged on, one had what was probably the lowest thing on earth. Nonetheless, I always suspected there was a bit of old-fashioned envy in there somewhere, especially where the '*inglés* – was concerned: after all, one did not win an important naval battle – thanks to lousy weather – and then have it tossed aside in a mere five hundred years.

Helen was called in first, and when she got up, instead of shaking her hand or patting her on the arm or bottom or anything, Férrer let her go in without a word of comfort or encouragement. As she followed him towards the critical room at the end of the corridor, he trudging more like an undertaker at the head of a cortège, than a proud officer leading his troops into battle, he did not even wish her '*suerte*' (good luck).

Although I was too far away to hear what was being said, because the Spiers and their party were seated right outside the open door of the room where the evidence was being taken, they could hear every question Helen was asked and every answer she gave.

Their interpreter, a German woman who spoke English infinitely better than Lew Spiers, translated everything Helen said and their whole party were excitedly discussing it.

I protested to several clerks about Helen's lack of privacy, before one finally went down and shut the office door. However it was almost immediately reopened and left open because there was no window in the tiny court room, and no air-conditioning. I tried to attract Férrer's attention, but either he could not, or did not, want to hear what I had to say, because whenever I waved to him, he disappeared behind the door. Had this been a proper hearing in an open court where everybody could hear exactly what was going on, fine. But this parody of a judicial process, with the Spiers sniggering outside the door while our evidence was being heard, supposedly in confidence, was something we could never have imagined. After about forty minutes, Helen came out. She was ready to use the toilet but that would have to wait several hours yet. Sr. Férrer was standing outside the little room, waving to me to come down.

'*Rapido, Señor! Rapido!*'

'Rapido, bollocks!' I wanted a word with my wife to see how she had got on. Also I needed a drink from the little bottle of water she had in her handbag. Space, privacy, toilet facilities, oxygen, rectitude and water, were all in desperately short supply here.

Typical of the Spanish way, the entrance to the court had been large and grand, with marble floors and staircase, flowery inscriptions and huge oil-painted portraits of expensively dressed, self-important people. Yet deep inside, where the real business was done, it was primitive and grotty, and when we asked where the toilet was, we were directed to a bar outside the court and down the street.

'*Rapidamente!*' Férrer kept repeating. '*Esperan!*' (They are waiting!).

'They can wait till I've had a drink,' I said. God knows we had waited long enough for him and the rest of them to get themselves together. Janet, who was acting as our court interpreter, suggested he might be concerned about the propriety of it, that Helen might be telling me the questions she had been asked and the answers she had given.

'What..? We had suddenly gone into moral mode? After the Spiers and their cronies had been listening to every word Helen and everybody in the interrogation cell had said, Férrer had all of a sudden become concerned about propriety?'

When I went in, I straightaway asked Sr. Férrer to have the Spiers party move up the corridor and, if necessary, exchange seats with our party. But he did nothing except stand in the doorway as though to prevent them coming in. And there he remained, behind me, like a third thumb, the least impressive figure in a room that contained Víbora-Masson and his assistant, apart from the judge, and Janet as interpreter. Had Férrer been waving semaphores, or whacking the sides of his nose with a hurley, I would have been none the wiser; I would have had to be holding up a mirror so I could see behind me. Where my man was supposed to be standing, Spiers's was standing close enough to touch me, with a leer he managed to sustain for a full hour and a half. There were six of us but only three chairs and no window, and it was red hot. The atmosphere was consequently insufferable, hence the open door and the Spiers hearing every word.

The questions were feeble and not phrased to discover truth. Patently their purpose was to trick and incriminate, but I answered exactly as I had intended, determined to cram in as many facts and arguments as I could. Even when the judge had had enough and ordered Janet to tell me to stop, I carried on until I was finished. As far as I was concerned, I would only hear what I wanted to hear, and say all I wanted to say.

When I came out, Trev Hall was called in: not as a *perito* but as an expert witness. He had been building a chalet across the road from the vivienda that Spiers and his gang were supposedly building for us, and had seen the gross errors they had made in the roof and elsewhere outside. Lew Spiers and his buddies were to be called in after lunch, but we had no wish to wait and listen, so when our side had all been heard, we left.

It came as a shock when Gilbert and Mildred telephoned that night to tell us the Spiers were throwing a party, shouting and yelling that they had won the case. And on the following day, when Helen was shopping in Pryca, Spiers ran after her between the aisles, shouting 'Loser! Loser!' She was so upset when she came back, that we decided to telephone Sr. Férrer. His staff said he was away for several days and that they could tell us nothing, so we decided to go to the police. Something must be seriously wrong. We had been told it would be weeks before judgement was passed, and that had seemed much more likely.

Because of the harassment the Forsyths were having to endure, as shamelessly as ever, Helen and Mildred decided to go together, though neither of the Forsyths had much faith in the police. However, the local variety were totally different to the *guardia*. They had very little authority compared with the other varieties of police, but were armed, and they were nearly always polite and friendly. Afterwards one of them called on the Spiers to give them a warning, and the Spiers never bothered Helen after that, although they continued to harass the Forsyths who were very reluctant to complain to any police; to them it would have been undignified. Gilbert, now eighty, had been the youngest major ever to serve in the British Army at the time of the Second World War when the Japs invaded the area of Burma where he was head of communications, and he still had several pistols and a rifle. I urged him to always carry one of the pistols when Spiers was in the vicinity, and to shove it in his face every time he bothered him. But he would not take me seriously.

'Have you any idea what the *guardia* would do to me?'

No, and I did not want any.

Nothing then happened, nothing at all for a couple of months, until one afternoon when Sr. Férrer telephoned to say he had received our *perita's* report and it was very favourable, but more money was needed before it could be entered into court and it was imperative we come in with it immediately, or we might have to go through the whole court palaver again with perhaps a completely different result this time.

When we got to his office, it was to find that Víbora-Masson and the Spiers already had copies of the report and had had them long enough for Víbora-Masson to make a written response which was surprisingly poorly put together; so bad, in fact, that it looked as though Víbora-Masson had thrown in the towel.

That Sr. Férrer had commissioned the *perita* on our behalf and we had already paid her a substantial sum, did not seem to strike him as of any significance. He said he did not know how the other party had come by a copy of a report which was intended for us, and did not seem to think it mattered. It was the same response he had made on so many occasions throughout the process when we had asked how, for instance, Víbora-Masson and the Spiers had come by various confidential documents we had sent privately to him.

The *perita's* report, illustrated by a very detailed aerial drawing of the roofs and houses, showed exactly – as mine had – the differences between the villa model and the *vivienda*. It also revealed that the land had not been properly levelled before construction had begun, necessitating therefore all kinds of unplanned and unrecorded changes that had resulted in serious faults in construction. It stated that the replacement of the walls, which had taken place long after the date for completion of construction, was highly consistent with our claim that they had been seriously defective, because in the opinion of the *perita* there would have been no other way of rectifying them, and the replacement work was obvious.

Of great importance was her opinion that neither the Spiers' architect, nor his building inspector partner, could have visited the site and confirmed that the *vivienda* had been properly built, before signing the documents declaring it to be in perfect order in accordance with the contract. The final construction, as her drawings and photographs clearly showed, did not even match the architect/builder's plan that Víbora-Masson had produced over a year after the completion date.

We could not have wished for anything better than this. On top of everything else, there was sufficient to warrant legal action against the architect and building inspector.

'This is it, then?' I said. 'After all this time…'

Helen and I turned to each other, so pleased and relieved we could hardly believe it.

'How long before we get our money back?'

Férrer suddenly looked grave; time for deferring to Spanish.

'*Todavía hay un problema grande.*' (There is still a big problem).

'Oh..?'

'*El juez es un amigo de* Víbora-Masson.' (The judge is a friend of Víbora-Masson).

'So?'

'It is going to be very difficult to win.'

'Why..? What difference does that make?'

He shrugged.

'What happens if we lose?'

'You'll have to appeal.'

'Christ..! I mean "*Hostia!*" How long will it take for the judge to give his verdict?'

'Two or three weeks at least.'

THIRTY-ONE

No sooner had the builder's rubble been buried beneath the plot next to our own, than families of Walloons – holidaymakers from the area the new owners lived in – started arriving, half a dozen or more for at least two weeks at a time. From now on, every summer – and for weeks before and after – we would have an invasion of yobs on both sides of us – Flemish to the left, Dutch to the right – shouting and yelling to each other across our premises and making a nuisance of themselves from the moment they piled out of their four-by-fours, until the moment they piled back into them two weeks later. Rarely more than a couple of hours later, by which time the cleaners would have been and gone, they would be replaced by the next contingent. They almost always came by car, and after their long drive down through France, Northern Spain and the long coast, they would be almost manic, especially the kids. They would be out of their vehicles and into the pool, shouting and shrieking within minutes, and from then on for the next two or three weeks, hell would be let loose. After a meal, they would go into town and come back with all kinds of huge plastic toys and boats to clash into the water, stopping only for drinks and to get the barbecue going. Sometimes there would be so many people they would have to occupy the pool in shifts, one lot yelling and splashing in the water, while the other got sunburnt. An hour later, all change.

The Walloons' pool on the left of our plot was too large and almost reached our wall because Trev, whose policy with anything dodgy was to build first and get permission afterwards, had bribed the *alcalde* into allowing him to install one of the biggest pools the law allowed, because the owners wanted to attract more customers; it even had underwater lights so the 'guests' could continue their antics during the night, by which time they would be thoroughly drunk and throwing their bottles over our wall.

Although the wonderful Mediterranean Sea was just a few miles away and the beaches never crowded, for most of every day the holiday-making hedonists would play in the swimming pool on huge inflated balls and toys specially made to make a highly vexing noise when they slapped them on the water, whilst their portable radios played Dutch or Walloon pop around the sides.

They would never have been allowed to do on a private housing estate in Holland or Belgium, what every one of them did on an *urbanización* here, and they were extremely rude and aggressive when we complained. One of a party of Walloons, a massively fat beast, would stand in the middle of the pool, bang his fists on his chest and roar, in broken English, 'I am a Viking! I am a Viking!'

One occasion they would be Vikings, the next, Walloons – quite a transubstantiation we thought. But they both made the same noises. At night we had to close the bedroom windows to reduce the incoming noise and the air would be stifling.

One particular gang who played several radios outside all day and night, were not only noisy but also aggressive. Ned was big and looked ferocious but like most of his breed and many other 'guard' dogs, when it came down to it he was more of a hand-licker than an ankle-biter, so because the police were disinclined to do anything about rowdy neighbours or holidaymakers whom they insisted on calling '*turistas*', i.e. sources of income, civilised, permanent and peace-loving residents had to defend ourselves the best way we could.

I confess that the very idea of using music as a form of torture was anathema to me, although I was aware the Americans used it for just that purpose at their hell-hole in Guantanamo. However, sensing that the kind of holidaymakers who rented the villas on each side of ours would be aficionados of neither Schoenberg nor Stockhausen, I recorded tapes of both, mixed them with total regard for dissonance, and when one night neighbour noise was at an intolerable level, played them back at maximum volume on the car radio while the car was standing in the garden with all doors wide open. Three minutes was all it took. First there were shrieks of horror, then shouts of fury, finally dead silence. Then Dutch pop started blaring at maximum volume accompanied by yelling and shouting. But they were no match for my Braun at maximum bass, and off and on went the various radios, ill-matched artillery on both sides of a battle front, until eventually, realising nothing they could throw at us could drown out what I was bombarding them with, they capitulated. Helen was concerned in case they attacked us during the night, but after a lot of verbal abuse and threats regarding our wellbeing, they drank themselves into a stupor, and that was the end of it. The following day might have been their last, but replacements were already on their way with exactly the same mentality and the same inclination to descend *en masse* at the local *guardia* to complain that we were spoiling their holiday; after all, two seventy-year-olds could cause mayhem when hemmed in by a couple of gangs totalling fifteen to twenty drunk and conveniently anonymous thirty-year-old hooligans.

Because their Riviera was such an expensive resort, large numbers of French holidaymakers came down to the Costa Blanca in August, though they did not even mix much among themselves, let alone with *rosbifs*, and caused very little trouble. As long as there was a plentiful variety of food – which of course there was – they were happy. Unlike Spanish men, French husbands were even more finicky about choosing comestibles in the markets and huge food stores, like Carrefour – a French store – than Spanish mothers. As long as they could discourse among melons and mushrooms and epicures' wine, the other holidaymakers were welcome to the sand and sea, paella and grog, and even the ineffable women. Occasionally expats of different nationalities made friends with each other, especially if they were neighbours, but holidaymakers generally stuck to their own kind.

By-laws prohibited the emptying of pools into the street because of the damage heavily chemicalised water did to the surface of the roads and pavements, but owners of pools, or the chancers they had looking after them, usually emptied the pools at night. Those who did not change the contents of their pool – and some boasted of not changing it for years at a time – would have pools containing all kinds of chemicals mixed with all kinds of bodily excretions produced by microbiome after microbiome of new organisms, their content no longer deserving the term, 'water', since it was composed of much more than two parts of hydrogen and one part of oxygen. Opaque and discoloured, it frequently stank. If the Dutch pool managers who used computers to justify their know-all attitude to everything, deluded themselves into thinking the sea was more heavily contaminated with human soil than were the densely contaminated swimming pools in which their holidaying countrymen, women and children flopped about all day and half the night, they must have been seriously browsing the wrong sites.

Villas rented to foreign holidaymakers were invariably owned by foreigners themselves, many of whom lived most of the time in their homeland and only visited Spain once or twice a year. By making the letting arrangements in their own countries, they avoided paying taxes to both their own government and the Spanish, but the whole business of renting to short-term visitors was in such a mess that it was quite beyond scrutiny and regulation.

It was living under these circumstances that spoiled life in Spain. By now we had nearly got used to minor irritations, like the judicial system, and had found so many people, places and things that we liked, not least the sun, language and health service, that were it not for our children being so far away, we would have happily spent the rest of our lives, not necessarily on the Costa Blanca, but somewhere in Spain. It seems a rather pathetic gripe to rate the health service as important, but had found that even without a background chronic illness, after three score years and ten, new illnesses multiplied and were usually incurable, becoming a nuisance that affected so many things.

Living next to bad neighbours, even on just one side of one's house, could be such a tribulation and was far worse than merely vexing. It was nowhere near a matter as simple as just packing up and going somewhere else, as most reasonable people suggest; not if one owned the house. We had bought ours in good faith, with no prospect of gangs of awful holidaymakers coming for two weeks at a time and creating havoc, but it happened within a year, as soon as we had the house the way we wanted and had spent a good deal of time and money on it, the garden, and the surrounds.

From then on, particularly between April and October it rapidly got worse until it became so intolerable that we were having to get in the car and go out to get away from it.

Like most expats, middle and working-class, we lived on an estate of mixed nationalities where the Spanish tended to be *nuevo rico* (new rich) and did not emerge before breakfast to sweep the area in front of their door each morning, the way the working-class women of the towns did, nor did they carry their chairs outside to commune with neighbours at night in the back streets, the way old people did. Nowadays, thanks to the many colonies of expats and hordes of tourists, an immigrant could manage without regard for the Spanish people or their way of life, and little or no facility with their language, by relying on better informed fellow countrymen.

Depending on their age, intelligence and sociability, immigrants everywhere probably underwent similar experiences, but in the case of people like ourselves who had pretty much retired from the dynamics of life, they would be encountering a situation for which they were totally unprepared. For a start, in Spain the *cucarachas* were quite a bit different from what we thought they would be, i.e., they were definitely not gourds filled with hard seeds that one shook rhythmically when singing South American songs. They were monster cockroaches that, like so many disagreeable species, had come by boat. And, like the cane toad in Australia, they had originated in America and rapidly colonised the whole country by consuming the relatively harmless indigenous species, the impact of which can best be estimated by comparing the substitution of a handful of house mice by a horde of bubonic rats.

We first knew we were unwitting hosts to the former when, in the middle of the night while searching in the kitchen for a Mars Bar to banish a nightmare, Helen stepped on one in her bare feet; and when I rushed down in response to her shriek, another dropped from the ceiling onto my incipiently balding crown. Why they should suddenly appear, I had no idea, I suppose this was the way it was with triumphant invasions.

But within days we were finding them behind pictures on the walls, skittering across tiled floors, and clumsily taking to the air in order to collide with our faces. Helen was mortified, especially after finding one inside her pillow case, and we tried everything to eliminate them, but the vile things were practically indestructible, proprietary deterrents seeming to act more like body-building supplements. They moved so purposefully that it took nerves of steel to stand one's ground in bare feet when a particularly gross behemoth with wire feelers and a bronze carapace decided it wanted to painstakingly search the area of floor one was occupying. A similar degree of red-badge valour was required to be able to close one's eyes within half an hour of seeing one of the blighters drop out of a crucifix and disappear somewhere in the room.

Eventually I found a remedy on the internet that recommended boric acid, an old wives' remedy for eye strain in humans, that apparently played havoc with the cockroach's nervous system which caused cognitive dysfunction and drove them insane. Although crazy cockroaches sounded worse than sane ones, the former were believed to forget the way into one's house and die of fatal disorientation. Seemingly they also carried the powder back to their nests where it ravaged the psyches of the whole family. With all this in mind, I bought the shop's whole stock – 5 kilograms – and dusted the spaces in front of all outside doors, all damp areas, such as under the sinks in the kitchen and over the chinks in the bathroom floor and walls, plus anywhere else I thought they might frequent. It did the trick, but only after spreading it around night after night for weeks.

Ants were another summer visitor, though a mixed blessing, because once they had route-marched and the column been located, remedial action could be taken. At least they were not malign, although Helen was not so sure. The main species we had was a voracious devourer of canine excrement, which was a boon if one were hostage to a voluminous crapper like Ned. When it first started it was as though Ned had suddenly reneged on all bowel functions.

I would say, 'Did you clear away Ned's business, dear?' and Helen would reply, 'No, I thought you must have. There's not a trace of it anywhere. Do you think he's all right?'

We could never discover whether the ants had consumed it, or carried it off, but in just a few hours it would vanish without a trace.

There was also the tiny leishmaniasis-toting sandfly which was dangerous to humans, and quite a few dogs in our area carried it; but by regularly spraying a dog with nasty insecticides that also killed honey bees and damaged peregrine egg shells, it caused no problems. One would be advised by 'well-meaners' not to use anything for animal and plant parasites except the expensive and utterly useless pyrethrum.

Ticks were other parasites that attacked dogs and humans, and were a menace in spring when they proliferated rapidly. However, there were several injectable insecticides that were very effective if administered properly. They had to be given in the correct area of the skin, or they could kill the dog, and could make the human administrator very sick if his or her own skin were penetrated.

Tough and persistent hornets were also common, and their sting could be really painful, especially just behind the ear. We had a nest – or, rather, they had one – inside an old garden hose, and after every winter, by which time I would have forgotten about it, they would emerge very angry if I unfurled the hose clumsily. Their nests were best doused with Dettol, paraffin or carbolic, best done on the run. Infestations with the foregoing were a matter of luck, but nowhere was free from the infuriating mosquitoes whose bites so easily became infected. They could be 'mopped' during the day when they were resting upside down on the ceiling, digesting the household blood bank, but the mops could leave unsightly marks. I had a small pond loaded with rice-water fish and paradise gourami – little fish which love mosquito larvae – but they could only deal with mosquitoes that landed on the water, and it was their larvae or pupae that the fish really went for. One of this irritating vector's most annoying features was the racket its wings made when it was approaching its quarry at night. Instead of merely thrusting its proboscis into the tenderest part of one's exposed body, sucking out a small aliquot of blood and pumping in various microorganisms, such as malarial protozoa in exchange, it made a screeching noise which got increasingly more voluminous as it approached, like a fully fuelled and recently serviced Messerschmitt zoning in on a disabled Lancaster.

Notwithstanding the fauna of a Spanish garden, there was the flora, which included the Prickly Pear and other excruciatingly finely spined, hooked and painful cactii whose spurs entered the skin a lot easier than they exited.

The Costa Blanca was a lot colder than aged holidaymakers and new expats anticipated, and from November to February it could be colder indoors than out. There was no insulation built into average accommodation, so no matter how much heat was engendered indoors, the vast majority of it went straight out through the walls. Floors were tiled and there was little in the way of carpets, so winters could be really uncomfortable. Fortunately gas was cheap. Unfortunately, the heaters that went with it were devilish to operate, always going off, making a lot of noise, and producing unpleasant odours. The good thing was that during the day the sun usually shone even in winter, so conditions outside were often pleasant.

Although I liked the period immediately prior to sunset when the light was so entrancing and the atmosphere balmy, Helen preferred it shortly after dawn when the light was soft and everything nice and quiet. She did her housework then, and afterwards her shopping, completing both before mid-day when in summer things begin to heat up. At dawn the light of day always seems freshly laundered, whereas at twilight – although there really was no such thing – it would often show all the colours that had been used to paint the day and were quickly blending into dusk.

As with their weather and topography, Spaniards themselves could be thoroughgoing extremists. On television I once saw a middle-aged man at a *valencian falla* waving a flag around his head while walking backwards on his knees in front of a statue that was being carried in a procession. It must have been sheer agony, and at the end, quite a few bystanders came up to kiss him with seeming great warmth; whether it was to absorb something spiritual, or express sympathy for his zeal, I could not determine, but from the look in his eyes it was plain he was in a different world from the one I was in. I could not but think that penitents who lacerated their bodies with various kinds of flail, did it for the entertainment of the crowd. They would occasionally pause for the application of what appeared to be tincture of iodine, by somebody who was standing by with a swab and bottle; though it would have been more impressive and not much less effective were they to have used sea salt, in which case there would have been lots of attendants standing by with buckets of white crystals from which they could cast handfuls willy-nilly, like confetti, or apply with a distemper brush.

During a vox pop, a priest was asked his opinion after viewers had been shown an eye-rolling young man of about thirty who had just received his first aid and was returning to take up his position in the procession for another dose of his particularly fiendish-looking lash. The priest, who was about fifty, chubby and well-preserved with exquisite skin himself, refrained from replying but produced a series of facial expressions that more eloquently spoke of the asininity of mankind, than anything I could ever recall having witnessed, heard or read about.

Contrariness was very much a part of the extremism. For instance, no matter how good or bad the weather was elsewhere in Europe, it was always better in Spain. No matter how good or bad it was in the rest of Spain, it was always better on the Costa Blanca. And no matter how good it was there, it was always better in Benidorm. With its occasional hurricane winds and deluges, the climate was not perfect but the Spaniard would nevertheless loyally defend it and deeply resent the kind of flippant meteorological comment that constituted the mainstay of much English small talk.

'Cold..? Today..? Not at all!' a Spanish female estate agent retorted in her best English when Helen and I were in an elevator with her on our way to view a flat, and I was being amiable. 'This is warm! This is a warm climate, not a cold one. England is an example of a cold place. Spain isn't. That is why you English come here!'

Well… Stick that up your jumper..!

Tolerance is also part of it. The Spanish especially have a reputation for tolerance of various sexual mores. On our third day in Spain, in the middle of the afternoon in Alicante, we had seen two men urinating on trees in a plaza near the bullring. When we expressed surprise, someone told us there was a law whereby men could stop their cars and pee by the roadside if they felt the need, though they were pretty sure it did not apply to women.

Both men and women pretended not to notice the vile stench of sewage which every so often came up, like a demonic miasma, from between the paving stones of old Spanish towns. On several occasions I had paused to observe the reactions of an elegant woman passing through such an invisible cloud of mixed quadrillions of bacteria and viruses, and nary an eye or nostril had twitched – perhaps a flicker of an eyelash, but certainly no more. But I am not sure how this should be interpreted.

On our return from town one Saturday we saw our fax machine had been very busy. Sr. Férrer had telephoned asking us to call back urgently but must then have decided he could not wait for our return call, and sent us an eighteen-page fax giving the results of our court case. Apparently we had won, but naturally I could hardly believe it, so I telephoned him.

He sounded as though he could hardly believe it himself, and in any case got the names all mixed up, so I got him to repeat it several times. So many things had gone wrong, people lied and stupid mistakes made, that this had to be the final blow: the wrong name of the winner relayed. But he must have checked it a hundred times himself because he was positive we had won hands down and the Spiers lost on every count.

It seemed there was a God after all, even though I was pretty sure we had not brought Him with us. Maybe He had been keeping an eye on us from Ireland. The children had probably been on to Him non-stop, as they said they would, and He had been paying attention. 'Suffer little children to come unto Me.' It was right. That particular command had always stayed with me from the Catechism, the first thing I can ever recall Him having said.

All the while, as our dear friend and brilliant counsel, Sr. César Quintiliano Férrer de Rossa, and I were exchanging blessings and praising the inevitability of Spanish justice, I was struggling to prevent any silly little sobbing or shrieking sounds from escaping and sullying my normally urbane tones. I would show him how we English handled a win-win; there would be none of the 'Gooooooooaaaaaallllll!' mentality from our side. We would treat it like any other item of news, such as the temperature in Madrid at 1310 hrs., the Dow Jones Index, or the condition of Ronaldo's cartilage…

The judge had awarded what we had claimed down to the last peseta – 6,362,100 ptas (€38,236.99) plus costs – and Férrer now said it was up to us to reach an agreement with Masson regarding how much the defendants would actually pay.

'The lot, *por supuesto*,' I replied.

Férrer then began his customary expostulating, saying it was normal practice to round things down to the nearest thousand. I said I did not care much for traditions like that and we should all simply obey the law and have the Spiers pay what the good judge had ruled they should pay.

Helen was over the moon with the judgement but the Forsyths were much more circumspect.

'Make sure he hasn't got the names mixed up,' Gilbert warned. 'One foreign name's the same as another to these people.'

A couple of days later Férrer called to say the Spiers had declared themselves bankrupt and could only pay two thirds of the money, enough to cover our expenses but not the penalty. Plus they could only afford to pay in small emoluments over what sounded like an eternity. Plus Masson warned that if we did not agree, his clients were likely to diddle off to the Philippines. They were pleading poverty because Lew was unemployed, Val likely to lose her job, and for half a dozen other spurious reasons. The trouble was, of course, and always had been, that the Spanish system, where the advance deposit on a property had to be paid directly into the hands of the prospective vendor, rather than to a neutral party with the legal authority to hold such moneys until the proper time came to hand it over. Had even the estate agent been holding it, in this case, Roberto Hernandez, he would have returned the money years ago when it was obvious the Spiers were not going to meet their obligations.

Whatever, I sent documents and information to Férrer to show the Spiers had more than enough assets to be able to pay the fine and the other expenses, but he felt we were lucky to have got this far and should not stand on principle. The court would expect us to accept whatever the Spiers offered, any further demands being construed as greed on our behalf. His continual remonstrations as to the 'generosity' of the award, exasperated me. Right from the start, he had sought to reduce the amount the Spiers should have to repay, and for him to now talk in terms of their 'generosity' after all they had done, stuck in my craw like a chopping axe. I had always understood that the aim of lawyers was to extract, by one means or another, as much money as possible from defendants, yet we seemed to have the only lawyer in the world whose objective was entirely the opposite. Where I was totally convinced he was in the wrong business, my wife was beginning to feel sorry for him. At least the Forsyths had no time for him.

While Helen wanted to accept and end it all because she had had enough and felt we would only be hurting Gilbert and Mildred, as well as ourselves, if we continued, Gilbert, who with Mildred had already suffered a lot more than we had, urged us not to let them off with a single peseta. Mildred, as tough as she was shrewd, was nevertheless clearly wearied by it all but was not one to seek the easy way out, and stood by Gilbert. He and I had not always agreed on tactics, but he had never complained about his own lot, his loyalty had never wavered, and he was prepared to continue to the very end without the slightest concession.

We had won the case which had occupied so much of our lives in Spain, but we were now faced with actually getting hold of the money. Although it was ours that the Spiers had in their bank – or wherever – and the Forsyths would not accept a penny from us for all their time, labour and expense, the reality was that it must have cost them plenty and they felt they had a right to see justice done.

After all of this time, years now, Gilbert had hung on, health palpably deteriorating, and when Férrer said he could not get any more out of anybody and did not want to continue, Helen and I decided to settle for most of what the judge had awarded, which included Val Spiers' signing over the car. It would have taken years to get every last peseta and there was no guarantee that we would have succeeded in doing anything other than throw away more in legal expenses, blood and sweat. I did not like to admit we were quitting before everything was completely wrapped up, but it had to end sometime.

Never mind the time and effort we had put into presenting the case, testimony from good witnesses like Gilbert, Mildred, Roberto and Trev Hall, constant help, loyalty and support from Edmundo, and countless, sometimes very difficult-to-obtain documents, from many sources, it seemed it was the report of our young *perita*, who had come onto the stage so late in the drama, that had made the difference between our winning and losing. In plain but very well written language, using all the formatting features available on her obviously very modern computer, to enlarge, embolden, accentuate, italicise and whatever else to emphasise her points, she made it very clear that the *vivienda* was very different in design to the original model to which the Spiers had contracted themselves. Not only different in the ways we had claimed, but different in other ways too, ways she had been able to divine with her superior skill and equipment. For instance, it was not only aesthetically different, but different in ways that affected the security and longevity of the building and safety of the occupants because of what she was able to prove were inferior materials and methods.

She challenged the claims the architect and his building-inspector, *de-facto* spouse and colleague had made about the legally required inspections and supervision of the construction, maintaining such checks could not have taken place, given its finished condition. She even challenged the affixed dates and details to which the two of them had applied their signatures, and demonstrated how they had deceived their College of Architects. She said both of them could and should be charged with having broken the law and committed criminal offences. She claimed they were incompetents, unfit for the positions they held on behalf of the Government and town council, and made it abundantly clear that both were pathological liars. However, unless the police or government decided to act on this, they would both escape any penalties because that was a matter to be dealt with by a different jurisdiction, one concerned with justice, abuse of authority, morality and corruption. As opposed to ours.

In Spain, an *extranjero* of average bent was unlikely to be able to comprehend how the judicial system worked: what the law allowed and disallowed, how lawyers and judges operated and courts functioned. To him or her, who would have been brought up to think bias and bribery should have no part in legal process, it would seem criminally unfair, and for a judge to accept that everyone would automatically be lying, lawyers encouraging their clients and witnesses to dissemble and pay witnesses, was pure corruption.

THIRTY-TWO

Generally my health was not bad. I was doing no heavy work but doing a fair amount of walking and gardening, getting plenty of sun and ample good food, and having no trouble getting the necessary medication I needed. But one particularly hot day we had been standing waiting rather a long time for a bus, and shortly after we got on, I collapsed.

According to Helen, immediately and without anything being said, everybody on the bus got up from their seat and went to the back of the bus. The driver called the police who appeared within minutes, carried me into their car, tore across pavements, siren wailing and lights flashing, and delivered me to the local general hospital.

I was examined straight away, found to be in no danger, and discharged. As we went walking through the market, our original destination, because I had been unconscious during the episode, Helen told me what had happened, explaining that the very concerned fellow bus passengers thought I had died and were talking about it among themselves. That night we were in a local supermarket when we came across several people who had been on the bus; we did not recognise them but they recognised us. One woman nearly fainted and several others gave a little cry and crossed themselves as though I was risen from the dead. When we explained that I was all right, they were so pleased and hurried off excitedly to tell their friends. And when we went back to the hotel where we were staying for a few days, the owner was similarly shocked to see me alive after having been told that I had gone to heaven. From then until the end of our stay, every time we went in or out she crossed herself and was full of smiles.

Weekends, which were manifestly so joyful times for our Spanish neighbours, were often periods of melancholy for Helen and me. With the holiday season over and Spanish residents back working and living in Alicante during the week, the *urbanización* was quiet apart from the dogs. However, come Friday when they returned to be hosts to their families, it was a different matter. The children would be glad to come into the *campo* where they could run about without parents having to worry about traffic, villains, and other menaces of the city, and grandparents would do everything they could to ruin them – they were already spoilt. It was a time therefore when we very much missed our own children and grandchildren, especially when we could hear grandfathers teasing grandchildren and grandmothers calling them in for the big Sunday meal.

On Saturday nights we would go to the local Centro de Cultura (Art Centre) if there was a show on, or down to the beach if there was a concert, the latter events frequently being of a high standard and very entertaining, especially the musicians and dancers. Big jazz bands, on a tour from South America, would come down from Valencia and play on the beach until well into the early hours, and it was entirely free. Nowhere in the world had we enjoyed this sort of entertainment, let alone under such wonderful conditions as free car-parking, warm sea air, ample seating, perfect audience behaviour, itinerant refreshment sellers of everything from sausage burgers to ice-cream, and all around the wonderful music and concert atmosphere.

To be able to dance in the semi-darkness on a lovely night on the warm sand, with the moon and artificial lights shimmering on the sea beyond and the lights of the city illuminating the hills behind us, surrounded by hundreds of music-and-dance-lovers of various nationalities and all ages, was wonderful. The seated *jubilados* and *pensionistas* would mostly be expats, the dancers mainly young local Spanish. And never any trouble: no drunken fools, no yobs looking for somebody to beat up, nothing. Even in Ireland, renowned for its friendliness and 'hundreds of thousands of welcomes', there was nothing like it: not the wonderful Latin big bands that garnered such a wide audience of dancers and music-lovers, not the sobriety, and never, of course, the paradisiacal weather. We could get in the car, drive down to the beach and park free anywhere, have a drink at one of the many sociable bars along the shore where one could already hear the music, amble on to the beach to find a pair of the numerous seats that had been provided at no expense. *Perfecto*!

One Saturday afternoon we went to a recently opened *vivero's* (horticultural nursery). Driving to somewhere new, having a look at their stock and then, over a coffee, considering buying something interesting, was a pleasant way of filling in a couple of hours and getting away from the vexations where we lived. Venus fly-traps fascinated me and I was always looking for something fragrant, with beautiful flowers, that would gobble up cockroaches and mosquitoes, rodents as well if possible. Such were on order, we were told, and would be in in a couple of weeks – 'weeks' being Spanish for 'eternity'. In the meantime would we like one that would snaffle ants and by Christmas probably be mature enough to take on horseflies and hornets.

No, we would try one of their new *ficus* (fig) hybrids, one that would bear fruit next year, enough to keep a whole family regular. Already at seven feet they were too big to get in the car, so one of the assistants helped us put one in the passenger side and arrange it so that it poked vertically out through the window, a way of transporting that the girl assistant assured us would be ideal. She got some twine and the three of us wound it round and around the passenger seat, seatbelt anchor and door so it would not budge before we got home. I drove, Helen sat in the back, and the tree did not impede my view at all.

The road we took had only recently been finished and there was very little traffic, so we headed straight for home, confident we would have no problem. There was no wind, not even a breeze, but I only drove at a moderate speed so as not to create any turbulence that might damage the foliage.

We had not gone more than a mile before two motorcycle *guardia* that we had seen earlier on the way there, came shrieking after us. They had clearly been looking for somebody to nail and lighten up an afternoon they would rather have spent at home with a few beers in front of the TV watching Real Madrid; and who better than two *jubilados ingléses*.

They maintained we were a danger to other road users because we were preventing the possibility of their overtaking us. I say 'possibility', but 'certainty' would be more apposite, because no Spaniard, old or young, male or female, would have been able to tolerate two white-haired and wrinkled English *ancianos* in front of them.

We were not obstructing anyone because the tree was going straight up in the air, and anybody passing would have had to pass on my – the driver's – side, not the passenger side where the tree was coming out from. But no one can win an argument with the *guardia*, and should not try; not even in a fairy story could somebody win an argument with these chaps. We had been told many times that the *guardia's* natural quarry was the Republican Spaniard, but nowadays it was the fearful, floundering and feckless Englishman, always with plenty of the ready in his pocket, or an ATM card, who provided these hunter-gatherers of the Spanish highway with the greatest rewards; Spanish drivers tended to be 'bankrupt'.

I was ordered to take out the tree and shove it in the boot where it would project horizontally straight out and behind the car, dragging along the ground, sweeping the road and swiping off the top and ends off the highest, youngest and most delicate branches. They then asked for the car's documents, and several years disappeared from the ends of our lives; it was the sort of request that caused a benign mole to change direction and start becoming malignant.

We knew that as soon as they saw Hilary Spiers' name, which had not yet been changed because of the complexity of such a task, they would realise they were on to a winner. At this point, a shrewd liar would have resorted to a tale about a cousin having lent us the car for the weekend, or something equally corny, but that was not our style. My Spanish went to hell and Helen's went nowhere better. Because we only had a British driving licence, even though we later had it confirmed that a British one should have sufficed, we were apparently committing several offences. While I was trying to explain, Helen was trying to contact Férrer, but his office was closed.

In Spain, problems like this could not be rectified by post or internet, everything had to be done by the individual in person or their *gestor*, doing the business at government offices in Alicante which often took half a day at a time, required several visits and, unlike in most EU countries, no translation or interpreter would be provided. Helen was by now able to deal with most things, even acting for friends, but serious matters demanded serious interpreters.

No matter what the transaction, punitive or routine, the procedure would be pretty much the same: documents in duplicate signed by a *notario*, plus three passport-sized photographs, copies of *cedulas* (identity cards), utility bills, several copies of whatever application forms were being submitted, and cash. In Spain, even banks did not like dealing with 'odd' amounts, preferring to round fees up if the customer were paying, and down if the bank were giving change, so it was as well for the customer to be carrying a range of denominations of currency if he or she did not want to be 'done' every time they settled an account. Because of the way they conducted business, with their predilection for paper, photocopying was a roaring trade and that was why there would always be several very busy photocopying shops near a government building.

In England, matters like these were usually dealt with civilly and efficiently, in Ireland almost always sympathetically whatever the subject's nationality. But in Spain one would be lucky to get back out of the door without tearing some hair out, or wanting to rip somebody else's heart out.

We were fined not only because of the tree, but because we did not own a Spanish driving licence and the *guardia* refused to recognise our British equivalent. Naturally, acquiring a Spanish driving licence was very different to acquiring a British one, not least because it required assessment at a special medical centre where most of the tests were absurdly perfunctory. The one we went to, which was one we had been told never failed to deliver, did the eye test first. This was carried out by an optician who called himself 'Doctor' but looked and sounded more like a sergeant major. After he had finished with me, I called out aloud to the receptionist to ask the name of '*El Toro*' of the eye department, and everybody, including the staff, giggled, albeit nervously. He was standing in the middle of the corridor where everybody could see him, and when I put my two hands up in imitation of a *banderillero* getting ready to place a pair of darts, the office staff had their hands over their mouths to stop themselves laughing. The other applicants, about thirty in number, looked as though they thought he was going to attack me, but he just huffed and puffed and disappeared back into his office.

I was then sent in to see the physician, an elderly and obviously long-since retired gentleman who, while having me standing in front of his desk, asked if there were anything wrong with me. I said 'No', which he wrote down and dismissed me as perfectly fit.

Then I had the hearing test which consisted of sitting in a dark and tiny cubicle, not unlike the confessional in a poor church, but not big enough to turn around in. After a couple of minutes the door was opened and I was called out without realising I had completed the test. When I asked what had happened, I was told I had been subjected to various sounds although I had not reacted to any of them.

'What was I supposed to do?' I asked.

'I told you. Raise your hand when you heard the sounds,' the audio technician replied.

'But I didn't hear any.'

'Well, that's the result.'

'Shouldn't we do it again, now I know what to do?'

'There's no point. It's over now,' he replied with a friendly smile. 'Has anybody checked your blood pressure yet?'

'No.'

'Come over here, then,' he said, and did it himself. '*Dios mio!*' (My God!) he said, and repeated it. Then he told me I must go to my GP the following morning to report the fact that my blood pressure was well over 200.

Finally, I was sent into a room with a computer where my reactions to various virtual driving conditions were to be assessed. As far as I could make out, nobody, be they English, Spanish, or anything else, had understood what they were supposed to do in this room. Whether it was new software, or the woman operating the equipment was new to the job, I had no way of telling, but she did not seem to know what to do either. However, we were very assured to overhear somebody tell somebody else that everybody passed or they would not pay. So it seemed like a good system after all.

When the time came to pay, the receptionist said to Helen, '*Muy buen, Señora! Muy buen!*' (*Very good, Señora!*)

She was congratulating Helen on having been given a licence not only to drive motor cars, but for motorcycles, cranes, large vans, tractors, and articulated lorries as well. Seemingly she had read off the categories on our English licence, which were quite differently coded to the Spanish, and Helen had thus been given credit for having passed driving tests for categories quite different from what she was qualified for. Everybody sitting waiting clapped their hands, especially the women, but although I was given the same, I received no ovation, presumably because I was a male.

The extra categories cost us more, twice as much in fact as the standard licence, but we decided not to make a fuss in case we ended up with nothing at all, a very easy thing to do, so we just paid the difference and came away heavyweights. I said to Helen that maybe we should have put down for a pilot's licence as well. I would have bet we would have got one, though God knows how much it would have cost.

The following day I went to see our GP who sent me into his *practicante* (nurse assistant) to have my blood pressure taken. This fellow nonchalantly waved me to a seat where he kept me waiting quarter of an hour while he tried to sell his car over the telephone.

I was sitting there with my arm on his desk, sleeve rolled up, monitor and cuff attached but not connected yet, while he bartered and argued with the prospective buyer, sometimes scoffing, otherwise almost pleading.

Eventually, I stood up, tubing dangling from above my elbow, and began to pull it off. At this point he must have remembered he was supposed to be urgently measuring my blood pressure, because he also stood up, and because I would not sit down again, he quickly attached the monitor.

He was shaking with foreboding when he saw the reading indicating I was suffering some kind of hypertensive crisis and in need of emergency treatment. In a panic, he repeated the measurement and then ran into the doctor's office. From there I was rushed to the hospital where, after a battery of blood tests, they started me on blood-pressure lowering medication. The next time I saw your man, when visiting the GP, I asked him if he had managed to get the price he wanted for his car, and it was a very sheepish smile he gave me as he hurried past. From then on, he always avoided me.

THIRTY-THREE

ONE NIGHT HELEN HAD to drive me to the Emergency Department at San Juan Hospital because of an agonising pain in my spine that suddenly came on about 2 a.m. and lasted for over an hour despite everything I did to try to relieve it. Within half an hour of arriving at the hospital, where I was seen immediately, I had had a physical examination, a sample of blood taken for comprehensive analysis, been given an X-ray, and put on a morphine drip. Two hours later I was on my way back home with the X-Ray plates, the result of the blood tests, a medical report beautifully typed up, a prescription, and an appointment to see a specialist in a fortnight – all in a large, unsealed manila envelope.

The results of a subsequent scan showed extensive damage throughout my spine due to herniated and disintegrating vertebral discs, but I was told there was nothing remedial that could be done. Consequently I was put on a slow-release opioid, and informed that I would have to remain on analgesics of gradually increasing strength for the rest of my life. Like most opioid medications, the one I was given caused side effects, though none of the oft-hailed euphoric effects, unlike with the dihydrocodeine I used to take in Ireland which was apparently not available in Spain.

Wise, multilateral advice on opioids was not easy to get, and doctors were generally timid or pig-headed about using them, but I could not see how the treatment of chronic or severe pain could be considered without them. They would ask me to rate the intensity of my pain on a scale of 1 to 10, but pain is so subjective as to render such an assessment worthless, if not ridiculous.

Although I used to smoke and drink, I had ceased the night before we had left England for Ireland thirty years previously, and never taken any other recreational drug. But now that we were in Spain and using the internet, Telefónica permitting, I read everything I could about analgesics, including marijuana, a drug I had never sampled but understood to be pleasant as well as efficacious in various medical situations. There was a serious and very informative Spanish periodical, called *Cañamo*, which was sold in all the big bookstores, and good quality pharmaceutical grade marijuana plus all the necessary accoutrements easy to obtain. Marijuana was recommended by many medical authorities around the world for various medical conditions, including chronic pain, so I tried it and found it helpful.

THIRTY-FOUR

As far as learning Spanish was concerned, I was quite happy with my somewhat restored arrangement with Edmundo; we did not meet every week as before, but frequently enough to maintain the friendship. I was still getting 'El Jueves', the witty satirical political comic, every week, reading good Spanish books and listening to Radio Clásica, the music programme whose presenters spoke such beautiful Spanish, and joking with sales staff in shops – self-deprecating cracks about old Englishmen always went down well. I was also very interested in the Civil War, though very few Spaniards were prepared to talk about it.

I had given up learning Spanish from books, although this method of learning had always suited me, and good teachers were hard to find. Our previous one, Vera the Venezuelan, had gone to France to find a man because she had been married to a Spaniard and reckoned Spanish men of her age were not properly educated because they had been brought up during the *Franquismo*. She maintained they might have florid manners but were all philanderers underneath.

Although I was happy enough to carry on, slowly picking up the language as we went along, Helen preferred to go to a proper language class and went to one which had a good reputation and was provided free by the *Ayuntamiento* in Muchamiel. There were two teachers: a man and a woman, both of whom taught general subjects to Spanish children during the day, and the Spanish language to immigrant adults in the evening. They apparently preferred the adult *extranjeros* because they were better behaved and keener to learn. In the case of *jubilados*, students were mainly women because women were more in need of it, and, according to the teachers, more conscientious.

There was a wide range of nationalities but only a few English. Not only were the English less keen to learn another language, but the conversational mode of teaching did not appeal to them, probably because it meant making their mistakes in public. The two teachers were of primary school standard and spoke no language but Spanish, making learning difficult for most of the students, especially as, for some inexplicable reason, Diego, the male teacher banned the use of dictionaries. Although she thought that rather silly, Helen did not let that bother her because she liked making friends of people from different cultures, and the facile way the lessons were conducted afforded plenty of humour.

According to Helen, Diego was lazy, rather pompous, and fancied himself an intellectual and historian, but was entertaining in spite of it. In Spain, as in America and some other European countries, the term 'professor' was used to denote 'teacher', but the English were very reluctant to use such a grandiose title for those they considered to be academically unworthy.

Maria, his female colleague, was timid but apparently not lazy like he was, and a far better teacher. While employed at the school she adopted two Russian boys, thus winning the sympathy of most of the class. Having no children of her own, she had no idea about rearing and had, without sufficiently investigating what it entailed, joined what was practically a craze at the time, for adopting Russian children. We often saw her when out shopping: they were like wild animals and poor Maria had absolutely no control over them. We had been used to spoilt Irish children behaving badly in public, and Spanish ones who were worse again, but these were altogether different.

The Spanish relished hearing the English ridiculed, but, as with the Irish, it was a habit they rarely exercised with regard to themselves. Mind, the comprehensively patriotic and monarchist Edmundo, who never criticised Spain or the Spanish, always winced whenever I launched into a blistering attack on the English Royal Family or average commoner even.

Most of the English, be they expats or tourists, did not like to hear me criticise England either, but I thought it typical of expats whose patriotism was often heightened abroad, no matter where they came from. Most amusing for me, was to hear the Spanish criticising the English regarding the Armada. I thought it ludicrous until I heard Edmundo saying much the same. Within days of arriving in Spain, we had several times heard English people in shops, cafes and other public places, who had been niggled by something a Spaniard had said or done, mutter: 'Just because we sank their bloody boats!'

'Hear that..?' I would say to Helen, 'I'd have expected the likes of them to have thought the Armada was a football team.' I suppose it was a tad cynical but at least it helped balance the Brit jingoism.

The Forsyths were very different from the usual expats, and had there been more of their ilk, the average Spanish might have regarded them more generously. Might. They had lived and worked in the Far East and Africa for most of their lives, and when independence came and the colonists kicked out, like many others who could not settle in England after a lifetime in the sun, they retired to the Mediterranean. So their reasons for coming to Spain were entirely different from those of the lower-class hedonists who largely made up the English expatriate populace.

Aside from the Forsyths and one or two other couples, there were very few English we met in Spain that we liked, and we could well understand why the Spanish tended to dislike them. Like with the Irish, those Spanish who had lived and worked in England tended to have a more generous view, but relatively few of them were back in Spain. Right from the start, whenever we were dealing with Spaniards, whether in an airline office, hospital, department store or bar, if they thought we were Irish, they were always, and without exception, much friendlier or more obliging than if they thought we were English. The proof was when they thought we were Irish and we told them we were in fact English, whereupon their expression instantly changed.

There were so many tales of perversely mean and selfish acts among expatriates that one could not but believe them, and sagas of family breakdowns, no matter from where the protagonists originated, were among the most common. People would come to Spain to get away from dire situations, to find some situations could not simply be walked away from. They would find that longstanding and previously strong relationships were not strong enough to survive the stress of moving to another country with all that that entailed, especially when there were so many alternative temptations waiting to welcome them with open arms. Men in their sixties no longer wanted partners who might have made good housewives and mothers forty years ago but were now hiding prostheses. A widowed bimbo with a house or car, a bit left in the bank and no progeny hanging about, would do fine considering the abundance of sexually active casuals. Good women might be scarce but good men were much scarcer.

In one way, retiring to Spain at a mature age was not that different to emigration to places like New Zealand and Australia in the early 1960s when we emigrated, where one of a couple wanted to emigrate, and the other did not; or one wanted to go back 'home' after a time, and the other wanted to remain. Trying to adapt to a completely different culture, where even the language was different, and it was countless miles from home, family, colleagues and friends, put strains on relationships even without hardship, bad luck or tragedy. With transport being much quicker and cheaper, visits back to one's homeland were much easier now, but mistakes ipso facto probably much easier to make.

Although Helen did not take to the sea very often, mainly because she had a thing about jellyfish, she was fairly fit, with a very good appetite and a capacity for walking surprisingly long distances. And apart from my affliction, now of nearly thirty years vintage, I was in reasonable fettle myself. Like most chronic illnesses, mine was a relapser and I could go quite long periods without it bothering me too much; then it would suddenly return and I would be re-reading my anthologies on mortality. The bacteria that caused it were only sensitive to certain antibiotics, and because of their iniquitous characteristic of being able to conceal themselves in particular tissue, such as bone, where they could not be reached by standard antibiotics, they could only be confronted when they exposed themselves by making forays into other more accessible areas of my body. A life of remissions and relapses is easier to contend with because of the sun, excellent food and unwitting exercise, remissions being longer, relapses shorter, and symptoms less irksome.

Notwithstanding that little ode to radiance, sometimes at night when I was lying in bed, Ned would give out a harrowing groan in the way of Rottweilers and bull terriers, that lasted several minutes and summed up my feelings exactly. I had been getting older without reaching any particular watershed, like the sun gradually cooling but never getting cold, and had come to realise that I would never again be middle-aged; from now on I would be either elderly or off stage altogether. I recalled the times when, as a callow youth, I had boasted to similarly callow mates that I only needed to last until I was sixty, but now that I was past that particular milestone I was aware that perhaps I was hanging on by my fingernails. Multiple minor flaws and blemishes had stealthily appeared and the medication that went with some of them so confused my overall pharmacological state that I did not always know which of my symptoms were due to the basic defect and which to the side effects of the treatment. They were frequent enough to make me think about writing something along the lines of 'The Tribulations of an Old Twat,' without too much tongue in cheek.

Helen was first to be diagnosed with cancer and neither of us had the slightest doubt that we were in the best place to deal with it. Within days she was admitted to the university hospital in San Juan, twenty minutes drive from the house. There was no whining about wishing we were back in Ireland with God and the praying nuns, or back in England where for half a lifetime I had worked among so many medics who never doubted they were the best in the world; one could tell by the way they so often proclaimed, 'I'm not God, you know,' meaning 'Maybe I'm not God, but, by Christ, I'm the best there is down here.'

Everything in San Juan University Hospital was done coolly and efficiently by a superabundance of staff, all of them homegrown, very few able to speak English, yet all of them – doctors, nurses and technicians – ever ready to give every patient an affectionate pat on the shoulder or gentle rub of the wrist.

The night after Helen's operation, our two daughters, Alice and Medbh arrived by plane around midnight, Alice from Belfast and Medbh from London, and I brought them straight to the hospital and into the ward via *Accidentes Y Emergencias*. My explanation to the doctor in attendance was accepted immediately and we were permitted to stay the night, sitting in the extendable armchairs that were provided in all wards for visitors to Spanish hospitals. The girls were delighted at the ease with which they had gained admittance to find there was no disturbance of any kind in A & E, it being very quiet and civilised, and they were astonished to see 'public' patients were accommodated two to a room, sexes separate, and never deserted for more than quarter of an hour.

'You wouldn't get checked on that often during the day, let alone in the middle of the night in Belfast,' Alice mused.

'Nor in London,' agreed Medbh.

The day after they left, Helen's fellow patient, the wife of a retired *guardia* colonel, but friendly, was discharged, and late at night a young, highly neurotic and heavily pregnant Romanian was given her bed. As soon as she had had her initial examination and the examining doctor and nurse had left, her husband sneaked in, and with the exception of brief sorties for cigarettes and 'recces', he never left the ward, spending all of his time sitting by his wife's bed, sleeping in the armchair provided for visitors, or smoking in the bathroom. He shared the food provided for his wife, showered and smoked in the bathroom, and slept with his head on the bed, more to obtain comfort than provide it. Whenever anyone came in to talk to Helen, whether staff or visitors, he and his wife would fall dead silent as they listened intently to whatever was being said. And when Helen was talking on the telephone to any of our family in Ireland, he would afterwards tell her that he and his wife wanted to go to Ireland and could we help him and his wife get in. Whenever Helen received a letter or document from the hospital, he would always ask what it was and if he could read it because it might be of help to him.

Helen stopped using the bathroom because he was using it so much and leaving his stuff in it, and instead went to a communal bathroom down the corridor. Then when she came back, there would be a scatter as he hurried from her side of the room to sit by the side of her bed and beguilingly rest his head on his hands like a spaniel. She was very nervous and hardly said a word but he boasted to Helen how they had left their parents to look after their children in Romania while they were trying to find a home somewhere in Western Europe, and their first move had been to wait until she was almost due to give birth before coming into the port of Alicante by boat where they knew they would not be turned away if they claimed emergency medical treatment because of 'pregnancy problems'. They had thus pleaded '*no comprendo*' to the Spanish authorities and demanded to be taken to A & E.

Constantly he nagged on to Helen for help in dealing with the Spanish staff, and although at first she did not mind, when she realised what they were up to, she tried to deter them. In the finish I had to tell them to leave her alone or I would have to do something. Helen hated having him in the room all of the time, but this was the drawback to allowing anybody, male or female who claimed to be a close relative of a patient, to stay in the ward, a little room for only two patients, in this case two sick women. Eventually the staff moved them elsewhere and the police became involved even though the Spanish were very tolerant towards anybody who was sick. I am not so sure about Ireland, but in England patients and visitors would have been more firmly dealt with.

Expats who could not speak Spanish were more troubled by medical appointments than anything, and would bring interpreters when they needed to enter hospital – usually much put-upon friends or neighbours with a smattering of the language, who would also drive them there, thus saving taxi and expensive interpreter fees. These angels of mercy would also be expected to negotiate rooms containing other patients of their nationality.

There were screens to go around the beds but the Spanish did not like them at all, regarding them as necessary only for certain procedures; so if Helen wanted a bit of privacy and drew hers, it would not be long before her *compañera* (room-mate), or *compañera's* visitors, would have pulled them back and were waving to her like a long-lost friend.

Helen's greatest embarrassment was to discover how candid the Spanish were about body parts, and when the buzzer was pressed for a nurse to bring the bedpan: '*La cuña, por favor!*' the voice would come over the intercom for all and sundry to hear, be they husband, son or daughter, in-law, friend or neighbour, or all of them together; and then: '*Pipi o Caca?*' The appellant would then have to reply so that the nurse would know which receptacle to bring, visitors paying close attention in case there were any difficulty with communication, in which case half a dozen voices might well be raised to make sure everyone within hearing distance was aware of the kind of emergency going on. A bedpan might then be brought to a grandmother and shoved, with only slight sleight of hand, under the bedclothes in the presence of everybody, and she would immediately go to work on it as unselfconsciously as if she were peeling an apple. After her exertions, one of her visitors would call for the nurse who would come to remove it, and guests would gleam at how successful she had been, or flinch in sympathy. On several occasions, with the curtains drawn back, Helen would be brought her dinner while her room-mate was undergoing an enema.

By now Helen had sufficient Spanish to deal with her situation, apart from the occasional predicament with a medical term; it was her room-mate and the room-mate's visitors that truly tested her ability. Not only would a second language quickly desert one in a stressful situation, even one's own language was unintelligible at times, and mellifluous though it might be for singing in, Spanish was no exception when it came to expressing anxiety. Frequently when Helen wanted a nap, to read or rest, her *compañera*, or *compañera's* visitor – when her *compañera* had gone to sleep – would jabber on until the *compañera* awoke.

Whichever room she was moved to, or whoever was moved in with her, whether *ex-franquistas* or republicans, her fellow patients were invariably warm-hearted and compassionate. Mind, for people so romantically attached to the sword, she was surprised at the fuss some of them made when confronted with the sharp end of a hypodermic needle, and how often they abused the *enfermera* (nurse) who wielded it. For all their machismo, the men, whom Helen reckoned were the worst, would frequently grapple with the *enfermera* holding a syringe, as though it were a fight to the death, and sometimes squeal loud enough to be heard rooms away.

Whenever I visited I would pump Helen for interesting tales, not least for variations on deathbed confessions from old *franquistas*, but although they would tell her many personal things about their families, the politics of the past were invariably being withheld until Judgement Day. The matter of the Spanish Civil War seemed to have more personal dimensions to it than any conflict I had ever read about, and as a consequence we never met any Spaniard as old or older than ourselves that I did not mull about in terms of which side they had been on.

Although I hated wars, I found civil wars fascinating, and none more so than the Spanish Civil War. I did not know whether it was because civil wars were more compact and easier to record, or whether the opposite was true and the truth harder to extricate even though the memories seemed to last longer and were often more bitter. I thought there was more to be learned regarding the nature of people during internecine, rather than international, conflict. Apart from anything else, civil wars never seemed to terminate with anything like the same clinical and legal finality as wars between nations, and their antagonists had to live and work together afterwards with the same intimacy as before hostilities began. So for me, the Spanish Civil War was endlessly fascinating, even if nobody – and that certainly included expats – wanted to talk about it.

Helen made a good recovery after her operation and went through chemotherapy without any trouble, impressing everybody by her quiet fortitude, which was just as well, because not long after the chemotherapy ended, her knees gave out. Once again she submitted without qualm to what both English and Spanish acquaintances correctly confided would be a painful experience as the remains of her own knees were removed and replaced with bits of metal and plastic. The only thing that really bothered her was that because the anaesthetic was delivered by epidural, she was aware of what was going on and being said, and had to listen to what she considered to be an amazing amount of claptrap as they discussed things like pop love songs and Real Madrid vis-a-vis Barça Barcelona.

It was my turn next.

THIRTY-FIVE

IN CONTRAST TO OTHER waiting rooms, the radiotherapy antechamber at San Juan was small and dingy and the walls glossy mortuary green and nausea cream. Decoration consisted of an old print of Van Gogh hanging cockeyed, moments after he had purportedly hacked a slice off his ear, unframed exhortations to seek help from a doctor when in agony rather than stoically enduring it – an appropriate exhortation for an alpha-male authority, I thought – plus a series of luridly coloured diagrams of tumours in their favourite sites. Additionally there were the usual prohibitions about smoking and unprotected sex, as though there were any likelihood of either here, except with regard to staff after hours. I never saw anything carnal but quite often smelt smoke and saw a young fellow in an operating gown pop his head guiltily from behind a screen or a door into a little dark room.

Entertainment comprised a tiny fixed-maximum-volume television permanently locked into Los Simpsons – oddly enough the Spanish seemed to think they and Señor Bean were hilarious – plus a couple of dozen ancient gossip magazines that could only have been creased to such a degree by rolling them into balls and playing football with them before putting them out on the table.

The male patients who sat in this room, sometimes for hours, were severely depressed. They had come in the hope that the invisible ray they had been brought up to fear might one day wipe out mankind, would now, through a little gun thing, dissolve the vile lumps in and around their most valuable parts and ignore everything else, so that they would be able to enjoy the remainder of a long and fruitful life. Few, however, seemed to have the faith to match, and clearly resented spending their precious last afternoons in here. If they no longer believed in God, how could they be expected to believe in something else they could neither see, hear, smell or touch? Cynicism was the only reliable doctrine one could count on these days. Even the wives, old women and today's only Christian disciples, showed little optimism. At one time they would have been rattling rosaries as if in the front row of a passion band, now they mostly grasped a battered mobile phone and stared at the floor instead of towards heaven. Most patients had at least one person accompanying them, but some a coterie, with the consequence that one or two patients could be leaning against a wall, unable to find a seat.

Helen and I were becoming experienced at dealing with the family on mortal matters, and had decided it was best to tell them while things were going on, rather than after they had 'run their course', so to speak, so I telephoned them one by one, and their response was to come over with their families to see us as soon as possible. By the end of the summer therefore, we had had them all over, and that was great, even though, there could have been more joyful reasons for a get-together.

I had not swam for years, nor been down to the beach for almost as long, but knew all the grandchildren would want to go there, so made up my mind to go down and get in with them, even if only long enough to receive a couple of jellyfish stings.

I had not started the treatment when Alice and her family came, but was able to construct a castle that turned out to be quite unappreciated in an age when grandkids made international calls on their own personal mobile telephones to say 'Hi', but not 'Hello', any more. Because I sometimes still referred to myself as a sculptor, Alice expected me to raise exotic creations out of the most unsatisfactory sculptural material on earth, but at least I was not heckled into replicating St John the Baptist or doing any crucified Christs, images rarely seen in sand even in a religious past.

I could see that once my back was turned, the building materials of my castle would soon be returned to their former state, 'dust to dust, and sand to sand', sort of thing, and the odds were that my own disloyal brood would be the exterminators, so I peeled off, already clad in navy blue trunks underneath, and headed for the brine, marvelling as I went, at the grossness of old men's bodies and wondering if I would ever be so transformed. One of the advantages of being male, was that although one could so easily recognise ugliness in others, one was quite incapable of perceiving it in oneself, yet it was the diametric opposite with the female.

Helen had insisted we set down our towels and whatnots within a child's arm's length of the life-guard's wooden tower so that help would be readily at hand, yet excruciatingly kept calling out to me to remind me of the serious risks of a heart attack, something she had never worried about in all the years I had plunged in seas, lakes and rivers all over the world, and warning me of the killer marine predators, albeit minute, that colonized the area in her imagination. For good measure she would quote graphs of deaths of men over sixty in this region of the coast, adding that I was seventy two, without once pausing to reflect that fatal embarrassment might pose the greater threat. She knew my hearing was no longer comparable with that of a dolphin, and was making allowance for it, notwithstanding there would have been plenty of listeners able to understand every frantic word.

 A microbiologist would not have bothered about such things when he was knee-deep in toddler water; what he would far more likely have feared would have been the used contraceptives, rubbish, and effluent of man and dog. And when he came ashore after swallowing mouthfuls of it, it would be on to a beach with almost as many fag-ends as grains of sand, indestructible debris that had a half-life longer than most types of radiation. When we were there, a lifeguard was wandering around with a kiddy's shrimp net which every now and then he shoved in the sand in front of him in, but even the huge cleaning machines that come on the beaches after dark hardly did more than mince some of them up into their constituent paper and tobacco so they would pass for sand when the sun came up.

One day I had an argument with one of the oncologists. I had read something on the internet by the NIH in America, one of the world's top authorities on cancer, stating that one of the chemotherapeutic agents I was taking was antagonistic to one of the others, and I wanted to discuss it with somebody. However, nobody wanted to discuss it with me, and I was told I had no right to challenge the treatment I was being given. But I persisted, any decent article on the treatment of a pernicious disorder always recommended discussion with the prescriber and, if necessary, his peers also.

 After a number of false starts and misunderstandings with various members of the oncological team, the one who eventually deigned to deal with me – presumably the oncologist bouncer – became very angry and started shouting, finally grabbing my arm and holding it down on his desk to make me listen to what he had to say, without having to listen to what I had to say. Whenever an *extranjero* is in an argument with a Spaniard – no matter who, why or where – a coterie, especially of women, will soon gather to support him or her, and abuse the *extranjero*; it frequently happens in a shop when the *extranjero* is disputing a purchase.

Bellowing was one thing, but laying hands on me was a different thing altogether. So after grabbing his and holding it down, I told him what I thought of doctors who were too arrogant to discuss patient's illnesses and treatment and lost their tempers when, however civilly, their treatment was queried. For good measure, I quoted parts of the Hippocratic Oath I considered relevant, and pointed out that the last thing a patient with a life-threatening disease needed, was a doctor who behaved the way he and his staff were behaving towards me. Was it because I was English, I asked, confident this was bound to locate a sensitive nerve. Without waiting for an answer, I then laid on about how, in half a lifetime of working in the health service in other, though non-Hispanic, countries which I listed, I had never lost my patience with a patient, nor witnessed a medical doctor all the way down from consultant to intern, lose theirs. As for applying a martial arts hold to subdue him, well…

Arm pinioning seemed to be catching and Helen was now holding my other arm while appealing to me to control myself.

'Can we not speak to somebody more sympathetic? There's bound to be a specialist somewhere who is prepared to discuss your treatment with you in a proper manner,' she appealed to him through me.

Because of the commotion, the head of department appeared. What was the row about, she wanted to know, though I suspected she had been listening outside the door for a while. Other patients in the waiting area outside, who would have been able to hear everything, were standing up, gabbling to each other and gesticulating towards us. I had no doubt they would be one hundred percent behind my antagonist, even though they probably could not understand what we were talking about.

Speaking in pigeon-English, he now told me I should speak in proper English because his English was better than my Spanish, which it most definitely was not. So I spoke to him in what he regarded as pigeon Spanish, and he spoke to me in what I considered was pigeon English and communication could hardly have been worse; it would have been funny if it had not been such a serious matter.

He was a big man and when he suddenly rushed around the desk and put his arms around me, I thought he was going to crush my rib cage or throw me to the floor. Instead, he was almost in tears and began pleading with me to forgive him.

I was astounded. He was shaking my hand and embracing me and I could hardly get him off. He told me he wanted to be my friend and his only wish was to help me. Imploring me to sit down, he retrieved a copy of the paper I had given him, which he had discarded into the wastepaper basket, spread it out on the desk and flattened it. Again and again he ironed it with his hand, smoothing out the creases as though he were smoothing out the creases in my personality at the same time. Then he got a notepad and drew diagram after diagram to explain the reason for his treatment, and could not have been more friendly, affectionate even, and neither Helen nor I knew quite where I stood, except that all along he had obviously seen the American paper to which I had been referring, knew exactly what I was talking about but had decided to ignore it. It was a pity he had not just come out with that in the first place and explained that perhaps the department was in the midst of deciding what to do about the disputed hormone that was the centre of the issue. I would have accepted that. But at least our relationship was now much improved, and afterwards, when the consultation was over, whenever we passed each other anywhere in the hospital or when I was attending subsequent appointments, he would never fail to call out '*Amigo!*', come over, pat me, and declare his friendship.

I am not going to suggest he was typical of Spanish doctors, because he was typical of no doctor I had ever known, only that the Spanish were very passionate people and this was an example. For a medical doctor of any nationality to apologise is quite something; for one to go to the lengths he had, was quite amazing. Imagine being addressed as '*Amigo!*' by an English or Irish doctor. It would be easier to imagine them throwing you to the floor and stomping on your testicles.

Maybe this fellow was going through a hard time – I could not help noticing he was suffering from severe psoriasis. Whatever, I could not help liking him. I have always suffered from a kind of mental aberration which inclines me to laugh whenever I get annoyed, and at one stage during our contretemps when I had been almost shouting back at him, I had made a crack about his machismo, and although the female head of department was in the room, he had burst out laughing and so had I. Even she smiled and the whole thing played very much in his favour as far as I was concerned. Again, imagine if it had been in England or Ireland and a female consultant had been in attendance: likely as not she would have called Security.

If only I could have had both Edmundo's and Humberto's opinion of him. Years later in Ireland, I would be waiting in a corridor outside an ophthalmologist's examination room when a middle-aged chaperone accompanying her mother would be leading the mother out and the mother would be wishing the ophthalmologist farewell. Suddenly the mother would turn back through the closing door and call: 'God bless you, Doctor, and a Merry Christmas to you and your staff!' It would be the first week in November.

It had taken a while for us to get used to the way the Spanish greeted anyone who joined them in an elevator, especially an elevator in a hospital, which they did every time it stopped and somebody got in or out. In England, when administrative staff were involved, especially receptionists in GP practices, even simple cordiality usually went wanting. Yet so often, one would hear telephone calls on the radio expressing fulsome gratitude to 'all the doctors and nurses' for treatment the caller had survived. Much though I liked to see gratitude expressed for favours bestowed, I never considered medical treatment under the National Health Service to be a favour.

For a while after my treatment I had not taken Ned for a walk. It was not easy where we lived because the nearest campo was hilly and very stony underfoot. If I went around the streets I encountered too many dogs, most of them not on a leash and often in threes, and if they were accompanied by women, as they usually were, the women would shriek because they thought it was the best thing to do when a Rottweiler appeared on the horizon. The fact that their freely running dogs included two Alsatians and a Golden Retriever did not seem amiss to them, and if a mêlée followed, I would be the one to sort it out because they would have no control over their own dogs.

Every yapping little thing we passed would rush up to annoy Ned, and because he was trained to back off, their owners would think he was afraid of their plucky little chap and comment aloud on this to their companions. But if Ned was annoyed by a squealing little runt, and growled, the tormentor would scatter, screeching, and its owner would go manic and demand Ned be put down and I be fined or imprisoned.

This particular afternoon, one when the sun was reluctant to go down, I decided to take Ned out. The Paradise Gouramis had started making their bubble-nests in my pond and I needed more plants, so we headed for the local reservoir where the water was supposed to be fit to drink. It was fenced with highwire chain link but there was always the odd place where one could slither under and drag a dog through, albeit upside down. A Border collie would have squeezed under, or deepened the hole by some furious digging, but a Rottweiler was too thick in body and brain.

When we reached the water, it was to find it quite dead as far as plants and every other kind of macroscopic organism was concerned, very probably because every now and then the *Ayuntamiento* 'treated' the ubiquitous faecal contamination by bombing it with rocks of sodium hypochlorite from a helicopter, and wiping out all fauna and flora. Sodium hypochlorite degrades quickly in ultra violet light and in the presence of organic matter, but that hardly renders it the perfect refreshment.

Having clambered uphill and over the walls that surrounded the reservoir, and slithered down others, I was drenched with sweat and tiring fast, so decided to return home, but Ned had somehow got himself on the wrong side of a wall and was unable to get back. I tried to signal him to go to where the wall was low enough for him to get over, but it was not an easy thing to explain to a dog, and eventually I had to go all the way back to get him, only to find he had got out and gone somewhere else to look for me. Former breaks in the fence had been repaired, so getting out meant circumnavigating the whole reservoir to the point where we had entered. It took ages to find him, and when I did, he manifested not the slightest iota of gratitude, preferring to keep his distance, presumably in case I did not find the whole thing all that funny.

Usually my walks were completed within an hour, and I was now an hour and a half overdue, so Helen would be worrying. These days she was always pestering me to take the mobile phone, but I felt such a sap taking it. I had assured her that if I happened an accident, such as a heart attack, her favourite prediction, I probably would not be able to use the phone and it might get lost or damaged. 'And don't ever send anybody,' I would tell her, 'because by the time they find me, I'll be past recuperation. And if I'm not, it'll be too embarrassing for words.'

But I knew that if I did not return soon, she would report it to the police. She never used to be like this, it was because of the cancer. She seemed to think I had lost my marbles as well as the tumour, when in fact, I had lost neither; I had merely been 'gunned' in the place I never revealed to anybody but a urologist.

On the way home I had just negotiated a bed of particularly thorny cactus, when I heard the sound of a helicopter. Ordering Ned to lie down, I dived down myself so that I could not be seen amidst the huge vicious thistles that grew all over the place. After a few minutes it disappeared, so I grabbed hold of Ned, hauled myself to my feet and we headed for home, both of us looking as though we had been flayed. Helen was waiting in a state of hysteria but then, as always the way with mothers whose children have returned after having gone missing for an hour, her first reaction was to rail at me.

'If I knew how to work the camera, I'd take a picture of the two of you... A crazy, knackered old man and his stupid old dog!'

'Ned's not old. He's just middle-aged. What do you think of this?'

I showed her the tiny aquatic plant I had clung on to, which might or might not survive, and all she said was, 'You mean to tell me you put yourself through all that for that? A bit of weed?'

No wonder I tend to boggle when I hear of a woman naturalist.

THIRTY-SIX

When we came to Spain, José Maria Aznar was prime minister, and although we had been led to believe he was a middle-of-the-road politician, the party he led, the PP (Partido Popular), was the remains of Franco's party, and as such, was probably as close to fascism as it was possible to get without the swastika. Spain's Socialist prime minister, Felipe González, had messed up by conspiring with the Guar*dia Civil* over the despicable way they had murdered several old Republicans, and Aznar, leader of the PP, took over from him.

On 11th March 2004 a series of bombs were set off at Madrid's Atocha Station, killing 198 people and injuring over 2000 more. Immediately the PP Government blamed ETA, the Basque separatists, and told its embassies around the world to inform as many governments as possible what ETA had done – or, rather, what the Spanish Government said ETA had done. It was only a matter of days before the General Election, so Aznar appointed Mariano Rajoy, a weak and unpopular individual, to be his successor, with Aznar still holding the reins. However, the stratagem failed when the populace discovered they had been misinformed, and there was an instant and dramatic response. Determined to prevent the PP from continuing in power by blackening the character of the Basques and Socialists (the PSOE), they contacted each other via their mobile phones and computers and in no time massive street demonstrations were mounted the way only the Spanish and French could do, and the PSOE, under José Zapatero, came into power.

Zapatero immediately began implementing policies he had promised were he to be elected: first of all, and within hours, he brought the Spanish troops back from Iraq. This brought widespread criticism from America, Britain and their allies, but was very popular among socialists and peace-lovers the world over, not least the majority of Spaniards. Regrettably, though fair-minded and humane, Zapatero proved weak on a number of other counts, singularly failing to implement a crucial promise he had made to the families of Republicans murdered by Franco, which was to exhume bodies dumped by the roadside fifty years previously and give them a proper burial. But because of resistance by the Catholic Church, as well as the PP, he now totally backed down. Then, when a few breakaway ETA individuals carried out a minor assault on an airport, he actually called on Mariano Rajoy for advice, and this earned him nothing but contempt from all sides.

He then tried to halt Spain's notorious ill-treatment of women by husbands, boyfriends and employers, by introducing all kinds of legislation to try to ensure equality between men and women. But policies, like making exactly half his cabinet female, and a small, very pregnant pacifist the new Minister of Defence, who, as part of her duties, had to walk through the ranks inspecting soldiers and other members of the armed forces, did not seem like a good idea to anybody but himself, and simply did not work. Like so many a Socialist leader, he was decent but weak. Every now and again in politics there comes a decent man who is a good politician, like Tony Benn in England, Noel Browne in Ireland and Jose Zapatero, all of them socialists, who had failed to achieve very much because they were not ruthless.

The monarchy in Spain had been in a parlous position for a very long time, and because of King Juan Carlos's unavoidable association with Franco, the current Royal Family were by no means universally popular. But if one were to compare them with the rest of the caste in Europe, not least their English cousins with their Nazi connections, they fared favourably well. After the atrocity at Atocha, for which Al-Quaeda eventually admitted responsibility, every member of the Spanish Royal Family attended the memorial service in Madrid, and not only did every one of them shake hands with both victims and bereaved, they warmly embraced and kissed them and spent considerable time talking and sympathising with them. No-one, no matter how imaginative, could conceive of the Queen of England kissing and hugging members of the British working-class, one after another, no matter what tragedy they had suffered. Even a brief note of sympathy would have had to have been written by a civil servant. There was still much Republican sentiment in Spain, and Juan Carlos's relationship with Franco had never been satisfactorily explained, but when it came to occasions like this, which called for a humane response, he always won – to use the awful American phrase – their 'hearts and minds'.

Spaniards had very ambivalent feelings about King Cabra. Nobody admired him, but because he was handsome and charming, everybody liked him. As playboy par excellence, he spent his time humping beautiful women and killing beautiful animals, especially exotic species threatened with extinction; the former the true blue approved of, the latter they did not care a fig about. As President of the Spanish chapter of the World Wildlife Fund, he felt he had a duty to carry out culling willy-nilly, mostly other countries' stock of wildlife.

Zapatero's special failure to honour the pledge he had made to the nation, regarding the Republican remains, in addition to his mismanagement of the country's finances and general lack of resolution, resulted in Rajoy and the PP, with its residue of the old guard, being too quickly voted back.

Many expatriates – very few of whom had experienced life under Franco – were supportive of the PP without knowing or caring anything about its history or policies, because they felt the PP would better look after their financial interests, and most strove to pay neither Spanish nor English taxes. Mind, there were many Spaniards who likewise did not care about such things, because even after all the years, the country was still very divided, a particular that was desolating considering the many wars world over.

Although many, if not most of the people in the various countries we had lived in, had avoided taxes wherever possible, Spaniards had a reputation for it, and had developed procedures that had become traditions where lawyers and notaries were involved, and were 'legally' built into the conveyancing of property,

From our first few days in Spain, the variety and quantity of wildlife, diurnal and nocturnal, in the air, on and under the ground, in inland waters and the sea, had never ceased to amaze me. Rabbit populations had been reduced by about seventy percent in recent decades because of epidemics; but rabbits, like many prolific creatures and plants, had a habit of rebounding even though they had many efficient predators, man not the least of them; so many of them were they at one time, that the Phoenicians had devised the term 'I-shepan-im', which means 'Land of Rabbits' and became 'Hispania' under the Romans. There were now more than 30,000 private hunting estates in Spain, and every autumn, hunters – or rather, 'butchers' – descended from all over Europe, especially Italy and Germany, to annihilate anything sprouting fur or feathers.

The only reason they had not eliminated whole genera was because of their superabundance combined with the country's topography, ecological controls being unenthusiastically enforced or non-existent. Young boys were encouraged to shoot, and fathers, grandfathers and uncles carried on into old age. It was a miracle that the likes of the bear, wolf, lynx and eagle, were not extinct.

On the road home after our first visit to the local theatre late on a Saturday night, an eagle owl took a hare in our headlights. It was spectacular in the dark with both sets of eyes glinting, and as is so often the case with raptors, instead of the predator abandoning the quarry in the strong light and close proximity of the car, it continued its pursuit, grabbed the hare without touching the ground, and made off with it as though it were a child's stuffed toy, neither bird nor mammal making the slightest sound.

So important was it to be able to handle a rifle in Spain, that during the Civil War, Villaneuve, a rich playboy and aristocratic father of a sixteen-year-old boy, arranged with the officer in charge of an execution squad that was going around exterminating Republican men and women, to have his son 'blooded' by murdering prisoners – often who had never been given a trial – and leaving them by the side of the road. The boy was still living while we were in Spain, and had become a rich and ageing roué himself, albeit a famous author as evil as his begetter.

Ireland also had plenty of rabbits, although, like in other countries where they were plentiful, every now and again they were decimated by endemic cycles of myxomatosis. The Irish were supposedly loath to eat rabbit because rabbits and blackberries, the only free wild food at the time, reminded them of the Nineteenth-Century famine. This, whilst possible, seemed to me to be even more irrational than the tale about the blind rat and the straw, and neither Helen nor I ever had such misgivings having been brought up during the Second World War when good food was scarce and such provender cheap and tasty.

One of the innumerable oddities of nature was the way cacti and succulents could store so much water and survive for such long periods during drought. At times, when shortage of rain meant that even mature specimens of common trees would die or be permanently maimed, all kinds of cacti and succulents survived without harm, and if sliced, their sap, which was as fluid and clear as water, would virtually gush out. Not only could they store water so long, but they were able to absorb it rapidly when the opportunity presented itself. There were other amazing features: both genera would grow on the poorest soil and put down roots from almost any part of the plant; all that was necessary was for the plant to make contact with the earth and it would germinate within days from that point. I considered this marvellous, coming, as we did, from daisy and dandelion land. Growth of cacti was astonishing as soon as they had put down roots, and just as some were edible when specially cooked, others were poisonous. As opposed to succulents, nearly all cacti had extremely sharp thorns that were frequently barbed, sometimes poisonous, and always difficult to remove once they had penetrated the skin where they could often cause quite agonising infections and pain.

THIRTY-SEVEN

Helen had surreptitiously started making the Sign of the Cross again when we passed a church and said she missed God and would make up with Him if ever we went back to Ireland; after all, she had never rejected Him the way I had. But Spain did not make me feel religious, and just as the paedophilia among priests in Ireland had been the last straw for me there, so the conduct of the Church during the Spanish Civil War kept me turned against it here.

On a Sunday morning many years ago I had been at Mass in the magnificent but stiflingly ornate cathedral of Seville, and had been astonished at the sparsity of the congregation; it was like a weekday service: very much a loose collection of individuals consisting mainly of ancient widows and quite a few disabled men and women, but very few families. The difference between the Catholic Church – supposedly a universal organisation – in Spain, in Ireland, and again in the north of England where we had experienced it at a working-class shack of a church, was immeasurable.

The time we had attended Mass in Seville, even people who appeared well off dropped a single coin of niggardly value into the collection plate, letting it fall from a height so it clunked. When, afterwards, I asked someone why so little was given and so ostentatiously, they smiled and said it was to show contempt for the clergy.

I did not think one could successfully rejuvenate old hobbies, certainly not with the same enthusiasm that had initially attended their being taken up, but if Helen, the convert, could manage it, so be it. However, I who was born a Catholic and had never experienced the ardour of the convert, had had enough.

I found Spain a difficult place to write in, though clearly many a writer had found it favourable. For me it was the same with Australia: I loved the sun but did not find it conducive to the kind of concentration required. A sunny latitude was more a place to paint or sculpt in, and when we lived in Australia and New Zealand, I likewise did quite a bit of both.

Spanish cartoonists were exceptionally good, as were their political satirists, though neither they, nor their public, considered cartooning to be real art. We met a really talented one at an exhibition of water colours that were all landscapes except for a couple of political cartoons that were brilliant, far better than the paintings, and we arranged to visit him at his home. His home and garden were so apt for an aged intellectual artist that one could have guessed his profession immediately on entering the premises, and his hospitality, surprisingly, was so warm that the whole experience was a delight. He showed us umpteen samples of work he had done for American and European comics during the Second World War: aeroplane battles, barracks, trenches, artillery and various nationalities of troops, all defiantly and anonymously done from his home in Catalonia. He was a very old man now but still working in a large studio cluttered with ancient drawings, paintings, sketches and comics, doing landscapes because he thought they were the proper things to do if one claimed to be an artist. And he was quite embarrassed about the superb cartoons and caricatures he had once drawn by the hundreds. His name was Rosando Franch and he turned out to be yet another friend of

Humberto. In Alicante, Humbert knew almost everyone in the upper echelons of visual art or literature, science or socialism, and they treated him with much affection.

Spain's visual artists seemed to have had strong personalities, and though often respected, were never revered in their time the way they became after their death, unlike their writers and composers. Writers were always respected.

I did not know what it was about postmen, but I always seemed to bring out the worst in them. I never had any trouble in England, but the Spanish were no better than the Irish when first we set foot on their soil. The main trouble in Spain was due to our man's semi-literacy in non-Spanish languages, and I am only talking about names, not grammar.

'Walters, Watson, Williams, Winfield, Winchester', for instance, were regarded as various spellings of the same name, thus adding to the confusion and delays caused by long Correos (Mail Service) holidays taken on the many religious anniversaries still observed in Spain, even though the reason for them had been largely abandoned. We had every reason to believe that Dutch, French and German expats suffered similarly and that many an item had disappeared forever after 'Bonfire For Badly Written Therefore Untraceable Letters Night'. And God help those whose mail was tossed over their wall simply because their mailbox did not appeal.

Gilbert did a *census gratis* and wrote out all the English names of residents in his *urbanización*, but got no thanks for it; in fact, his postman complained he had made his job much harder.

THIRTY-EIGHT

For a while now we had been seriously missing the children and considering returning to Ireland. Our encounter with cancer had made us think about life in a more discriminating way, and drifting from possible metastasis to probable metastasis hardly seemed a rewarding way of investing one's time.

I was a paper-boy delivering newspapers to people's doors twice a day when the headlines had bawled 'I licked the "Big C"!' It was a triumphant message from the hardest man in the Wild West in the days when the C-word meant something different to what it does today, and to be impudently told that John Wayne had beaten what nobody else had beaten and was once more in perfect killing health, was meant to be good news for the whole world: the Searcher would be scalping the scalpers for a bit longer. I had given up the paper round by the time The Duke had lost the power of speech and left it to Grub Street to eke us up to date. It was not so much that the big heart was wanting as it was a complete failure of material resources, and if he could not access them, who could. It was surely salutary.

No matter how long we had lived in Spain, we would never have been accepted the way we would had we been Spanish, exemplary or otherwise, and many expatriates told us they felt exactly the same. An *extranjero* must work in his adoptive country for at least half a lifetime to qualify as any candidate with a chance. Mind, it had been the same in Ireland, though to a less trenchant degree. And being English was far worse in New Zealand or Australia than it was in Ireland. Canada was the only country we ever lived in that liked us because we were English; not even the English liked the English. But we were not going back to Ireland because we thought it *Shangri-la* any more. The attraction was that our children and their children lived there, and that was why we intended to spend the rest of our lives there. Had our children decided to emigrate to Spain, we would have stayed, and gladly, but although they liked Spain as a holiday destination, it did not appeal to them as a place to live. Before we came to Spain we thought the children would have been thrilled to come and visit us; but although all of them liked the sun, none liked the mess Spain had made of its once lovely coast, and much preferred the way the French and Italians had so diligently preserved theirs. Mind, they all thought the beach in Jemina was the best they had ever swam from. They were still at an age when the fact that Spain had an infinite number of wonderful buildings – even though few had been properly maintained and most were decaying – was less important than its beaches. And they had survived not only because of the sympathetic climate but because, with the exception of Guernica, they never had to undergo the horrendous destruction suffered by neighbouring countries during two world wars.

We had once thought we would be able to come to Spain, absorb a few salubrious years of sun and Mediterranean food, enjoy something of the culture, and then return rejuvenated to Ireland. The reality, of course, was that we had superannuated ourselves, burnt our boats behind us and were becoming otiose entities increasingly aware of our senescence in an environment and era that was becoming increasingly hostile to people like us. Eleven years was a long time and it was impossible not to think we were growing further away from our family. We tried to kid ourselves that the weekly phone calls assured us they sounded 'all right'. We had made visits every year, but they were nowhere near enough, and we would never know what was really happening in our absence, what problems they were having with their work and their children and each other.

At first Spain had seemed a mere hop away, but that was just the flight, and even that, what with the constant tightening up of security, had in recent times become more of a hop, skip and a jump. The price of air fares rose and the whole bit, including various infirmities and advancing age, soon became something of a hassle. After sixty years of age, the years counted, and after seventy, ailments and illnesses were no longer curable and holdalls not the doddle they used to be.

We were a very closely knit family and kept in fairly close contact with each other but telephone and email were nowhere near enough. They needed us and we needed them. So when I finished the radiotherapeutic phase of the cancer treatment, which I was relieved to have had in Spain rather than Ireland, and against the advice of the people who were treating me and considered Ireland an unhealthy environment to recuperate in, we put the house up for sale.

As luck – or rather, rapacity – as far as buying a house in Ireland was concerned, and diametrically contrary to the situation in Spain, property prices had gone crazy, with everybody buying and selling houses from and to each other, and kidding themselves they were financially astute. We had only been in Spain a few months when, in its own ridiculous jargon, Ireland was calling itself the rider on the back of the 'Celtic Tiger', a claim as absurd as it was disingenuous. It was meant to imply that the country was in a very healthy economic state, something blatantly untrue. Nothing was being manufactured and exported any more, no extra services being provided, and those that were once satisfactory had deteriorated. All anybody wanted to do was have a good time: to drink, travel, squander, have illicit sex, and boast. The whole housing thing was a scam where, with the complicity of the Government, estate agents, banks, building societies and solicitors were creating the impression that the country was becoming rich through the previously unappreciated value of its property. In fact, all that was really happening was that ordinary people were selling their ordinary properties to each other at prices far in excess of their worth, and most of the newly-built stuff was less than ordinary, being awfully designed and thrown up by awful builders, sold by awful estate agents, legalised by awful solicitors and the money to buy lent by awful banks and building societies that behaved like bad banks.

As in Spain, houses in Ireland were being flung up far in excess of need by anybody able to plonk one concrete block on top of another, though, unlike in Spain, old corrugated sheds – often old animal sheds 'in need of some restoration' – were being called 'residences' by estate agents whose descriptions were as crass as they were counterfeit. Prices had soared to preposterous levels because instead of holding back until the situation had stabilised, people goaded by greed and vanity, who were manic about 'getting on the ladder' but could not afford to, were grabbing whatever they could lay hands on. The worst party in the business was an irresponsible, incompetent, greedy, power-crazy and corrupt government that cared for the welfare of none but the wealthy, and encouraged fools to borrow way beyond their means without regard for the consequences.

Again the situation was very different in Spain where properties, though not perfect, were infinitely better than their Irish counterparts – if they could be said to be 'counterpart' – very much cheaper and with prices falling rapidly and drastically. Many expats who were getting old and sick, or had simply become disenchanted with Spain or Mediterranean life and wanted to return to their homeland, were finding that although their apartments, villas and chalets were getting cheaper by the week, they were also – again – becoming increasingly difficult to sell.

As if bankers in Ireland and England had not already done enough to flay their customers – now called 'clients' – many were urging them to be highly cynical about property deals abroad, especially in Spain, a place few of them had any idea about. These blackguards were making the very criticisms about Spanish bankers – namely greed and chicanery – that they so richly deserved themselves.

The Catholic Church, at one time a pillar of morality was becoming an object of contempt because of the many disclosures about the physical and sexual abuse of the unmarried mothers and children who had been in its care for many years. Yet, as always in Ireland, nobody in authority would accept responsibility for anything, and nobody was punished. In America, at least some of the big swindlers were imprisoned and quickly; in Ireland they were given years to pack their bags and begin new lives abroad after taking their ill-gotten gains with them and arranging bankruptcy deals that would smooth their path for an eventual scot-free return.

While we had our Spanish house up for sale at a price much less than it was worth, and the opposite to what we would have to contend with when we were back in Ireland, we were soon grinding our teeth at the absurd criticism we had to listen to from people who claimed to be buyers but were either unable to buy or had no intention of doing so. If estate agents had been able to suss out the difference between the genuine article and the time-waster, which they should have been, things would have been different; but good estate agents, like good deals, were becoming hard to find. A few years after we came to Spain, when the prices of property were going up every week, the place was swarming with estate agents, just as it was in Ireland where everybody with a shop window was chancing their arm.

We had a couple of expats demanding we install an elevator so that the grossly obese woman could more easily get up the short flight of stairs. As Helen said, it was a wonder they did not all want a jacuzzi deducted from the price. One Spanish *comprador supuesto* (prospective buyer), in a highly annoyed voice, wanted to know if we had read all the books on our bookshelves, and why we should be wasting space buying such things when 'Spain has more libraries than any country in the world', the kind of boast Spaniards would have no qualms about making. Because if we had not read them, we had no right to have them taking up valuable space, and if we had read them we had no business hanging on to them. Goodness knows why our books should be such a sore point with the Spanish, given the respect they had for their own authors, but they frequently sought assurance that we would be getting rid of them, even if it meant the bonfire solution. Some made sarcastic comments about our taste in decoration and art, even including family photographs, but they were as likely to be expats as natives.

The 'husband' of a couple of women asked for details about the septic tank, such as where the effluent went, data beyond the ken of the architect who designed it and to whom we had paid one million pesetas – a nice round sum produced by entering a few simple measurements into a computer which then churned out a graphic image with a few pages of incomprehensible data; the same computer which could not even recall our names.

How should we know where the effluent went: whether it went to the left or right, north or south. Who else with a septic tank knew where their effluent went if they had a septic tank, as everybody in the street had. Like ours, did it not just disappear into the earth and fertilise it?

For more than a few potential buyers, a crucial drawback was that the arboreal sentinels on each side of the drive when one entered the front gate, did not match. Instead of having an orange on one side, and a lemon on the other, as we had, and thought was a good idea, the aesthetes who came to view our house required they be the same: either two lemons or two oranges, and they were prepared to stand and argue about it on the way out. When I suggested the situation could be rectified in fifteen minutes with a spade and a different sapling, they looked at me with disgust, but I had always found it hard to credit that somebody would put up with a bad dog for fifteen years, a bad tree, or one in the wrong place for a lifetime, rather than replace it.

A couple of French homophiles complained that, *naturellement*, they would have to rip out the entire kitchen and fit one more acceptable to Gallic tastes.

After nothing for months, the male member of a young German couple, scarcely more than teenagers, wanted to photograph every inch of the house, inside and out, and email the images to the father-in-law in Munich so he could decide whether it was worth his coming out for a look. The images must have passed the test because the father-in-law came the next day and immediately set about making a comprehensive list of price deductions calculated on the basis of changes they would want made, including things like having arches put over all the doorways because the eight-year-old granddaughter would want a 'proper Spanish house', a swimming pool and another balcony, making three rather than the existing two which apparently gave the place a rather 'boorish' appearance. Hmph, I was making allowances for his English and realised he might not be communicating exactly what he intended to communicate, and we could not afford to be too censorious given we were becoming desperate.

The following evening, at his office and their convenience, Roberto convened a meeting with very nice refreshments in his special conference room and we were all there: the very polite Roberto and his sweet female assistant who was handling the transaction and had been reduced to a state of intense anxiety, the Germans with their spoilt children for whom Roberto had to keep sending out for more ice-cream, Roberto's gentle Argentinian cousin with a large family who had been given a job because of the unemployment back home.

The father-in-law was the age and type of German who reminds anybody my age, of the War, and I could not help picturing him in his indestructible peaked cap, white-piped black uniform with whacking great, iron-cross medal, slapping his thigh with his riding crop. He launched straight into a list of what he referred to as the house's 'impediments', as though he were a lawyer arguing a case, and neither Roberto nor his young lady assistant knew where to put themselves.

However, I did not see that Helen and I had any further obligation to the client beyond the already expended basic courtesy, especially seeing as Roberto's wine and refreshments were now fully exhausted. A few more of the petit *führer's* silly jokes and I realised we would have to jettison any illusions about selling the house to him or his kin, so very frankly summed up the situation based on what Roberto's assistant had been telling us earlier about how these days her boss was being treated like dirt by foreigners claiming to be buyers. And the whole thing folded; whether they found a house that suited the eight-year-old *mädchen*, or returned empty-handed to the Vaterland, we neither knew nor cared. We only knew that once they had left his office, Roberto and his previously crestfallen assistants turned to me almost weeping with joy. To have had one of the scores of 'clients' that bowled into their office every day of the week to reduce them to tears of frustration and humiliation, told where to get off, in their presence, was obviously pure bliss.

'I wanted to clap!' Sandra, his longest serving assistant declared. 'So did I, so did I,' agreed Roberto. 'That was wonderful, Jack. We should have recorded it so we could play it back whenever we have had anybody like that in the office. It has really cheered us up. Oh, their faces..! Man..! What I would give for a photograph of the look on that man's face.' But for us it was back to square one.

Helen was convinced the real stumbling block to a 'Sale Agreed' was probably yours truly: though if Roberto thought so, he never admitted it. No matter how I dressed – casually or formally; whatever I was doing – reading, gardening, patting the dog; or whatever I said – speaking in educated tones, jocularly, amiably, or not at all 'because of an old stroke', I was, beyond all doubt, negatively affecting the outcome. So it was decided that in future, whenever we heard a potential viewer approaching, I would have the good grace and common sense to disappear with the dog, without delay, and disappear into the campo where I would remain with the mobile phone strapped to my ear – like most of my faculties, my right ear hearing had just about packed in – until Helen telephoned to say the viewing party had exited the property and every tip or touch we had implemented to conceal or rectify minute flaws, had once again been in vain and perhaps should be undone.

'*Vuelva otra vez, Whittington, vendedor supuesto. Mejore la suerte la proxima vez!*'

(Return again, Whittington, would-be seller. Better luck next time!)

Sometimes I would sit under a tree with Ned, praying and cursing at the same time, while a sudden shower drenched me;

he with an expression that so eloquently conveyed: 'What the hell are we waiting here for? Let's hit the trail, you miserable old plonker.'

Then, as we plodded home after Helen's all-clear, we would be listening to her description of whoever had been into every private part of our house, somebody, the likes of whom under normal circumstances would never have been allowed inside the front gate, let alone the front door.

Often enough the viewers would have constituted a small party, and if they were *extranjeros*, included a smart-alec who claimed to know everything there was to know about the place, its culture and its shysters – which probably meant the likes of us.

It was really difficult to pick a genuine wanna-buyer from a time-waster, even the time they spent viewing was not a reliable indication, and we were weary of books and articles by tiresome wiseacres in the English Sunday newspapers, on tips for selling property

Sterling, which was the currency British pensioner buyers were paid in, had dropped to virtual parity with the euro, and as a consequence Spanish inflation was making life difficult. The competition among property sellers in the form of expats wanting to return to England, was causing prices to drop so low that not a few were throwing in their cars, furniture and other expensive appliances, making buyers extremely greedy and encouraging them to make all sorts of demands, ones they must have known were not only unfair but ludicrous. Whether one regarded those who wore the seller's hat to be the Hydes and the buyer's hat to be the Jekylls, or the other way around, depended entirely on whether one was a seller or a buyer, but the stories being circulated were enough to make one vow to never again descend into either pit after getting out of this one; it was like having one's spaniel run over.

Only a short time previously many prospective *vendedores* (sellers) had negotiated mortgages from which they were now walking away, leaving the banks with cheap houses to flood the market with. There were always genuinely desperate cases, because when expats fell on hard times, which they frequently did, things were usually much harder to deal with.

When a spouse or partner suddenly died, was diagnosed with terminal cancer or dementia, or went off with somebody else, it instantly changed the situation for the remaining part owner of the house. At such times, Spain, which always seemed especially foreign to the expat, felt truly alien, and what was once a charming little villa with an exotic little garden and private pool in a lovely climate where food was cheap and medical services almost as good as Germany's or France's, could all too soon become a fragmented, sandblown, overgrown hovel with a mess outside, all kinds of bills coming in the mailbox, or over the wall impaled on the spurs of bougainvillea, with Catalan Shylocks forever knocking at the gate. At certain times of year the Sirocco wind brought incredible quantities of red brown Sahara dust which it deposited on balconies, walls and any other white areas, and was exceedingly difficult to remove. Naturally it got into the television, computer, 'player' and other electronic devices where it remained forever.

By the time we had been trying to sell for a year, every *urbanización* for miles was peppered with '*Se Vende*' notices, *inmobiliarias'* windows plastered with hundreds of pictures of all kinds of habitations, properties and *parcelas*, and inside, with brochures and websites containing many more. As *inmobiliarias* went bust, those like Hernandez's, who hung on grimly, were overwhelmed with clients wanting to sell, rather than was the case five years previously when everybody wanted to buy. Buyers capitalised on the fact that they had the upper hand now and demanded terraces upstairs and downstairs, a mountain view out of one window and a sea view out of another, at least four bedrooms, a double garage that could be converted into a fifth; a barbecue, satellite dish, garden filled with trees bent double with luscious fruit, and in between, bushes, herbs and flowers, with plenty of gravel or bark chippings to make it easy to maintain, plus, *por supuesto,* a large, self-maintaining, underwater-lit swimming pool with robot waiters and lifeguards.

Until this point, peripheral changes, like moving furniture and dumping Christmas and birthday cards more than four years old were about as far as we had been prepared to go to make the place more appealing, but we absolutely resisted taking down family photographs just because the Financial Times said such things turned people off. We did not have many photographs of ourselves or our children because we could not see the point, we had always preferred photographs of deceased people who had meant much.

According to property-wise newspaper columns, anyone wishing to sell their house should hide all personal items, such as toothbrushes and half-used toilet rolls – which apparently upset sensitive viewers – though items like condoms which we Catholics should not have been able to recognise, were presumably acceptable since they were not mentioned among the taboo items. To appeal, the house was to look minimally comfortable but as though plenty money had been spent on it despite nobody living in it.

Selling tips notwithstanding, it was astonishing how well informed English newspaper columnists and bank managers fancied themselves to be when listing the perils of living in Spain: not only about the swindlers that reputedly staffed all banks and estate agencies, but about the deadly wildlife – animal and plant – that had apparently evolved to check the numbers of *extranjeros*. So who could blame me when Helen read out from the Times that a single woman of twenty-eight was whimpering because her Camden flat had been on the market for three whole weeks, had had only five viewers, and I had urged Helen to change the paper, despite its Arts Supplement.

Many expats, some of whom had been living in Spain for decades, some for just a couple of years, felt impelled to go back home to spend the remainder of their lives with the remains of their family before moving on to the last paradise, one which would take far less negotiation. But much had changed and attitudes undergone metamorphosis. People were not invariably sympathetic towards those who had gone off for a few years in the sun and then come running when things got a little tougher. Only a few years ago these sundowners had never stopped boasting about their adventurous spirit, their wonderful life in the glorious sun with their own swimming pool, orchard of pineapple and fig trees, super-abundance of wonderful cheap food, dirt-cheap guzzle and little rows of white powder, back now with their tails between their legs and their pacemakers, plastic knees and colostomy bags dangling. Working-class hedonists who had got used to having breakfast in the sun, lunch in the sun, tea, dinner and drinks in the sun, followed by more drinks and naps in the sun, now found that drizzle on the windows while they once more ate take-away meals indoors in long grey chinos, required acclimatisation, as did the silly sentimental tattoos with which their right arms were covered.

After so long whining about the shops being shut in the afternoon, they had got to like it, got used to going out after tea to shop when the streets and shops were all lit up and presented a totally different and more relaxed atmosphere than during the day. Food shopping in the morning, beach and leisure in the afternoon, and then shopping for clothes and interesting impulse stuff in the evening, had something to commend it when wound up with a light meal or tea and coffee with cakes, all very tastily served, and, as always, cheap and served by lovely waiters. The same ones had left cars at the airport with keys in the ignition and a letter of explanation to their bank or HP manager because they could not afford to keep paying for either their houses or their cars and had not been able to sell them.

Not a few, who had what they believed to be a natural bent for country life, had bought *fincas* and a few hectares with lemons and olive trees in the campo with a view to becoming a grandee – albeit from Birmingham or Cardiff – but if the 'back to the earth' adventure was hard to accomplish in England or Ireland, where the soil was rich and well irrigated, the language comprehensible and the crops recognisable, it was a damned sight harder in Spain which was just the opposite. Skills, tools and methods were all different, electricity often serendipitous, and loneliness something they had never experienced before. Sixty and seventy-year-old lumps of five-toed gout stomping on berries among hard stalks and kernels had not proved too easy a task, and if we were having difficulty selling our place in an *urbanización*, the poor blighters who bought into self-sufficiency would be having one hell of a job.

THIRTY-NINE

Out of twenty-three years in Ireland, there was scarcely a day when I failed to do something useful, and when that happened it would invariably be because of ill health. I used to make and repair all kinds of things, deriving as much pleasure out of getting an old field gate to swing properly over sloping ground, or cutting a leather washer to fit an ancient hand pump for which parts could no longer be obtained, as working on a sculpture or writing the chapter of a book. I did not consider myself a craftsman because instead of acquiring a skill by the ideal method of apprenticeship, I was self taught; but I have always been pretty resourceful and determined, and that counted for a lot. We had all kinds of animals and plants and were always trying something different. Our life was fulfilling and in a small but definite way we believed ourselves to be useful contributors to the planet, as well as only moderate polluter-consumers.

Yet we had been in Spain for a whole twelve years and in that time I had done comparatively little that could be called worthwhile. I had written a couple of manuscripts, drawn a bit and painted a little, but done no sculpture. We had seen nowhere near enough of our sons and daughters and their sons and daughters, so our contribution as parents and grandparents had been negligible. My output therefore was scarcely different from the thousands of ex-pats who arrived with no ambition other than go through the motions of hedonism, so it seemed it was time to move on.

One particularly hot afternoon, two policewomen who seemed genuinely keen on the house, were viewing it for the third time; one had brought her parents and I was offering them Ned as a bonus. Introducing him as they stood in a line with him wagging his stump and licking their hands one after another, everything was going swimmingly until he reached the last one, *el padre* (the father), when for some inexplicable reason he turned broadside, raised his hind leg and squirted a thick jet of highly concentrated piss over the front of the old man's trousers. Later Helen would try to convince me that it had happened because Ned was claiming his territory and stating it directly to the head of the invading party, whereas I, the 'pucka animal authority', was certain it was pure canine cussedness, and had I brought my shotgun from Ireland when we came, might well have dashed into the garage, grabbed it and blown his bloody head off as an act of good faith, though it would not necessarily have proved a deal-clincher. Such reactive emotions might seem extreme but we were becoming desperate. As it was, whether the family had a commendable sense of humour, or had taken a liking to Ned despite his atrocious manners, they didn't say a word but eventually took the house but not the dog; they already had one they said.

We had hung on to see if the prices of houses in Ireland would drop, but the only ones dropping significantly were Spanish and they were dropping more and more every week. Helen had been against lowering ours any further but I felt we had waited too long already and unless we did something drastic, and soon, we were never going to get back to Ireland. Thus, after a couple of days going through all our calculations yet again and soul-searching like never before, we decided to drive around the streets in our vicinity to determine the price of every house that was up for sale and similar in value to our own, and then reduce ours to substantially less than the lowest. I could not recommend it as a way of doing business but it worked.

After our thrice dropping the price, the two young girl police, one of whose fathers had endured the hosing from Ned with exceptional grace, decided to buy. They were the loveliest looking police in the world, nothing like the *guardia civil*, and one of them was so excited she wept when we handed over the deeds. A week later we were back in Ireland, back to a different Ireland from the one we left in 1998 and to a very different place from the one we came to in 1976. It was now December 2009.

FORTY

It took seven months to find a little house in the country, during which time we lived with Walter and his family. It was crowded but they were all welcoming and Walt still very much the country lad though he now worked in town and lived the urban life. With him as chauffeur we scoured the county for a new home, the three of us unconsciously seeking somewhere like the place we had once lived in, even though finding such a situation and living in it was now quite beyond us for obvious reasons. Three of our children were still living in Ireland, though far apart, so we sought somewhere as equidistant from them as possible and found a cottage which happened to be not really far enough from where we had first come to live. We would always seek to avoid passing our original home when nearby, so that we would not see it modernised and devoid of animals and crops the way people would insist on telling us it was. Walt was stoic enough to take it, and Helen would have just turned her head away, but I, the big bossman, would have to stifle a whimper.

Our new home was not even remotely like the place we had first come to. Far from perfect, and lacking much potential, it was in the country, but instead of several hectares of good arable land, we now had less than a quarter of an acre exhausted by the few tired and almost unidentifiable old oak and ash that leaned along its borders and shed branches of rotten wood every time the wind got up, as it so often did. Grass was the only plant that grew well because of the septic tank system whose pipes were too close to the surface, inches rather than feet, and typical of the builder's frugality throughout.

But we had grown weary of traipsing all over the county, embarrassed by causing overcrowding in Walt's house and, unlike what grandpas are supposed to be – patient, encyclopaedic mules and table-tennis aficionados – my infirmities were truly coming into their own and my DIY skills had almost entirely vanished apart from issuing orders that were considered old-fashioned by forbearing sons.

Our children and friends had warned us of the changes that had taken place in so many areas of Irish life during the time we had been away, we had observed many of them ourselves during holidays and read of them in the newspapers and on the internet, yet were still unprepared for just how many and far reaching they were. Changes in the arrogant and unhelpful way banks, building societies and insurance companies treated customers were the most obvious, but changes in the attitudes of ordinary people towards wealth were also notable, particularly regarding the squandering of money on such things as weddings, birthdays, holidays, frequent eating out and most of all, on property.

The buying and selling of anything classed as property, and that included corrugated iron sheds and disused animal houses – anything with a roof – dominated conversation and had become almost a mania. But instead of being satisfied with renting, young married couples, unlike their European counterparts, wanted to immediately own their own house. Had there been proper state control over landlordism and the constant raising of rents, priorities might have been different, but Irish governments had always favoured landlords over tenants and penalised buyers with excessive stamp duty. It was as though accommodation was a newly discovered resource, like gold or titanium and everybody was mining it; a worldwide delusion more pernicious in Ireland than anywhere else.

Apart from the deterioration in services provided by financial institutions coupled with inexcusable increases in charges, much inconvenience had been created by the closure of rural post offices, police stations and medical facilities. The one thing that had improved beyond measure was the quality of main roads, even though public transport was as deplorable as ever.

Of the changes – which had taken place in an absurdly short space of time – none were more drastic than the attitude towards the Catholic Church because of the continuous disclosure of clerical paedophilia. A major reason for many of the problems, whether to do with corruption or incompetence, was the perennial reluctance of the Government to punish those in positions of authority for their acknowledged crimes and mistakes, and instead, incredibly, to reward them with promotion and benefits.

Our first coming to Ireland had coincided with the ending of the romantic age, and although there subsequently seemed to be more changes for the worse than for the better, not least there seeming to be nowhere near as many wonderful traditional musicians as there used to be, happily the ready friendliness of the people hardly seemed to have changed, and this has surely always been Ireland's saving grace. The Spanish are also friendly, but in a different way, and there is nothing superficial about it. It can take time to win them over, but once they have decided on one's worthiness they can make extremely loyal *amigos*. Otherwise, although one often hears it said that the Irish and Spanish are very similar in nature, we never found it to be so, not that it matters.

About the Author

JOSEPH ROBINSON WAS BORN in South Shields, educated in Newcastle and London, did two years National Service in the RAMC before emigrating to work in New Zealand, Australia and Canada, returning to work in Scotland and obtaining a PhD in Medical Microbiology.

He had sculpture and oil-painting exhibitions in England, Ireland, Germany and America and published several social history biographies. In 1976 he and his young family moved to live in rural Ireland. In 1998 he and his wife went to live in Spain for some years.

He now lives in Ireland.

Printed in Poland
by Amazon Fulfillment
Poland Sp. z o.o., Wrocław